PEACE MAKER

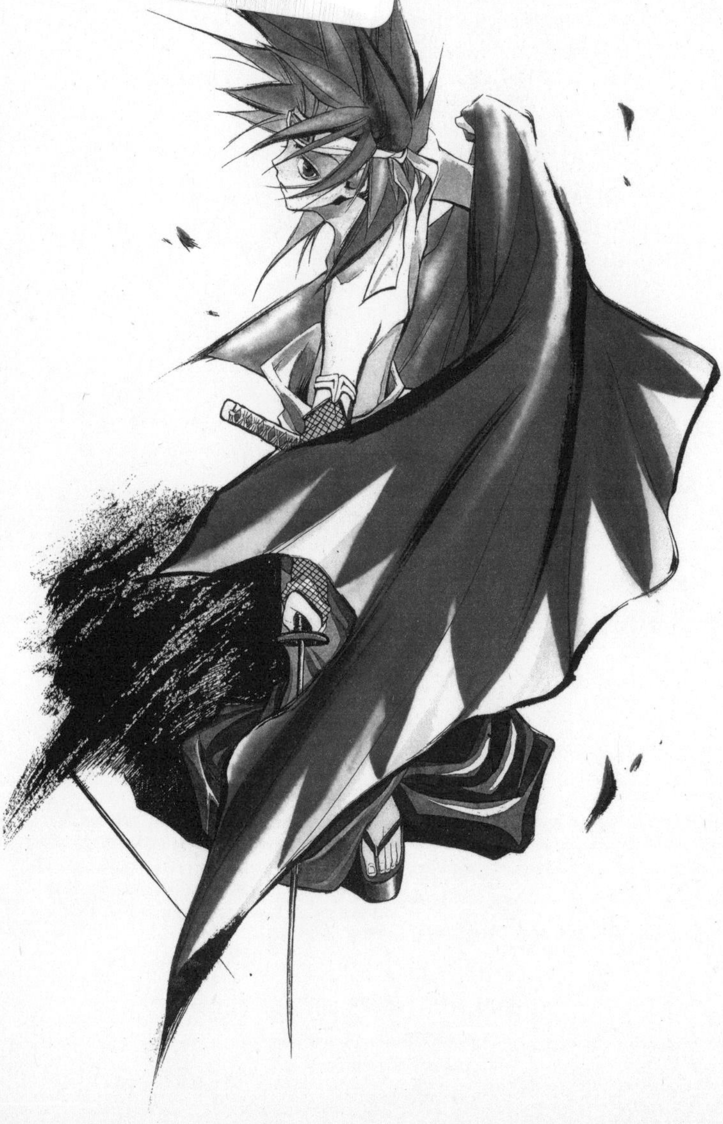

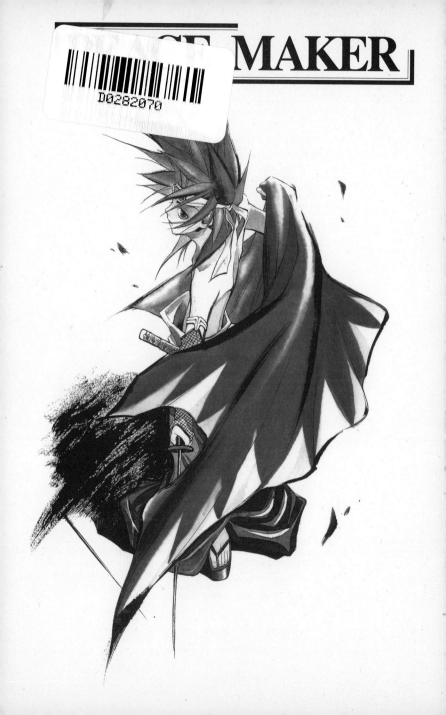

Peace Maker Volume 1
Created By Nanae Chrono

Translation - Michelle Kobayashi
English Adaptation - Christine Boylan
Retouch and Lettering - Star Print Brokers
Production Artist - Michael Paolilli and Bowen Park
Cover Design - Al-Insan Lashley

Editor - Hope Donovan
Digital Imaging Manager - Chris Buford
Pre-Production Supervisor - Erika Terriquez
Art Director - Anne Marie Horne
Production Manager - Elisabeth Brizzi
Managing Editor - Vy Nguyen
VP of Production - Ron Klamert
Editor-in-Chief - Rob Tokar
Publisher - Mike Kiley
President and C.O.O. - John Parker
C.E.O. and Chief Creative Officer - Stuart Levy

A **TOKYOPOP**® Manga

TOKYOPOP Inc.
5900 Wilshire Blvd. Suite 2000
Los Angeles, CA 90036

E-mail: info@TOKYOPOP.com
Come visit us online at www.TOKYOPOP.com

ISBN: 978-1-4278-0075-6

First TOKYOPOP printing: August 2007

10 9 8 7 6 5 4 3 2 1

Printed in the USA

PEACE MAKER
ピースメーカー

Volume 1
by Nanae Chrono

HAMBURG // LONDON // LOS ANGELES // TOKYO

CONTENTS

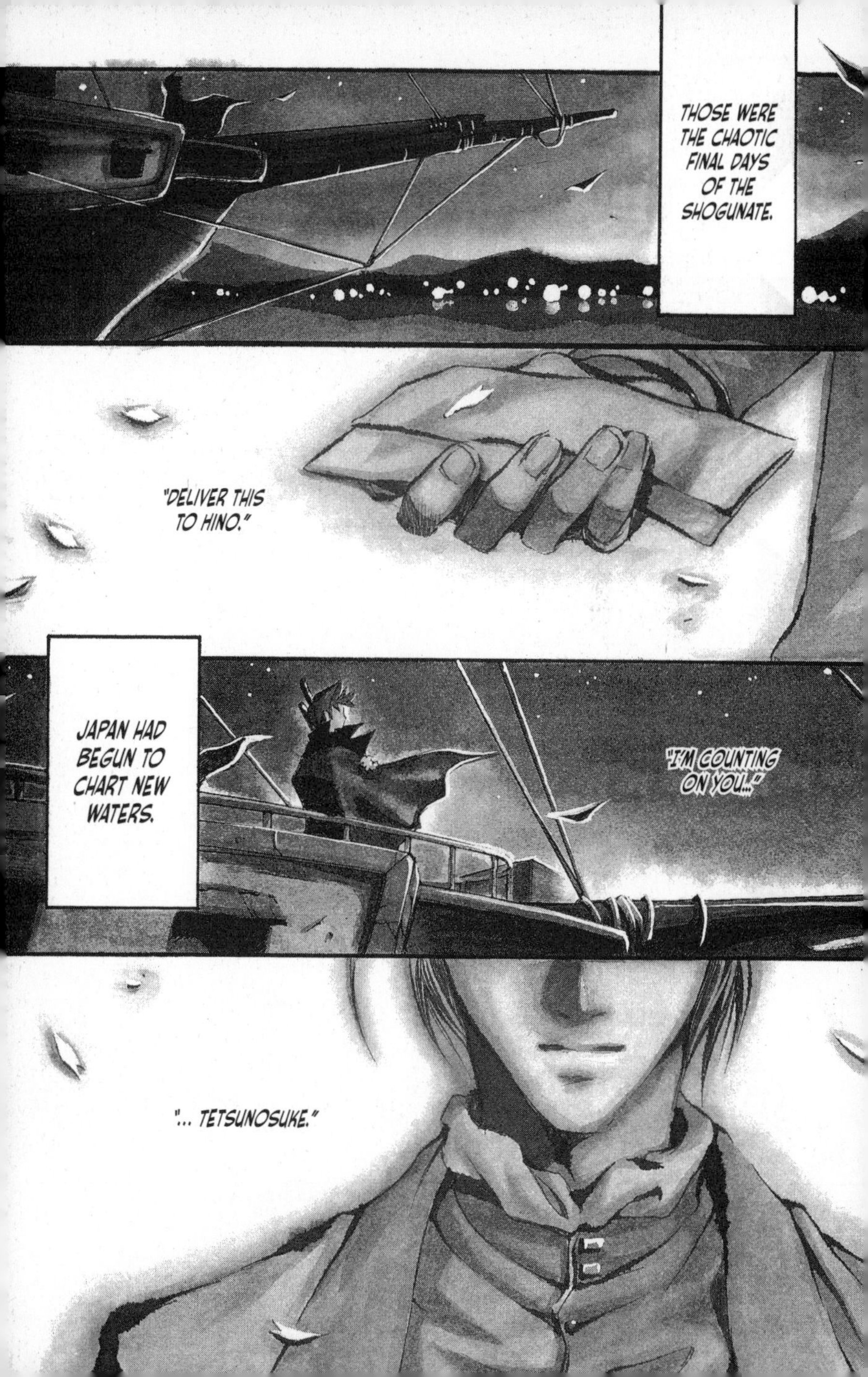
THOSE WERE THE CHAOTIC FINAL DAYS OF THE SHOGUNATE.
"DELIVER THIS TO HINO."
JAPAN HAD BEGUN TO CHART NEW WATERS.
"I'M COUNTING ON YOU..."
"... TETSUNOSUKE."

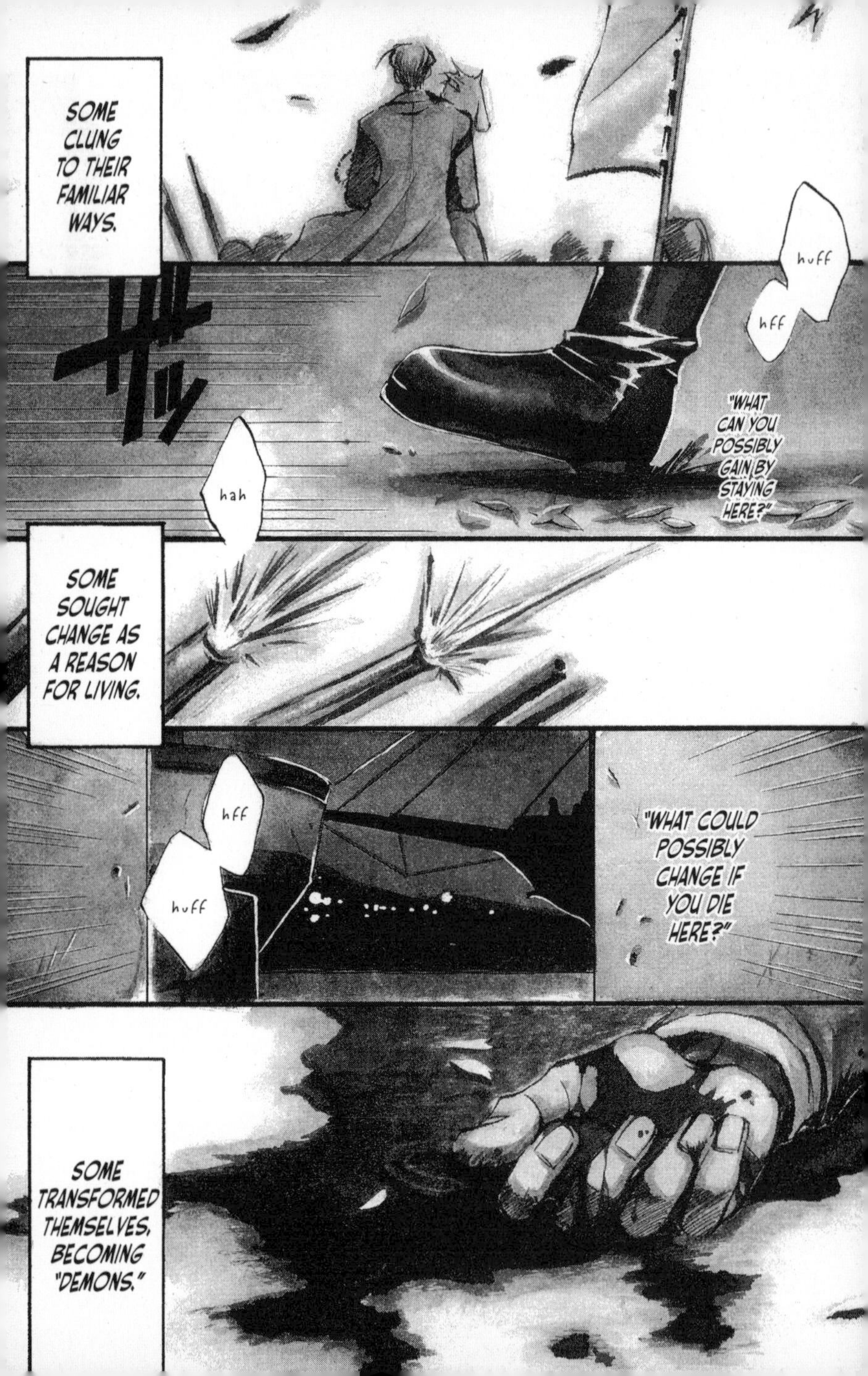
SOME CLUNG TO THEIR FAMILIAR WAYS.
huff
hff
"WHAT CAN YOU POSSIBLY GAIN BY STAYING HERE?"
hah
SOME SOUGHT CHANGE AS A REASON FOR LIVING.
"WHAT COULD POSSIBLY CHANGE IF YOU DIE HERE?"
hff
huff
SOME TRANSFORMED THEMSELVES, BECOMING "DEMONS."

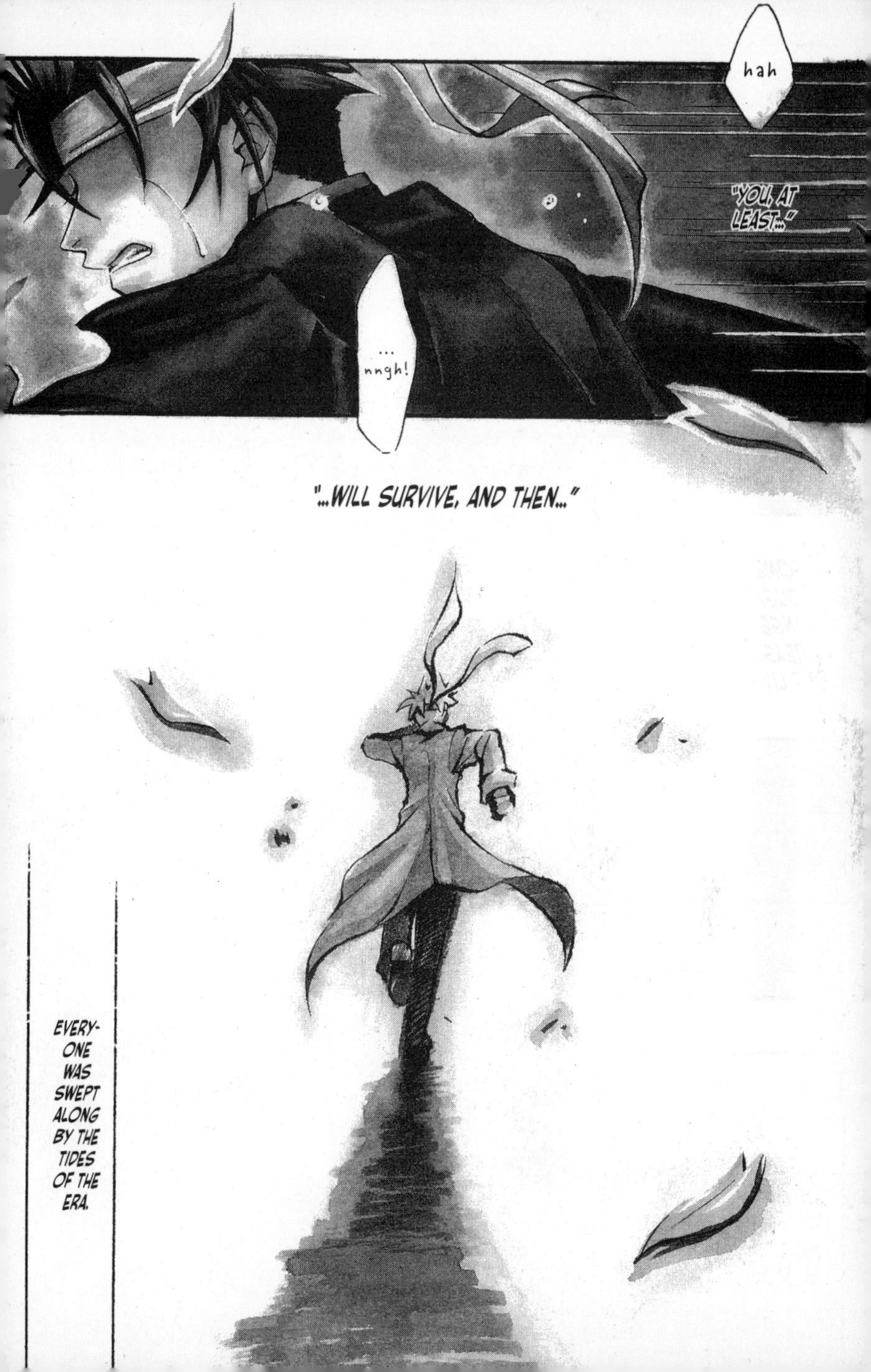
hah
"YOU, AT LEAST..."
... nngh!
"...WILL SURVIVE, AND THEN..."
EVERY-ONE WAS SWEPT ALONG BY THE TIDES OF THE ERA.

Act.1 I Will

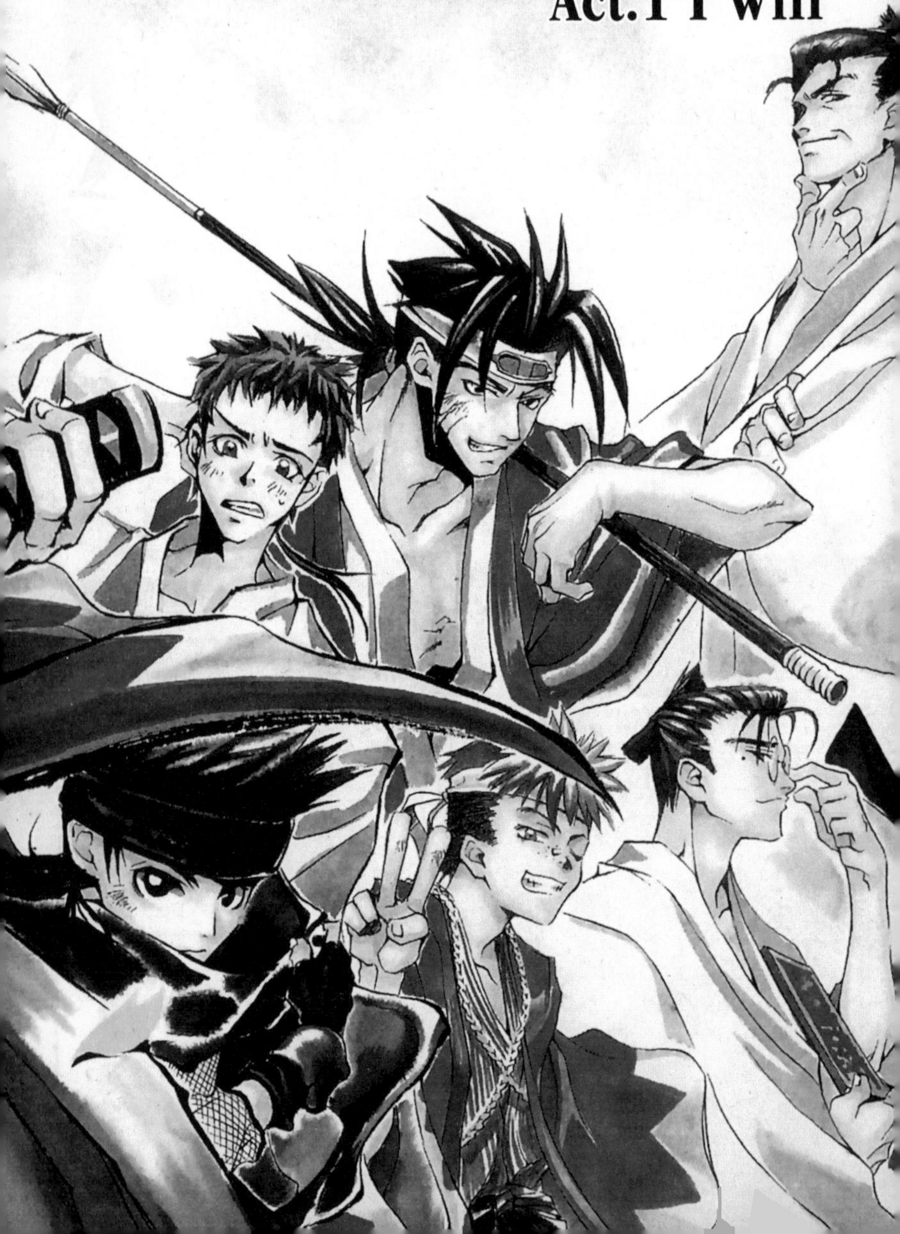

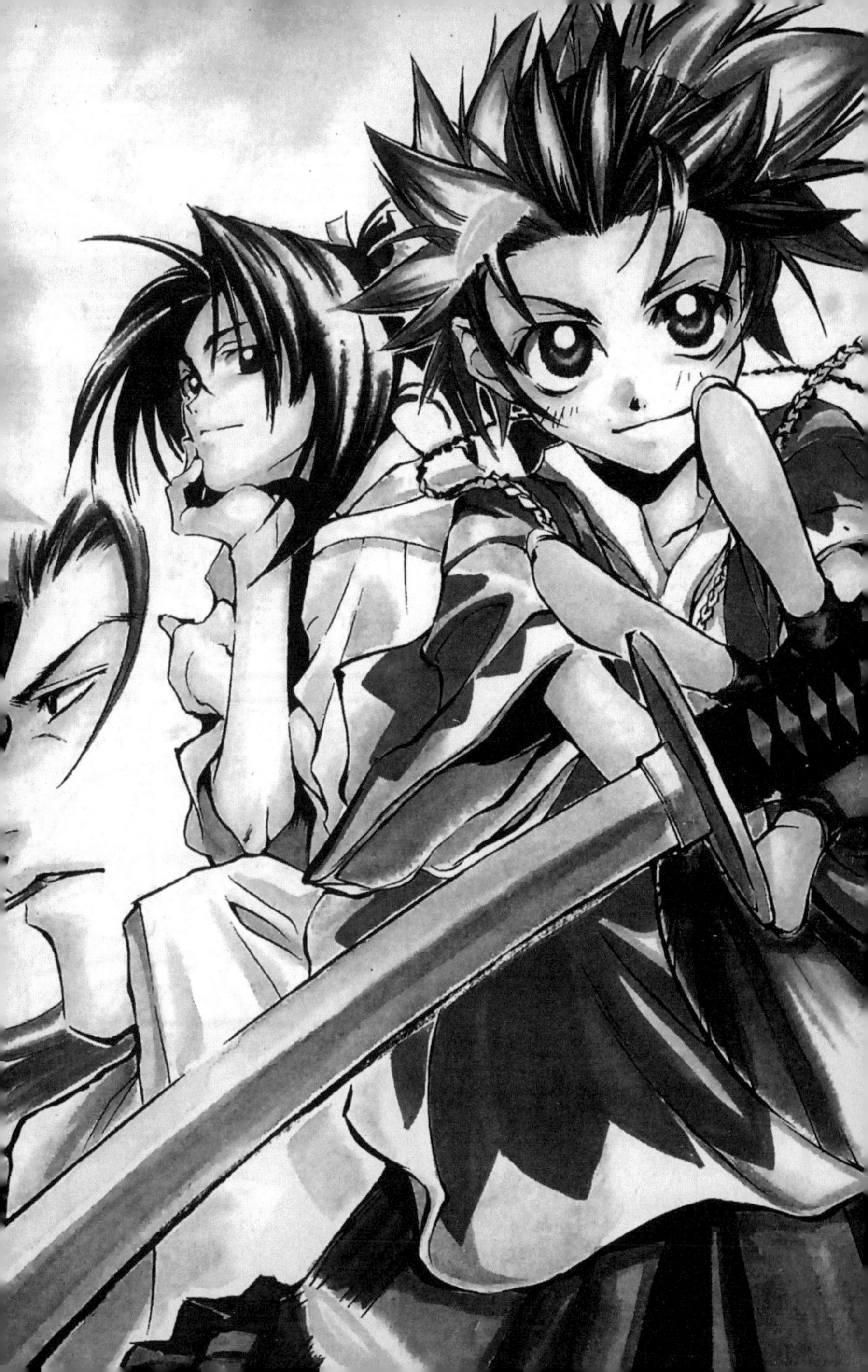

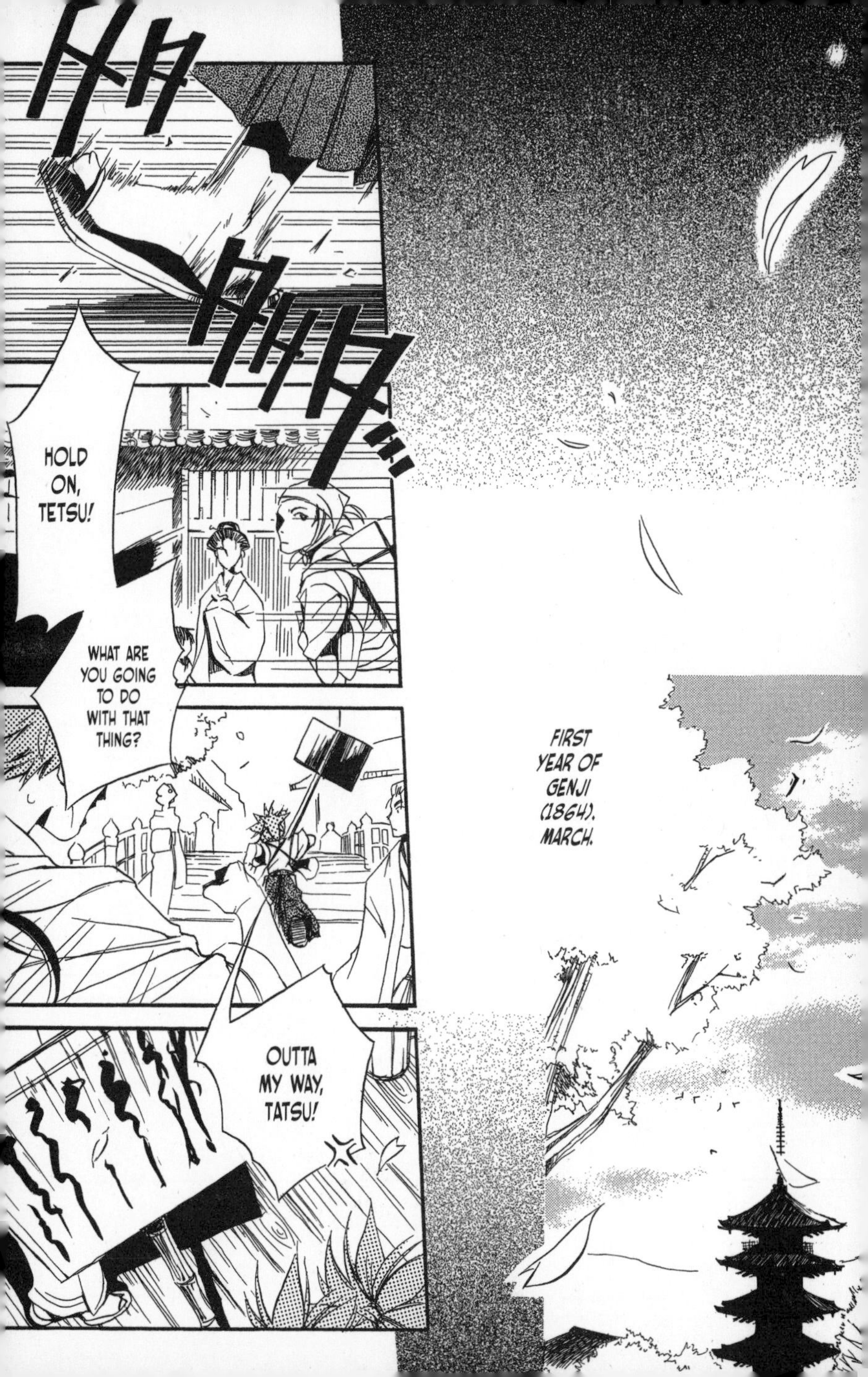
FIRST YEAR OF GENJI (1864). MARCH.
HOLD ON, TETSU!
WHAT ARE YOU GOING TO DO WITH THAT THING?
OUTTA MY WAY, TATSU!

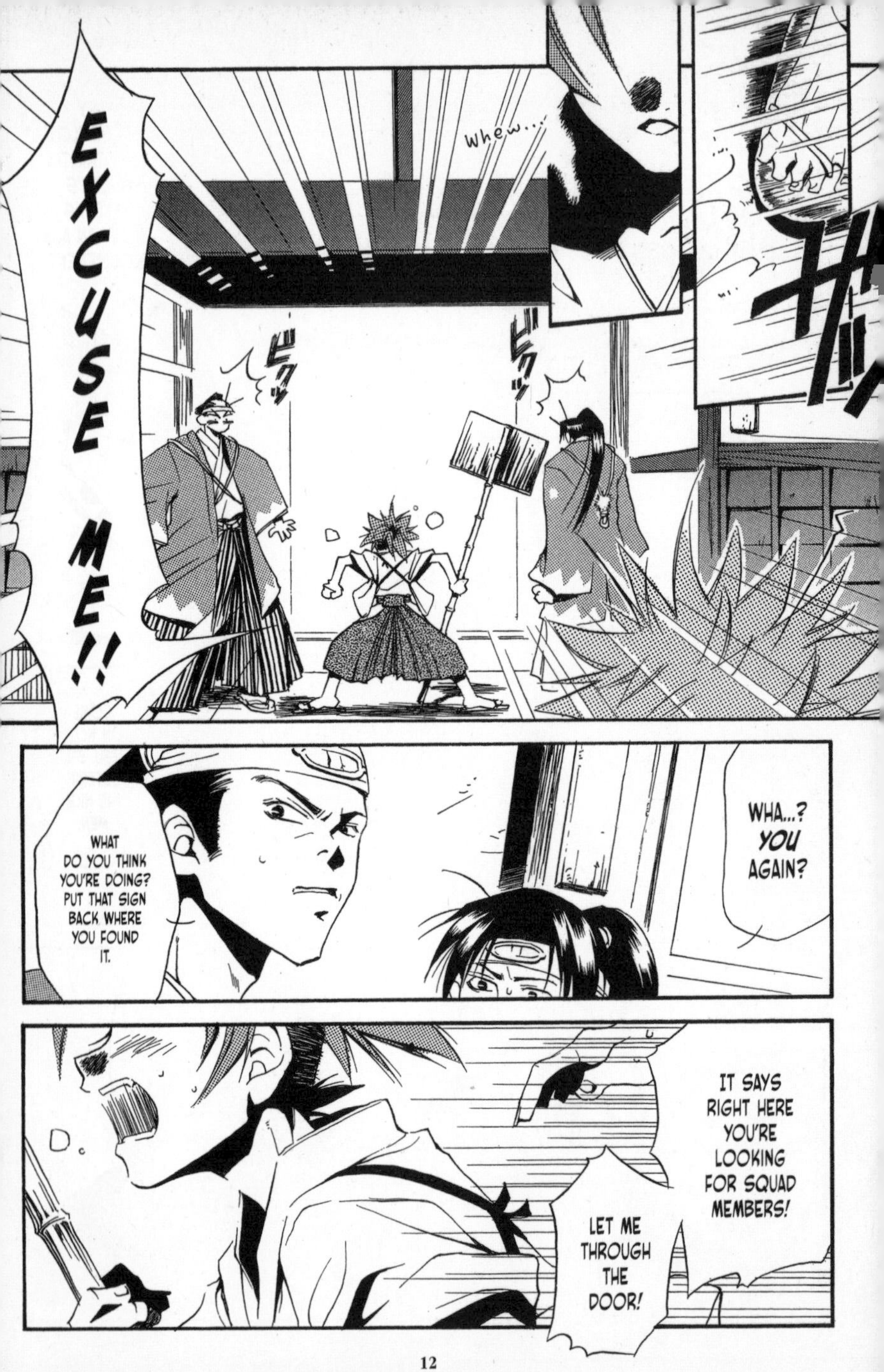
Whew...
EXCUSE ME!!
WHA...? YOU AGAIN?
WHAT DO YOU THINK YOU'RE DOING? PUT THAT SIGN BACK WHERE YOU FOUND IT.
IT SAYS RIGHT HERE YOU'RE LOOKING FOR SQUAD MEMBERS!
LET ME THROUGH THE DOOR!

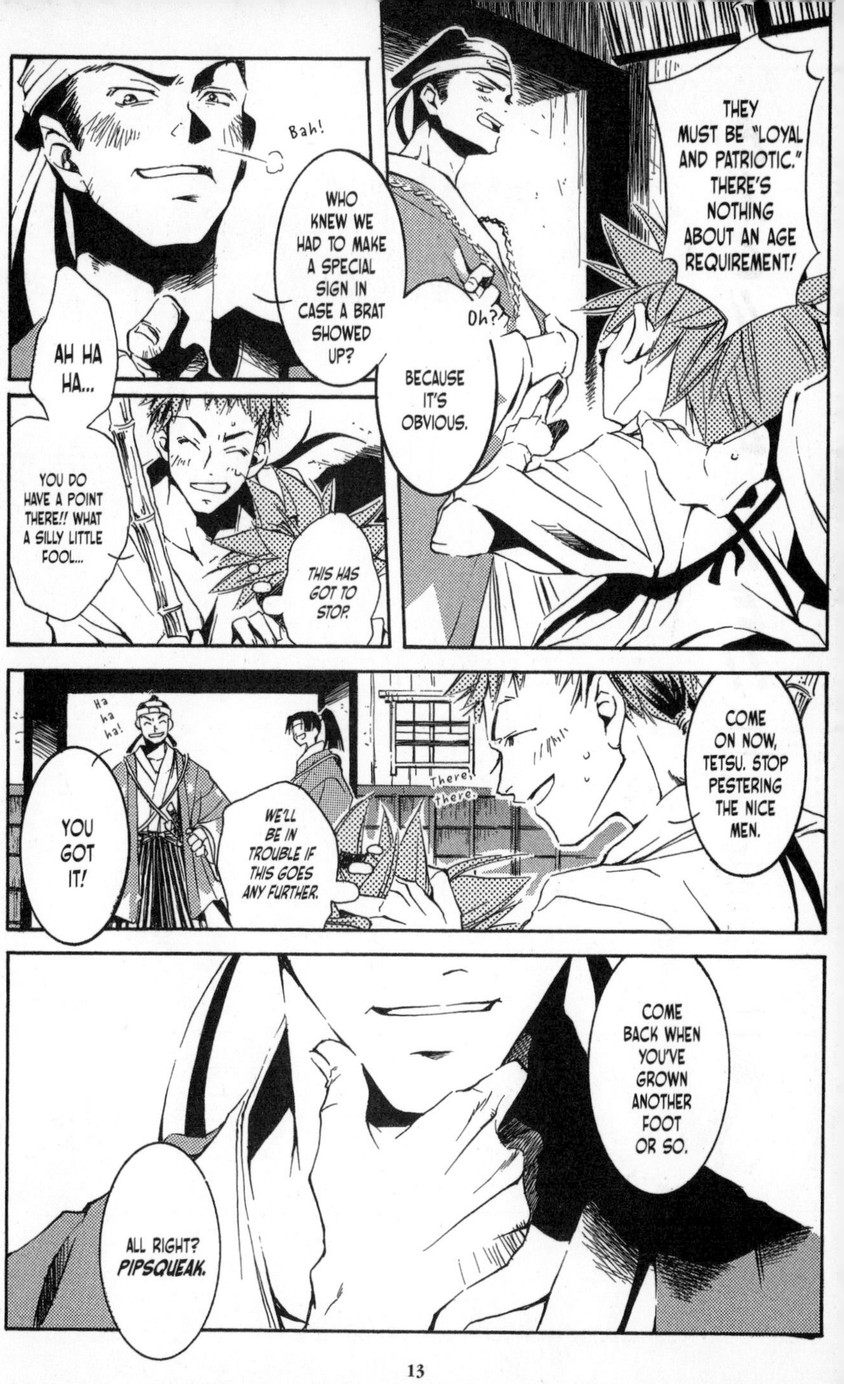
THEY MUST BE "LOYAL AND PATRIOTIC." THERE'S NOTHING ABOUT AN AGE REQUIREMENT!
Oh?
BECAUSE IT'S OBVIOUS.
Bah!
WHO KNEW WE HAD TO MAKE A SPECIAL SIGN IN CASE A BRAT SHOWED UP?
AH HA HA...
YOU DO HAVE A POINT THERE!! WHAT A SILLY LITTLE FOOL...
THIS HAS GOT TO STOP.
COME ON NOW, TETSU. STOP PESTERING THE NICE MEN.
There there.
WE'LL BE IN TROUBLE IF THIS GOES ANY FURTHER.
Ha ha ha!
YOU GOT IT!
COME BACK WHEN YOU'VE GROWN ANOTHER FOOT OR SO.
ALL RIGHT? PIPSQUEAK.

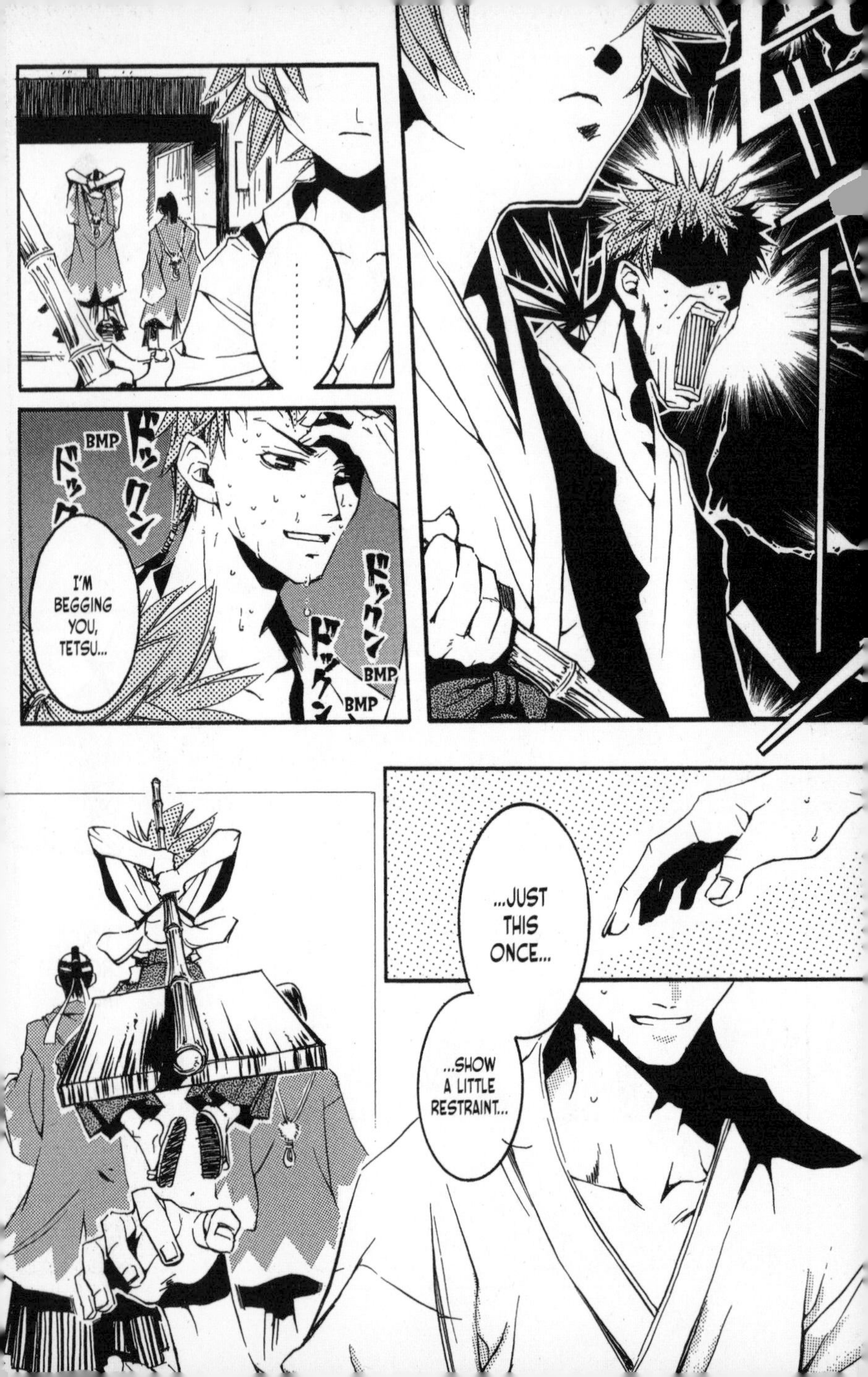
BMP
I'M BEGGING YOU, TETSU...
BMP
BMP
...JUST THIS ONCE...
...SHOW A LITTLE RESTRAINT...

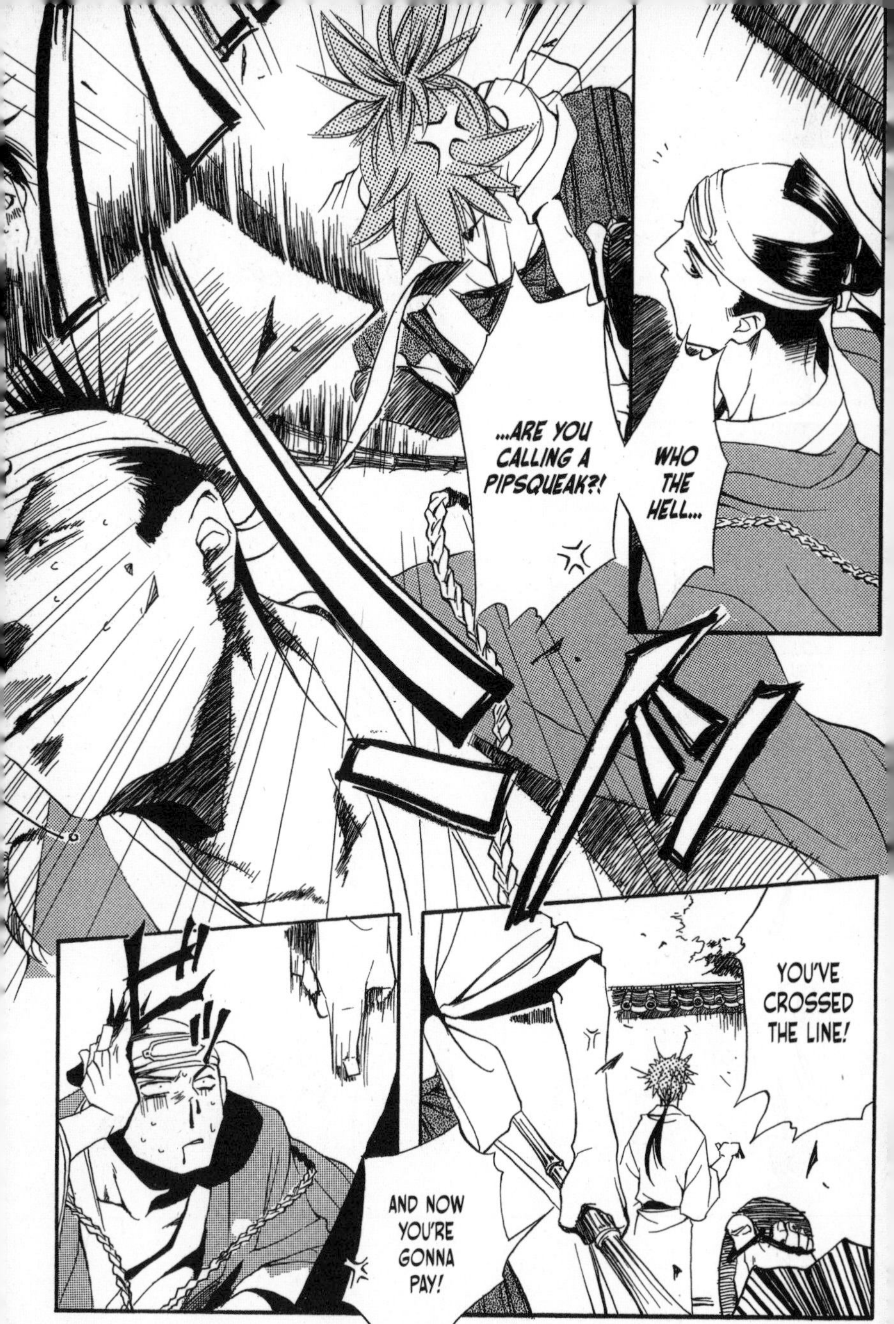
WHO THE HELL...
...ARE YOU CALLING A PIPSQUEAK?!
YOU'VE CROSSED THE LINE!
AND NOW YOU'RE GONNA PAY!

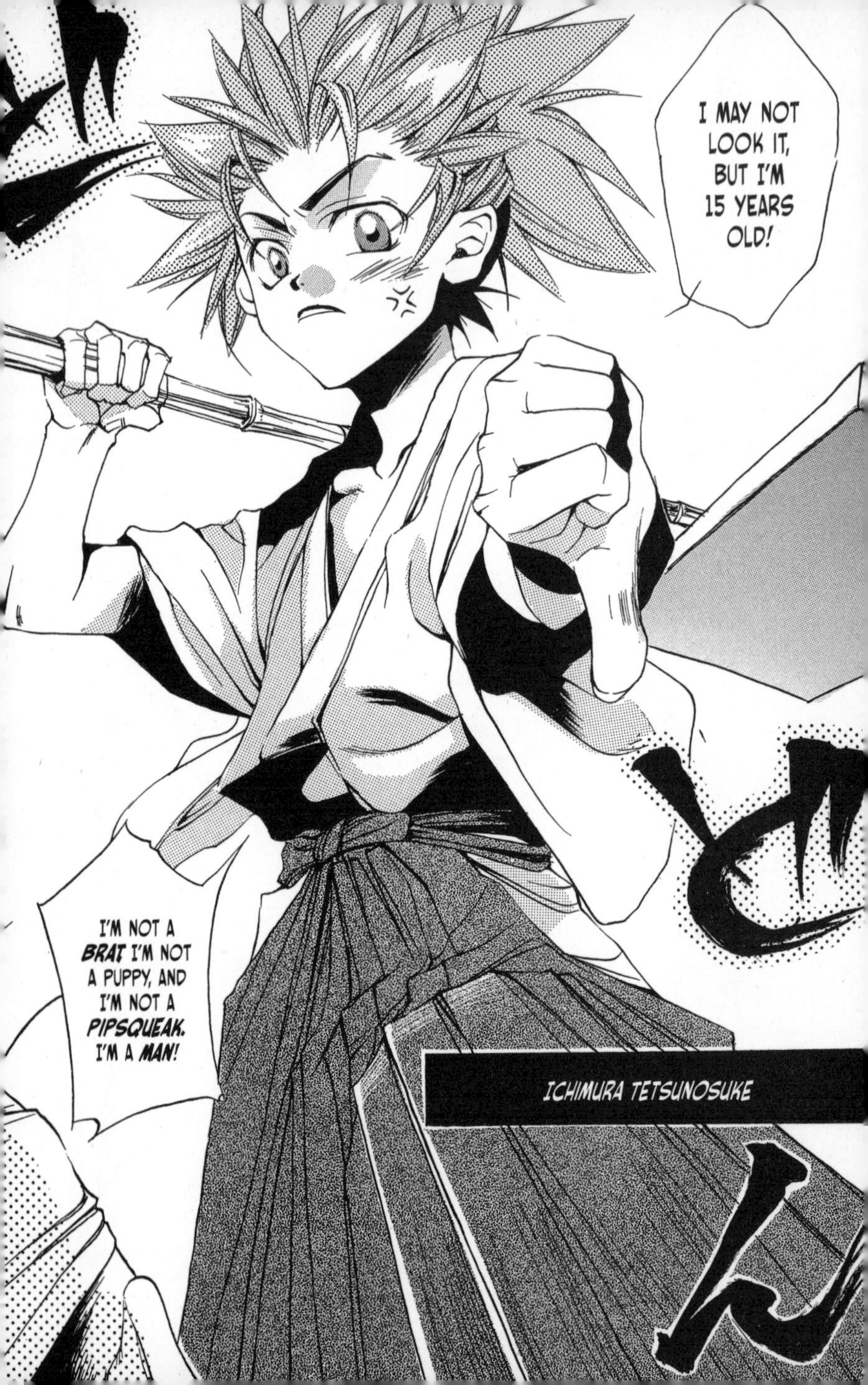
I MAY NOT LOOK IT, BUT I'M 15 YEARS OLD!
I'M NOT A BRAT. I'M NOT A PUPPY, AND I'M NOT A PIPSQUEAK. I'M A MAN!
ICHIMURA TETSUNOSUKE

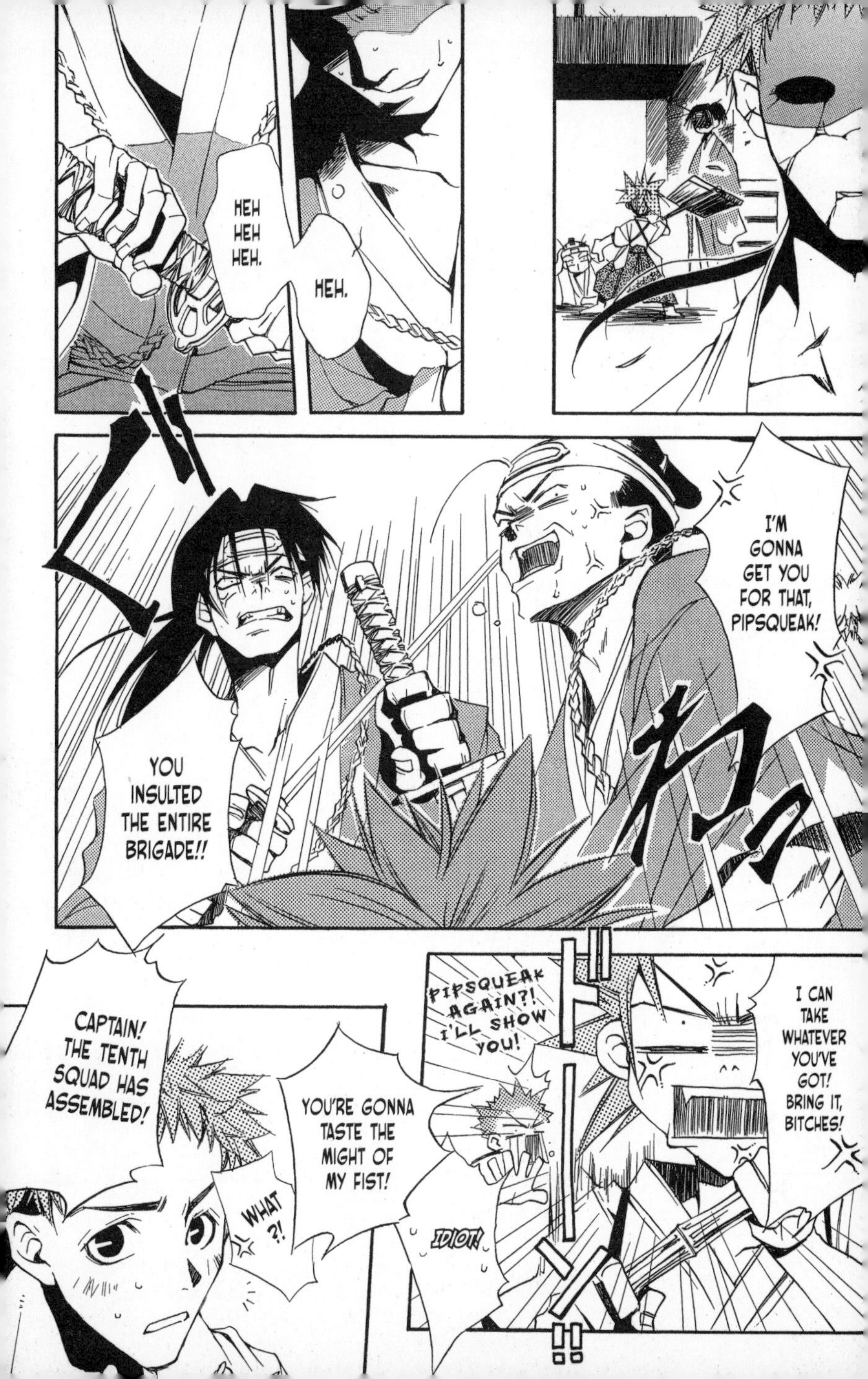
HEH.
HEH HEH HEH.
I'M GONNA GET YOU FOR THAT, PIPSQUEAK!
YOU INSULTED THE ENTIRE BRIGADE!!
I CAN TAKE WHATEVER YOU'VE GOT! BRING IT, BITCHES!
PIPSQUEAK AGAIN?! I'LL SHOW YOU!
YOU'RE GONNA TASTE THE MIGHT OF MY FIST!
IDIOT!
CAPTAIN! THE TENTH SQUAD HAS ASSEMBLED!
WHAT?!

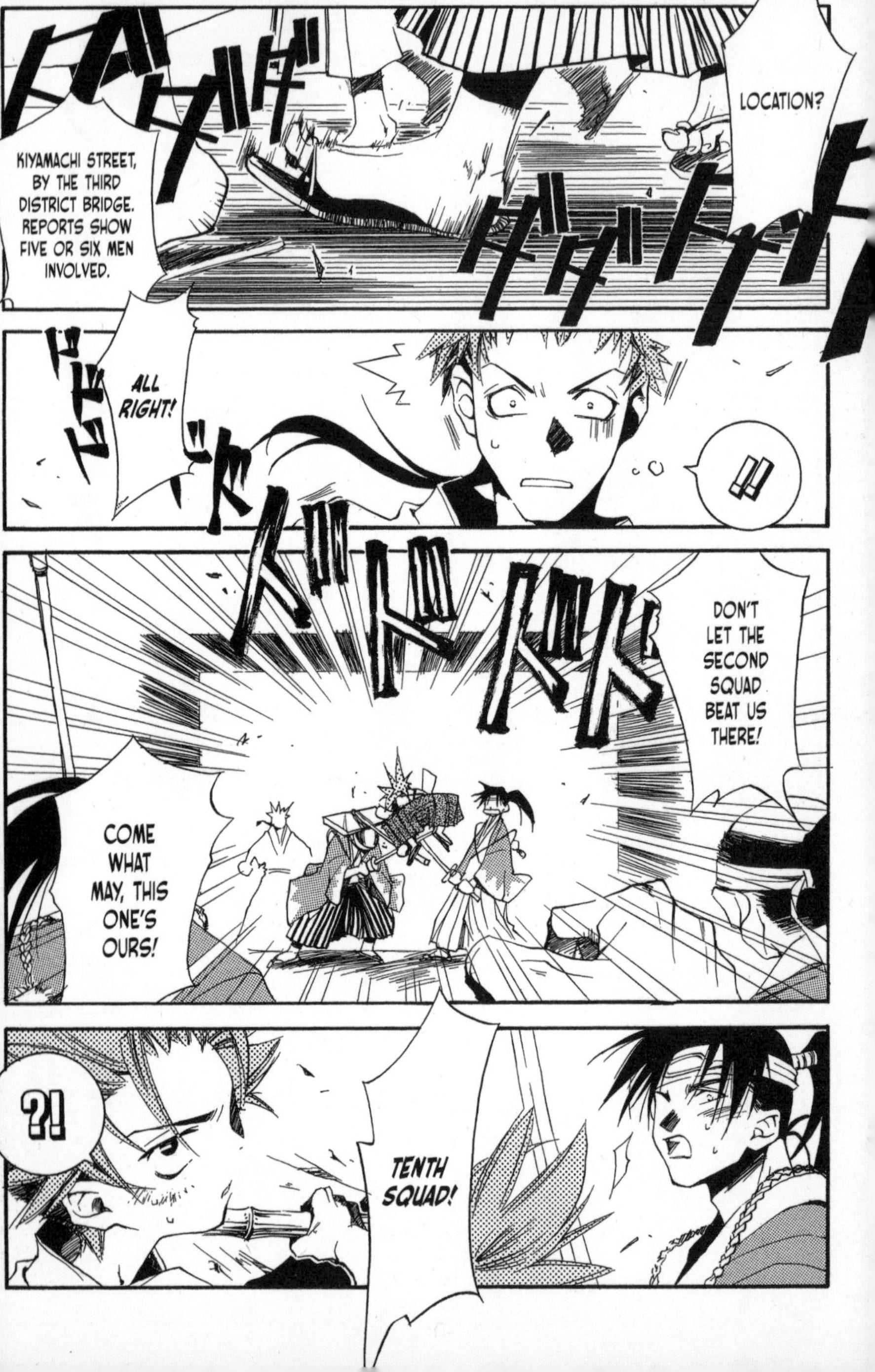
LOCATION?
KIYAMACHI STREET, BY THE THIRD DISTRICT BRIDGE. REPORTS SHOW FIVE OR SIX MEN INVOLVED.
!!
ALL RIGHT!
DON'T LET THE SECOND SQUAD BEAT US THERE!
COME WHAT MAY, THIS ONE'S OURS!
TENTH SQUAD!
?!

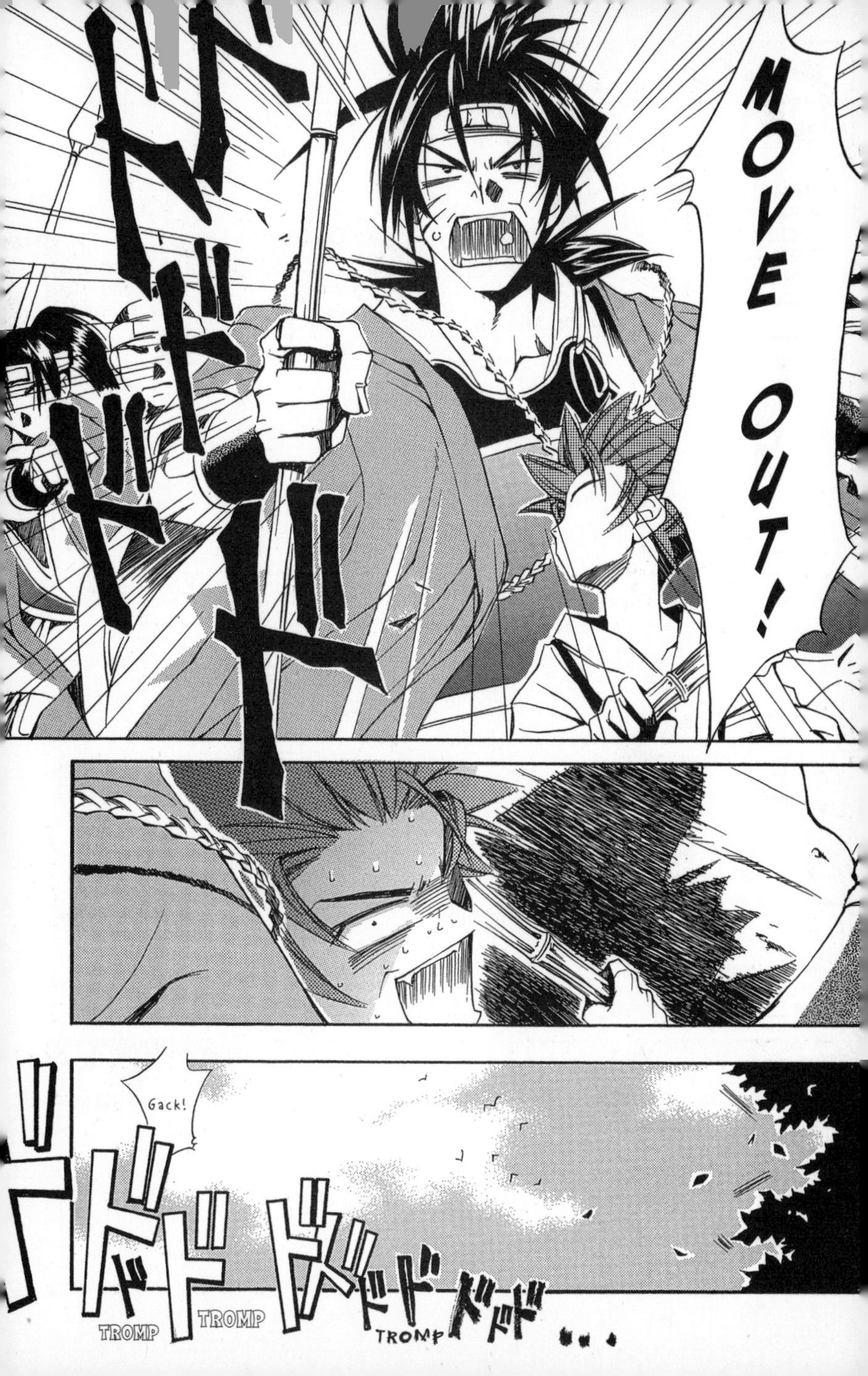
MOVE OUT!!
Gack!
TROMP
TROMP
TROMP

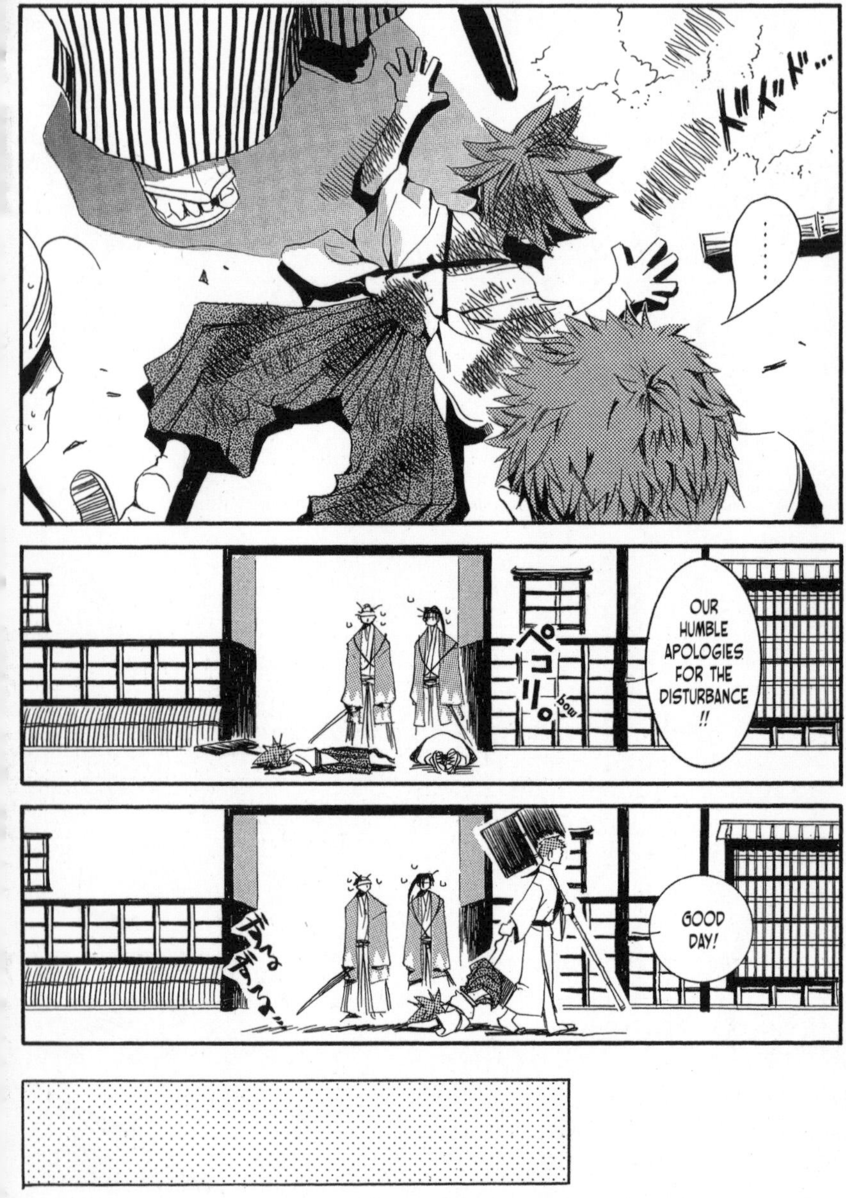
......
OUR HUMBLE APOLOGIES FOR THE DISTURBANCE !!
bow
GOOD DAY!

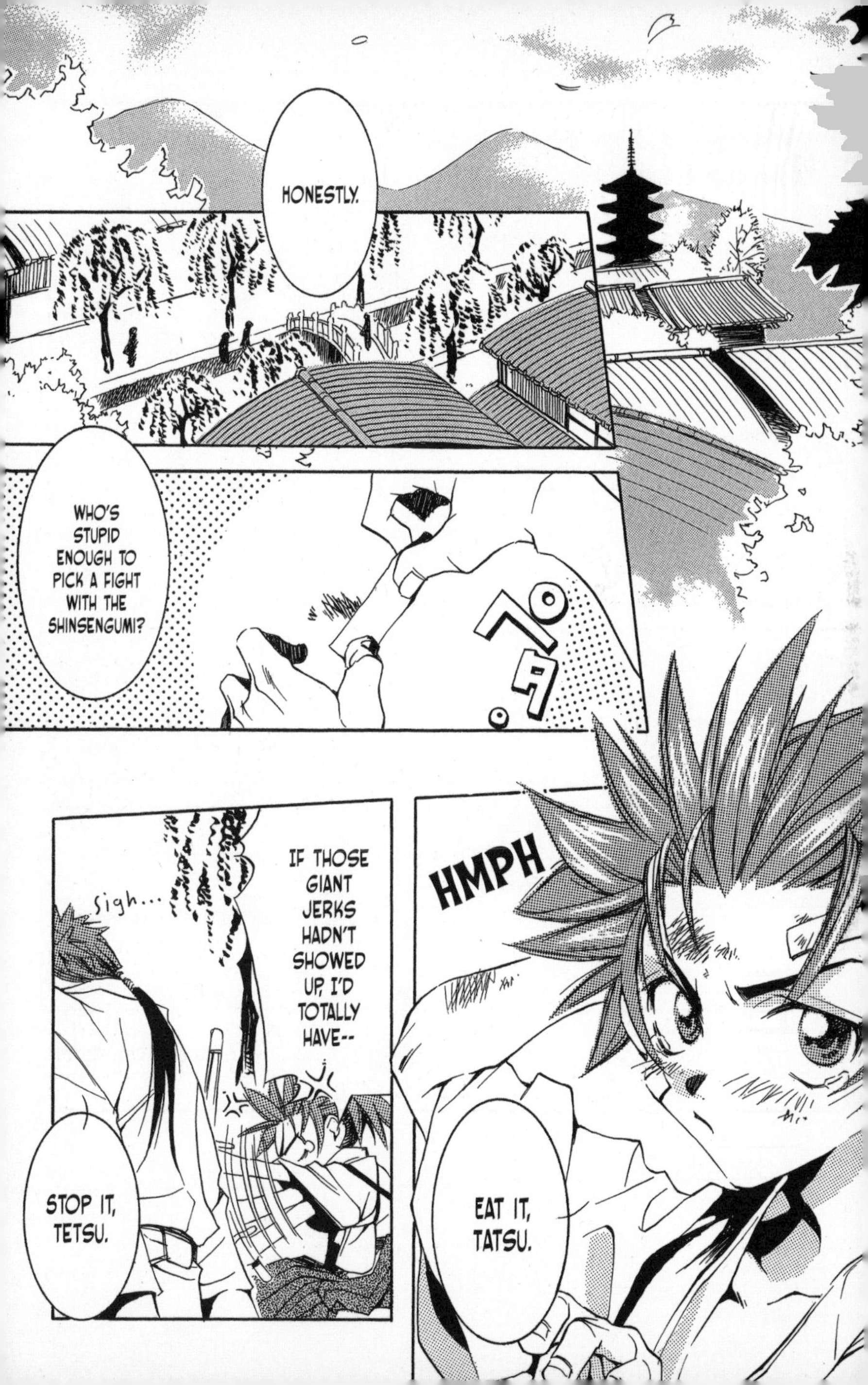
HONESTLY.
WHO'S STUPID ENOUGH TO PICK A FIGHT WITH THE SHINSENGUMI?
ペタ
HMPH
EAT IT, TATSU.
IF THOSE GIANT JERKS HADN'T SHOWED UP, I'D TOTALLY HAVE--
Sigh...
STOP IT, TETSU.

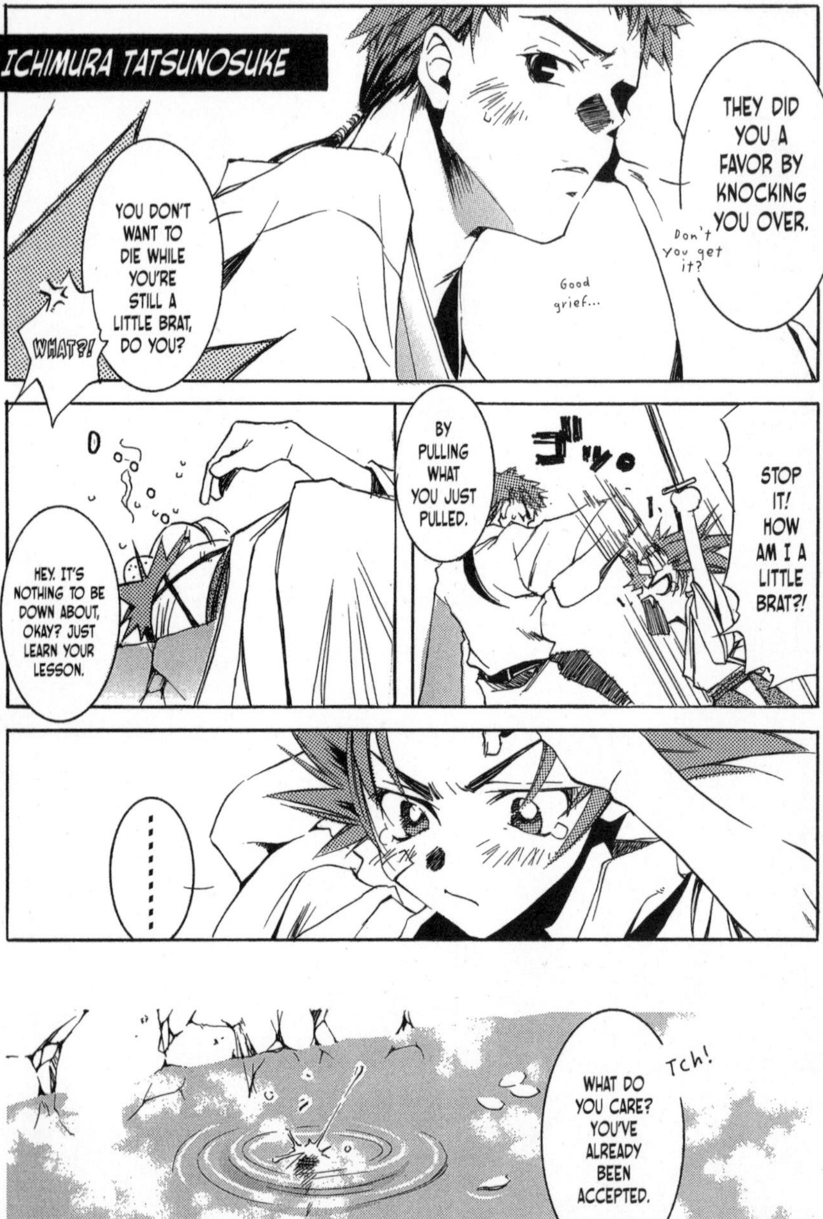
ICHIMURA TATSUNOSUKE
THEY DID YOU A FAVOR BY KNOCKING YOU OVER.
Don't you get it?
Good grief...
YOU DON'T WANT TO DIE WHILE YOU'RE STILL A LITTLE BRAT, DO YOU?
WHAT?!
STOP IT! HOW AM I A LITTLE BRAT?!
BY PULLING WHAT YOU JUST PULLED.
HEY. IT'S NOTHING TO BE DOWN ABOUT, OKAY? JUST LEARN YOUR LESSON.
......
Tch!
WHAT DO YOU CARE? YOU'VE ALREADY BEEN ACCEPTED.

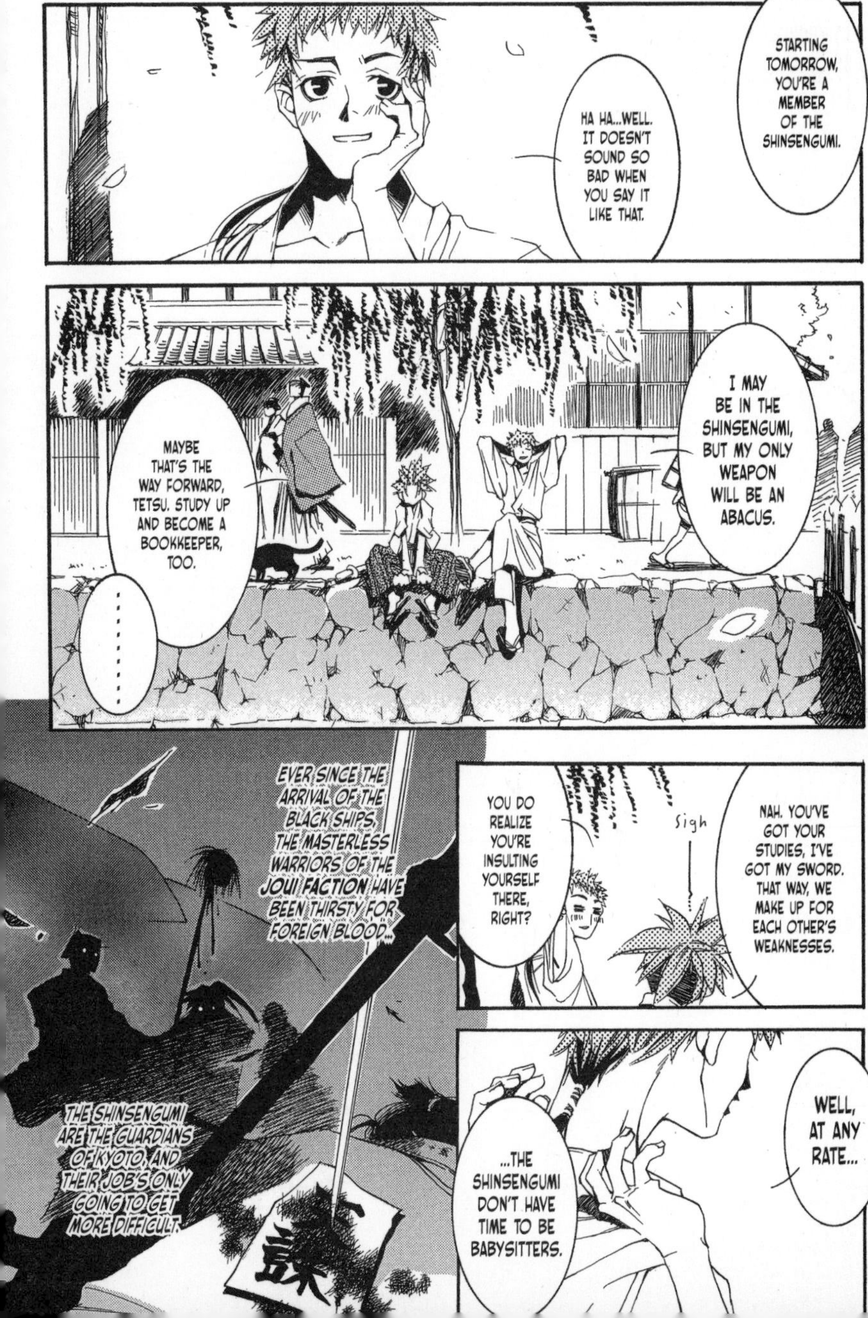
STARTING TOMORROW, YOU'RE A MEMBER OF THE SHINSENGUMI.
HA HA...WELL. IT DOESN'T SOUND SO BAD WHEN YOU SAY IT LIKE THAT.
I MAY BE IN THE SHINSENGUMI, BUT MY ONLY WEAPON WILL BE AN ABACUS.
MAYBE THAT'S THE WAY FORWARD, TETSU. STUDY UP AND BECOME A BOOKKEEPER, TOO.
......
NAH. YOU'VE GOT YOUR STUDIES, I'VE GOT MY SWORD. THAT WAY, WE MAKE UP FOR EACH OTHER'S WEAKNESSES.
Sigh
YOU DO REALIZE YOU'RE INSULTING YOURSELF THERE, RIGHT?
WELL, AT ANY RATE...
...THE SHINSENGUMI DON'T HAVE TIME TO BE BABYSITTERS.
EVER SINCE THE ARRIVAL OF THE BLACK SHIPS, THE MASTERLESS WARRIORS OF THE JOUI FACTION HAVE BEEN THIRSTY FOR FOREIGN BLOOD...
THE SHINSENGUMI ARE THE GUARDIANS OF KYOTO, AND THEIR JOB'S ONLY GOING TO GET MORE DIFFICULT.

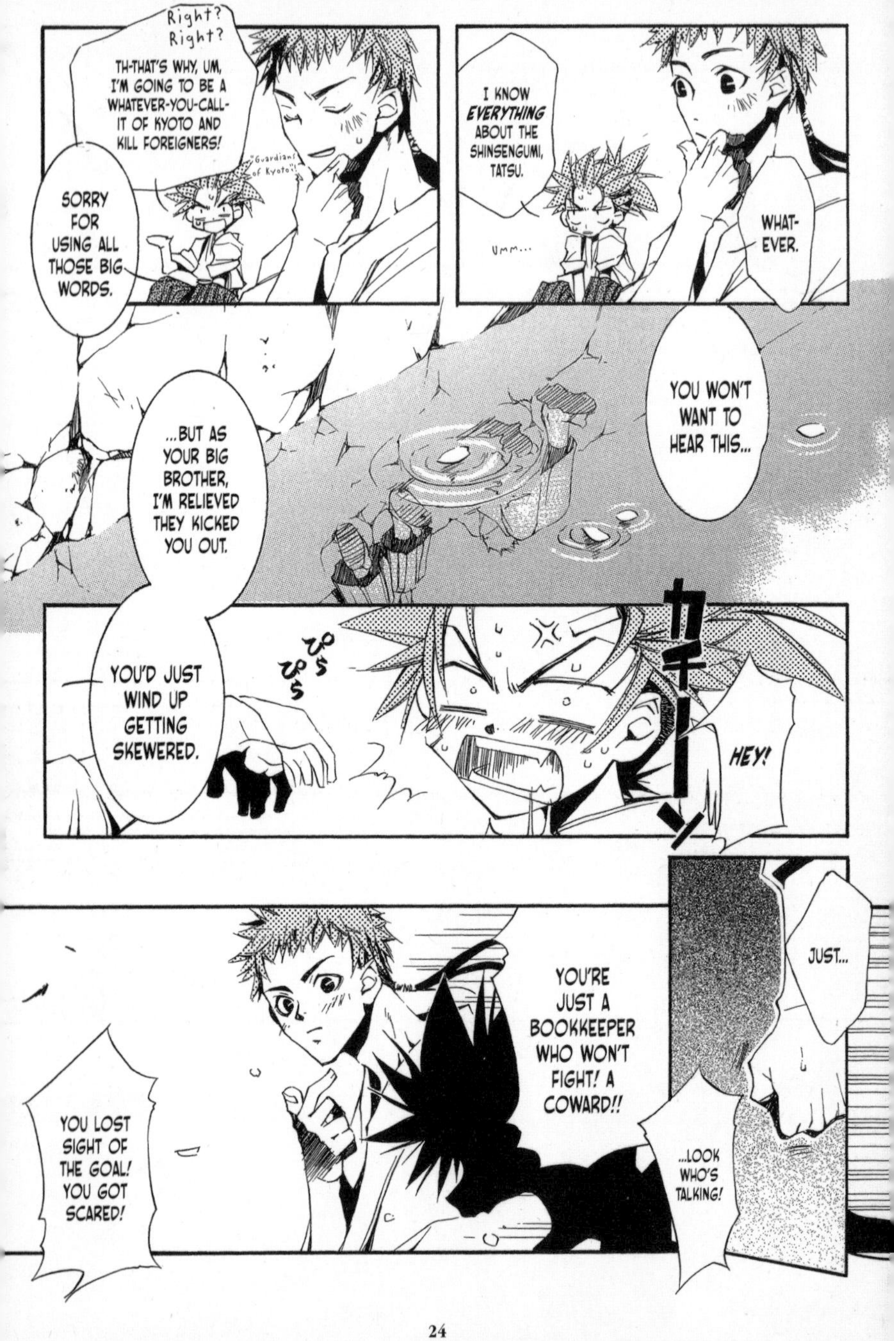
I KNOW *EVERYTHING* ABOUT THE SHINSENGUMI, TATSU.
WHAT-EVER.
Umm...
Right? Right?
TH-THAT'S WHY, UM, I'M GOING TO BE A WHATEVER-YOU-CALL-IT OF KYOTO AND KILL FOREIGNERS!
"Guardians of Kyoto"!
SORRY FOR USING ALL THOSE BIG WORDS.
YOU WON'T WANT TO HEAR THIS...
...BUT AS YOUR BIG BROTHER, I'M RELIEVED THEY KICKED YOU OUT.
YOU'D JUST WIND UP GETTING SKEWERED.
カチーン
HEY!
ぴらぴら
JUST...
...LOOK WHO'S TALKING!
YOU'RE JUST A BOOKKEEPER WHO WON'T FIGHT! A COWARD!!
YOU LOST SIGHT OF THE GOAL! YOU GOT SCARED!

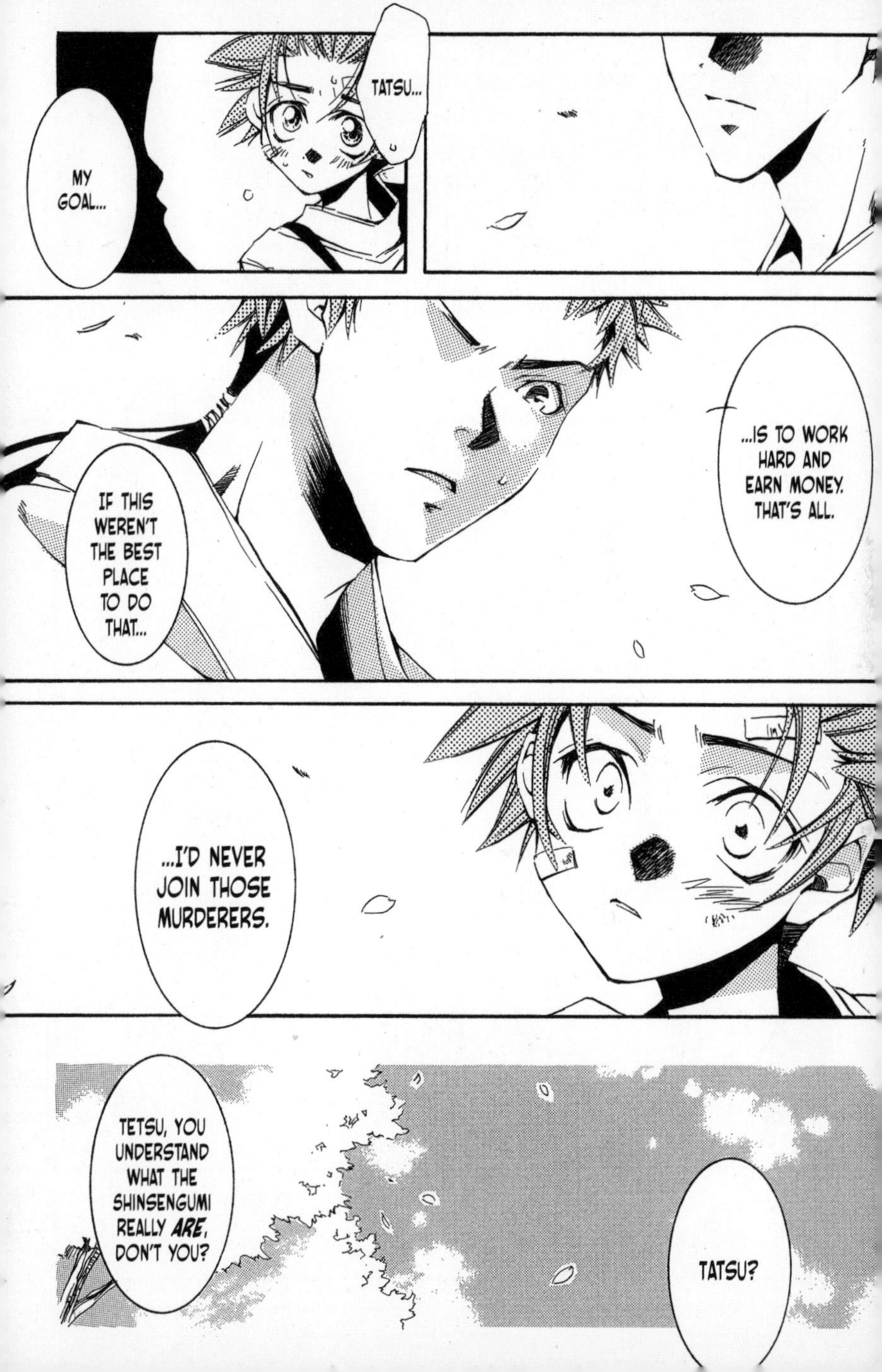
TATSU...
MY GOAL...
...IS TO WORK HARD AND EARN MONEY. THAT'S ALL.
IF THIS WEREN'T THE BEST PLACE TO DO THAT...
...I'D NEVER JOIN THOSE MURDERERS.
TATSU?
TETSU, YOU UNDERSTAND WHAT THE SHINSENGUMI REALLY *ARE*, DON'T YOU?

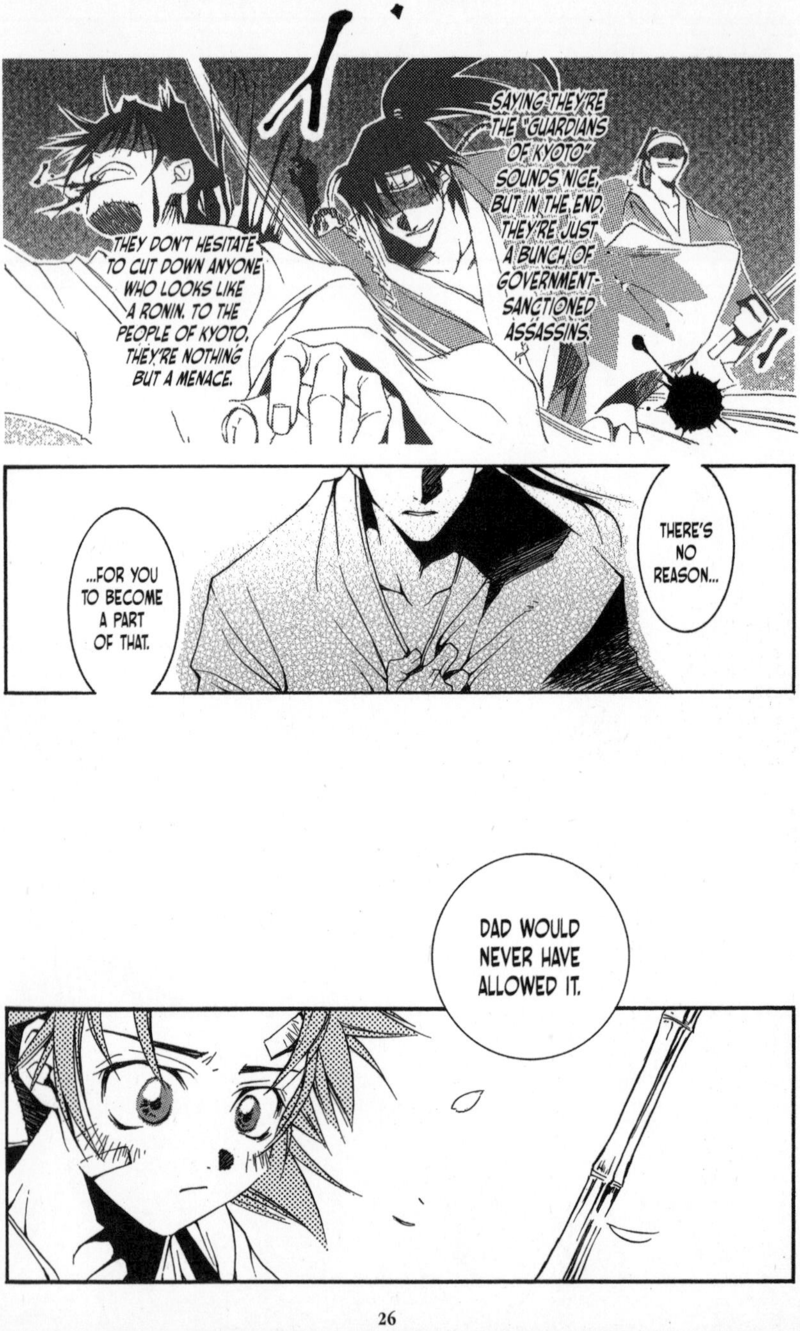
SAYING THEY'RE THE "GUARDIANS OF KYOTO" SOUNDS NICE, BUT IN THE END, THEY'RE JUST A BUNCH OF GOVERNMENT-SANCTIONED ASSASSINS.
THEY DON'T HESITATE TO CUT DOWN ANYONE WHO LOOKS LIKE A RONIN. TO THE PEOPLE OF KYOTO, THEY'RE NOTHING BUT A MENACE.
THERE'S NO REASON...
...FOR YOU TO BECOME A PART OF THAT.
DAD WOULD NEVER HAVE ALLOWED IT.

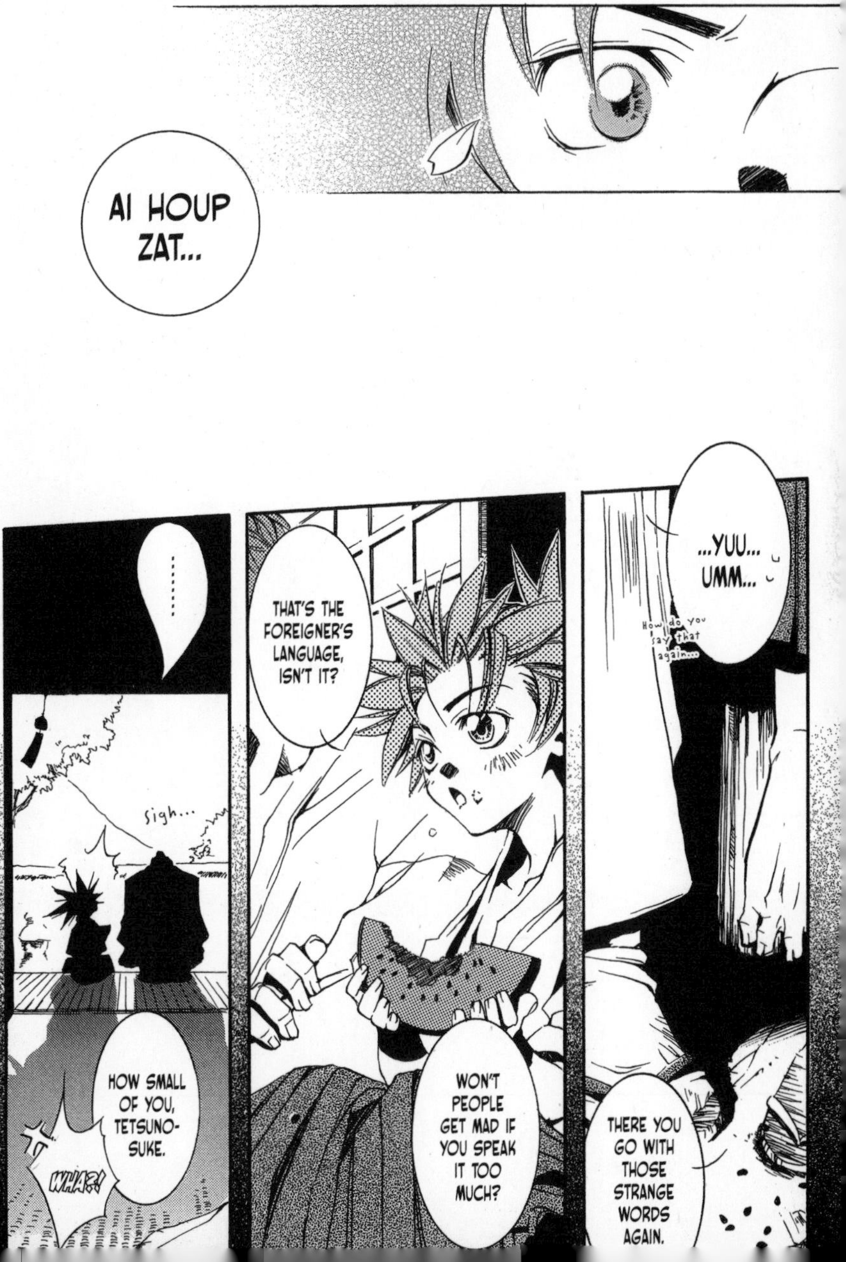
AI HOUP ZAT...
...YUU... UMM...
How do you say that again...
THERE YOU GO WITH THOSE STRANGE WORDS AGAIN.
THAT'S THE FOREIGNER'S LANGUAGE, ISN'T IT?
WON'T PEOPLE GET MAD IF YOU SPEAK IT TOO MUCH?
......
Sigh...
HOW SMALL OF YOU, TETSUNO-SUKE.
WHA?!

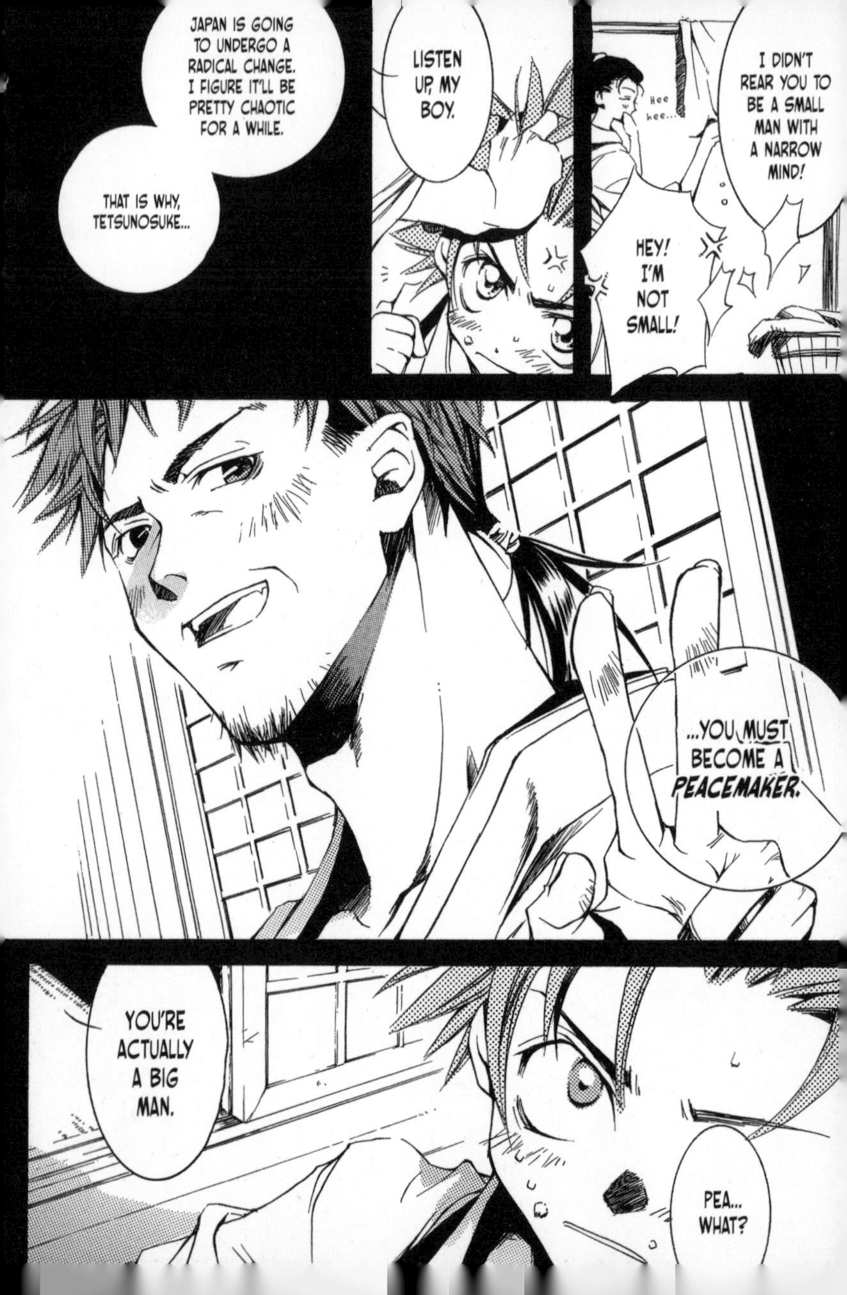
I DIDN'T REAR YOU TO BE A SMALL MAN WITH A NARROW MIND!
Hee hee...
HEY! I'M NOT SMALL!
LISTEN UP, MY BOY.
JAPAN IS GOING TO UNDERGO A RADICAL CHANGE. I FIGURE IT'LL BE PRETTY CHAOTIC FOR A WHILE.
THAT IS WHY, TETSUNOSUKE...
...YOU MUST BECOME A PEACEMAKER.
YOU'RE ACTUALLY A BIG MAN.
PEA... WHAT?

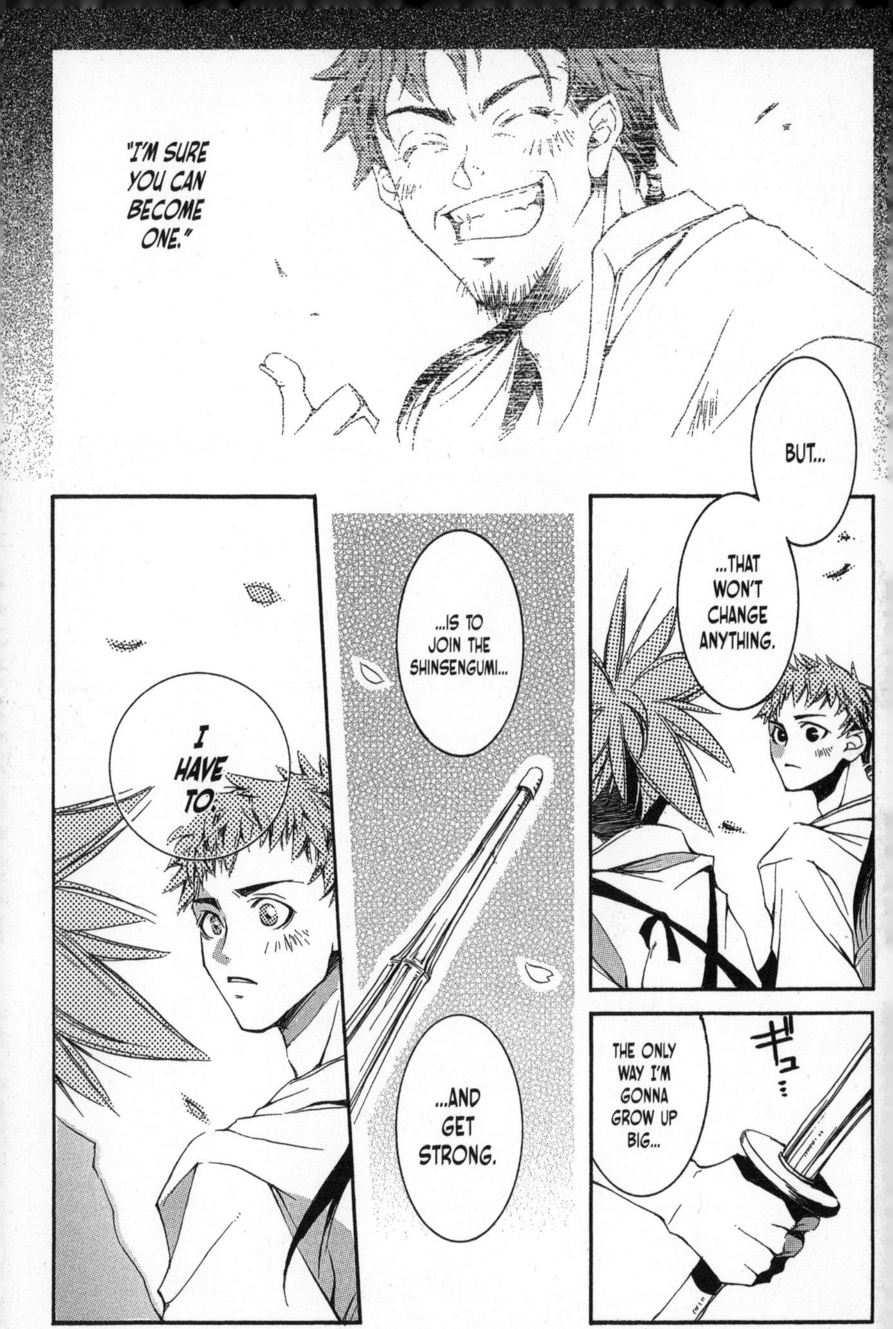
"I'M SURE YOU CAN BECOME ONE."
BUT...
...THAT WON'T CHANGE ANYTHING.
THE ONLY WAY I'M GONNA GROW UP BIG...
...IS TO JOIN THE SHINSENGUMI...
...AND GET STRONG.
I HAVE TO.

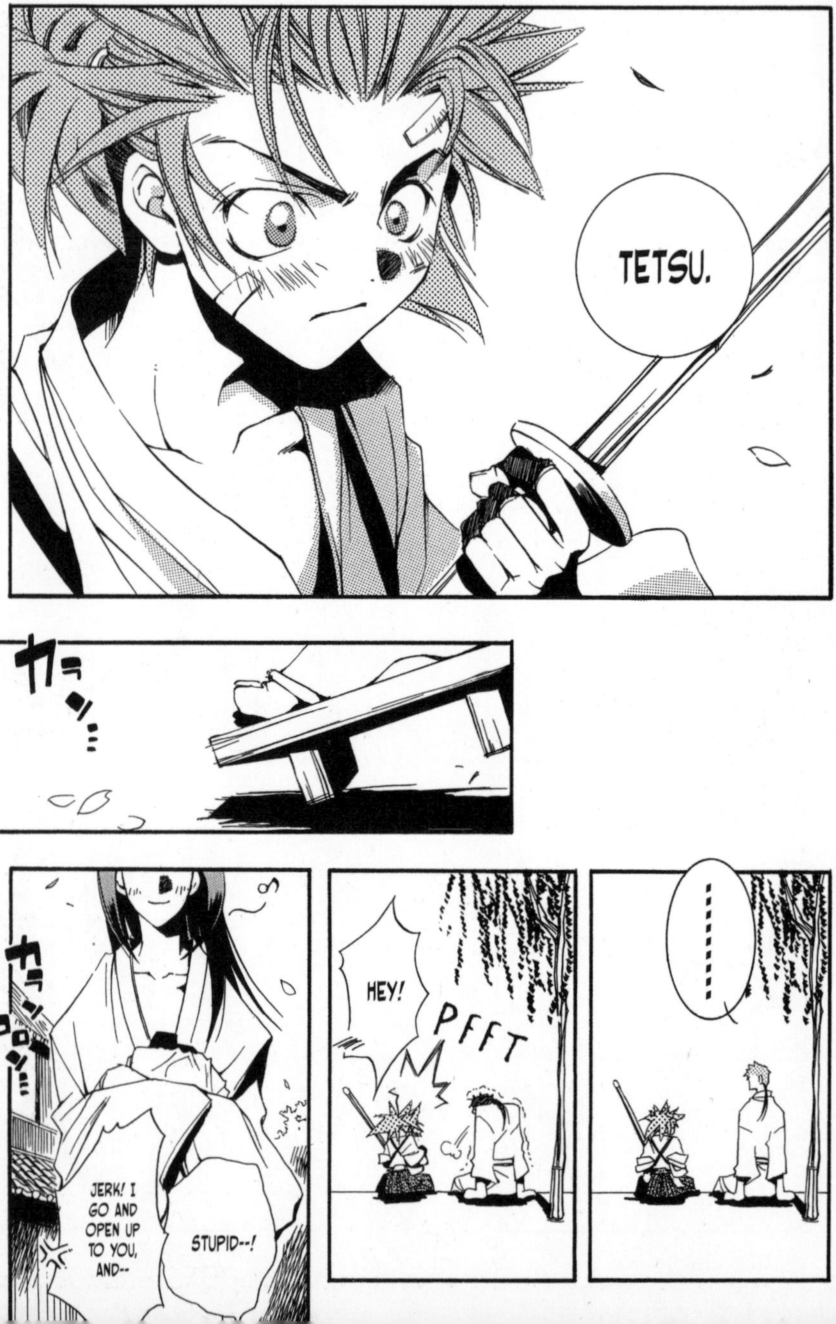
TETSU.
カラン
......
HEY!
PFFT
カランコロン
JERK! I GO AND OPEN UP TO YOU, AND--
STUPID--!

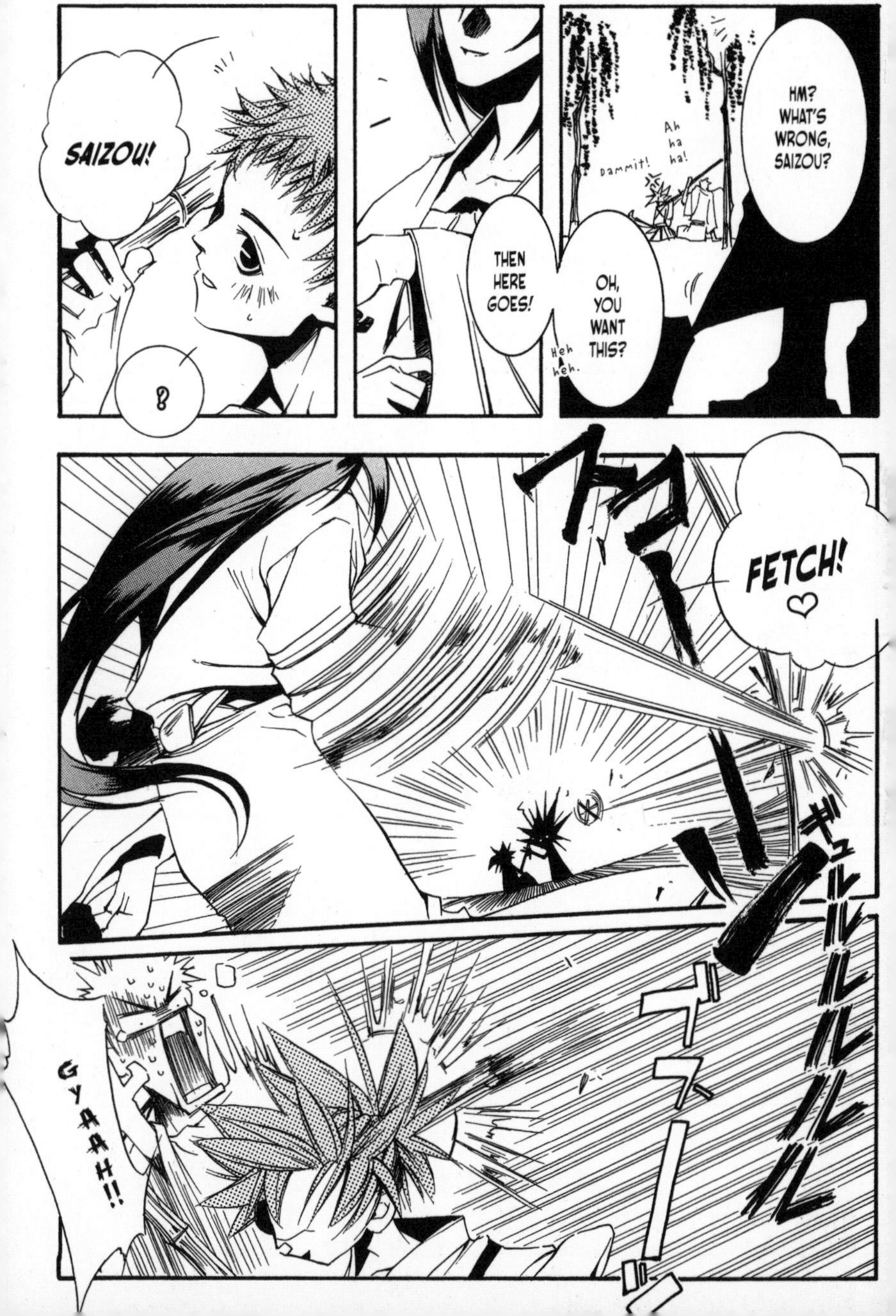
HM? WHAT'S WRONG, SAIZOU?
Ah ha ha!
Dammit!
OH, YOU WANT THIS?
Heh heh.
THEN HERE GOES!
SAIZOU!
?
FETCH! ♡
GYAAH!!

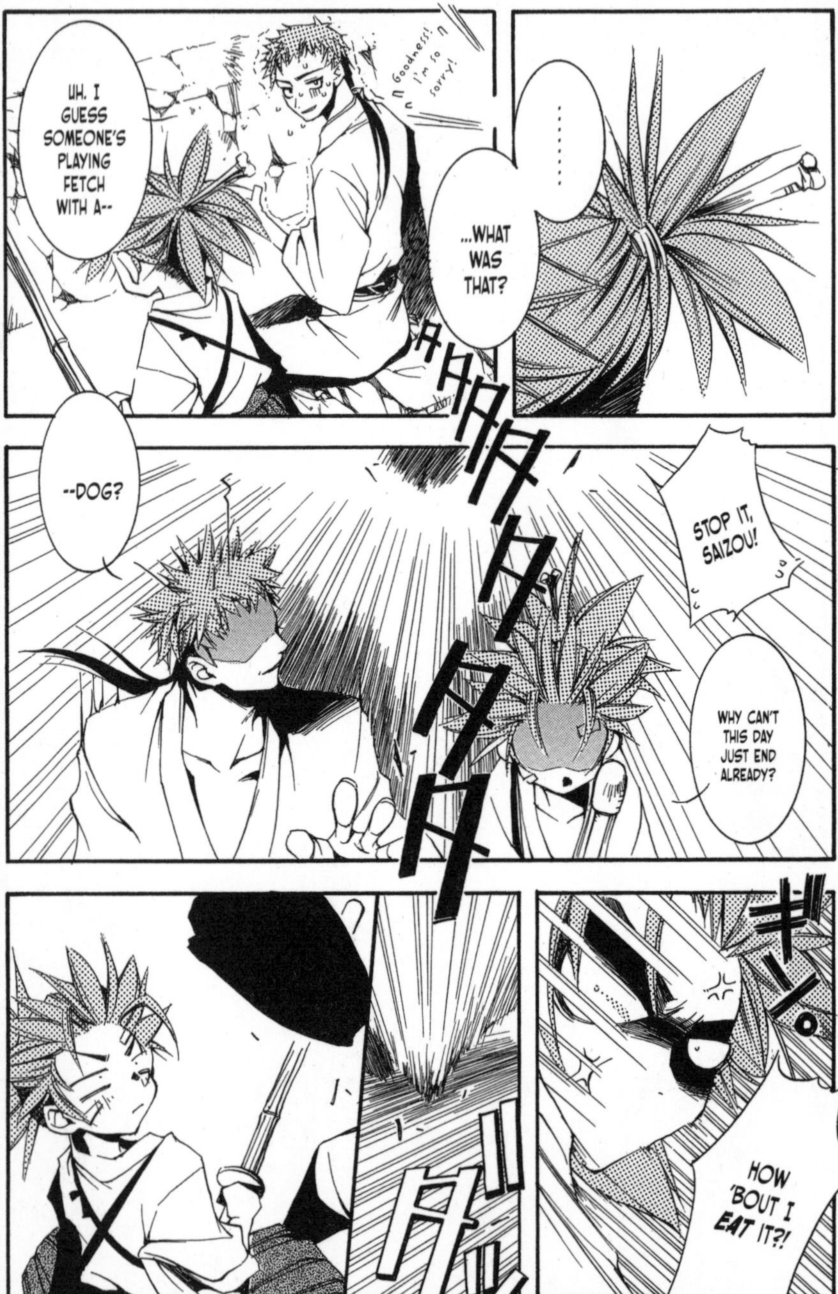
......
...WHAT WAS THAT?
Goodness! I'm so sorry!
UH. I GUESS SOMEONE'S PLAYING FETCH WITH A--
--DOG?
STOP IT, SAIZOU!
WHY CAN'T THIS DAY JUST END ALREADY?
HOW 'BOUT I EAT IT?!

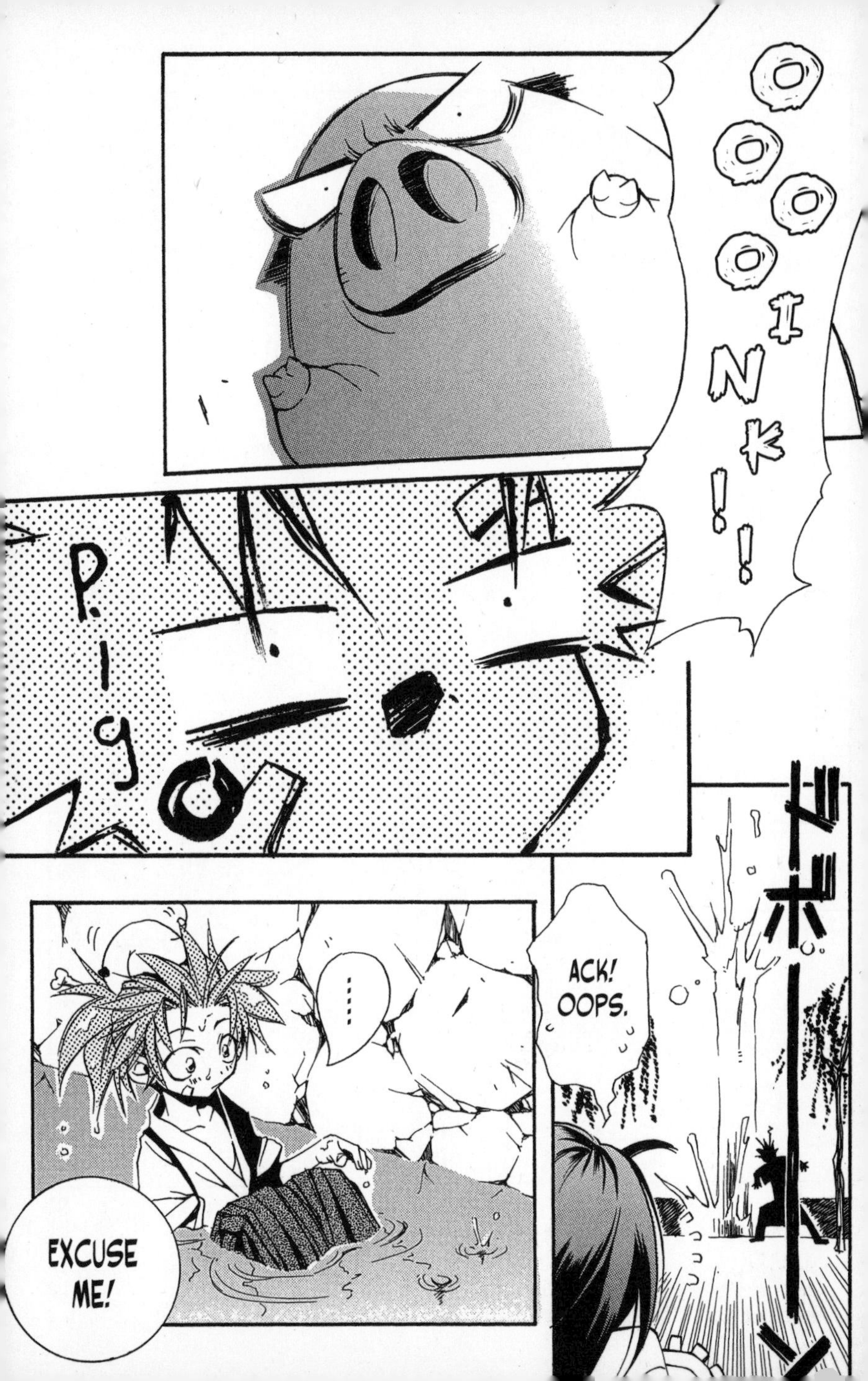
OOOOINK!!
P-ig
ACK! OOPS.
.....
EXCUSE ME!

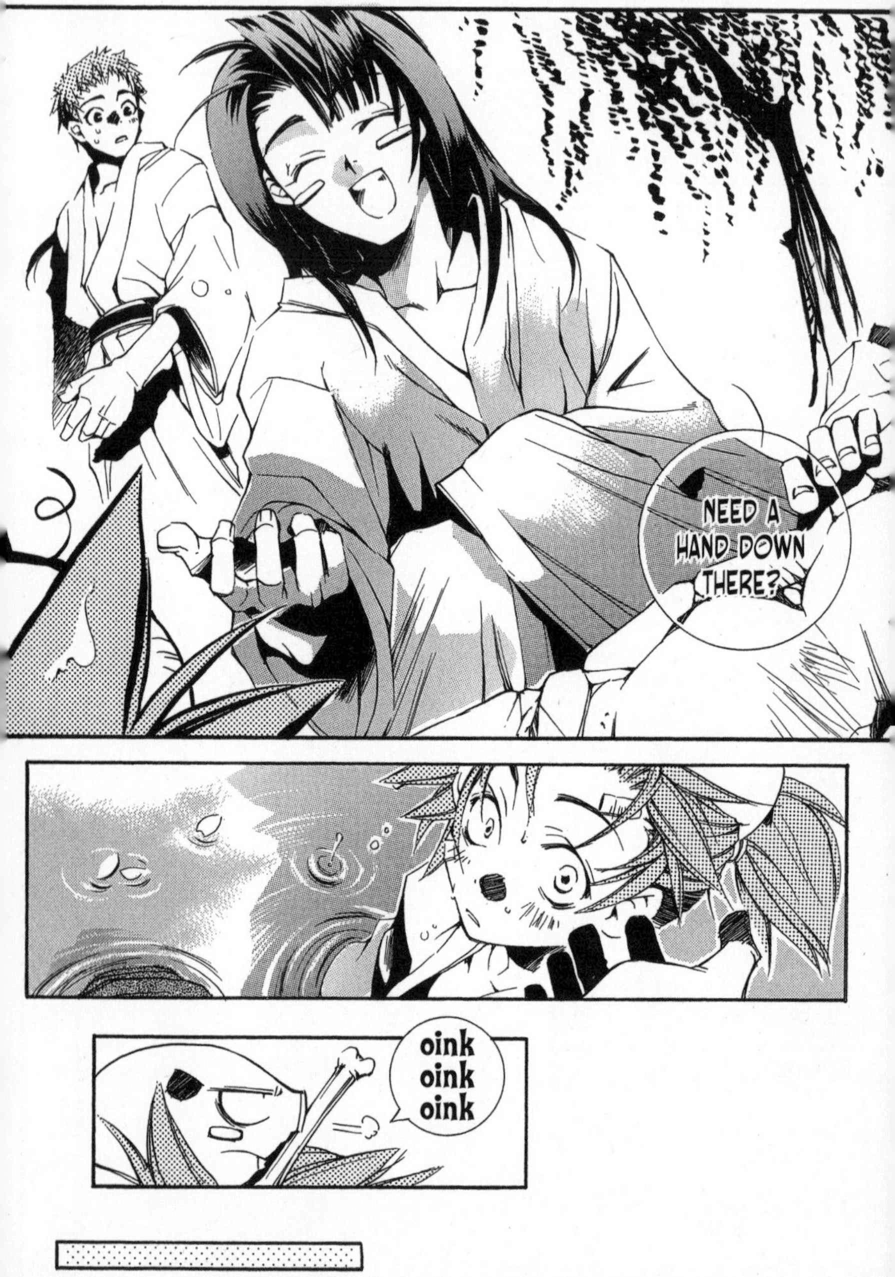
NEED A HAND DOWN THERE?
oink oink oink

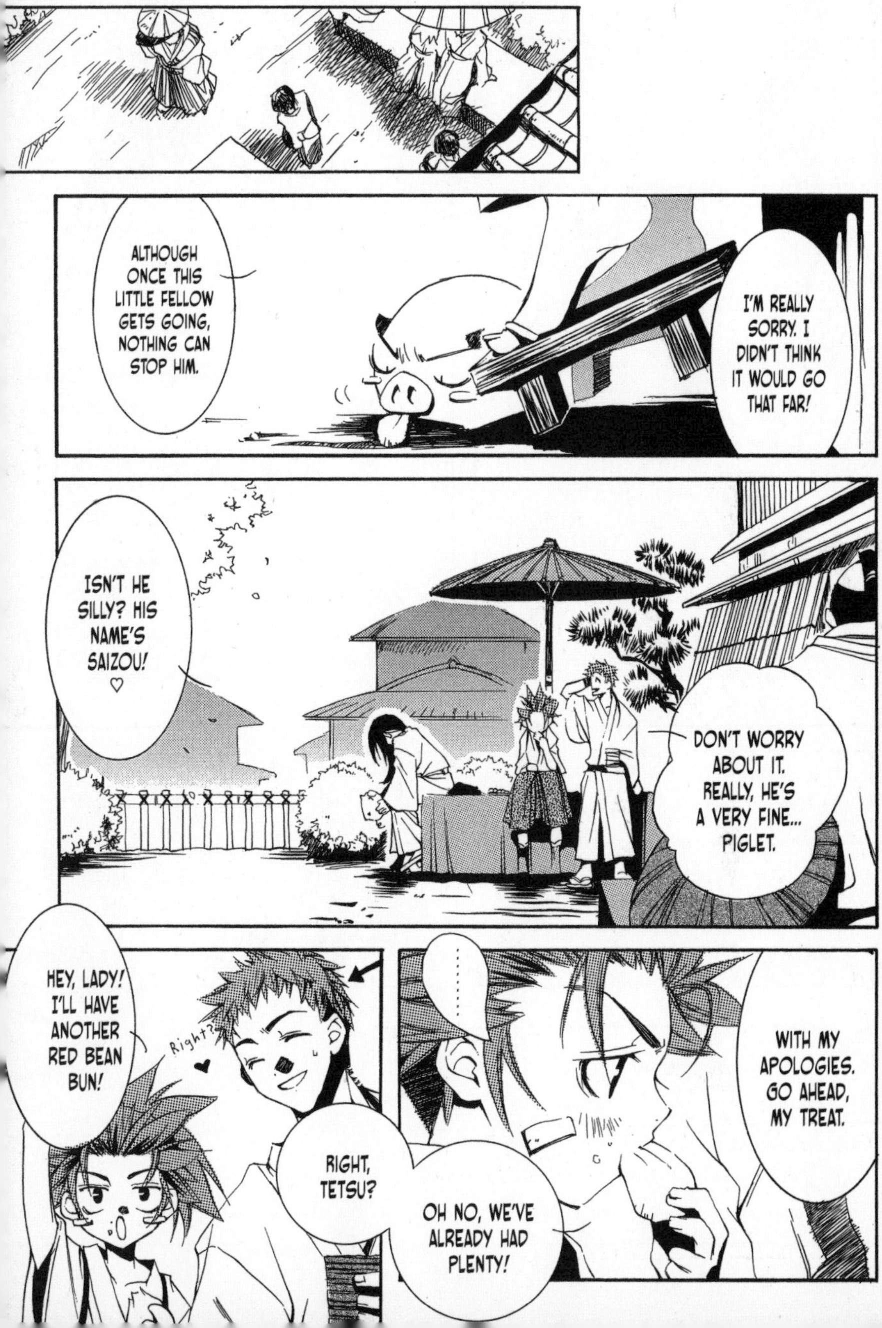
I'M REALLY SORRY. I DIDN'T THINK IT WOULD GO THAT FAR!
ALTHOUGH ONCE THIS LITTLE FELLOW GETS GOING, NOTHING CAN STOP HIM.
DON'T WORRY ABOUT IT. REALLY, HE'S A VERY FINE... PIGLET.
ISN'T HE SILLY? HIS NAME'S SAIZOU! ♡
WITH MY APOLOGIES. GO AHEAD, MY TREAT.
......
OH NO, WE'VE ALREADY HAD PLENTY!
HEY, LADY! I'LL HAVE ANOTHER RED BEAN BUN!
Right? ♥
RIGHT, TETSU?

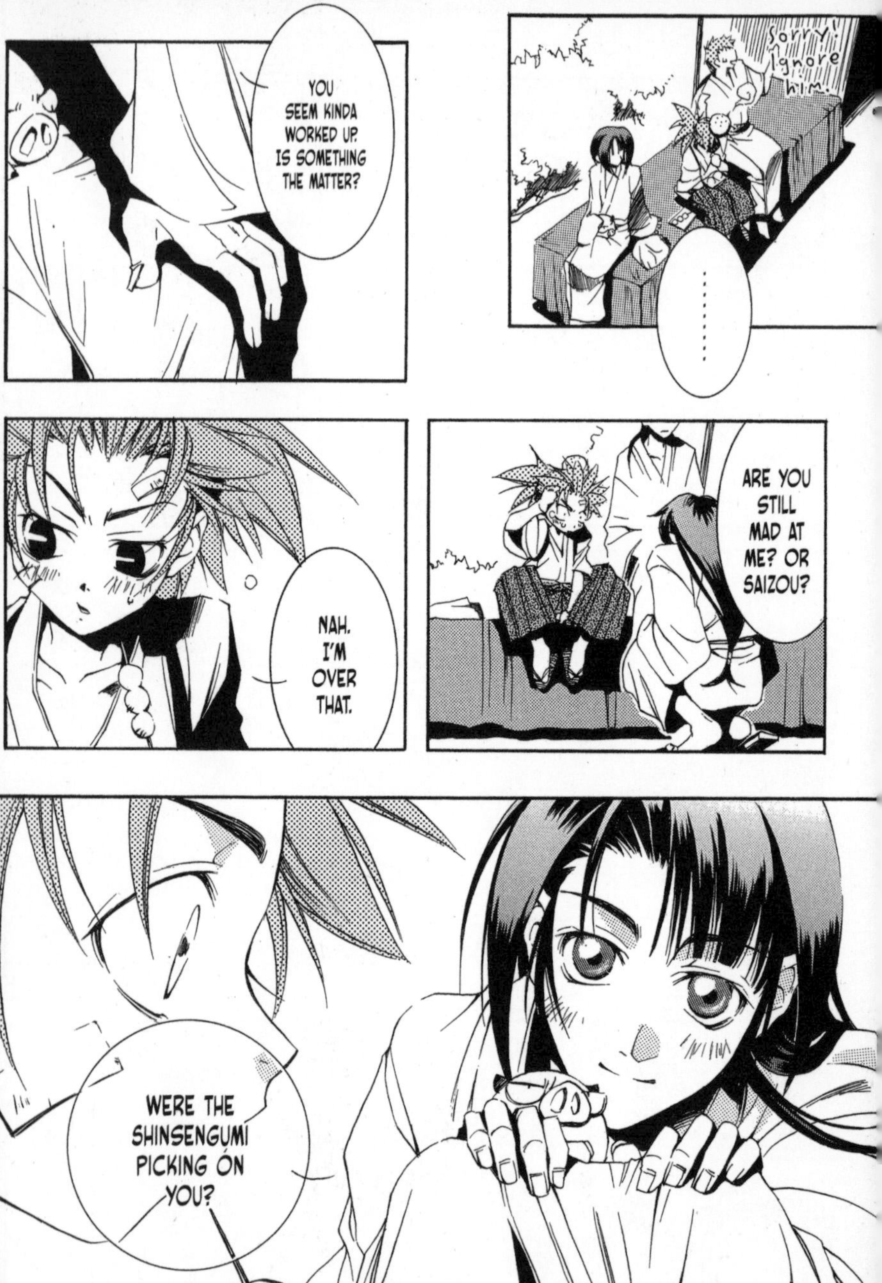
Sorry! Ignore him.
......
YOU SEEM KINDA WORKED UP. IS SOMETHING THE MATTER?
ARE YOU STILL MAD AT ME? OR SAIZOU?
NAH. I'M OVER THAT.
WERE THE SHINSENGUMI PICKING ON YOU?

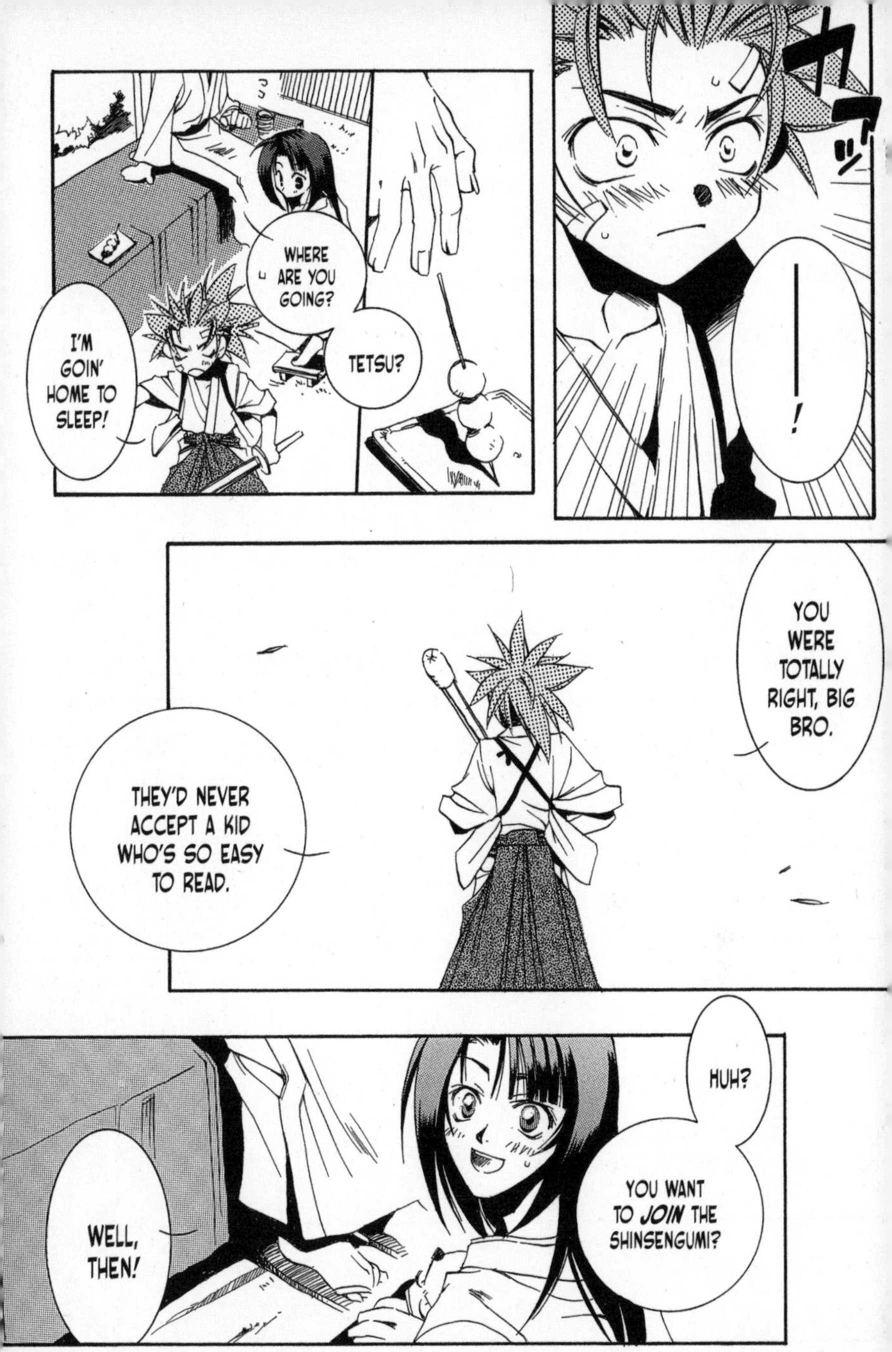
—!
WHERE ARE YOU GOING?
TETSU?
I'M GOIN' HOME TO SLEEP!
YOU WERE TOTALLY RIGHT, BIG BRO.
THEY'D NEVER ACCEPT A KID WHO'S SO EASY TO READ.
HUH?
YOU WANT TO *JOIN* THE SHINSENGUMI?
WELL, THEN!

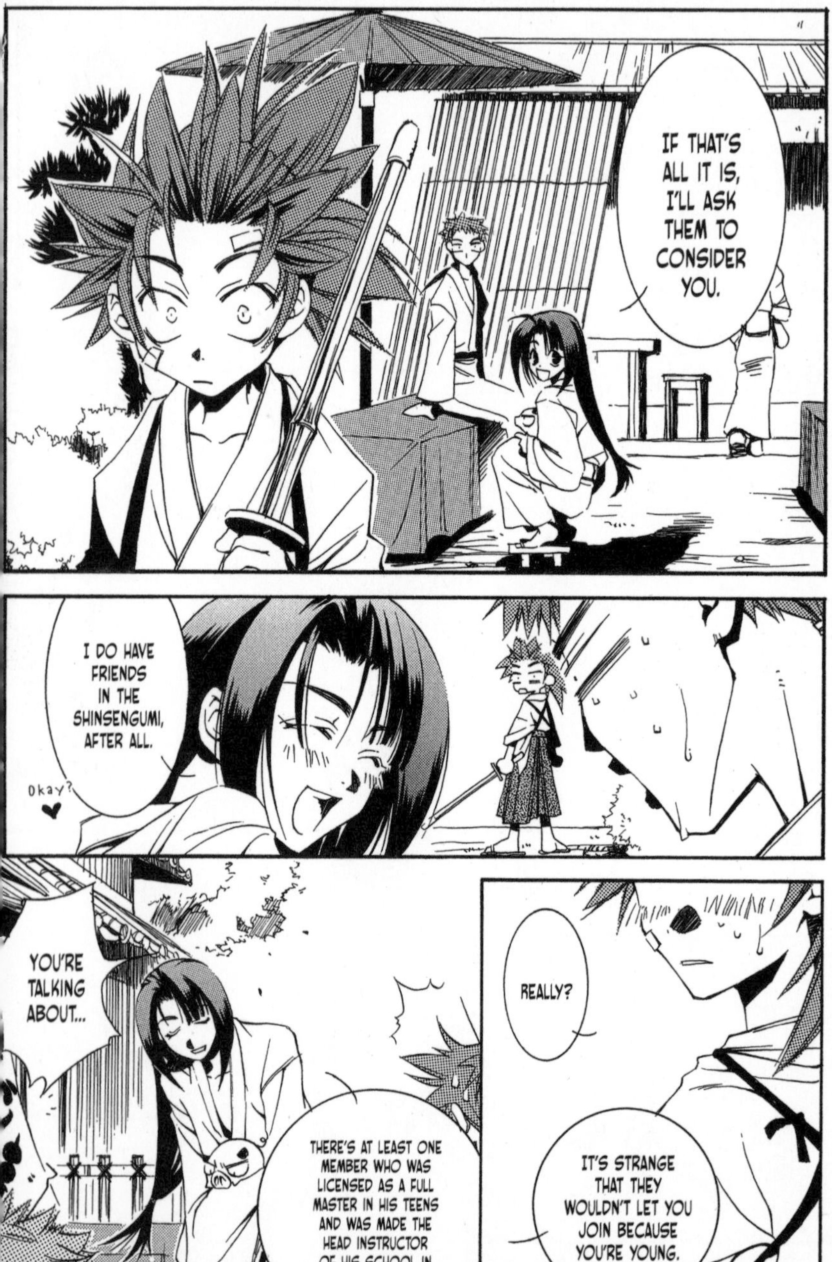
IF THAT'S ALL IT IS, I'LL ASK THEM TO CONSIDER YOU.
I DO HAVE FRIENDS IN THE SHINSENGUMI, AFTER ALL.
Okay? ♥
REALLY?
IT'S STRANGE THAT THEY WOULDN'T LET YOU JOIN BECAUSE YOU'RE YOUNG.
THERE'S AT LEAST ONE MEMBER WHO WAS LICENSED AS A FULL MASTER IN HIS TEENS AND WAS MADE THE HEAD INSTRUCTOR OF HIS SCHOOL IN HIS TWENTIES.
YOU'RE TALKING ABOUT...

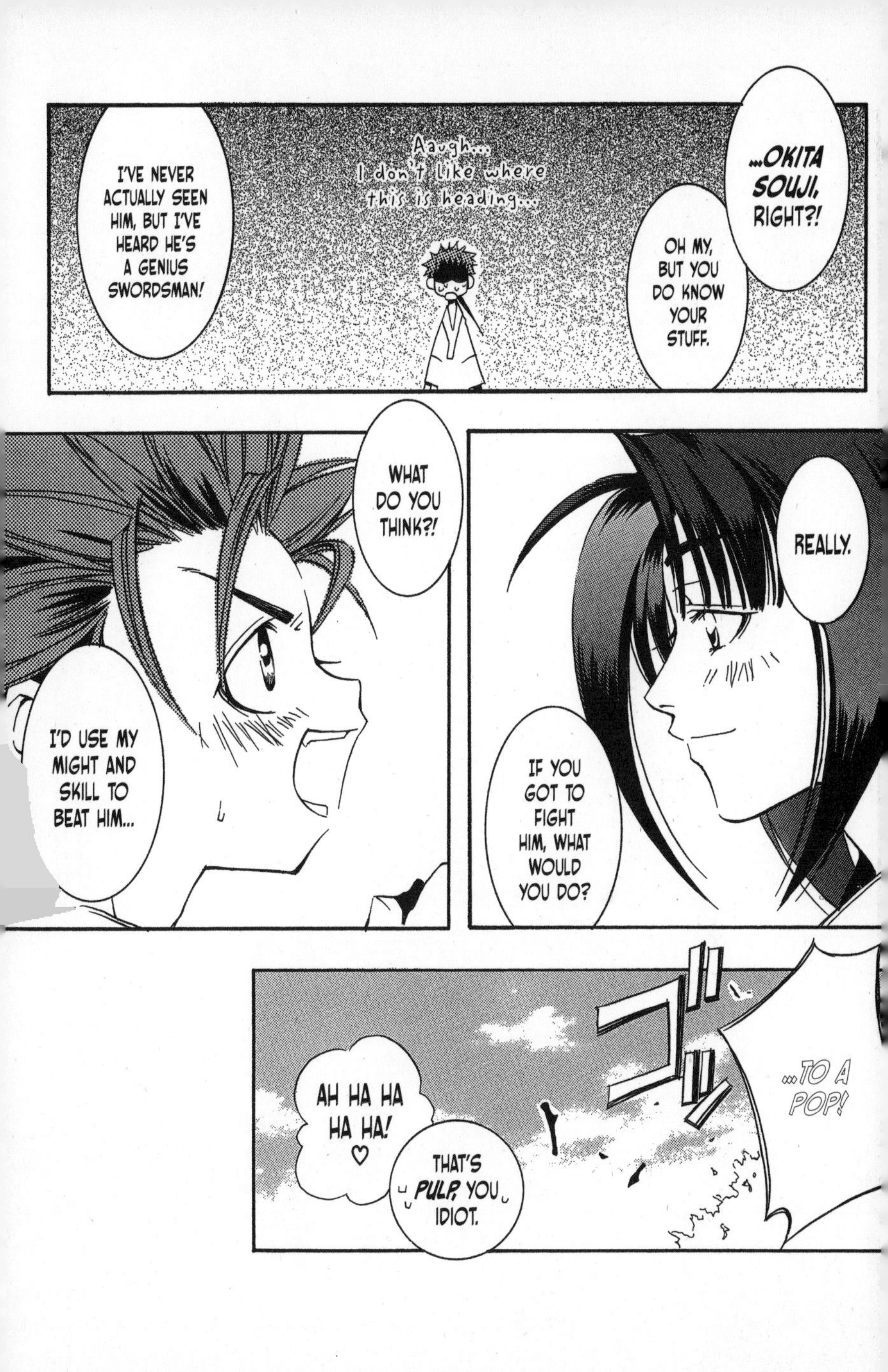
...OKITA SOUJI, RIGHT?!
OH MY, BUT YOU DO KNOW YOUR STUFF.
Aaugh... I don't like where this is heading...
I'VE NEVER ACTUALLY SEEN HIM, BUT I'VE HEARD HE'S A GENIUS SWORDSMAN!
REALLY.
IF YOU GOT TO FIGHT HIM, WHAT WOULD YOU DO?
WHAT DO YOU THINK?!
I'D USE MY MIGHT AND SKILL TO BEAT HIM...
...TO A POP!
AH HA HA HA HA! ♡
THAT'S PULP, YOU IDIOT.

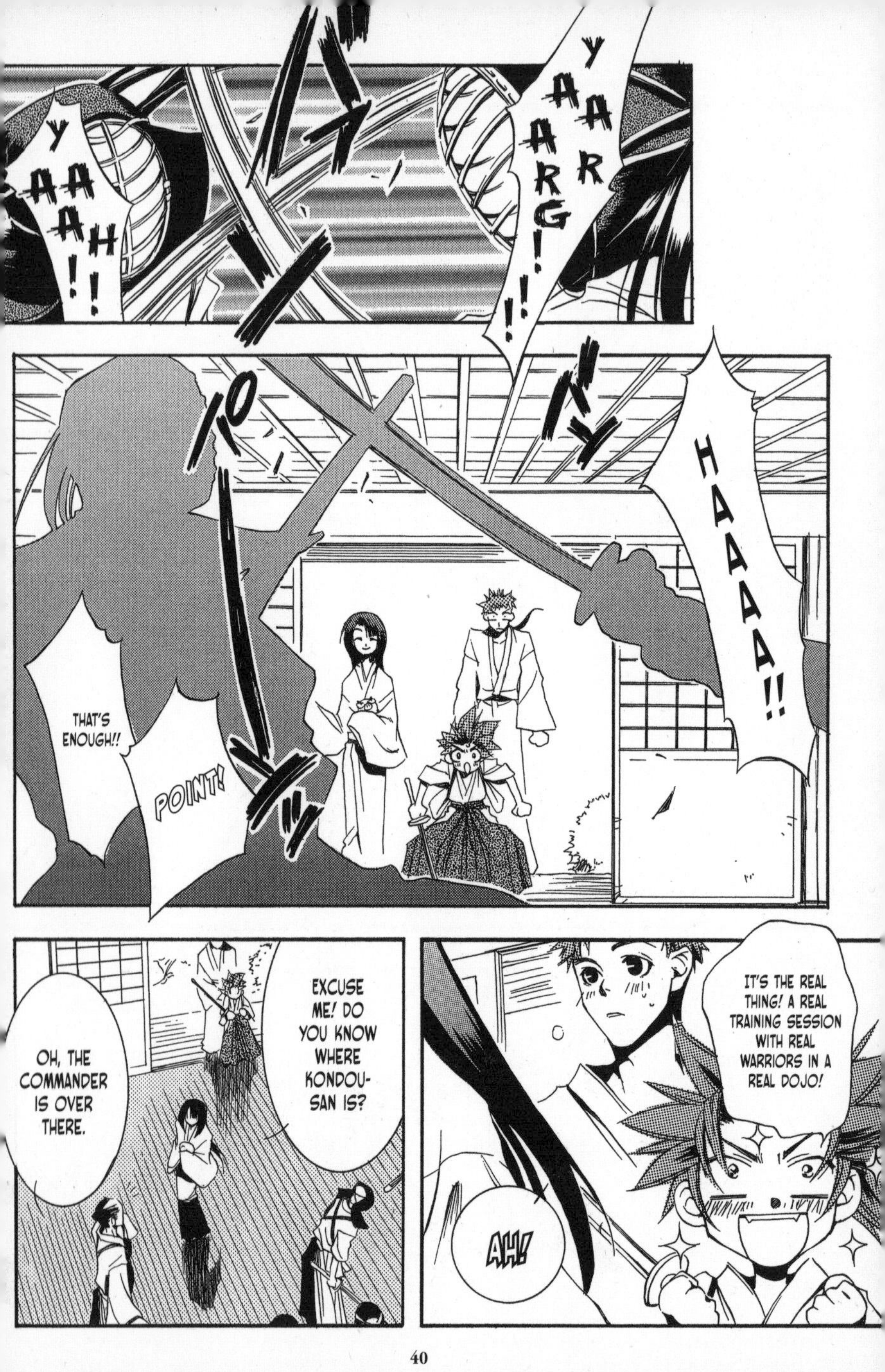
YAAARRG!!!
YAAAH!!
HAAAAA!!
THAT'S ENOUGH!!
POINT!
IT'S THE REAL THING! A REAL TRAINING SESSION WITH REAL WARRIORS IN A REAL DOJO!
AH!
EXCUSE ME! DO YOU KNOW WHERE KONDOU-SAN IS?
OH, THE COMMANDER IS OVER THERE.

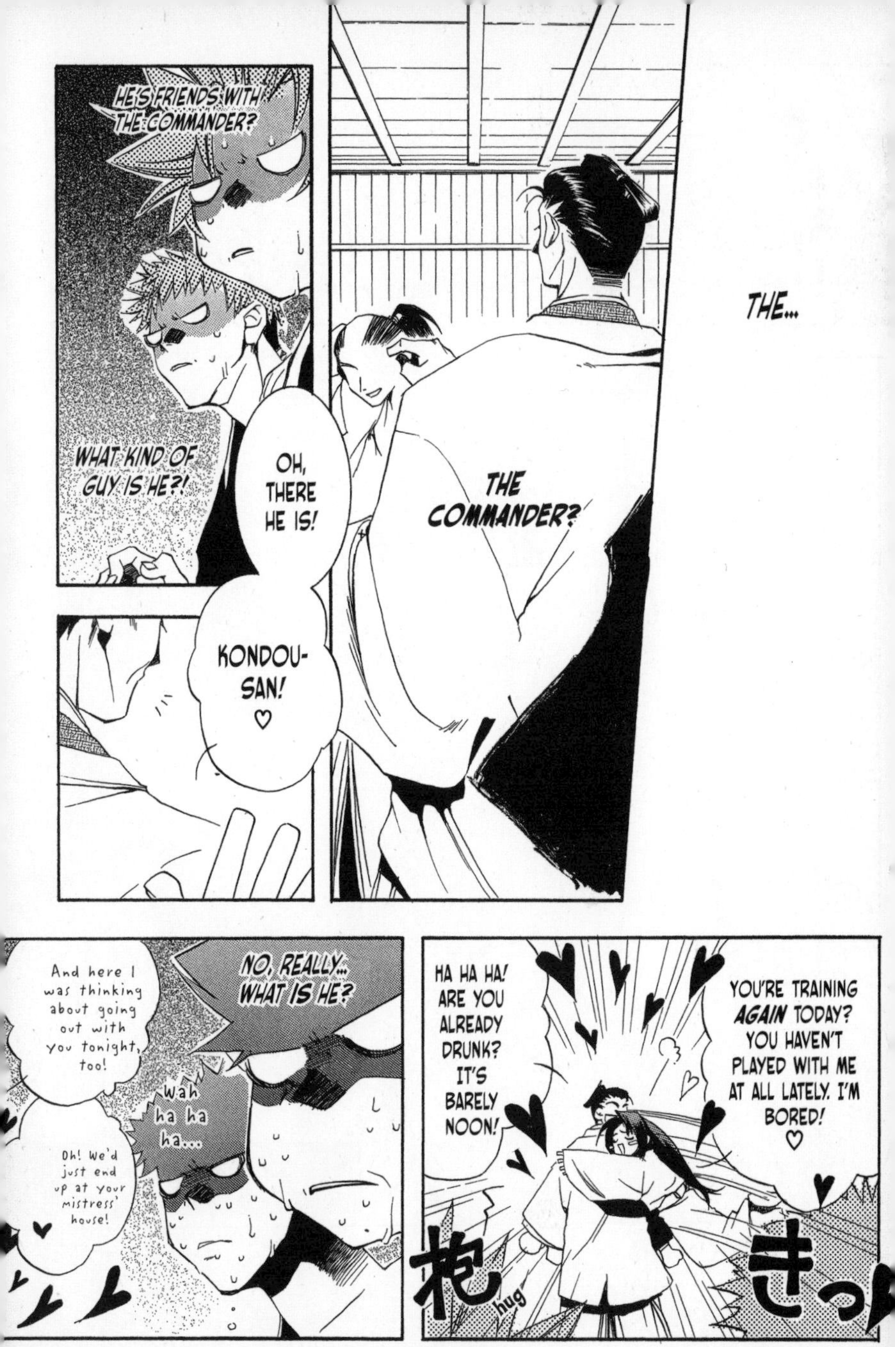
THE...
THE COMMANDER?
HE'S FRIENDS WITH THE COMMANDER?
WHAT KIND OF GUY IS HE?!
OH, THERE HE IS!
KONDOU-SAN! ♡
YOU'RE TRAINING AGAIN TODAY? YOU HAVEN'T PLAYED WITH ME AT ALL LATELY. I'M BORED! ♡
HA HA HA! ARE YOU ALREADY DRUNK? IT'S BARELY NOON!
抱 hug
きっ
NO, REALLY... WHAT IS HE?
And here I was thinking about going out with you tonight, too!
Wah ha ha ha...
Oh! We'd just end up at your mistress' house!

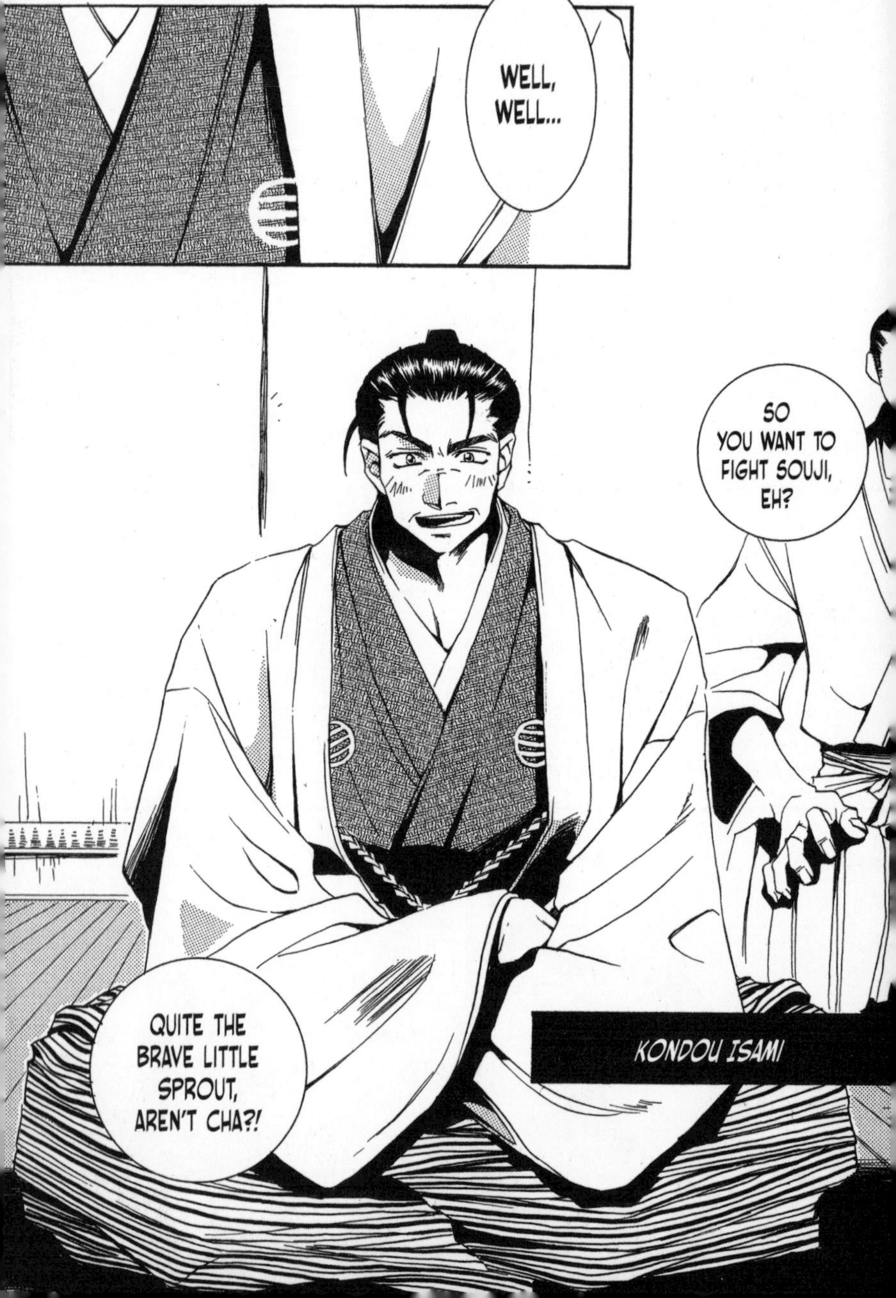
WELL, WELL...
SO YOU WANT TO FIGHT SOUJI, EH?
KONDOU ISAMI
QUITE THE BRAVE LITTLE SPROUT, AREN'T CHA?!

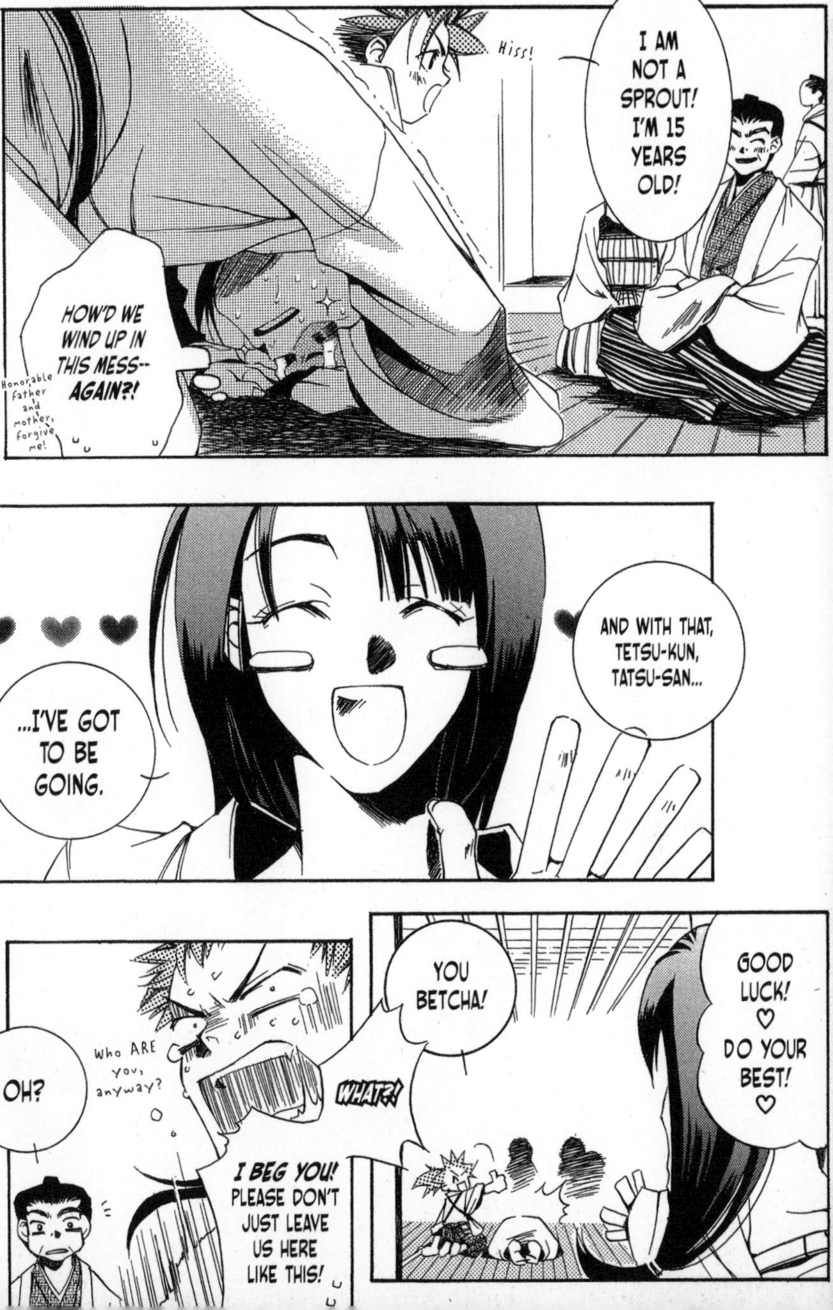
Hiss!
I AM NOT A SPROUT! I'M 15 YEARS OLD!
HOW'D WE WIND UP IN THIS MESS--AGAIN?!
Honorable father and mother, forgive me!
AND WITH THAT, TETSU-KUN, TATSU-SAN...
...I'VE GOT TO BE GOING.
GOOD LUCK! ♡ DO YOUR BEST! ♡
YOU BETCHA!
WHAT?!
I BEG YOU! PLEASE DON'T JUST LEAVE US HERE LIKE THIS!
Who ARE you, anyway?
OH?

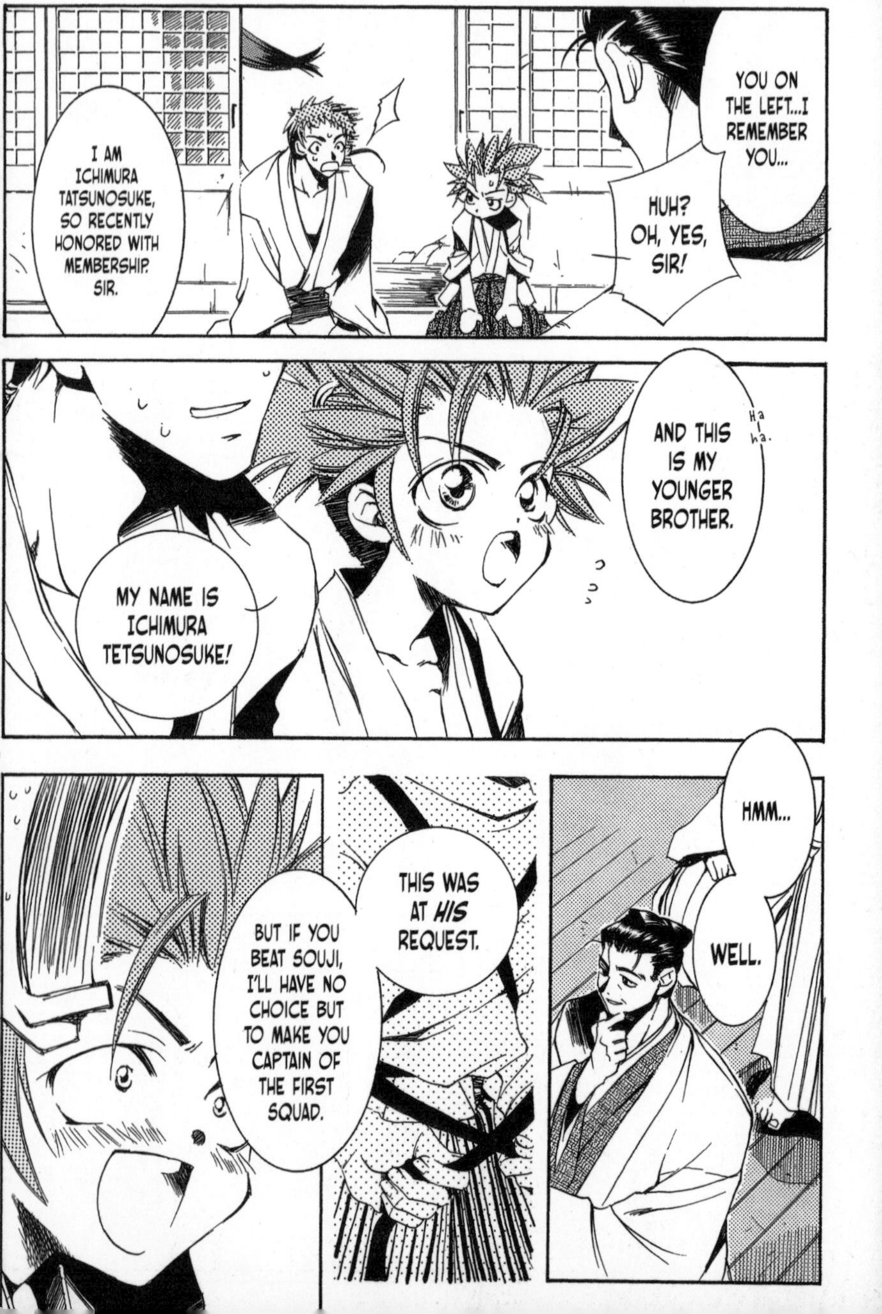
YOU ON THE LEFT...I REMEMBER YOU...
HUH? OH, YES, SIR!
I AM ICHIMURA TATSUNOSUKE, SO RECENTLY HONORED WITH MEMBERSHIP. SIR.
AND THIS IS MY YOUNGER BROTHER.
Ha ha.
MY NAME IS ICHIMURA TETSUNOSUKE!
HMM...
WELL.
THIS WAS AT *HIS* REQUEST.
BUT IF YOU BEAT SOUJI, I'LL HAVE NO CHOICE BUT TO MAKE YOU CAPTAIN OF THE FIRST SQUAD.

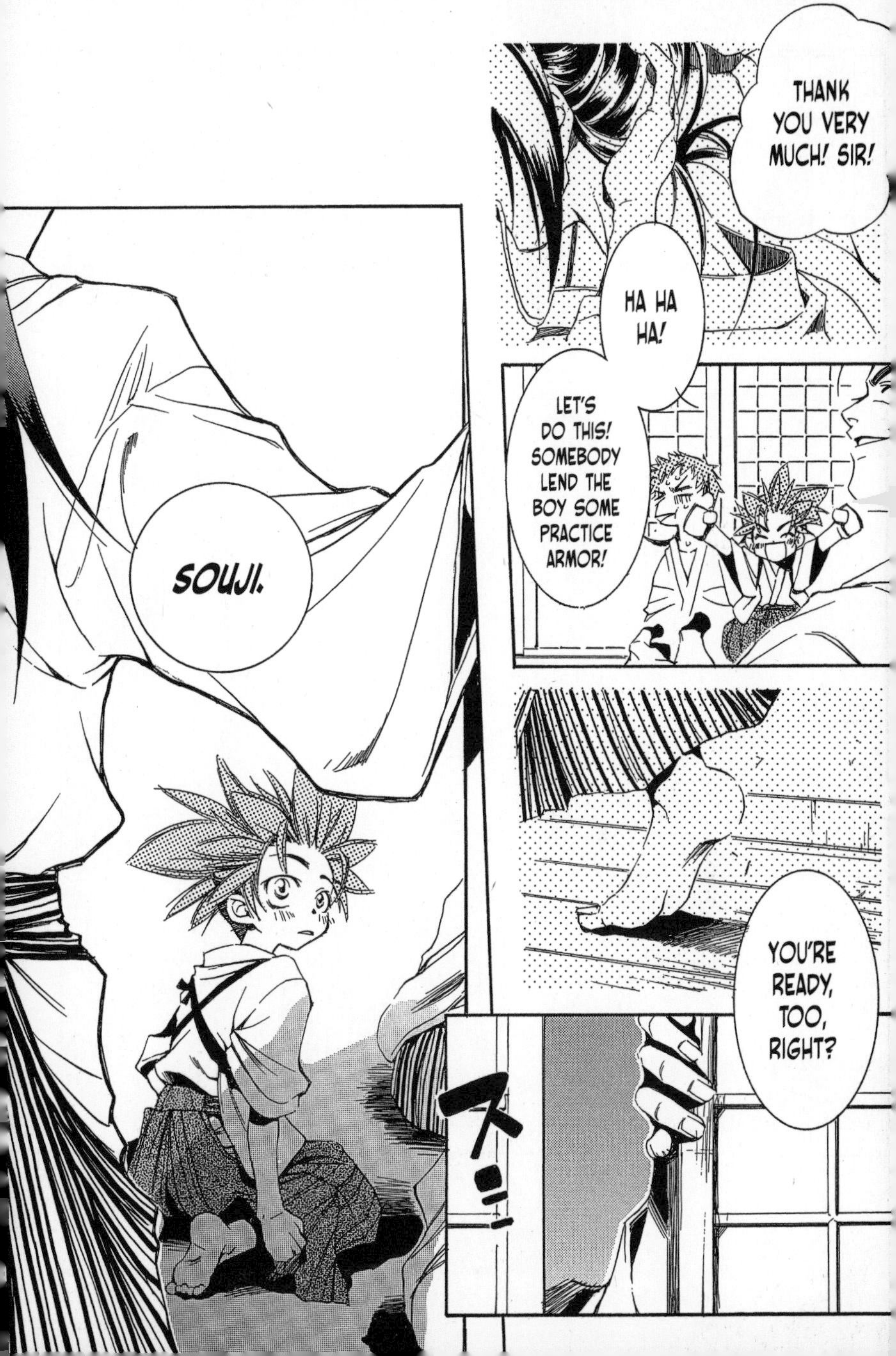
THANK YOU VERY MUCH! SIR!
HA HA HA!
LET'S DO THIS! SOMEBODY LEND THE BOY SOME PRACTICE ARMOR!
YOU'RE READY, TOO, RIGHT?
SOUJI.

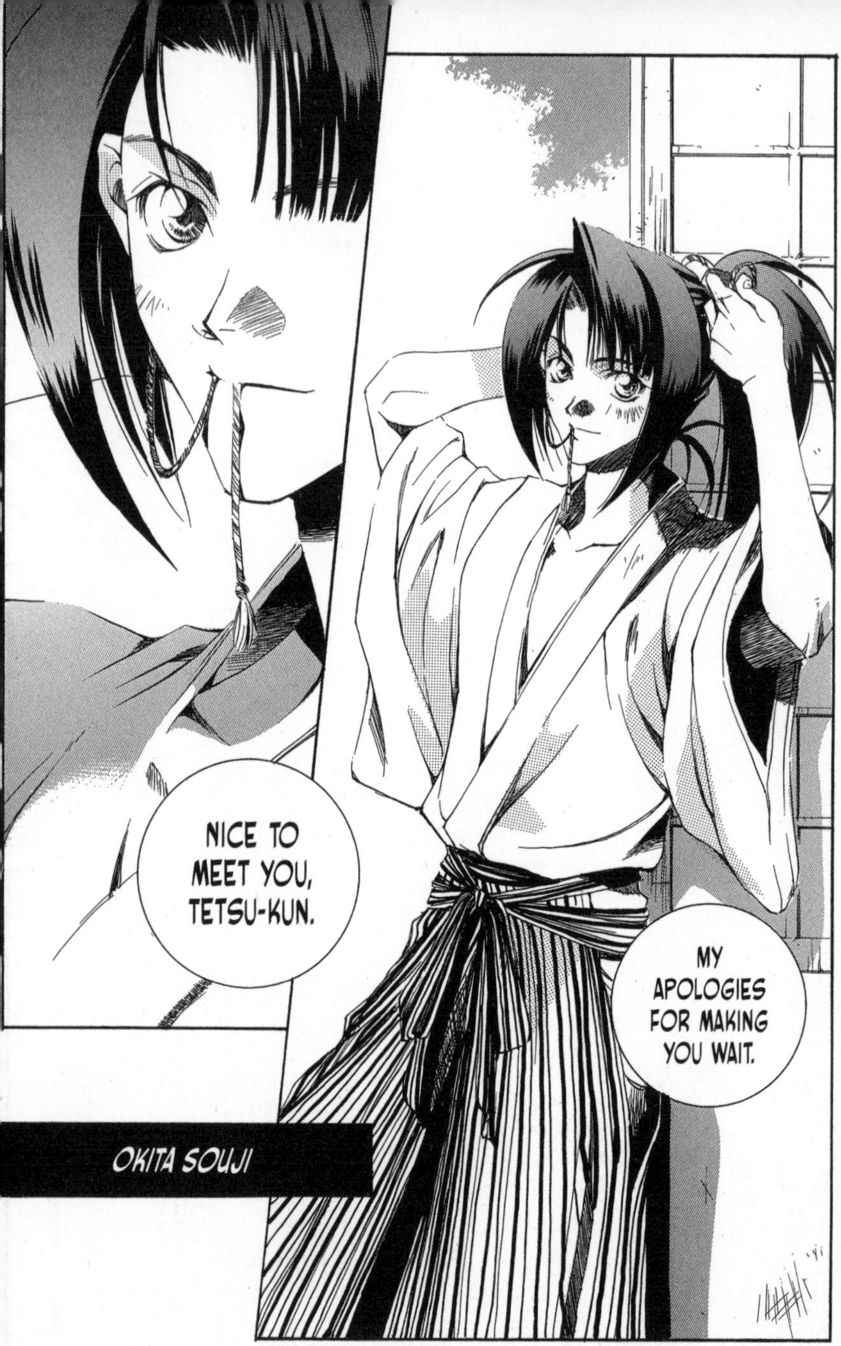
MY APOLOGIES FOR MAKING YOU WAIT.
NICE TO MEET YOU, TETSU-KUN.
OKITA SOUJI

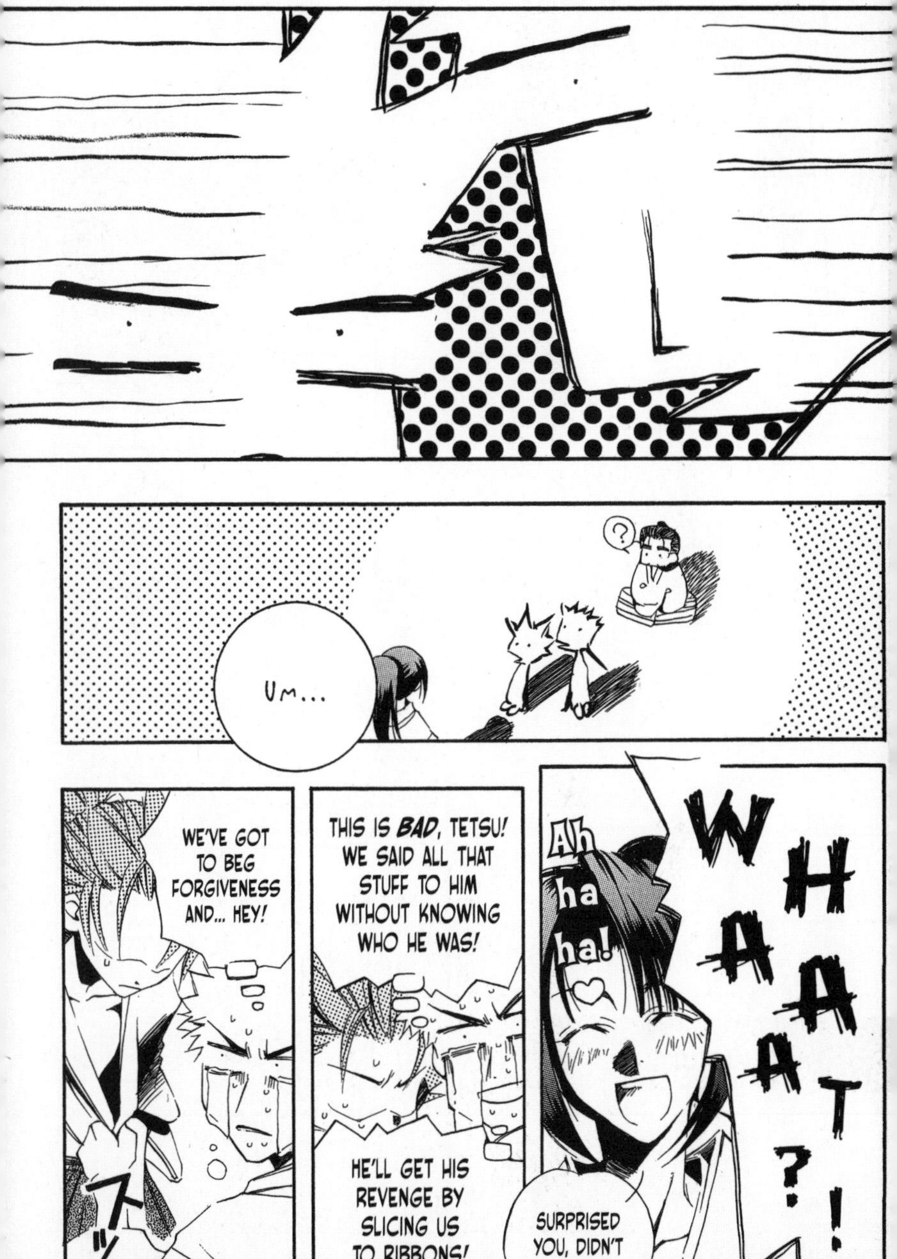
?
UM...
WHAAAT?!
Ah ha ha!
SURPRISED YOU, DIDN'T I? ♡
THIS IS *BAD*, TETSU! WE SAID ALL THAT STUFF TO HIM WITHOUT KNOWING WHO HE WAS!
HE'LL GET HIS REVENGE BY SLICING US TO RIBBONS!
WE'VE GOT TO BEG FORGIVENESS AND... HEY!
スッ

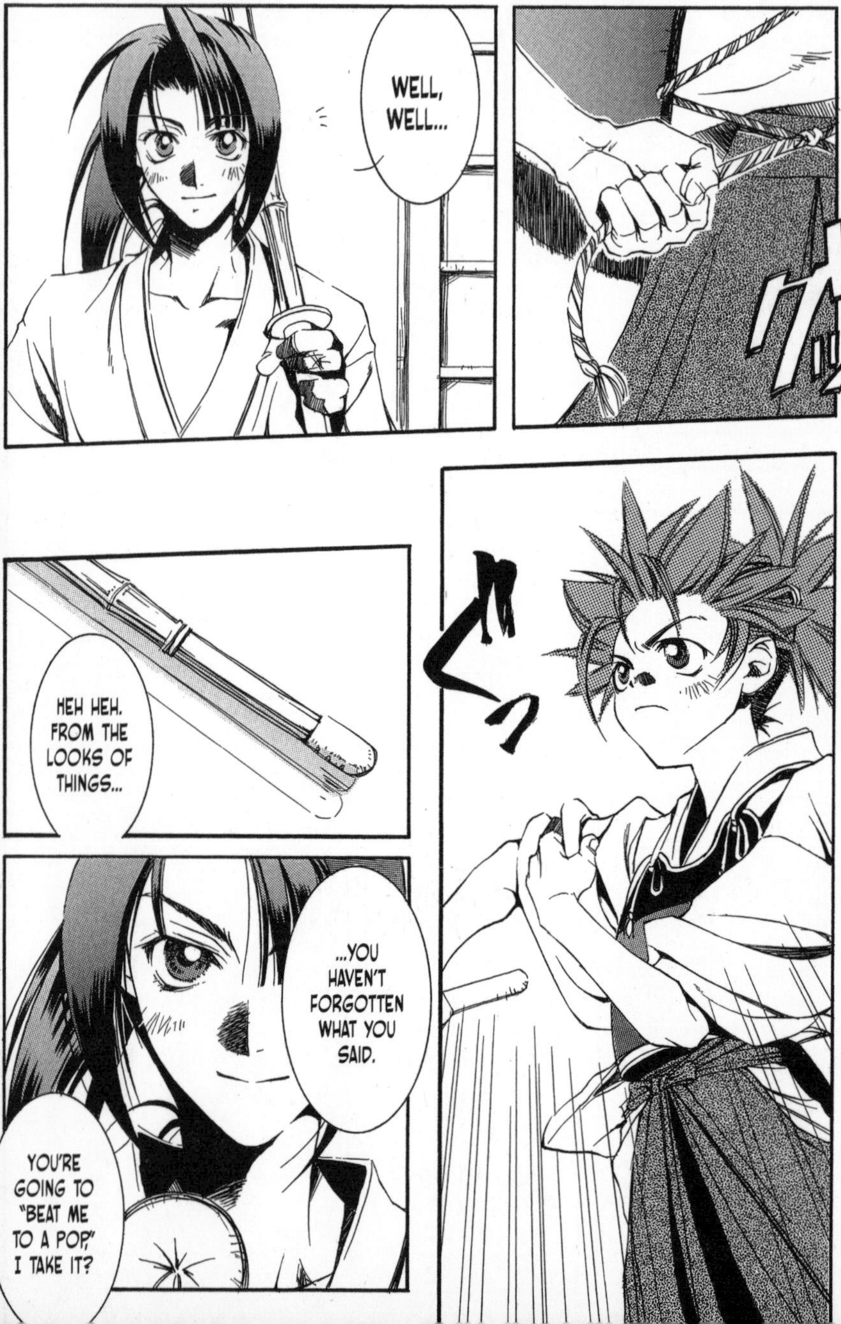

グッ
WELL, WELL...
ぐっ
HEH HEH. FROM THE LOOKS OF THINGS...
...YOU HAVEN'T FORGOTTEN WHAT YOU SAID.
YOU'RE GOING TO "BEAT ME TO A POP," I TAKE IT?

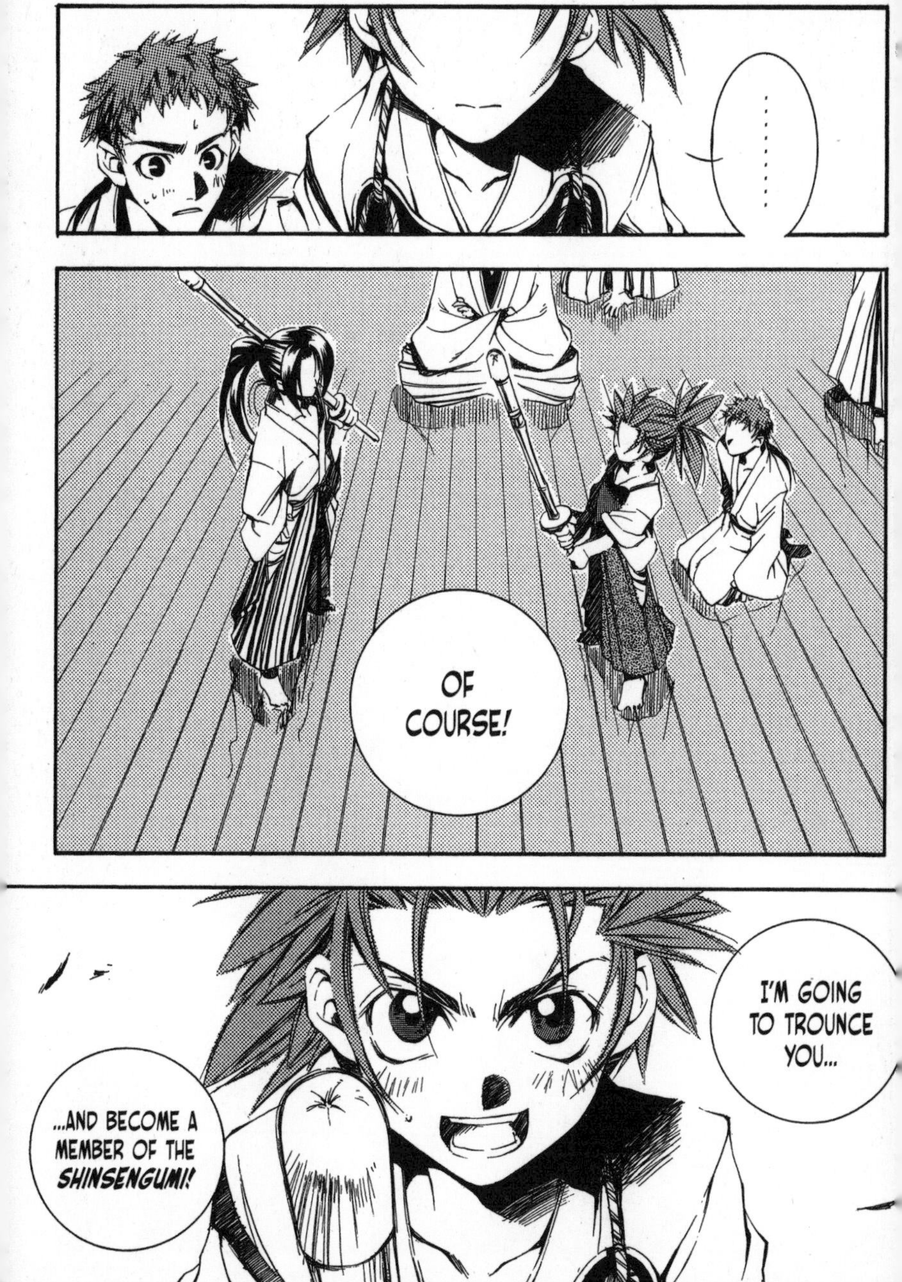
......
OF COURSE!
I'M GOING TO TROUNCE YOU...
...AND BECOME A MEMBER OF THE SHINSENGUMI!

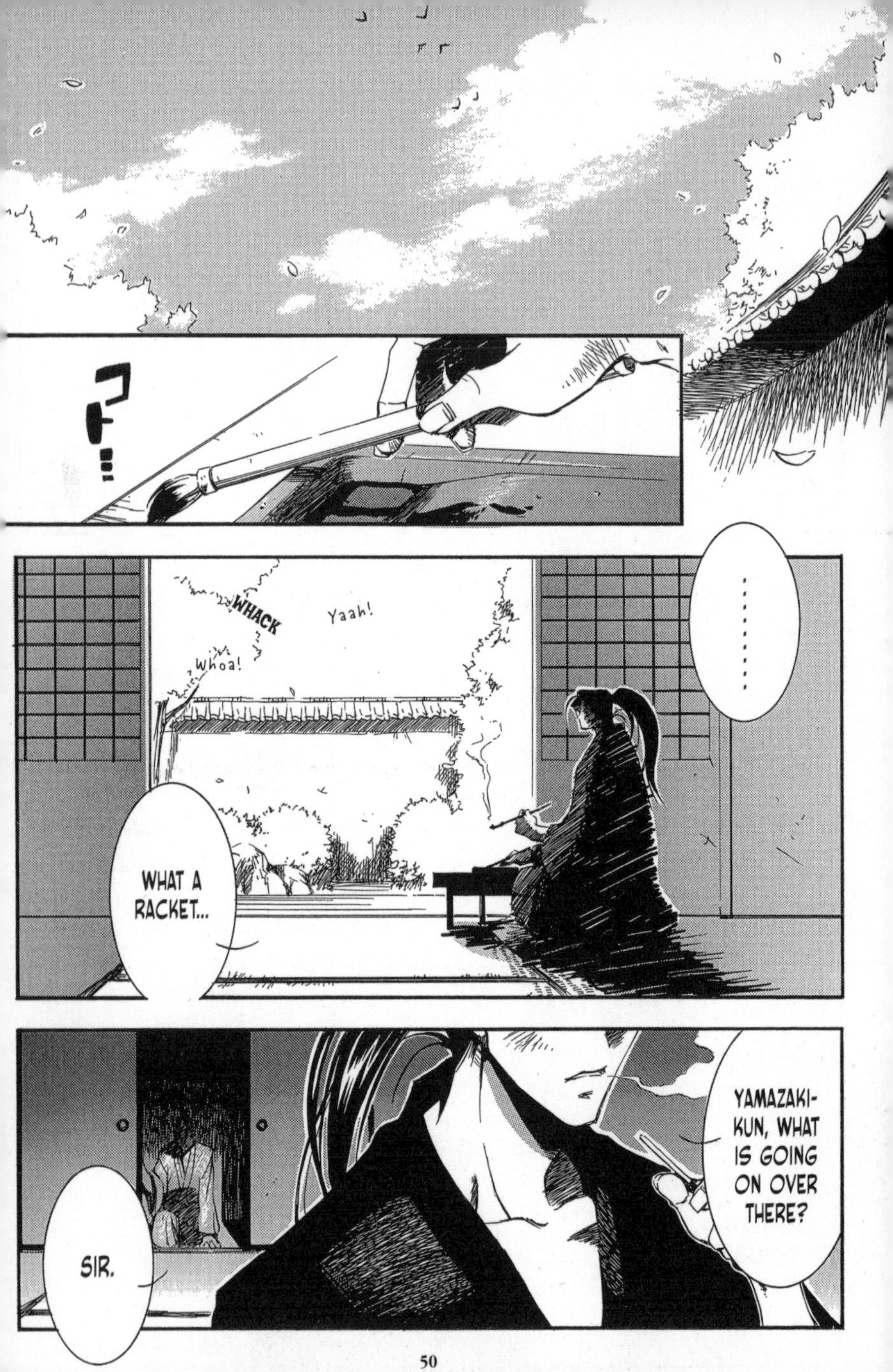

コト…
......
Yaah!
WHACK
Whoa!
WHAT A RACKET...
YAMAZAKI-KUN, WHAT IS GOING ON OVER THERE?
SIR.

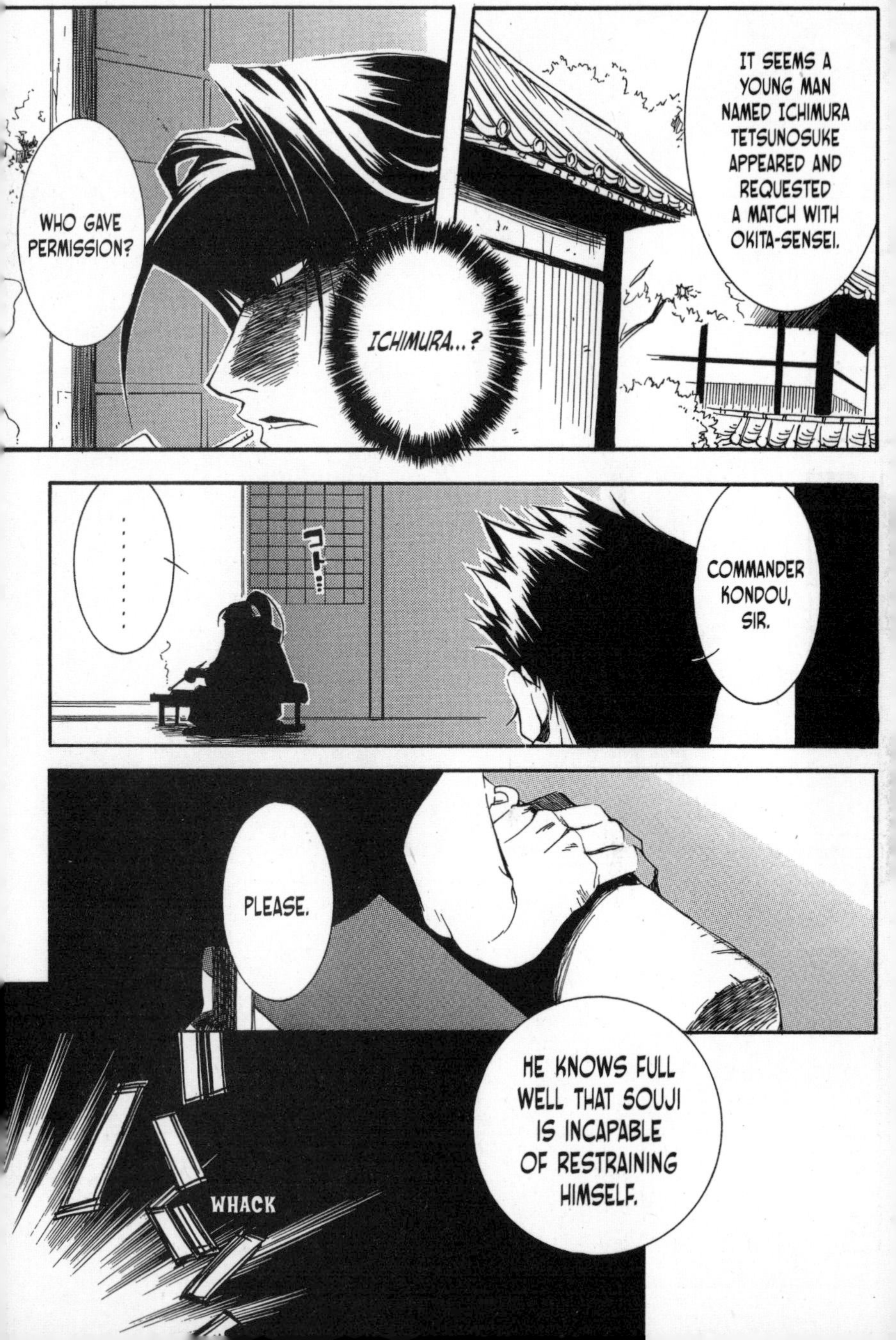
IT SEEMS A YOUNG MAN NAMED ICHIMURA TETSUNOSUKE APPEARED AND REQUESTED A MATCH WITH OKITA-SENSEI.
ICHIMURA...?
WHO GAVE PERMISSION?
COMMANDER KONDOU, SIR.
......
PLEASE.
HE KNOWS FULL WELL THAT SOUJI IS INCAPABLE OF RESTRAINING HIMSELF.
WHACK

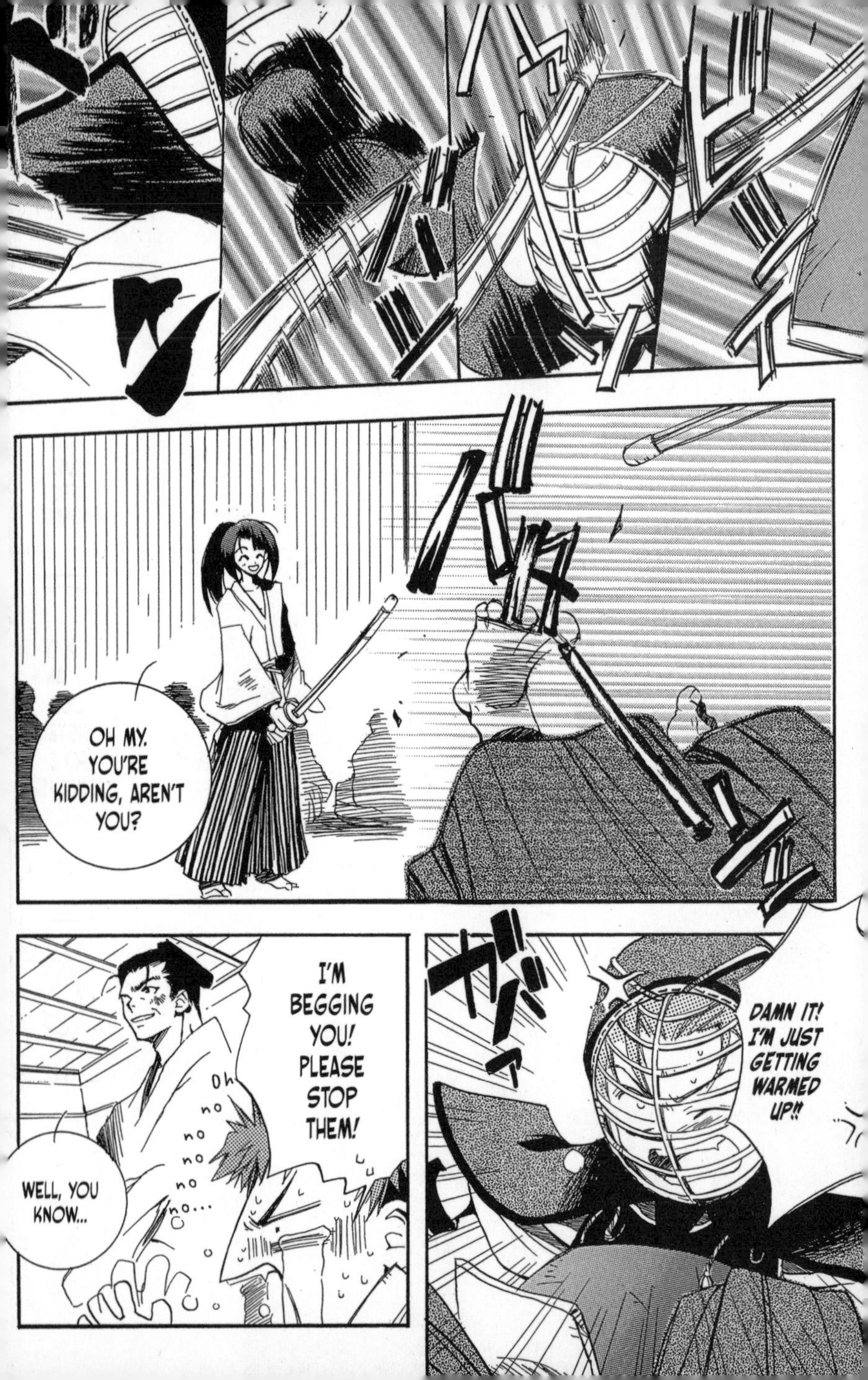
OH MY. YOU'RE KIDDING, AREN'T YOU?
DAMN IT! I'M JUST GETTING WARMED UP!!
I'M BEGGING YOU! PLEASE STOP THEM!
Oh no no no no no...
WELL, YOU KNOW...

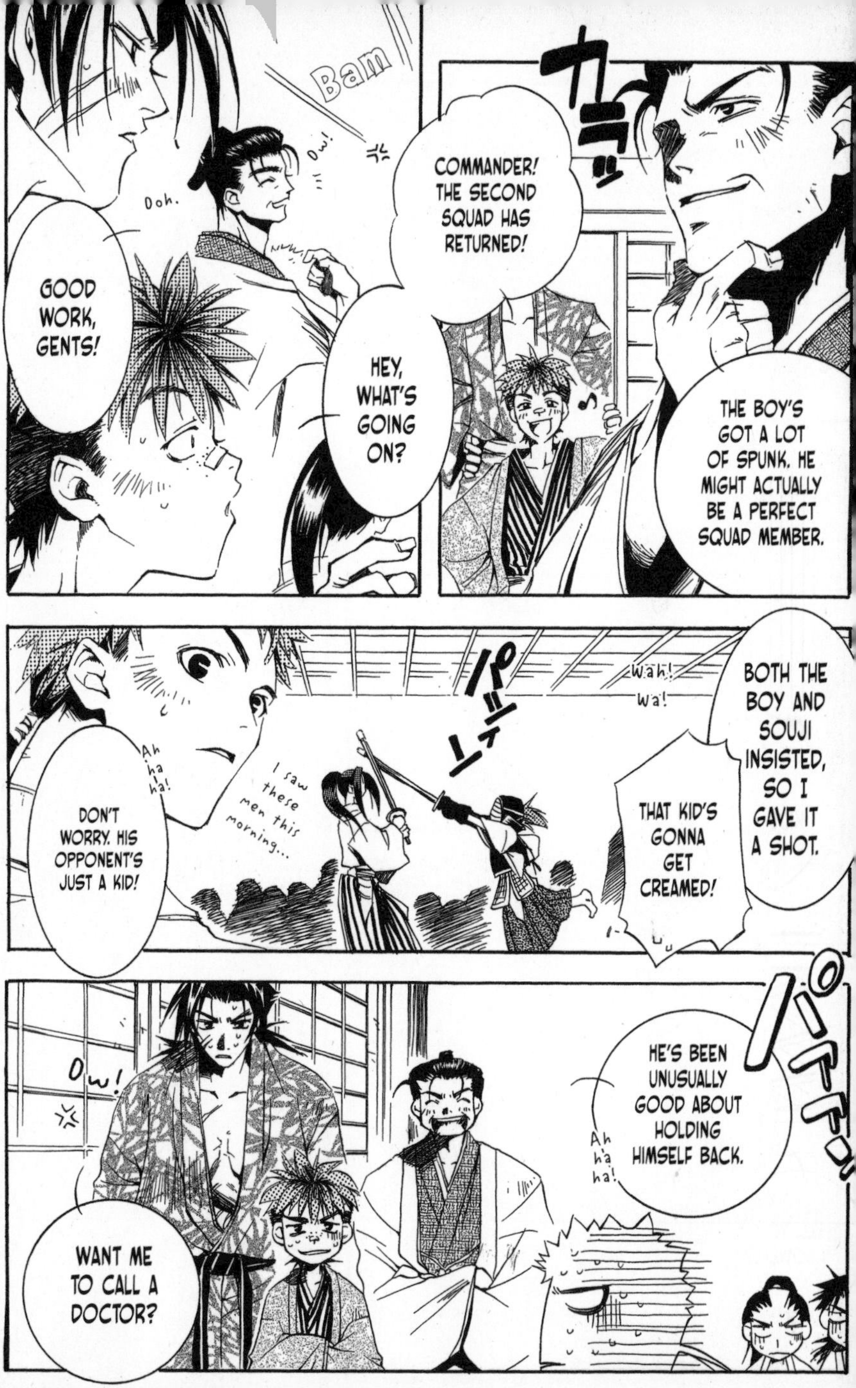

THE BOY'S GOT A LOT OF SPUNK. HE MIGHT ACTUALLY BE A PERFECT SQUAD MEMBER.
COMMANDER! THE SECOND SQUAD HAS RETURNED!
HEY, WHAT'S GOING ON?
Bam
Ow!
Doh.
GOOD WORK, GENTS!
BOTH THE BOY AND SOUJI INSISTED, SO I GAVE IT A SHOT.
THAT KID'S GONNA GET CREAMED!
Wah! Wa!
I saw these men this morning...
Ah ha ha!
DON'T WORRY. HIS OPPONENT'S JUST A KID!
HE'S BEEN UNUSUALLY GOOD ABOUT HOLDING HIMSELF BACK.
Ah ha ha!
Ow!
WANT ME TO CALL A DOCTOR?

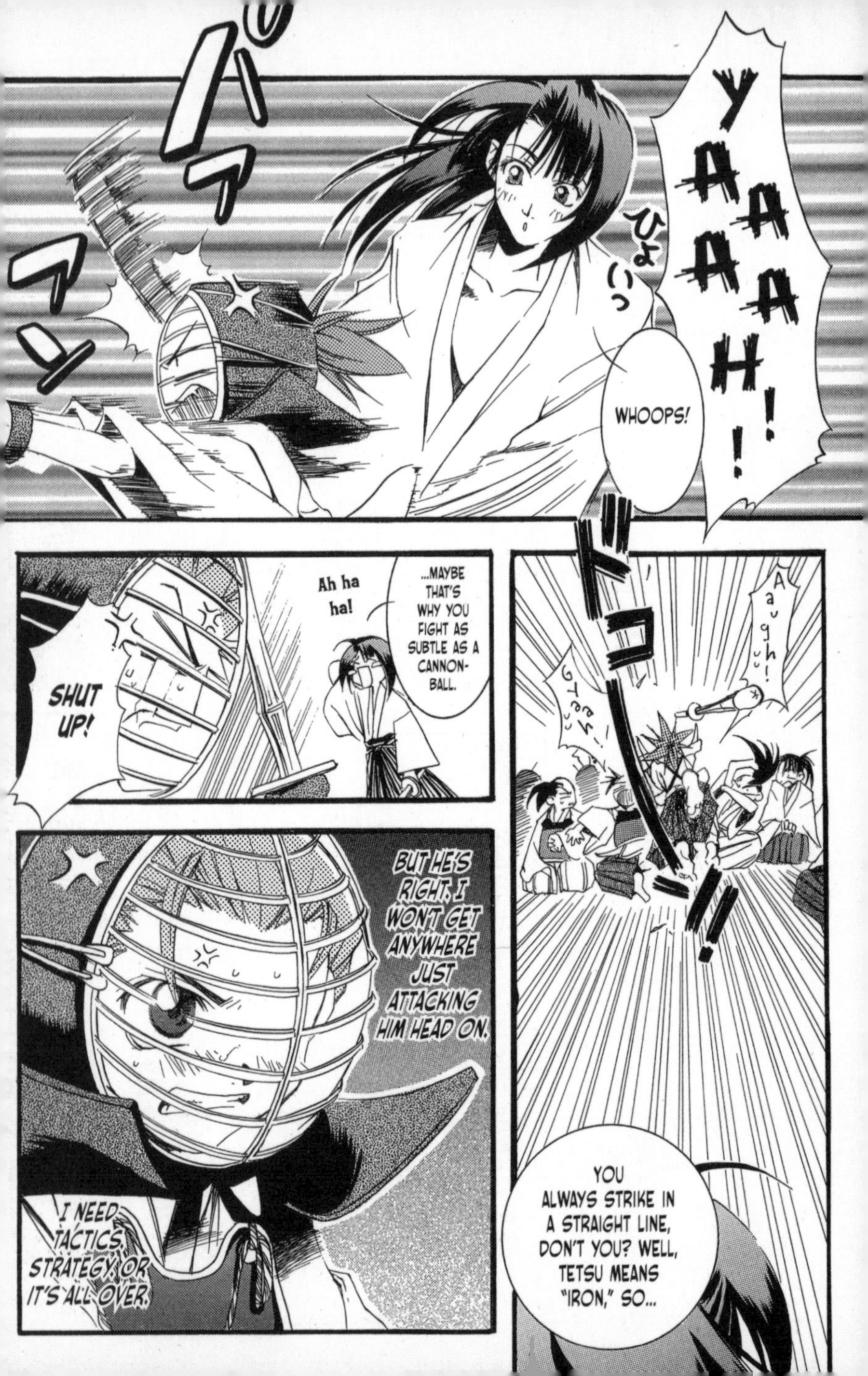
YAAAAAH!!
ひょいっ
WHOOPS!
バァン
ドコーッ!!
Aaugh!
Geez!
YOU ALWAYS STRIKE IN A STRAIGHT LINE, DON'T YOU? WELL, TETSU MEANS "IRON," SO...
...MAYBE THAT'S WHY YOU FIGHT AS SUBTLE AS A CANNONBALL.
Ah ha ha!
SHUT UP!
BUT HE'S RIGHT. I WON'T GET ANYWHERE JUST ATTACKING HIM HEAD ON.
I NEED TACTICS. STRATEGY. OR IT'S ALL OVER.

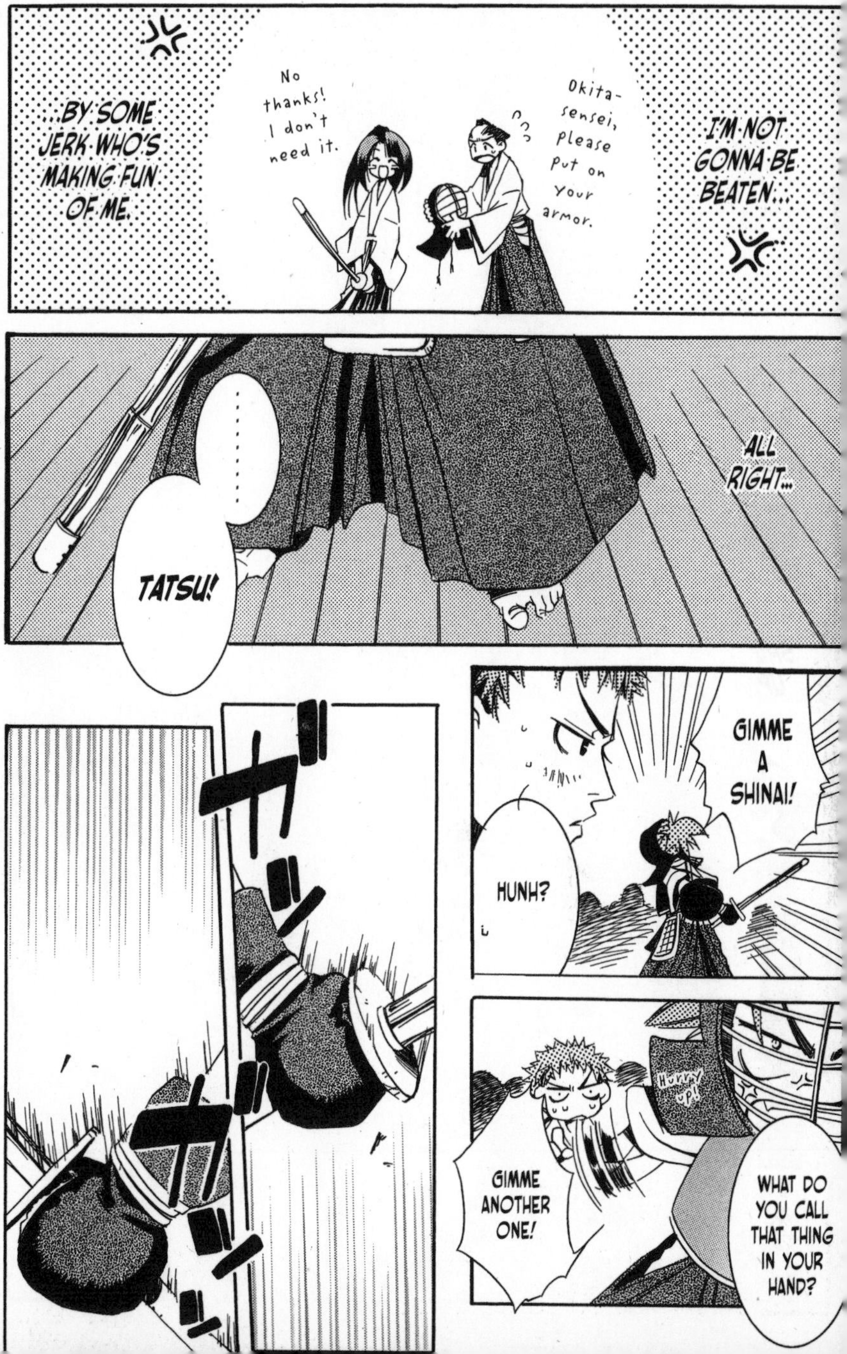
I'M NOT GONNA BE BEATEN...
Okita-sensei, please put on your armor.
No thanks! I don't need it.
...BY SOME JERK WHO'S MAKING FUN OF ME.
ALL RIGHT...
......
TATSU!
GIMME A SHINAI!
HUNH?
WHAT DO YOU CALL THAT THING IN YOUR HAND?
Hurry up!
GIMME ANOTHER ONE!

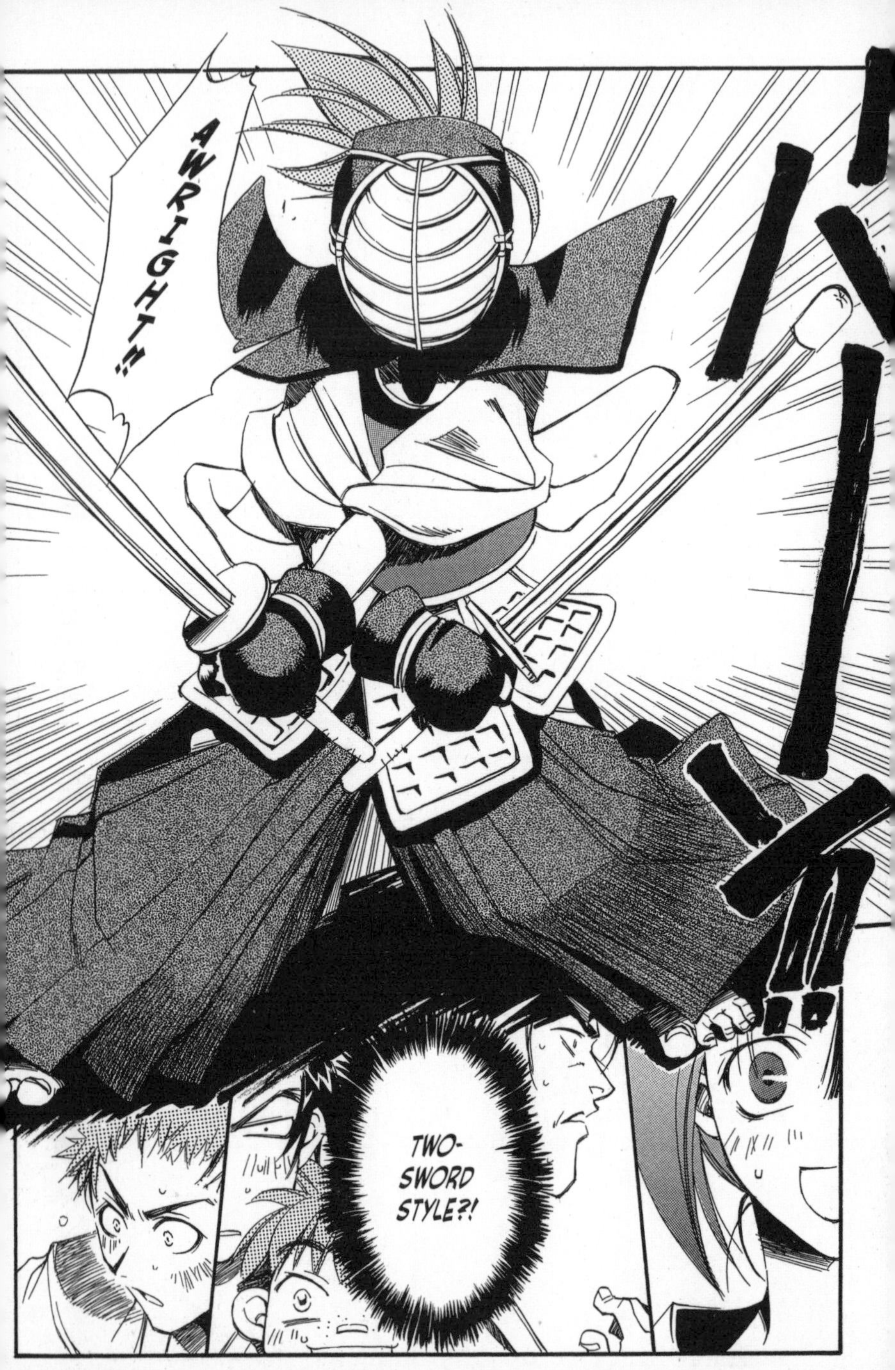
AWRIGHT!!
TWO-SWORD STYLE?!

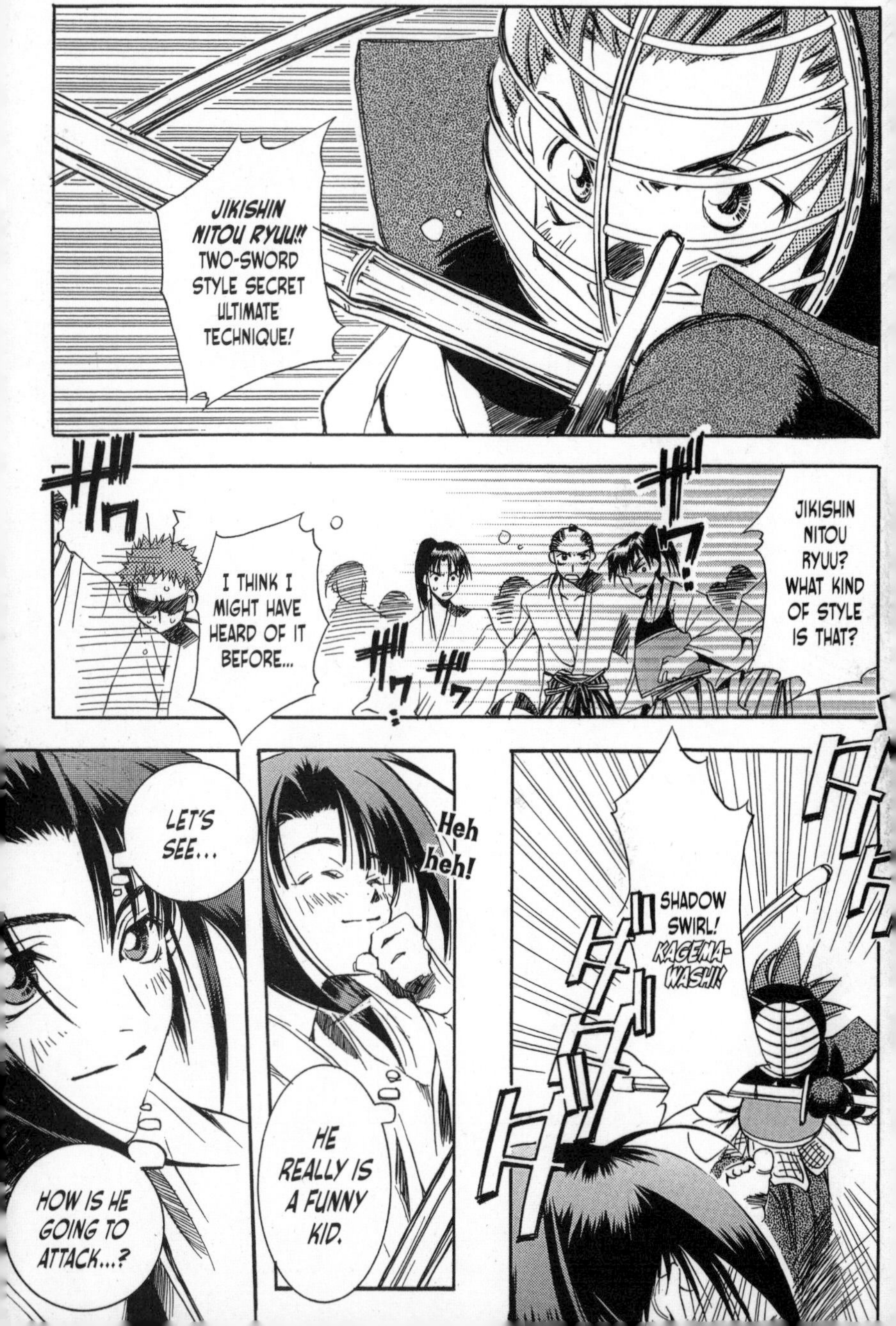
JIKISHIN NITOU RYUU!! TWO-SWORD STYLE SECRET ULTIMATE TECHNIQUE!
JIKISHIN NITOU RYUU? WHAT KIND OF STYLE IS THAT?
I THINK I MIGHT HAVE HEARD OF IT BEFORE...
SHADOW SWIRL! KAGEMA-WASHI!!
Heh heh!
HE REALLY IS A FUNNY KID.
LET'S SEE...
HOW IS HE GOING TO ATTACK...?

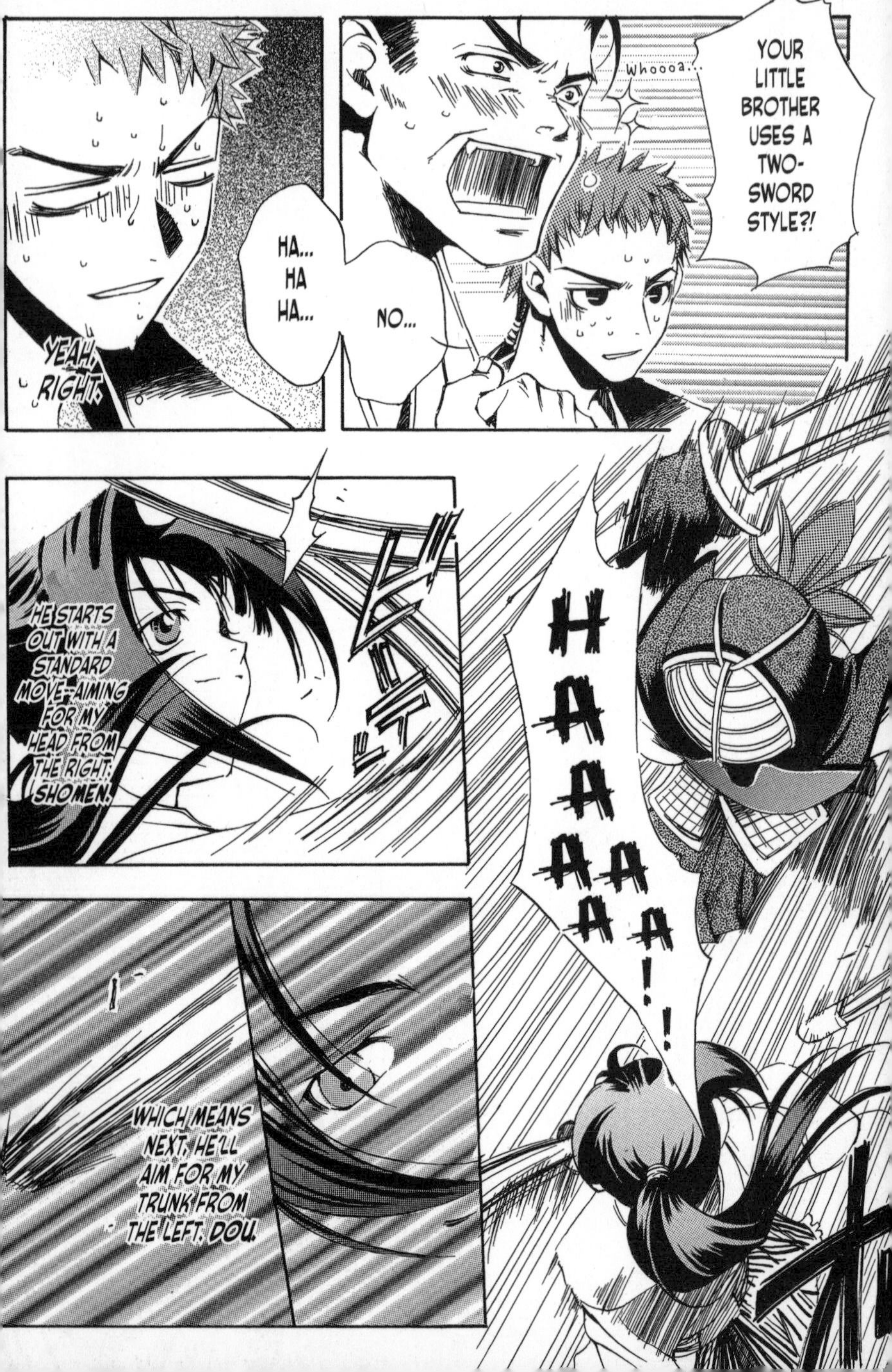
Whoooa...
YOUR LITTLE BROTHER USES A TWO-SWORD STYLE?!
NO...
HA... HA HA...
YEAH, RIGHT.
HAAAAAAAA!!
HE STARTS OUT WITH A STANDARD MOVE--AIMING FOR MY HEAD FROM THE RIGHT: SHOMEN.
WHICH MEANS NEXT, HE'LL AIM FOR MY TRUNK FROM THE LEFT: DOU.

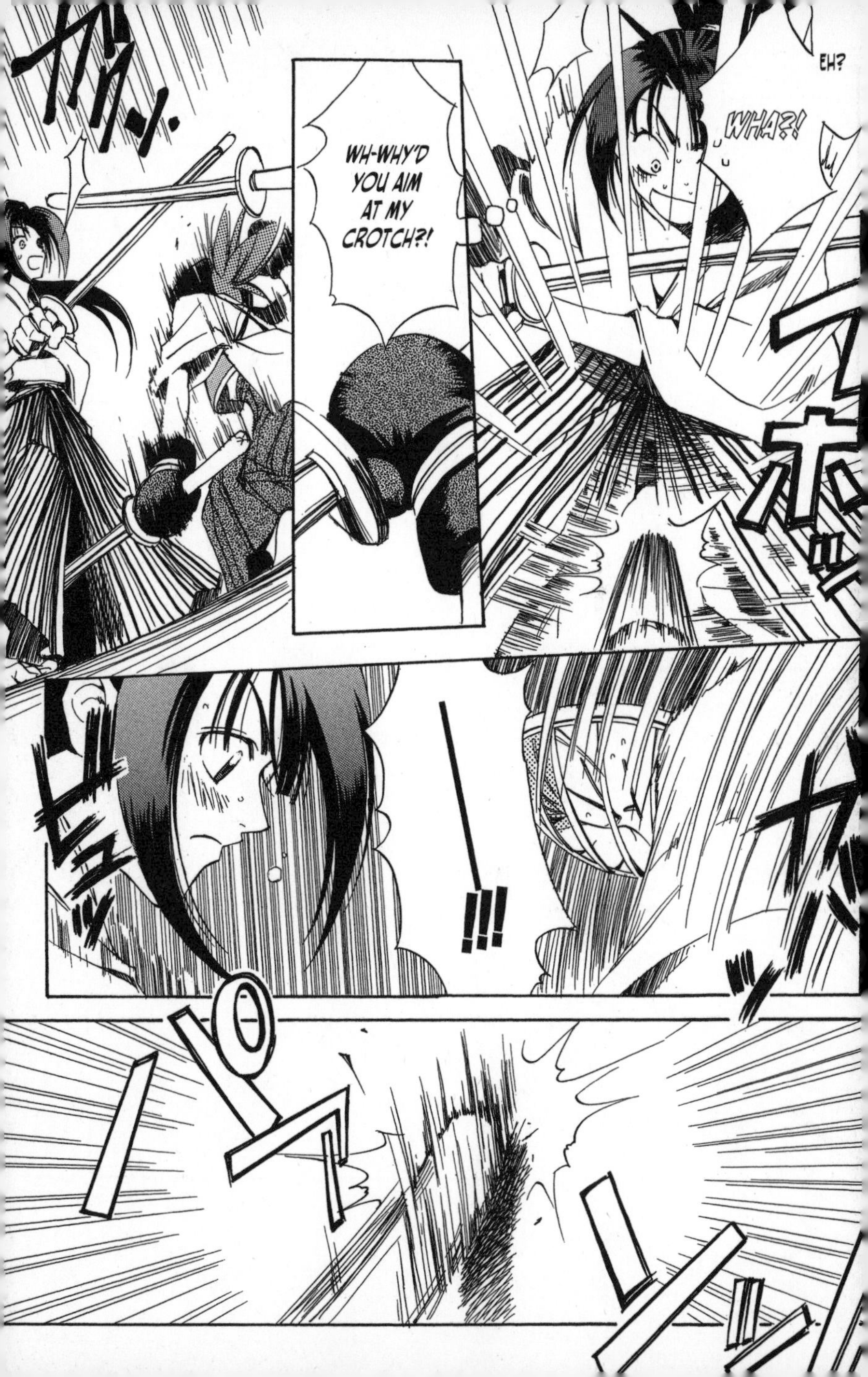
EH?
WHA?!
WH-WHY'D YOU AIM AT MY CROTCH?!
!!!

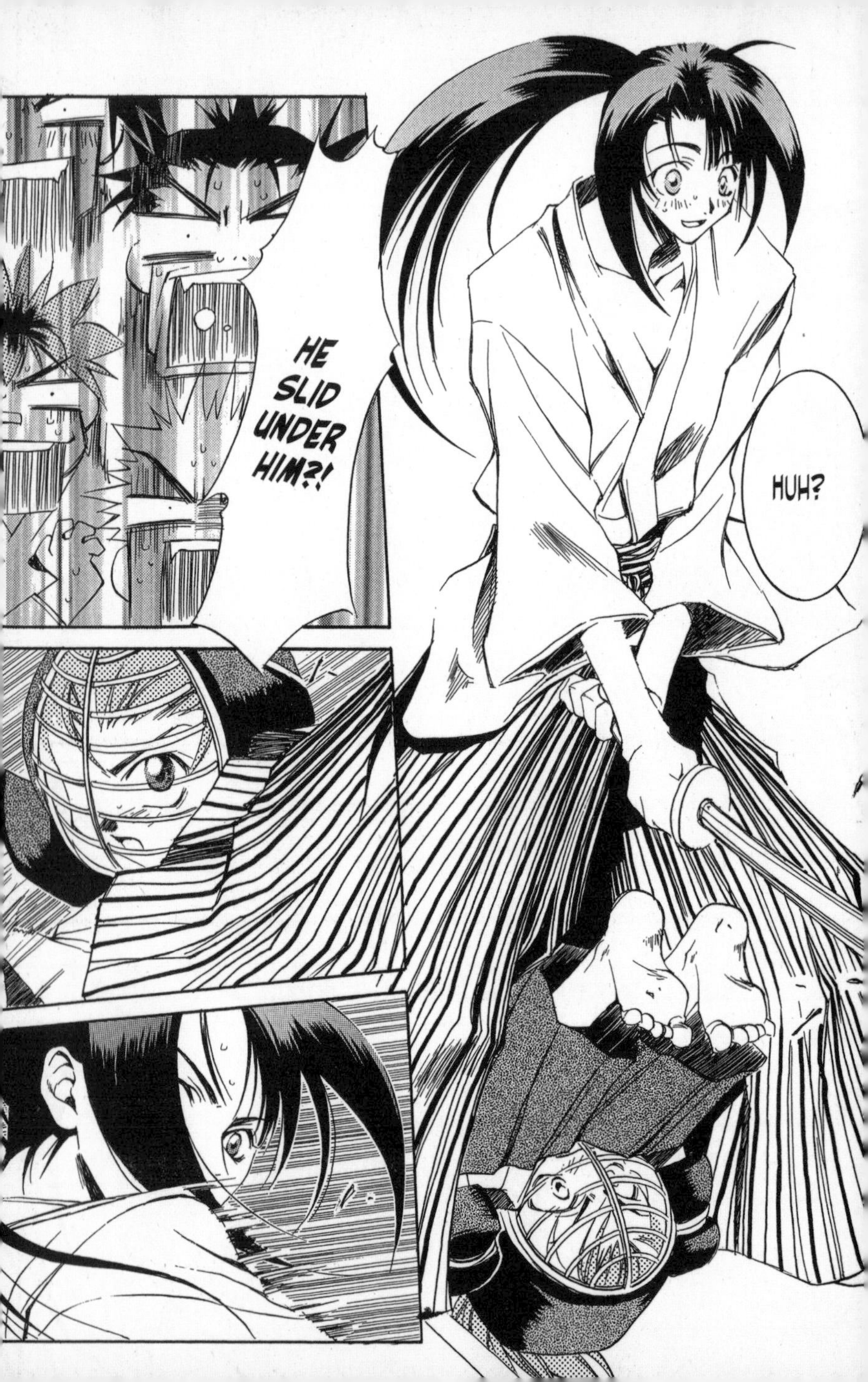
HUH?
HE SLID UNDER HIM?!

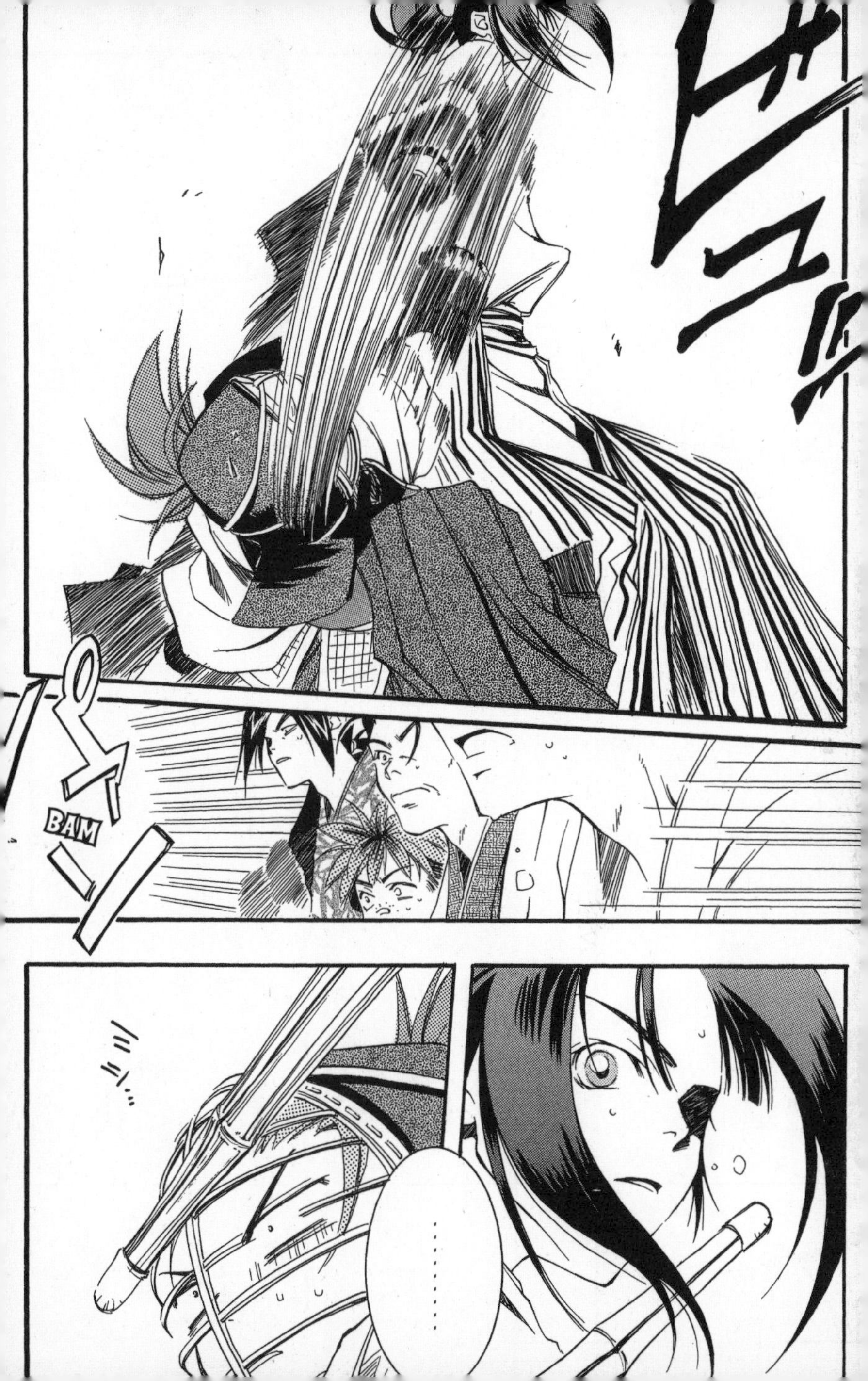
BAM
......

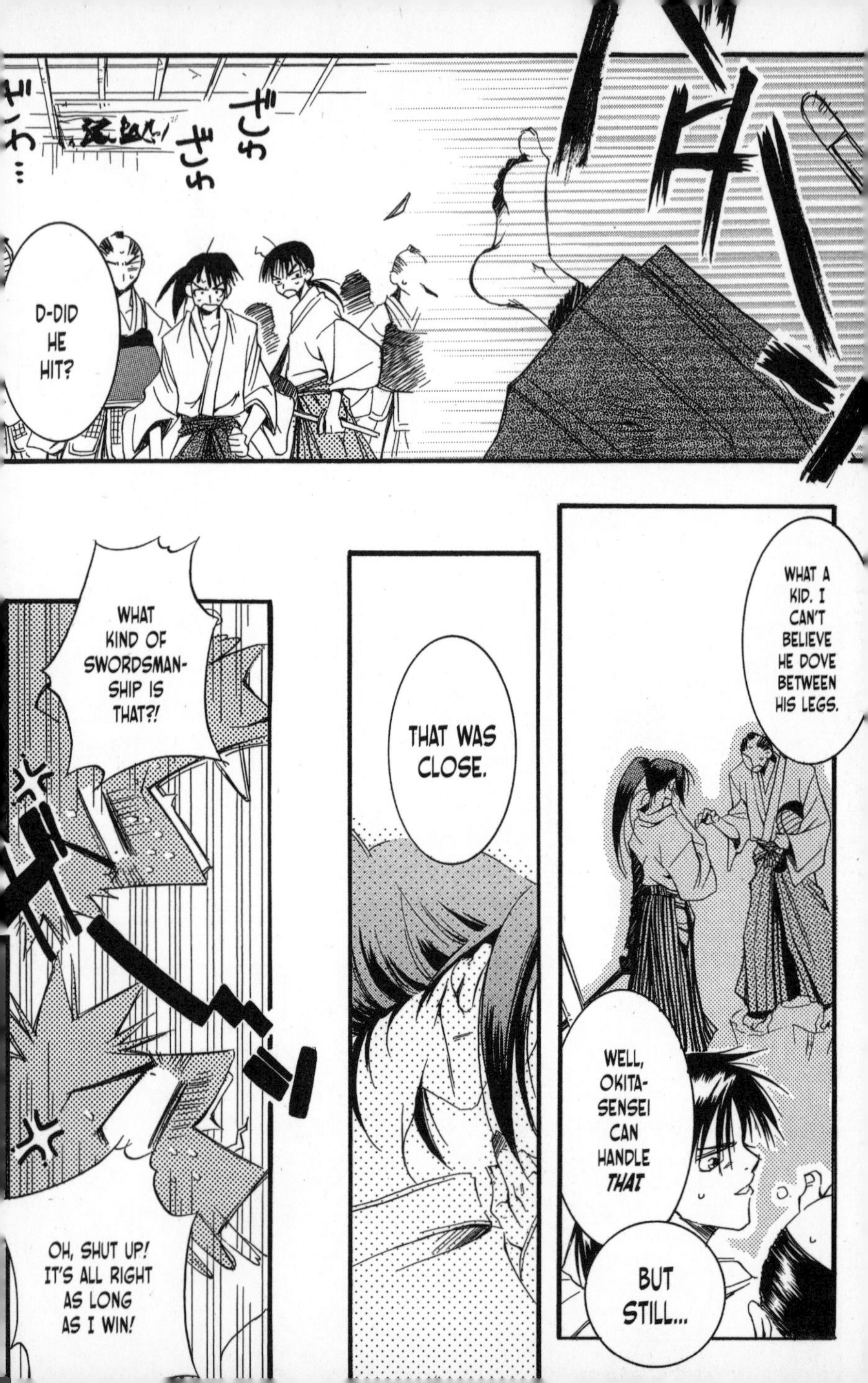
ざわ ざわ
ざわ…
D-DID HE HIT?
WHAT A KID. I CAN'T BELIEVE HE DOVE BETWEEN HIS LEGS.
WELL, OKITA-SENSEI CAN HANDLE *THAT*
BUT STILL...
THAT WAS CLOSE.
WHAT KIND OF SWORDSMANSHIP IS THAT?!
OH, SHUT UP! IT'S ALL RIGHT AS LONG AS I WIN!

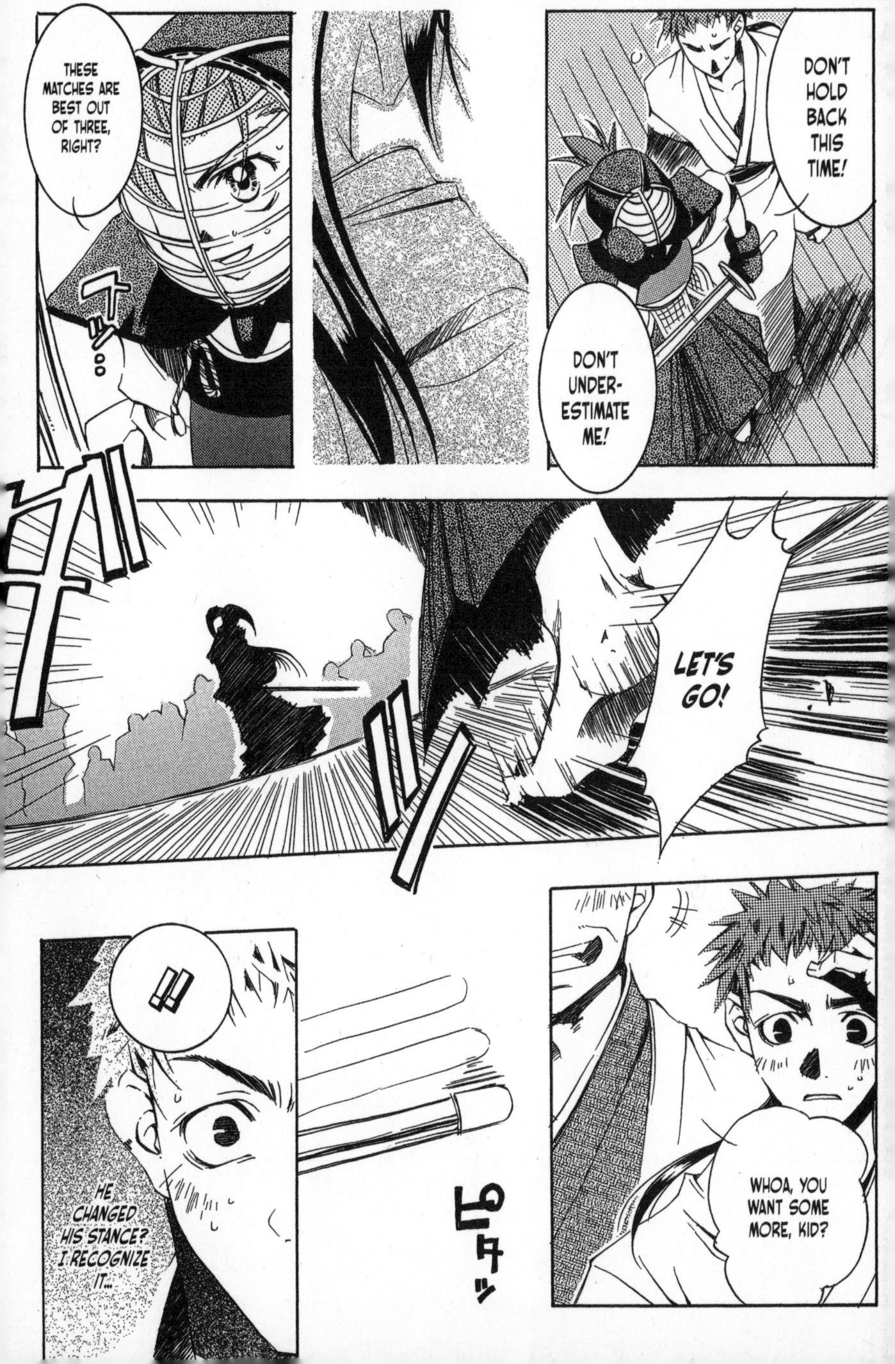
DON'T HOLD BACK THIS TIME!
DON'T UNDER-ESTIMATE ME!
THESE MATCHES ARE BEST OUT OF THREE, RIGHT?
フッ。。
LET'S GO!
WHOA, YOU WANT SOME MORE, KID?
!!
HE CHANGED HIS STANCE? I RECOGNIZE IT...
ピタッ

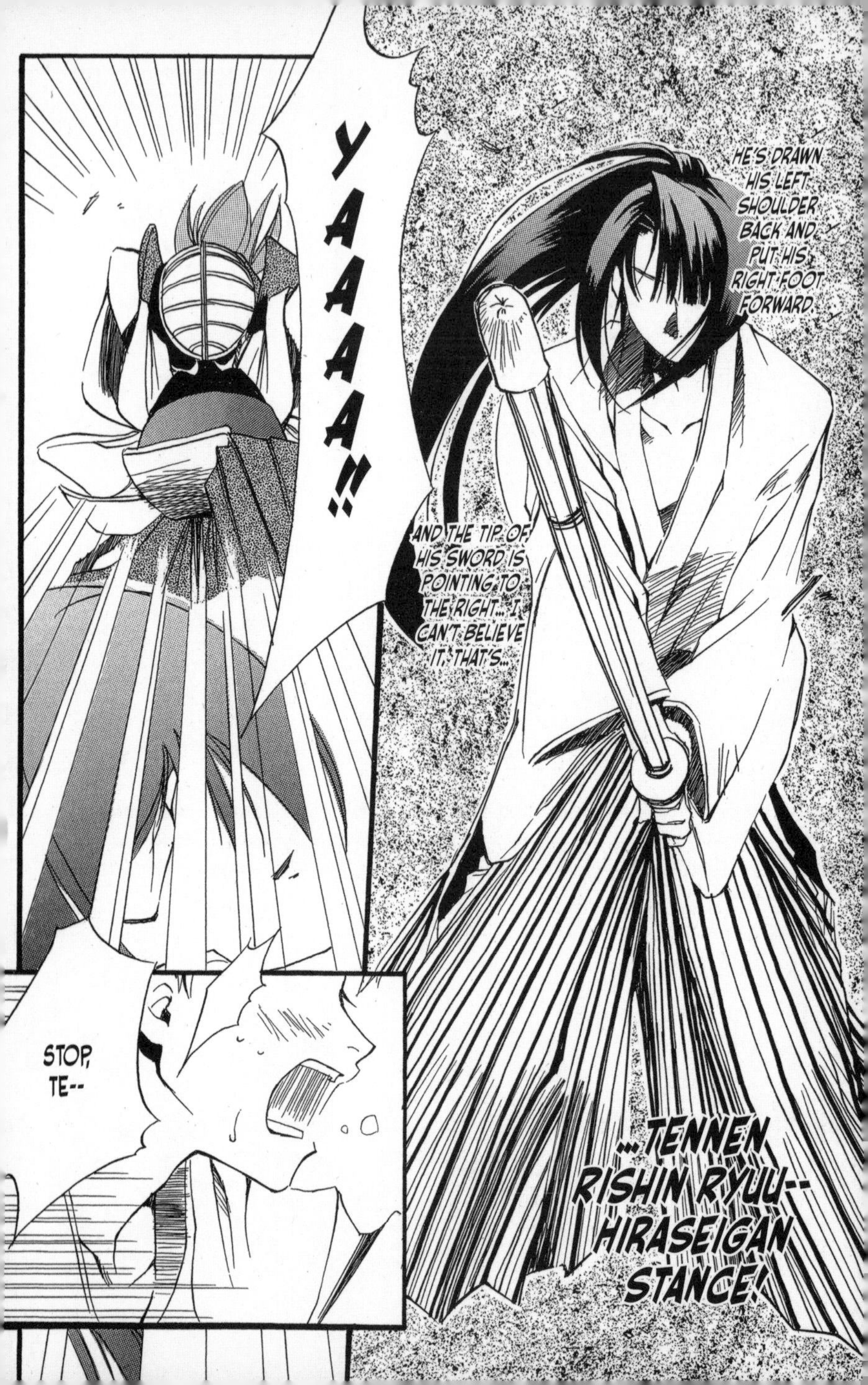
HE'S DRAWN HIS LEFT SHOULDER BACK AND PUT HIS RIGHT FOOT FORWARD.
AND THE TIP OF HIS SWORD IS POINTING TO THE RIGHT... I CAN'T BELIEVE IT. THAT'S...
...TENNEN RISHIN RYUU-- HIRASEIGAN STANCE!
YAAAAA!!
STOP, TE--

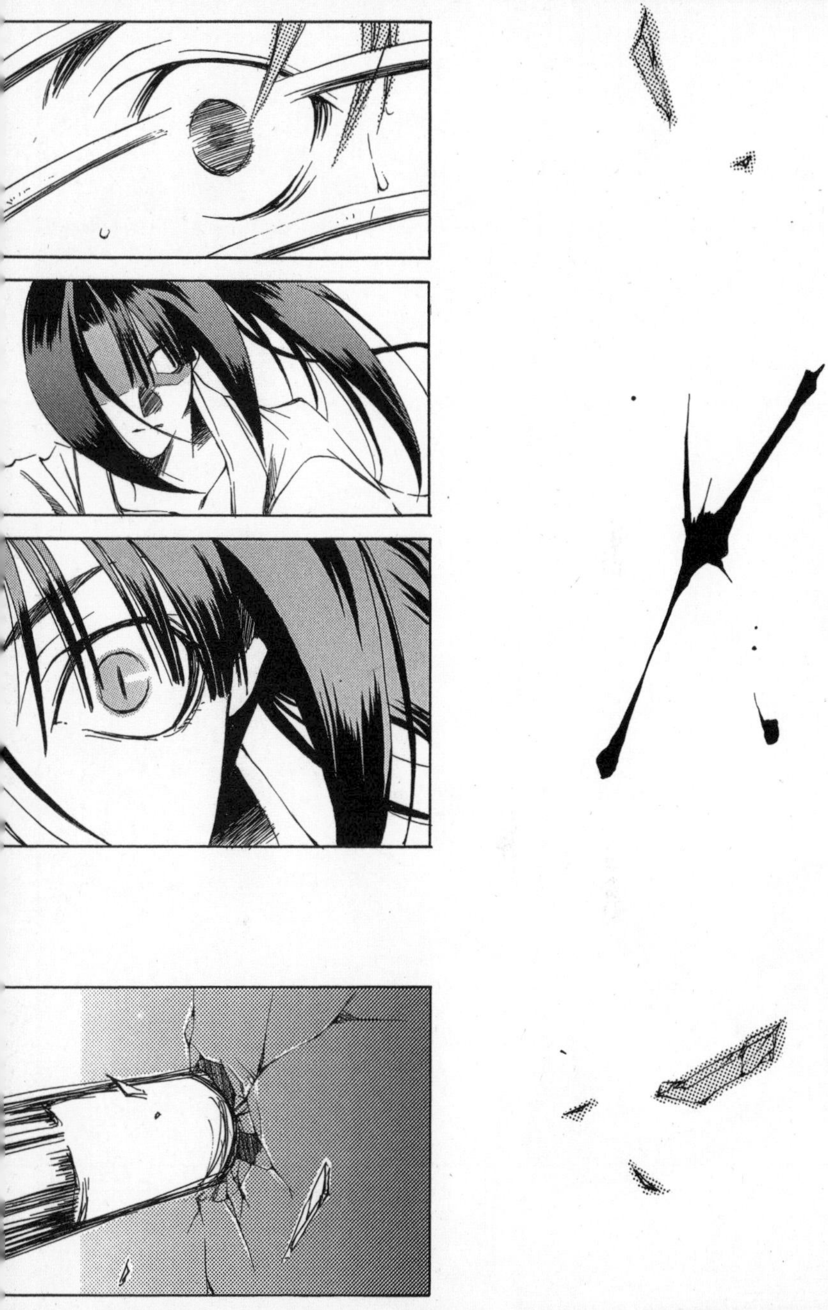

TE...

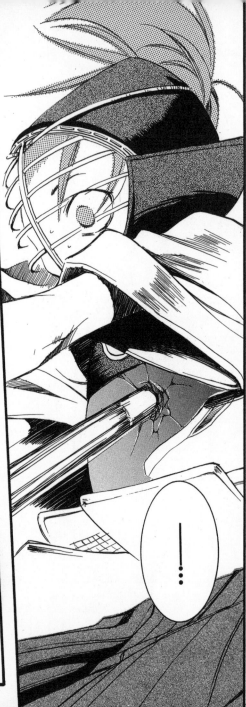

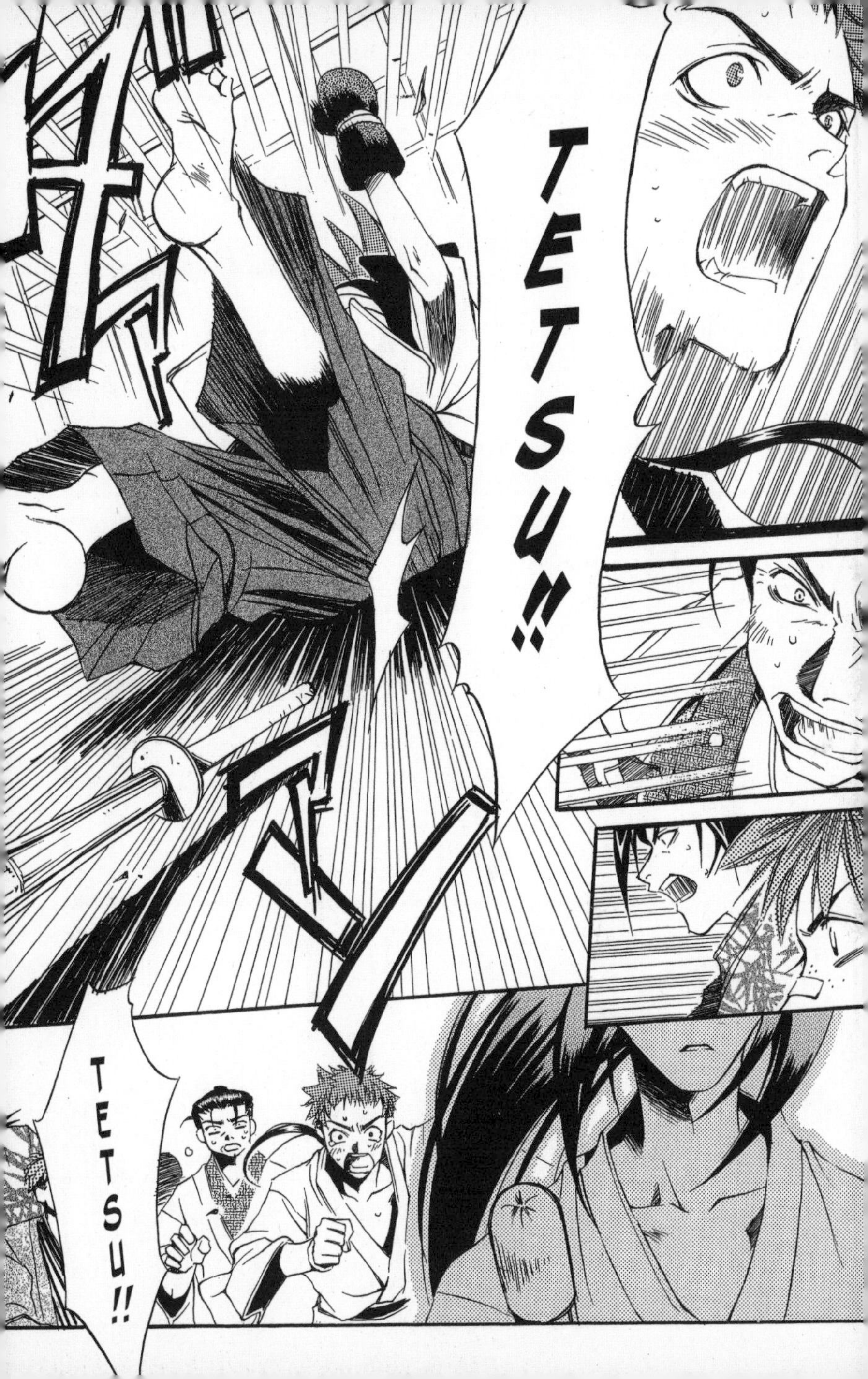
TETSU!!
TETSU!!

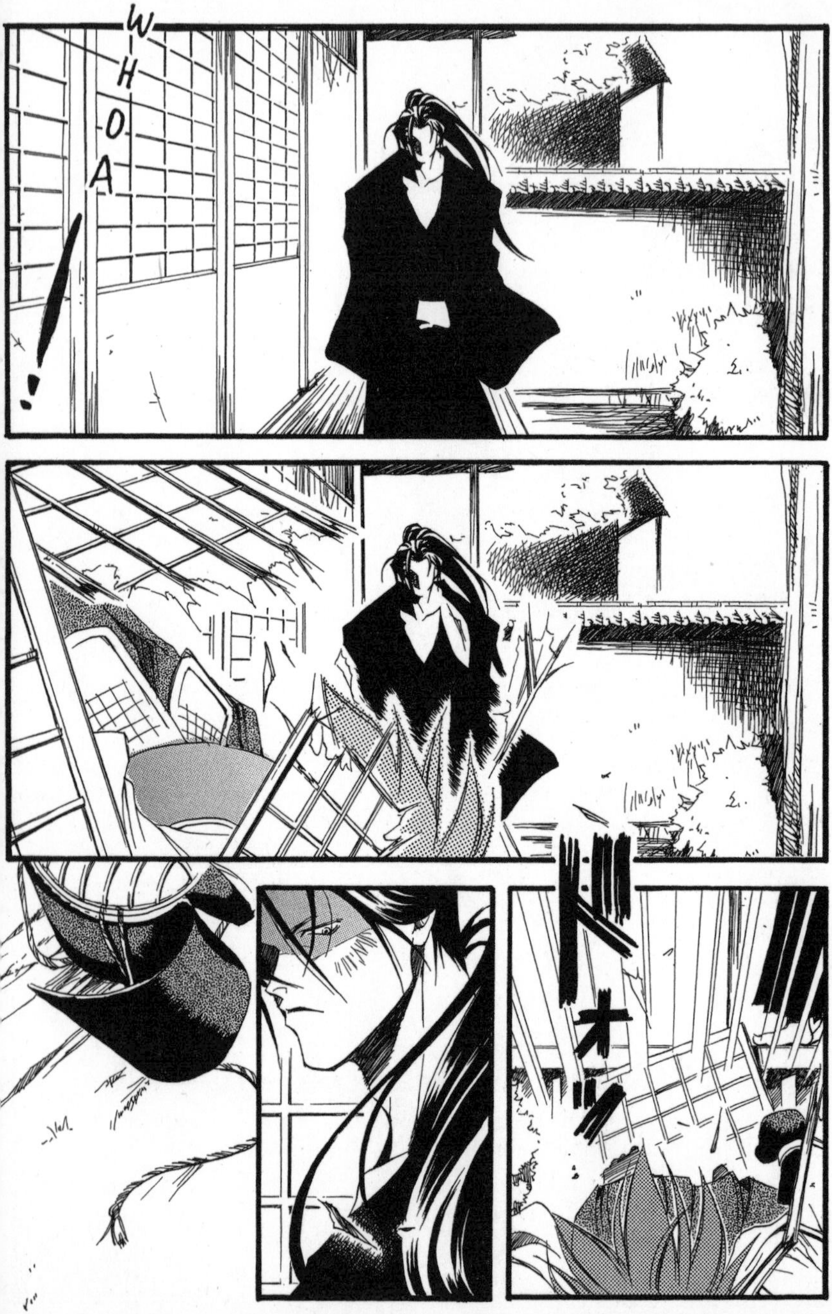
WHOA!!
ドオッ

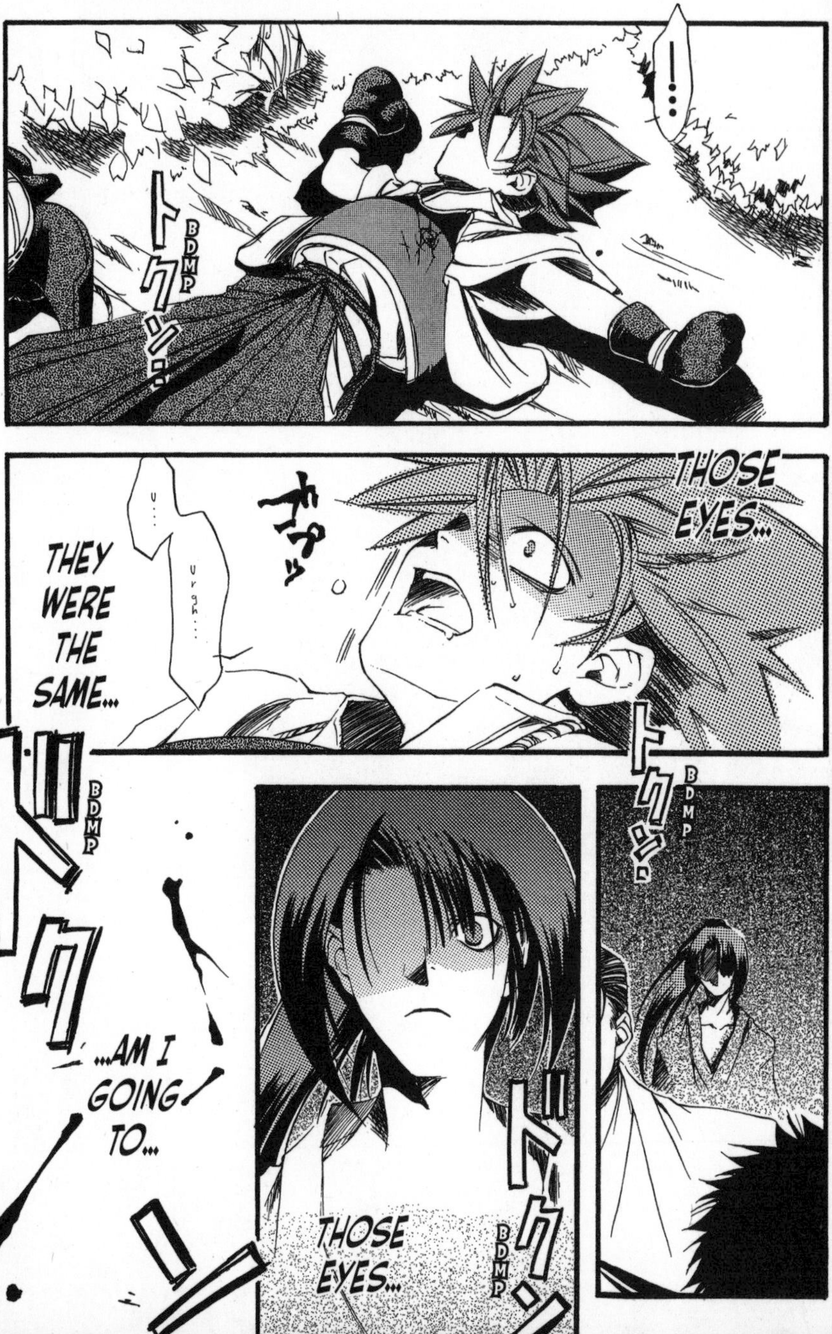
!...
BDMP
THOSE EYES...
U...
Urgh...
THEY WERE THE SAME...
BDMP
BDMP
THOSE EYES...
BDMP
...AM I GOING TO...

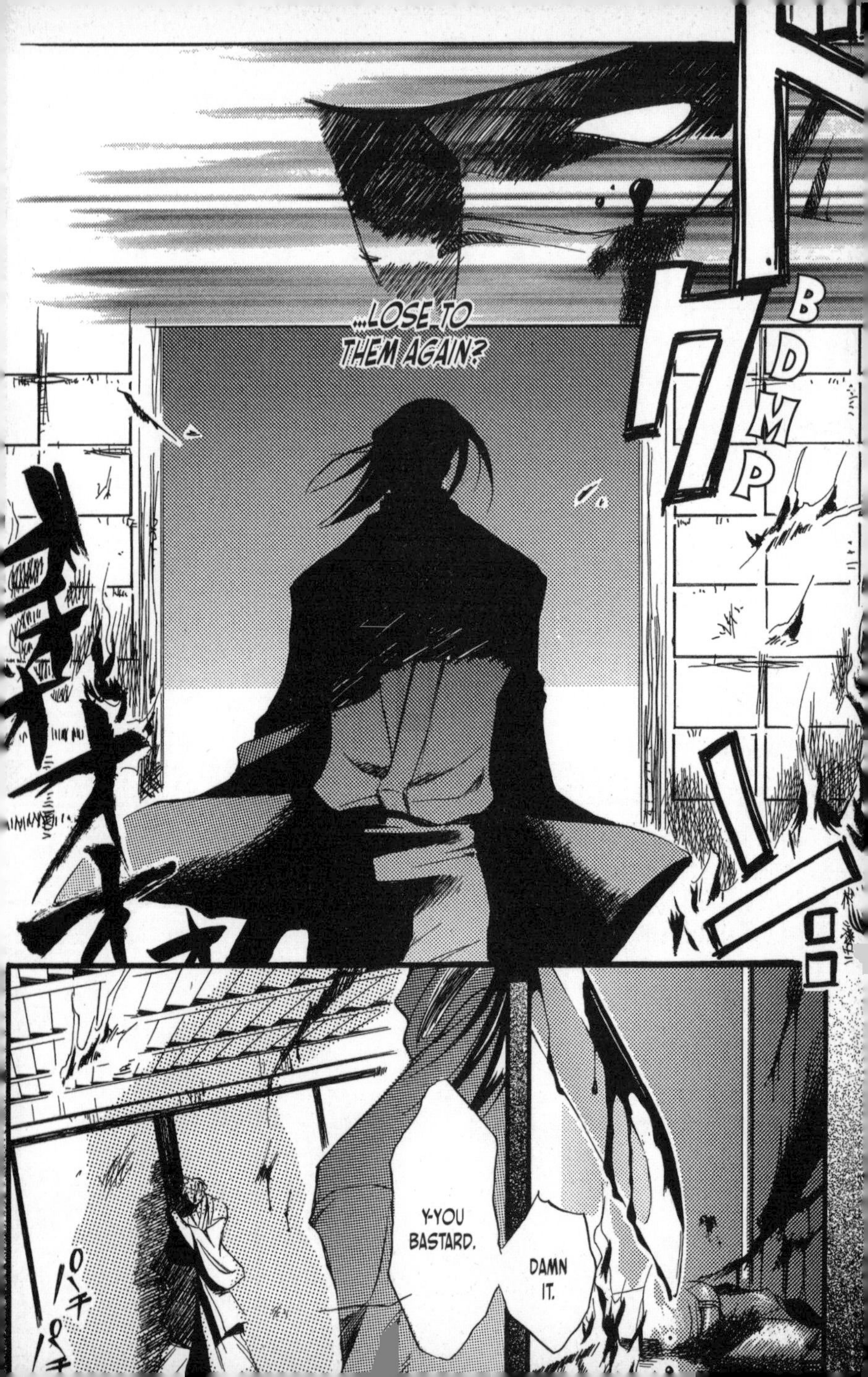
BDMP
...LOSE TO THEM AGAIN?
Y-YOU BASTARD.
DAMN IT.

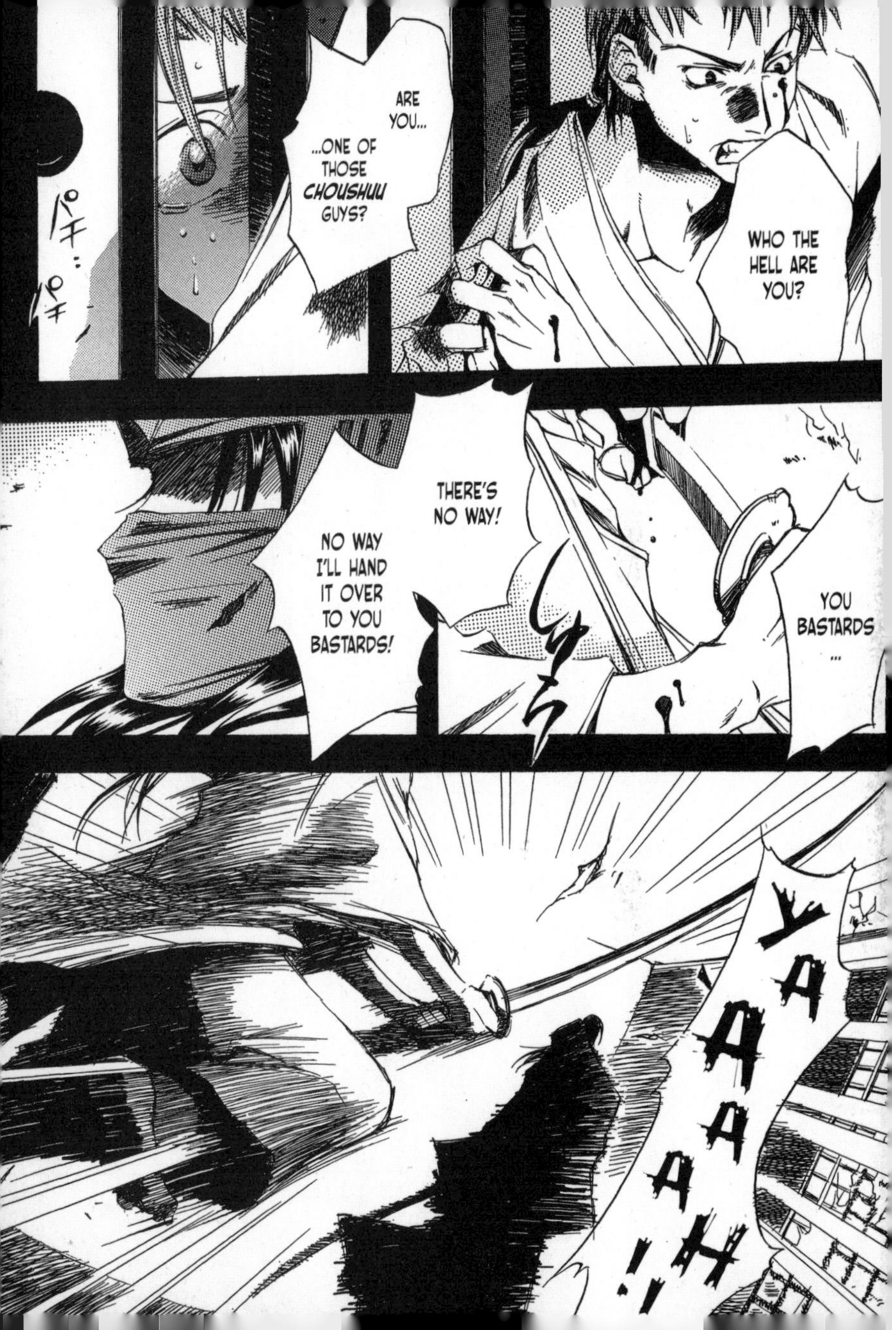
WHO THE HELL ARE YOU?
ARE YOU...
...ONE OF THOSE *CHOUSHUU* GUYS?
パチ…パチ
YOU BASTARDS ...
THERE'S NO WAY!
NO WAY I'LL HAND IT OVER TO YOU BASTARDS!
YAAAAAH!!

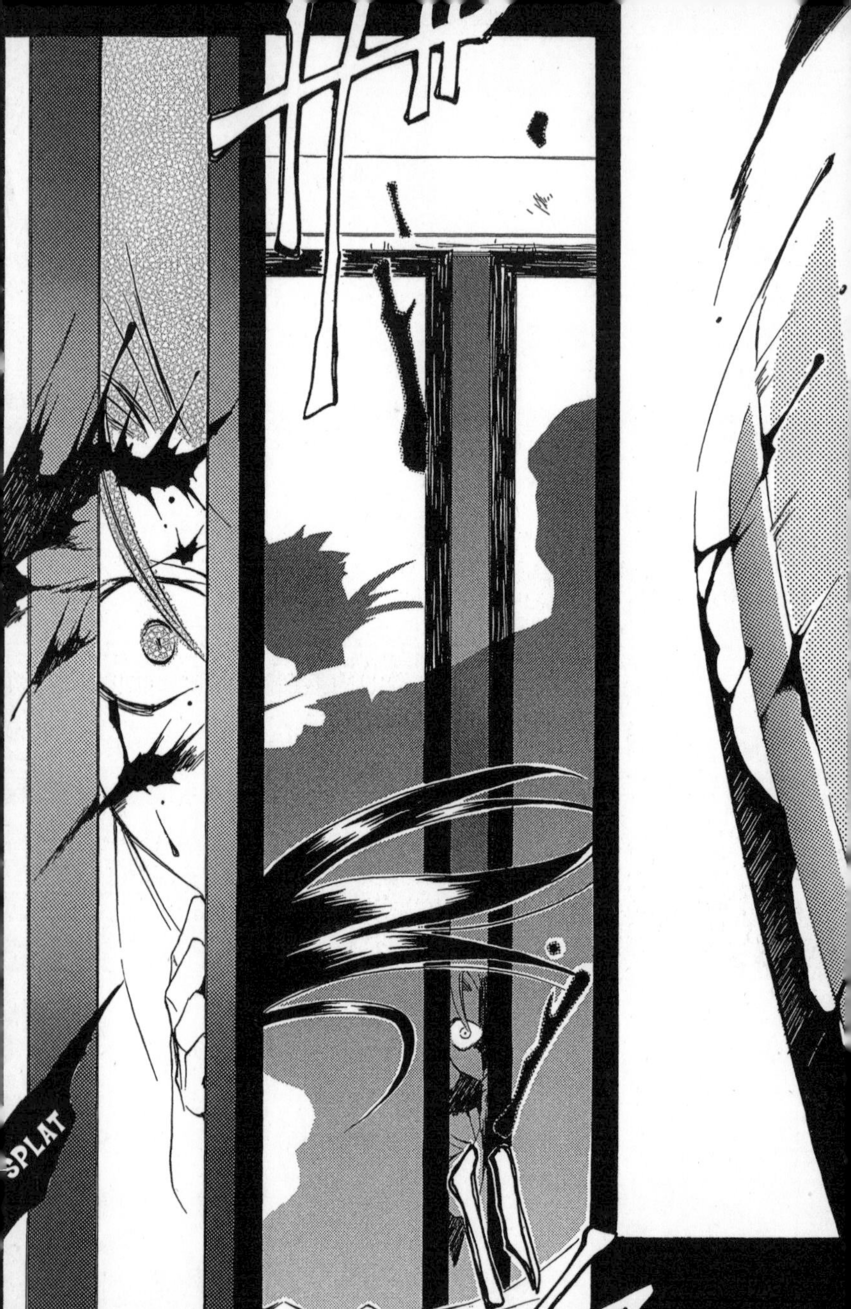
SPLAT

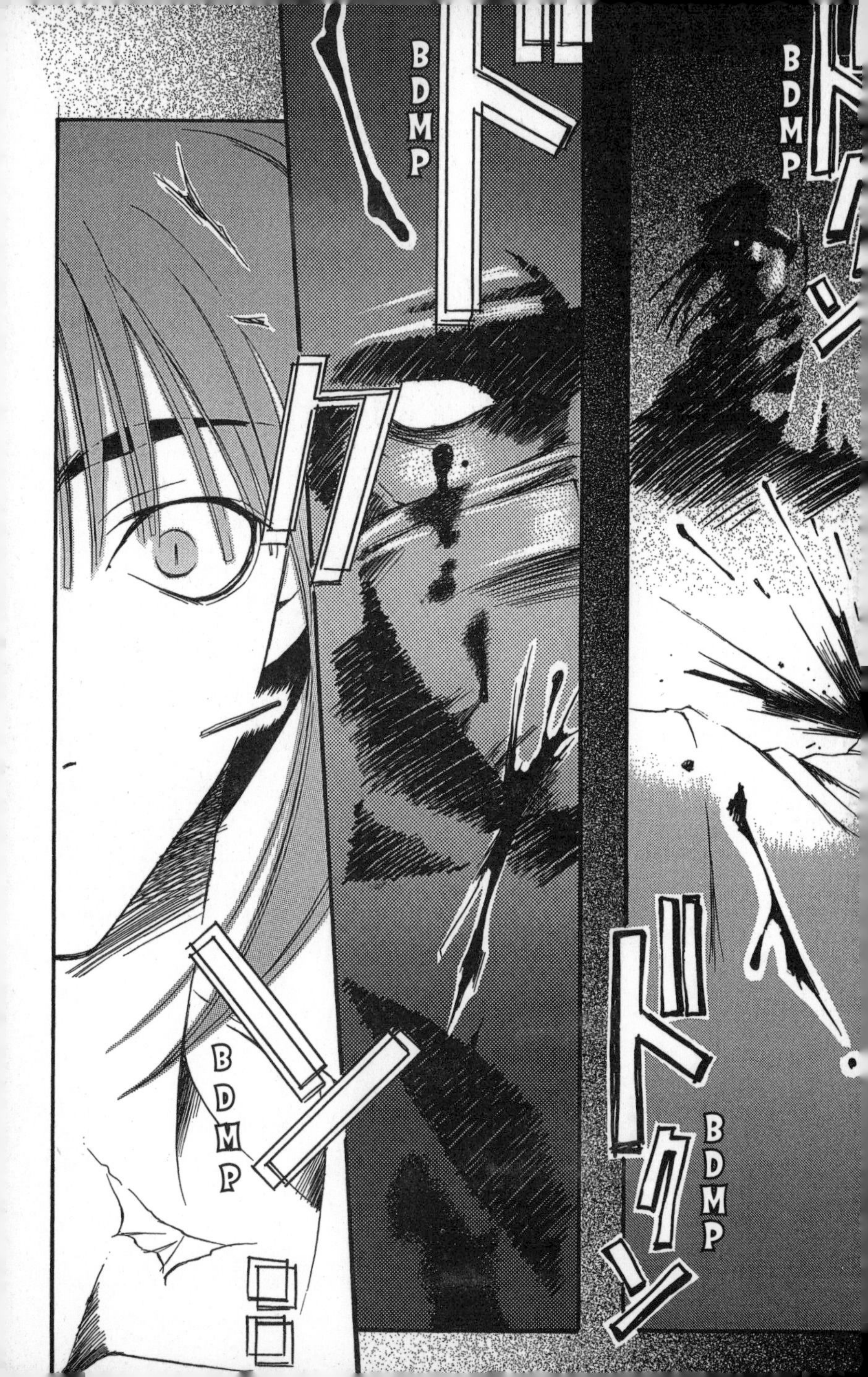
BDMP
BDMP
BDMP
BDMP

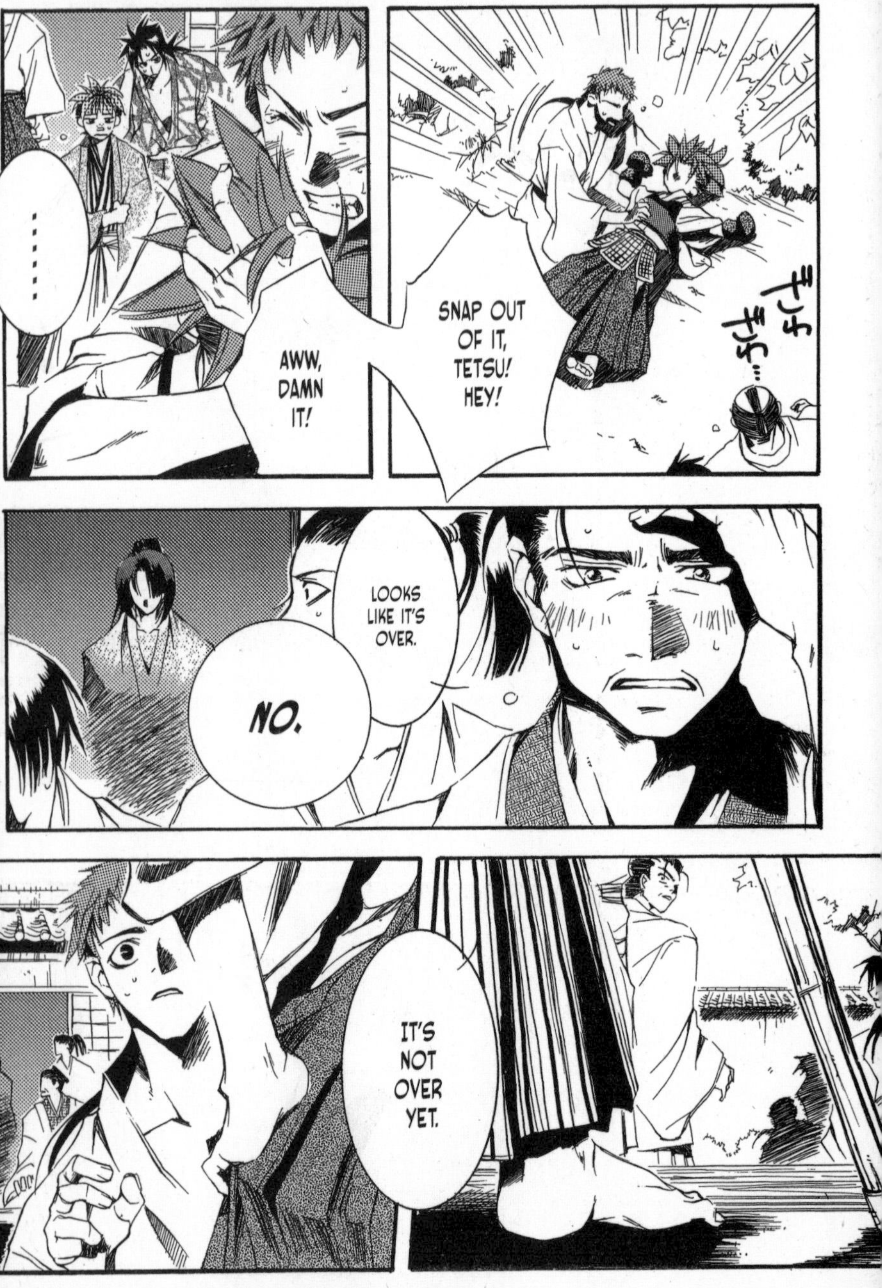
ざわ ざわ…
SNAP OUT OF IT, TETSU! HEY!
......
AWW, DAMN IT!
LOOKS LIKE IT'S OVER.
NO.
IT'S NOT OVER YET.

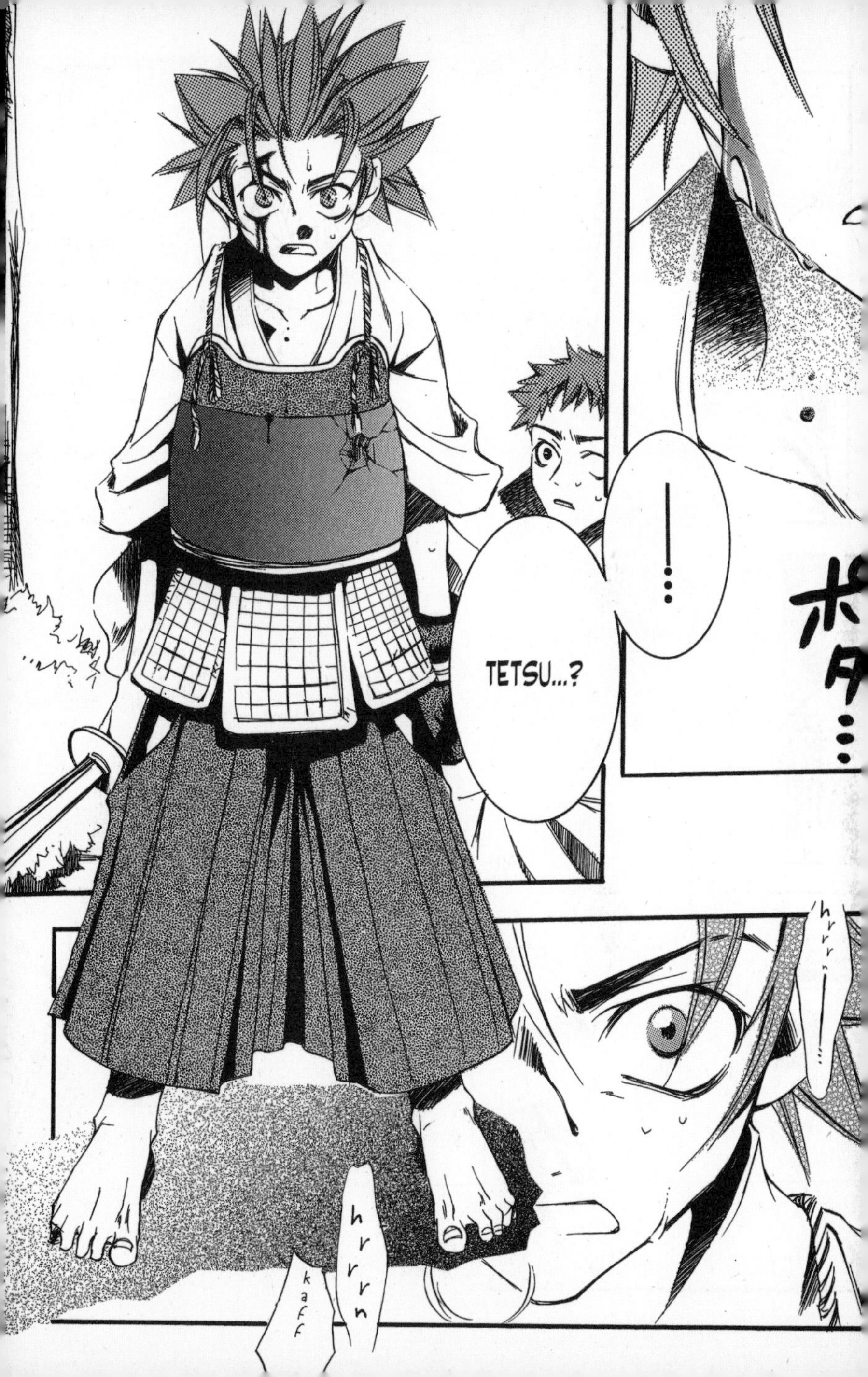

ポタ…
!…
TETSU...?
hrrrn—…
hrrrn
kaff

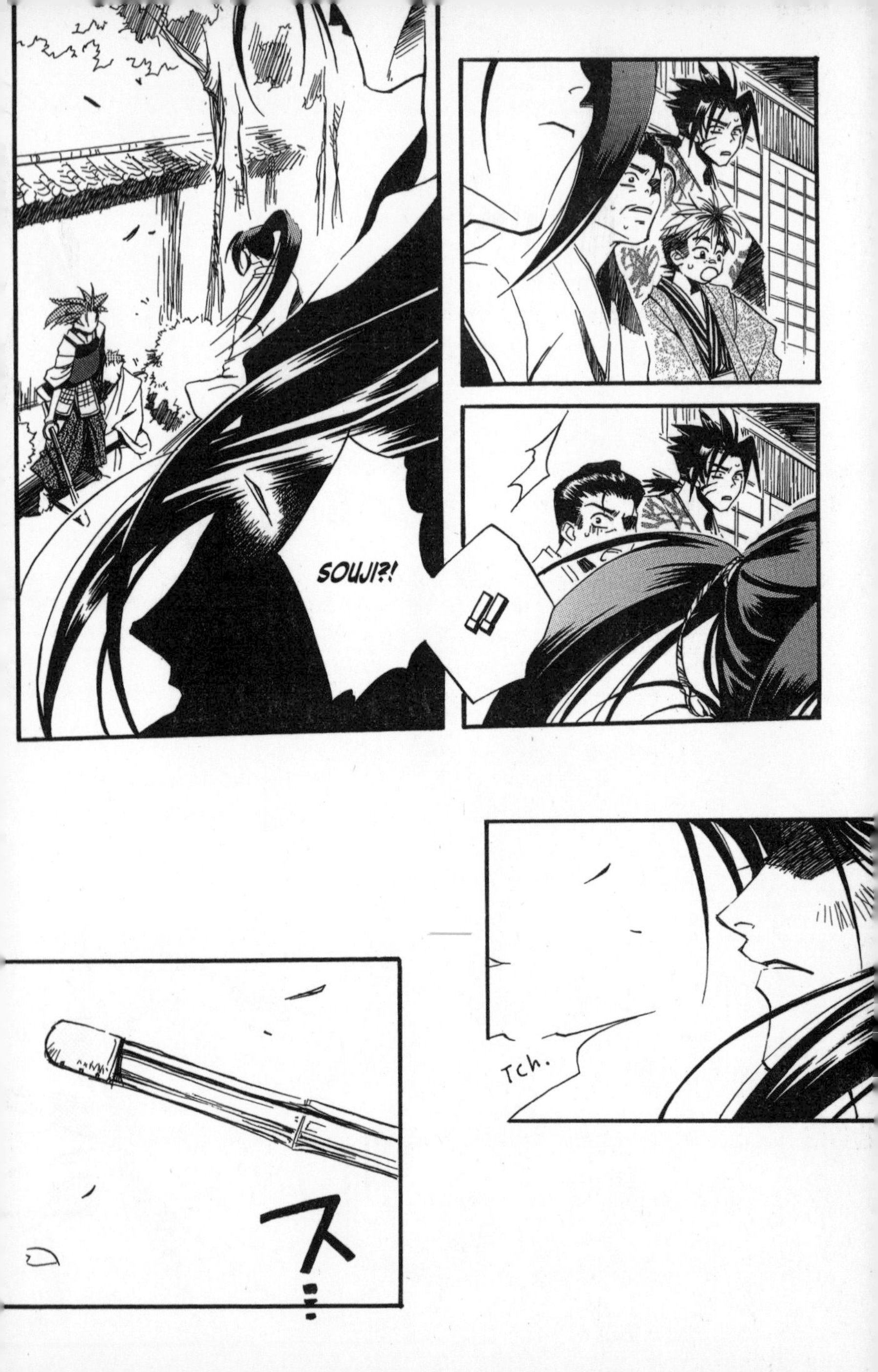
!!
SOUJI?!
Tch.
ス

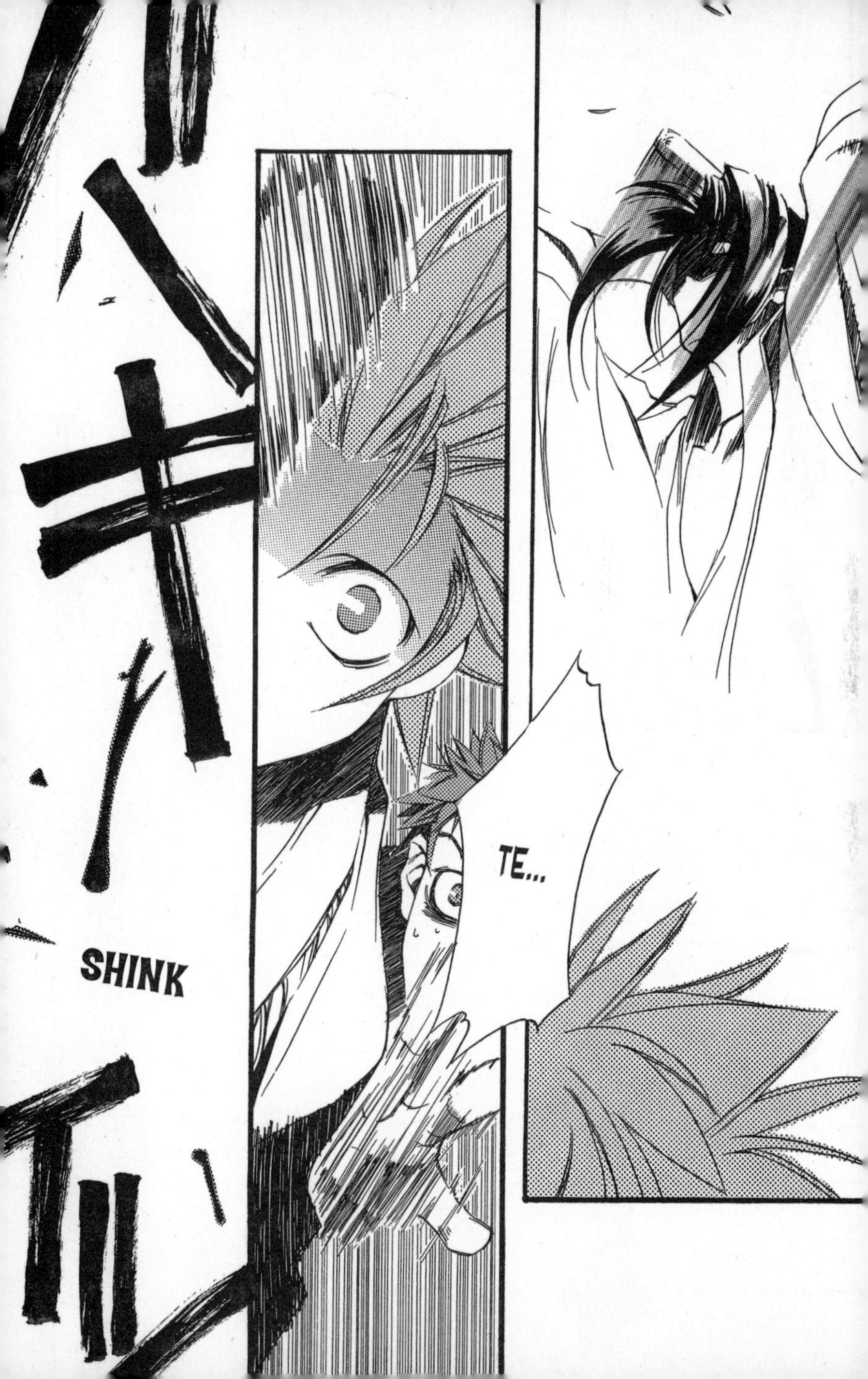
TE...
SHINK

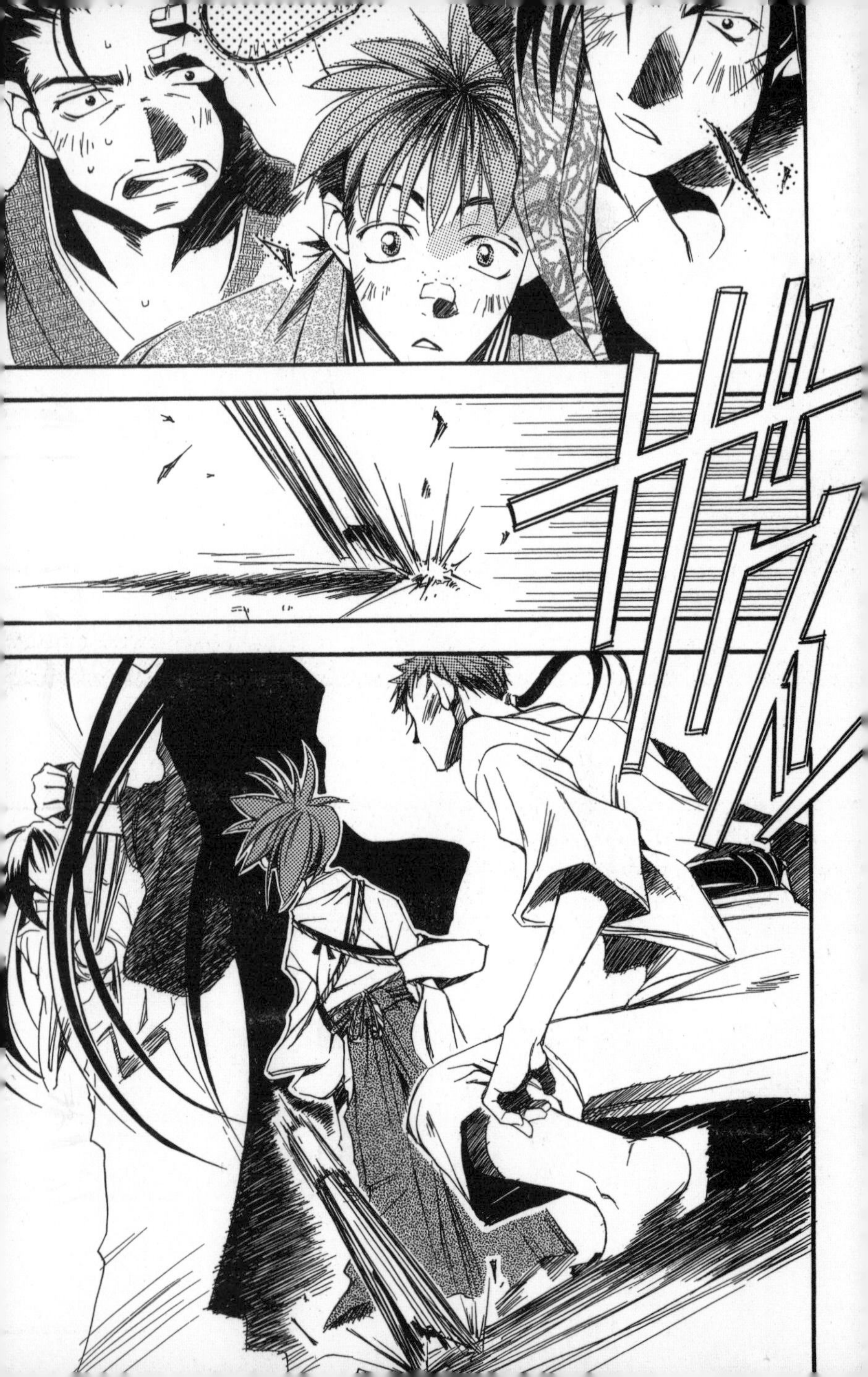

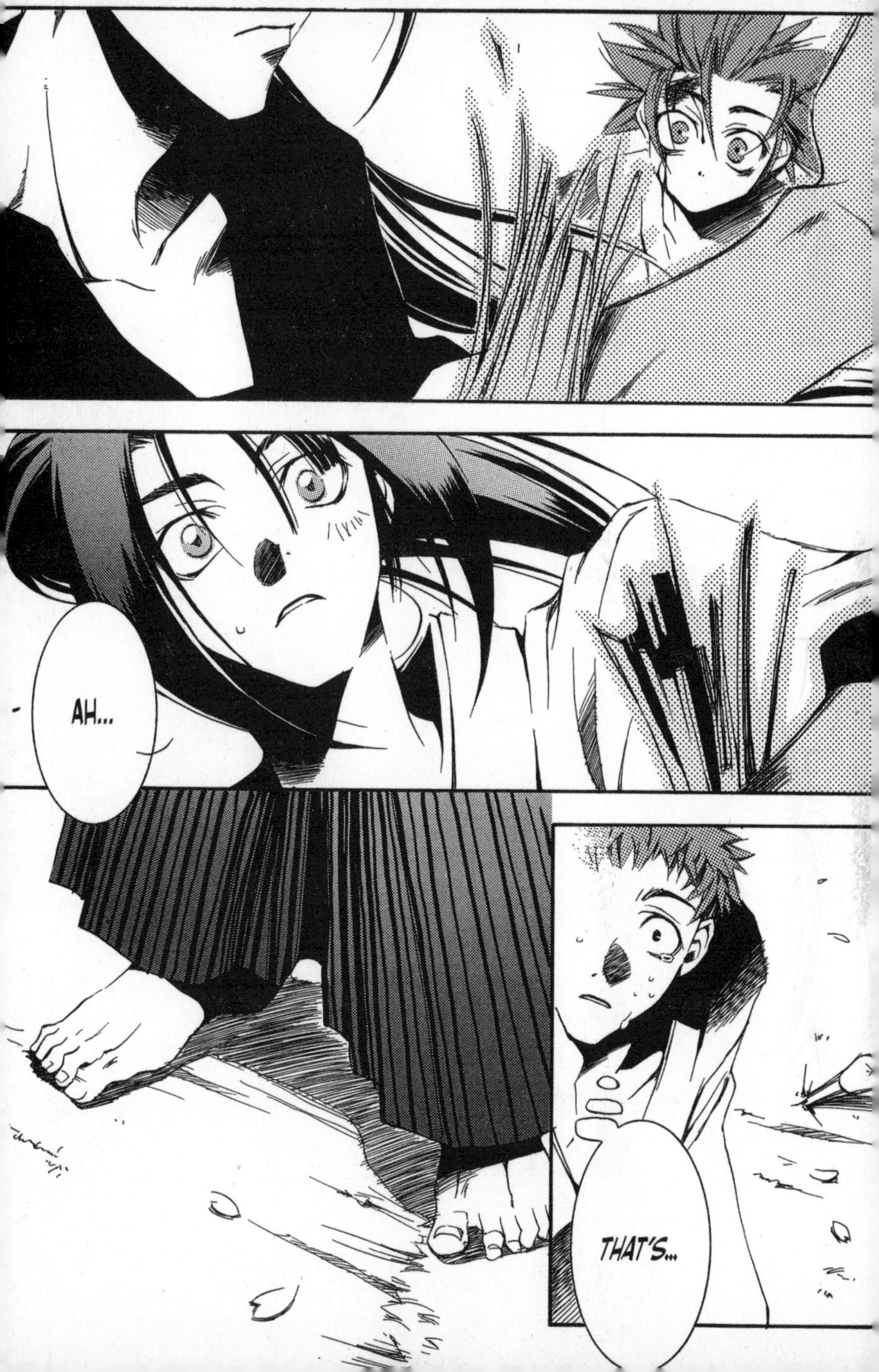
AH...
THAT'S...

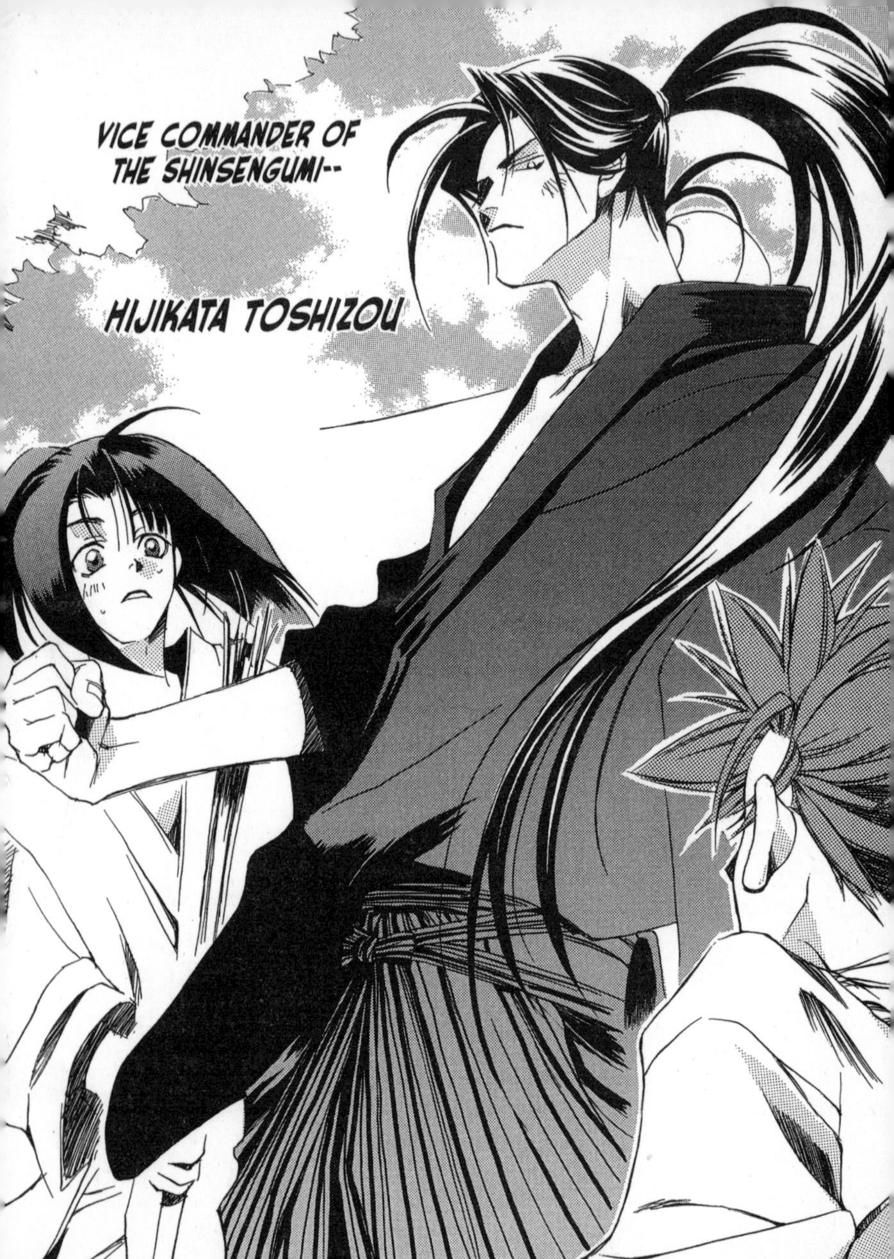
VICE COMMANDER OF THE SHINSENGUMI--
HIJIKATA TOSHIZOU

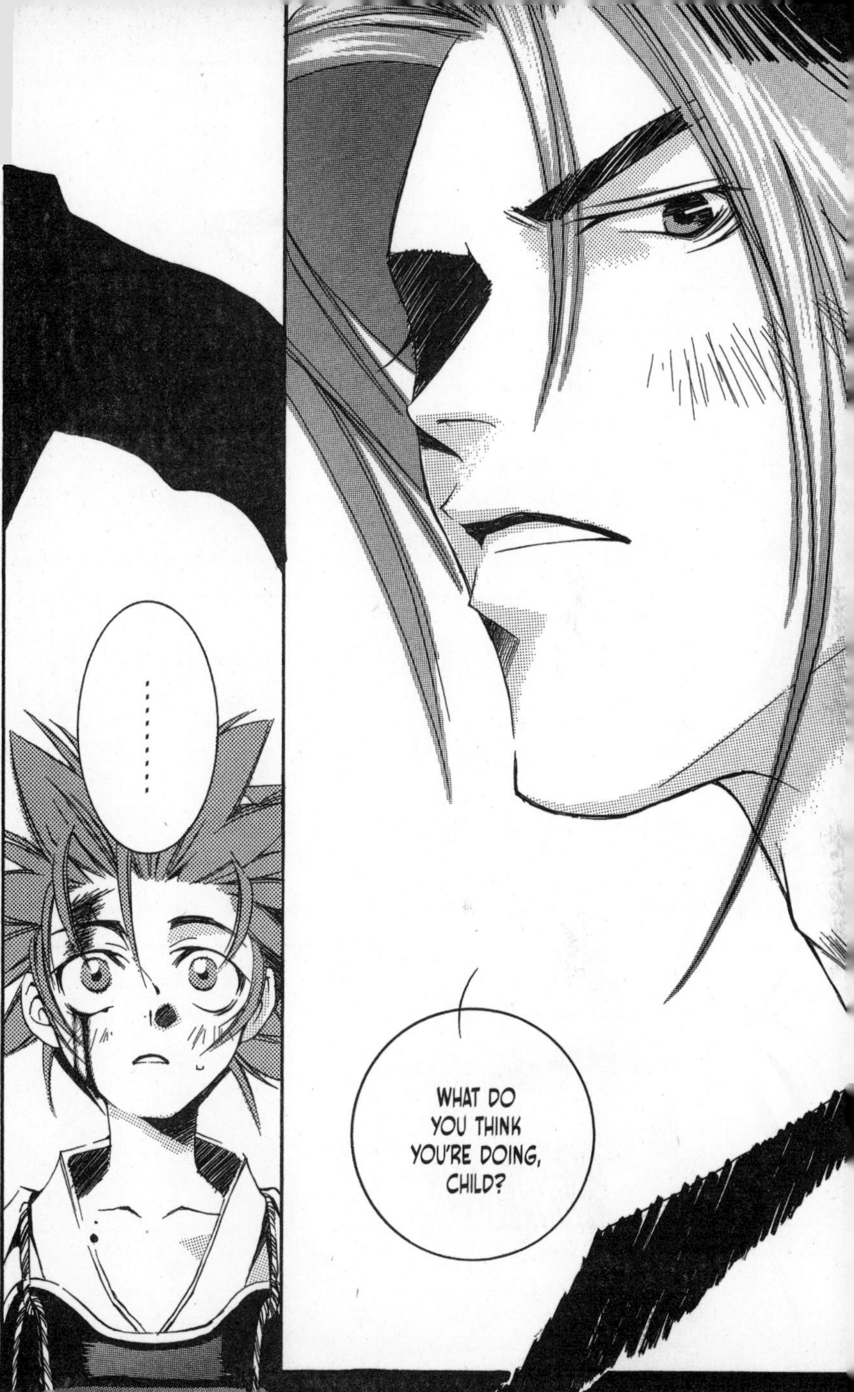
WHAT DO YOU THINK YOU'RE DOING, CHILD?
......

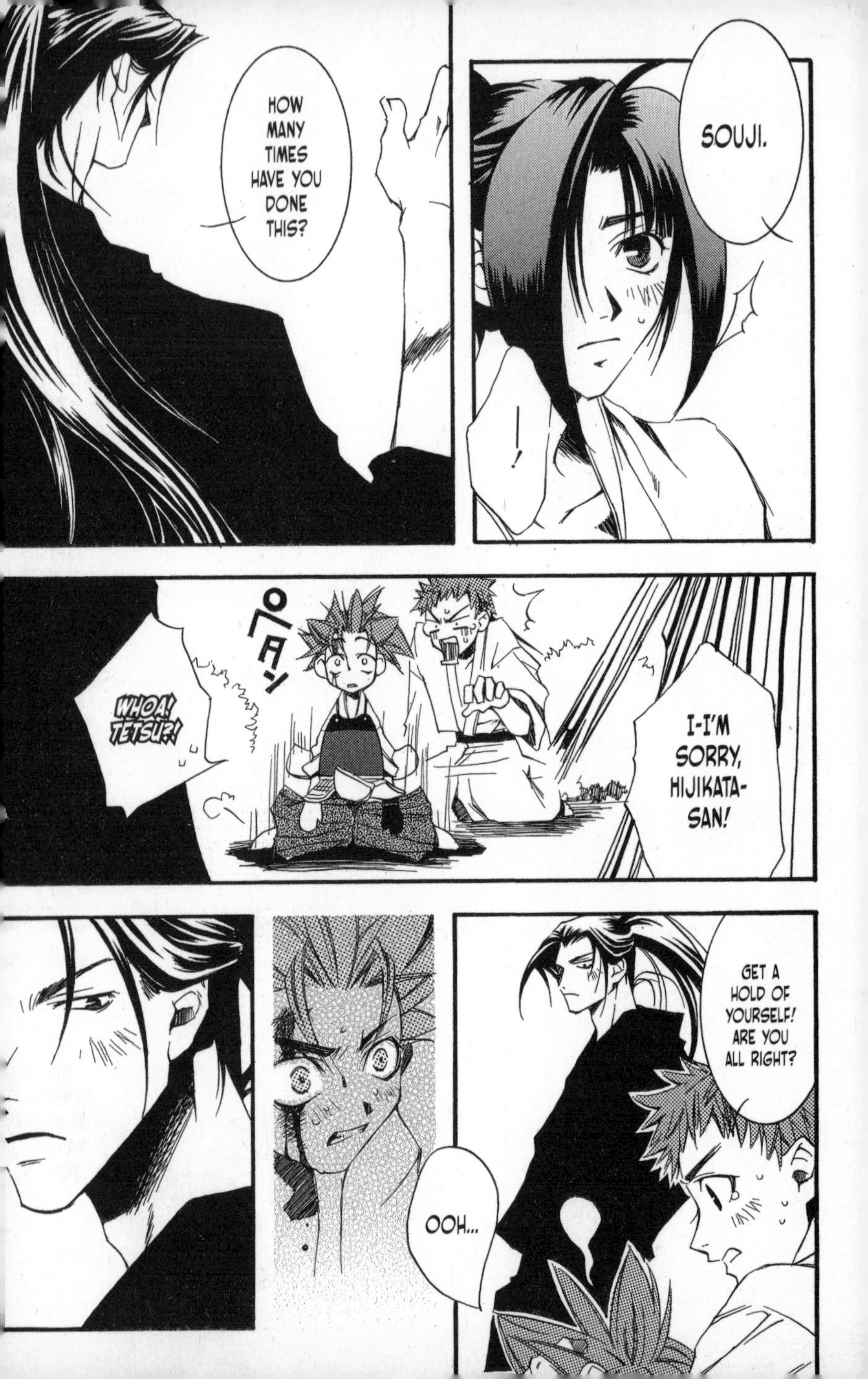
SOUJI.
HOW MANY TIMES HAVE YOU DONE THIS?
I-I'M SORRY, HIJIKATA-SAN!
ペタン
WHOA! TETSU?!
GET A HOLD OF YOURSELF! ARE YOU ALL RIGHT?
OOH...

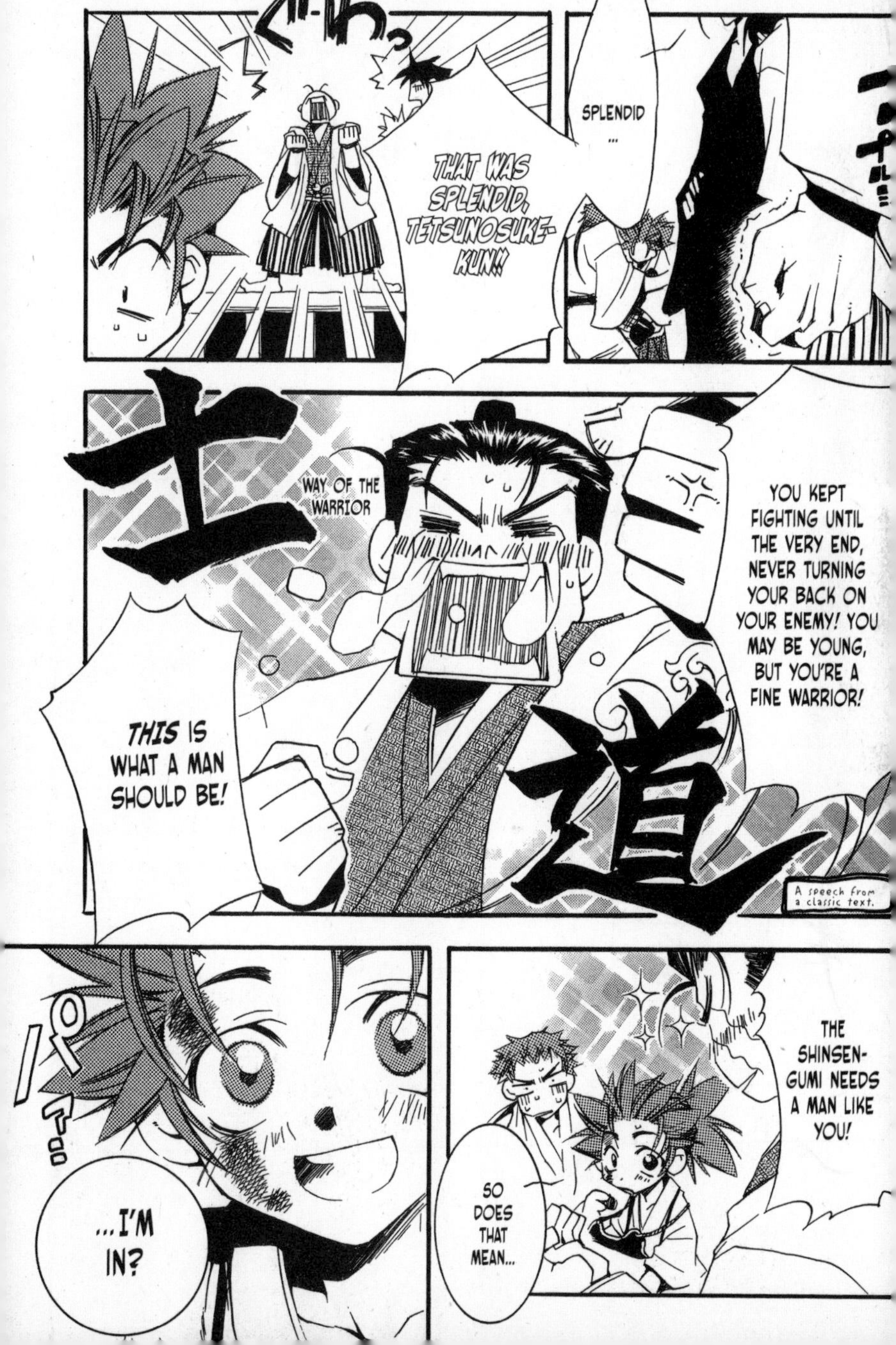
SPLENDID ...
ぐ-わっ
THAT WAS SPLENDID, TETSUNOSUKE-KUN!!
YOU KEPT FIGHTING UNTIL THE VERY END, NEVER TURNING YOUR BACK ON YOUR ENEMY! YOU MAY BE YOUNG, BUT YOU'RE A FINE WARRIOR!
士道
WAY OF THE WARRIOR
THIS IS WHAT A MAN SHOULD BE!
A speech from a classic text.
THE SHINSEN-GUMI NEEDS A MAN LIKE YOU!
SO DOES THAT MEAN...
...I'M IN?

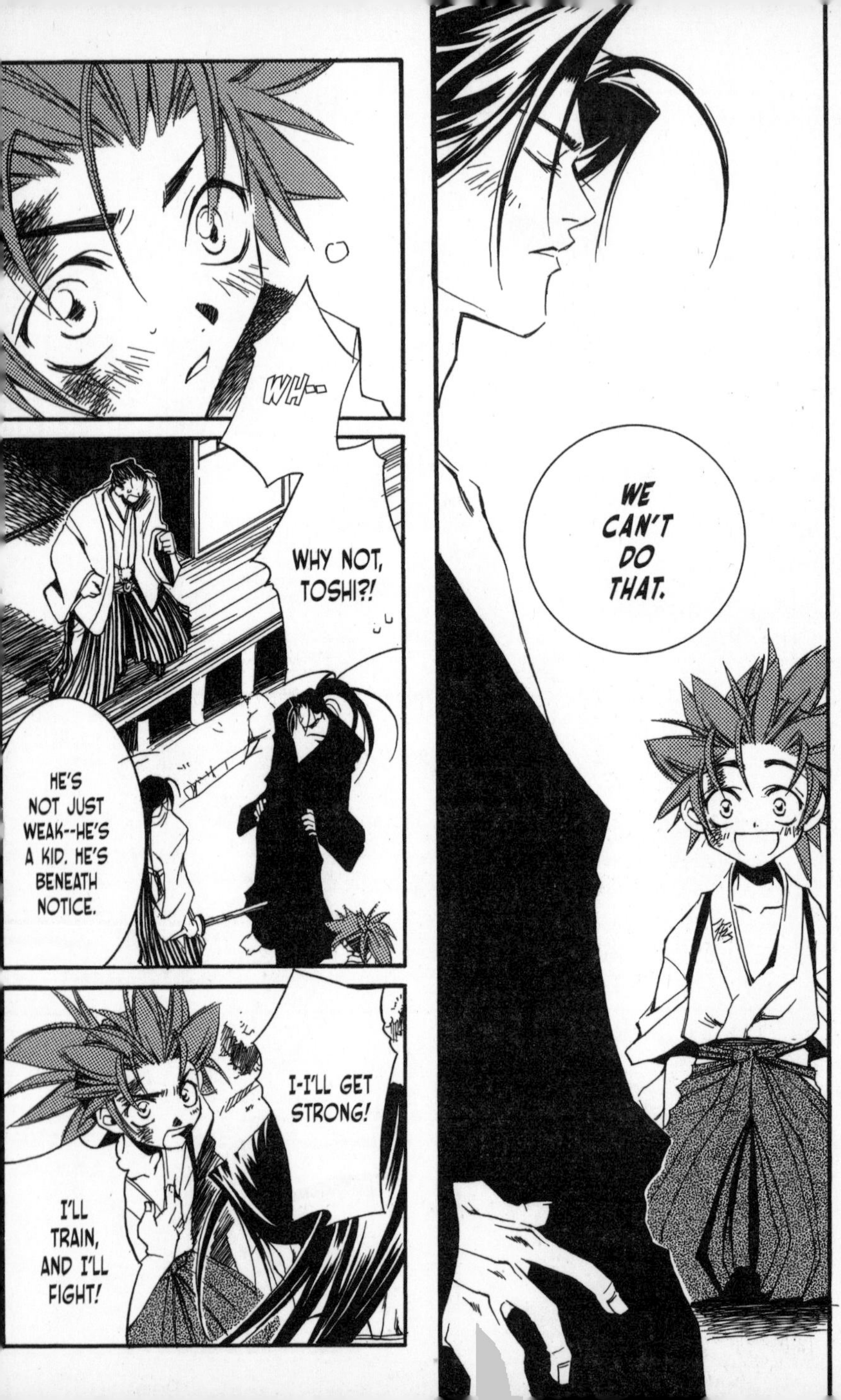
WE CAN'T DO THAT.
WH--
WHY NOT, TOSHI?!
HE'S NOT JUST WEAK--HE'S A KID. HE'S BENEATH NOTICE.
I-I'LL GET STRONG!
I'LL TRAIN, AND I'LL FIGHT!

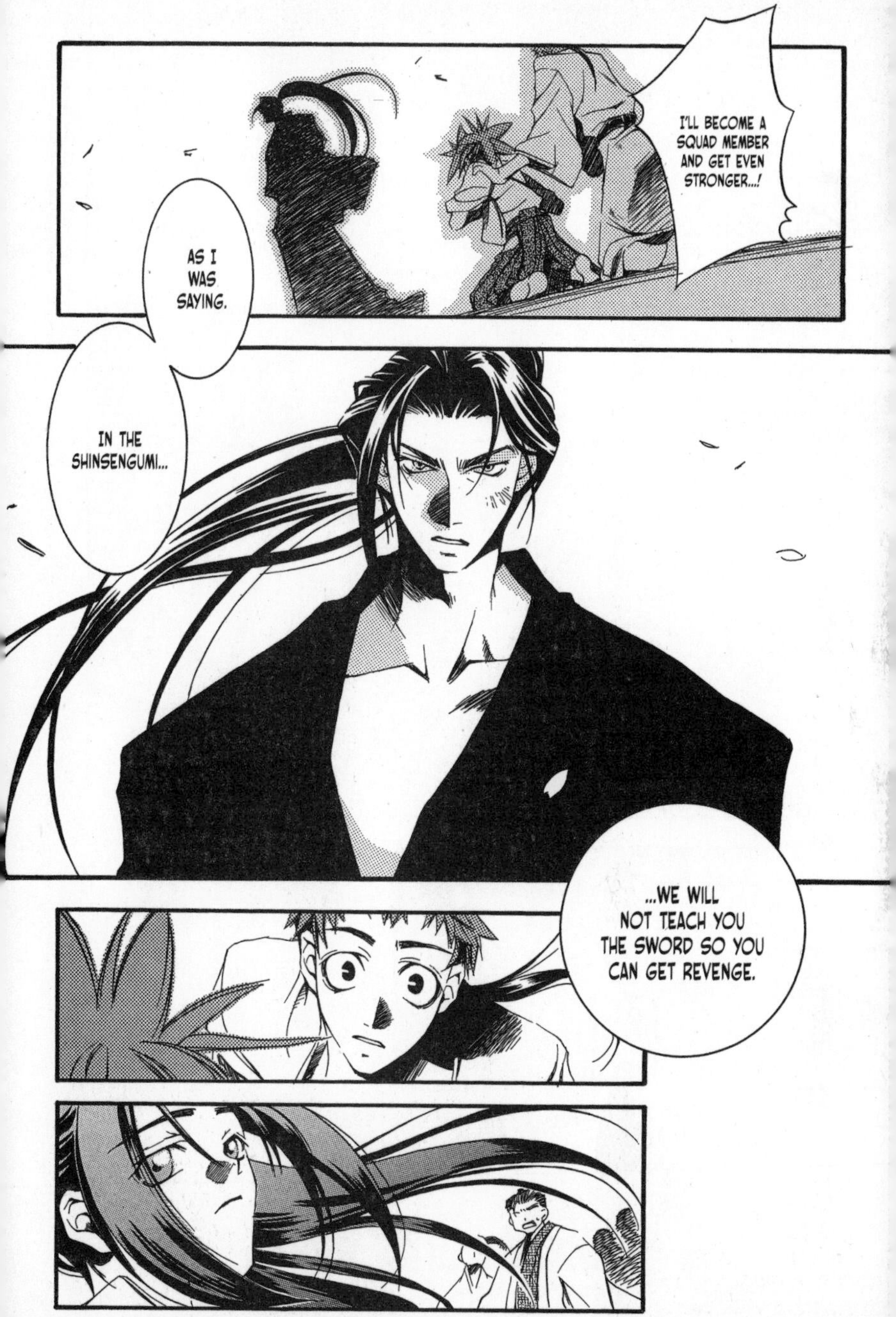
I'LL BECOME A SQUAD MEMBER AND GET EVEN STRONGER...!
AS I WAS SAYING.
IN THE SHINSENGUMI...
...WE WILL NOT TEACH YOU THE SWORD SO YOU CAN GET REVENGE.

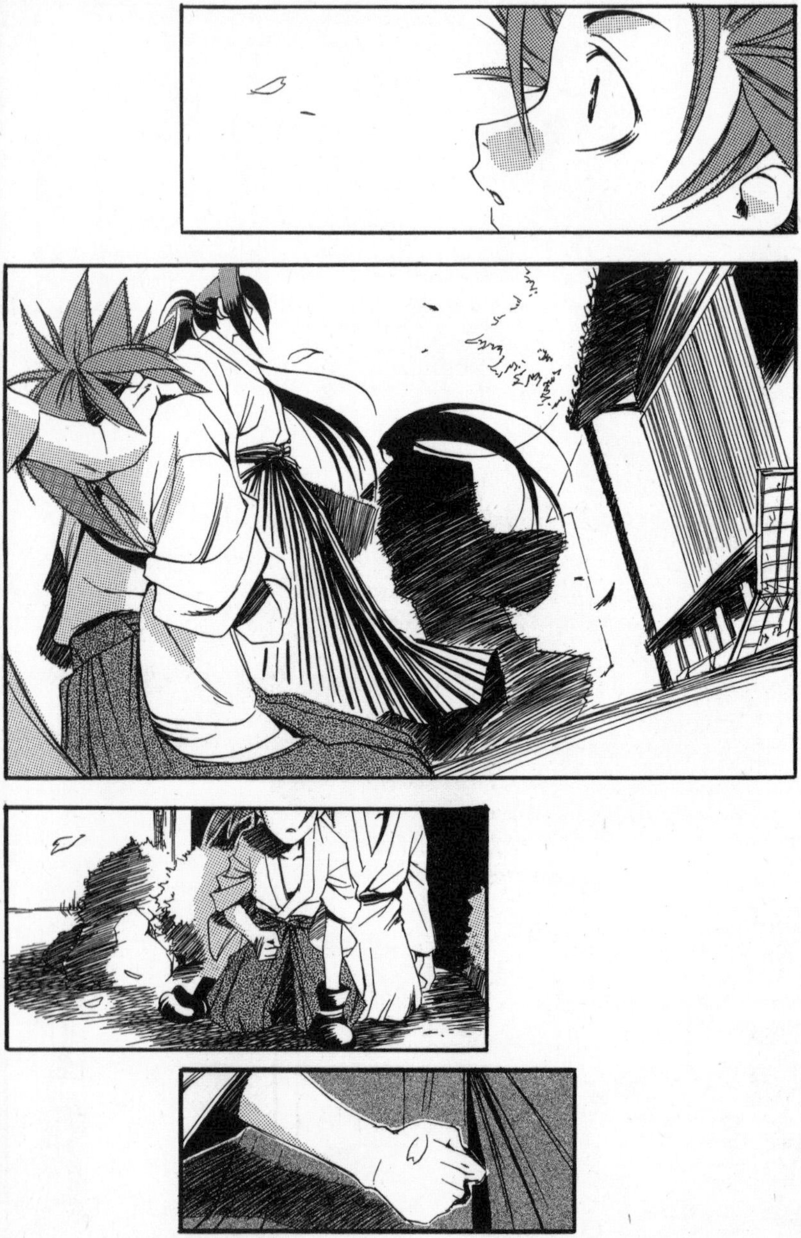

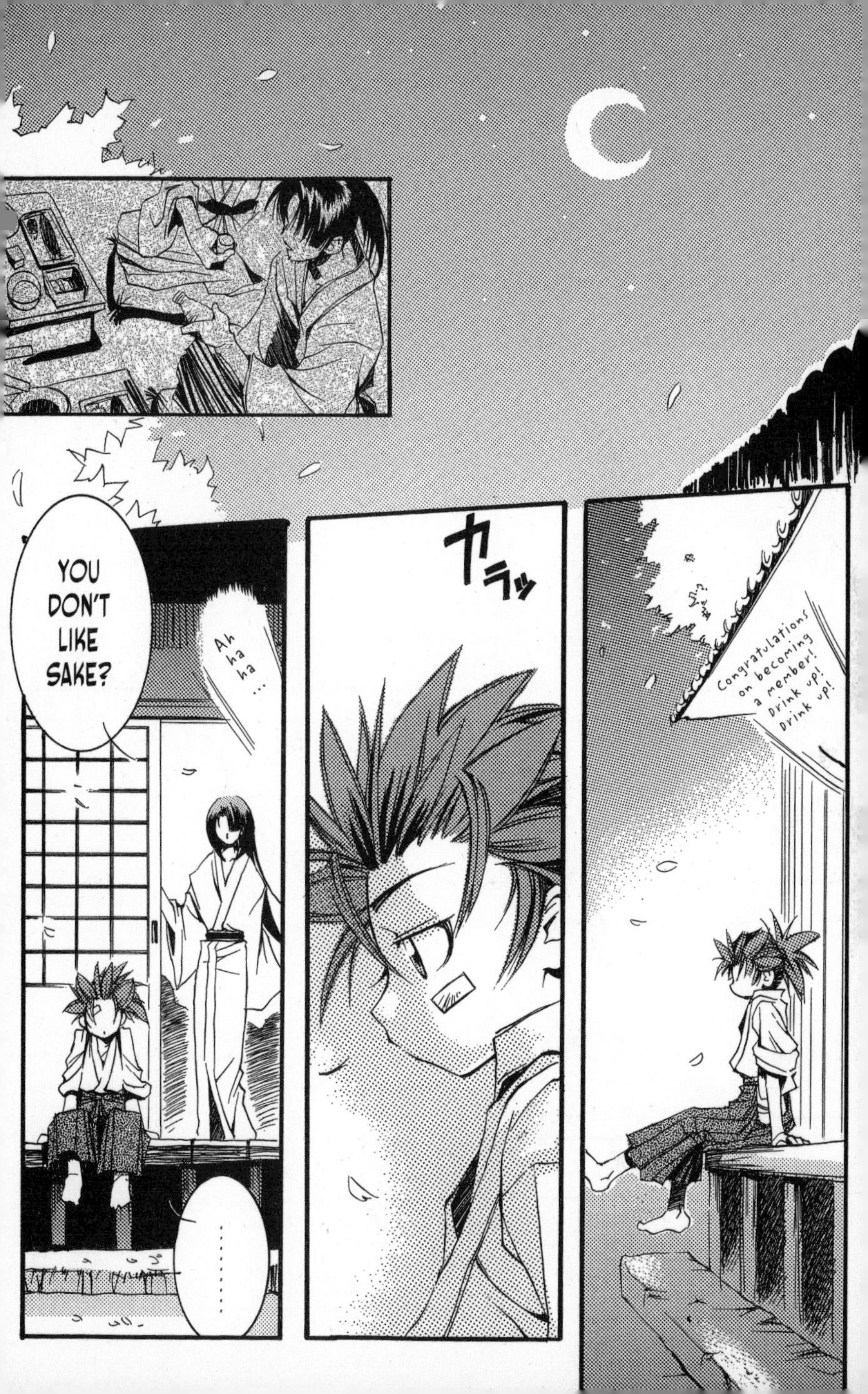
Congratulations on becoming a member! Drink up! Drink up!
カラッ
Ah ha ha...
YOU DON'T LIKE SAKE?
......

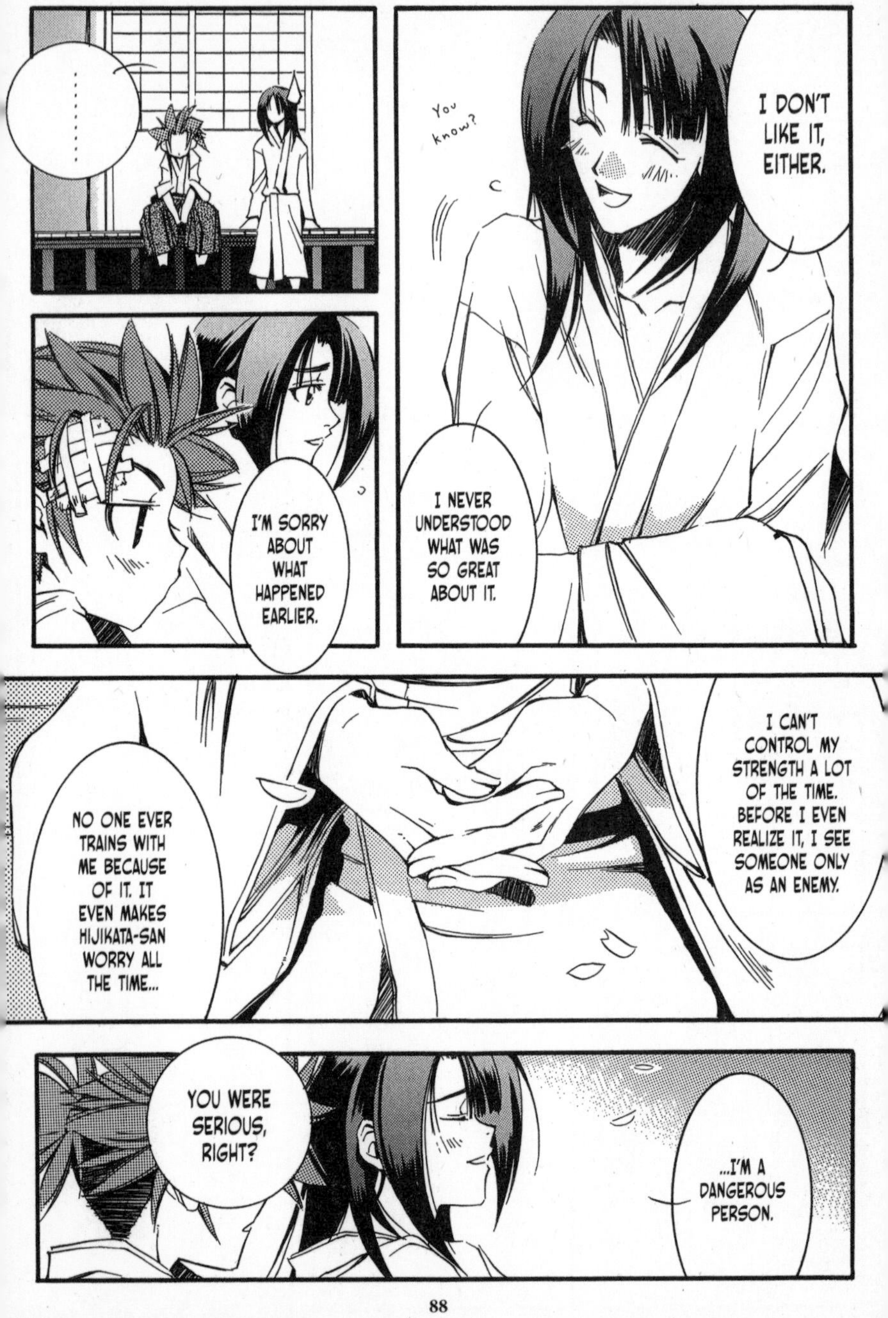
I DON'T LIKE IT, EITHER.
You know?
I NEVER UNDERSTOOD WHAT WAS SO GREAT ABOUT IT.
......
I'M SORRY ABOUT WHAT HAPPENED EARLIER.
I CAN'T CONTROL MY STRENGTH A LOT OF THE TIME. BEFORE I EVEN REALIZE IT, I SEE SOMEONE ONLY AS AN ENEMY.
NO ONE EVER TRAINS WITH ME BECAUSE OF IT. IT EVEN MAKES HIJIKATA-SAN WORRY ALL THE TIME...
...I'M A DANGEROUS PERSON.
YOU WERE SERIOUS, RIGHT?

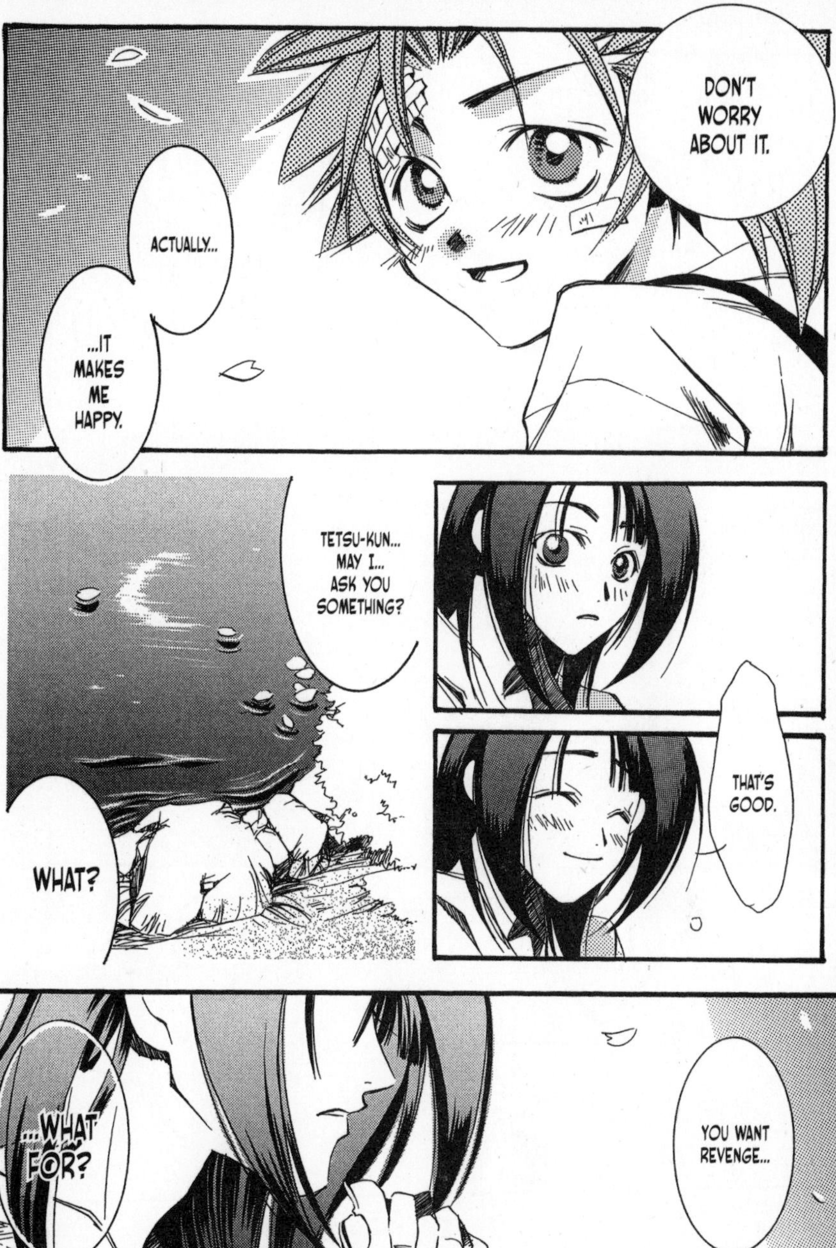

DON'T WORRY ABOUT IT.
ACTUALLY...
...IT MAKES ME HAPPY.
THAT'S GOOD.
TETSU-KUN... MAY I... ASK YOU SOMETHING?
WHAT?
YOU WANT REVENGE...
...WHAT FOR?

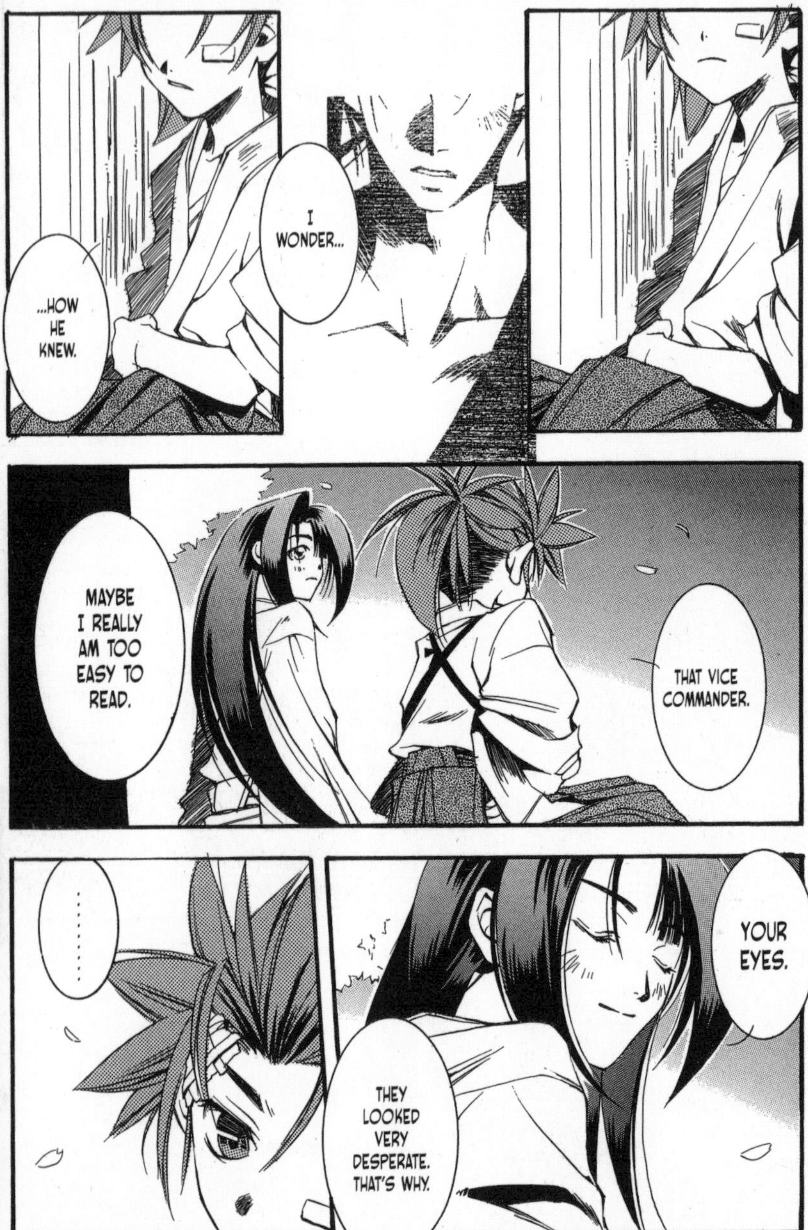
I WONDER...
...HOW HE KNEW.
THAT VICE COMMANDER.
MAYBE I REALLY AM TOO EASY TO READ.
YOUR EYES.
THEY LOOKED VERY DESPERATE. THAT'S WHY.
......

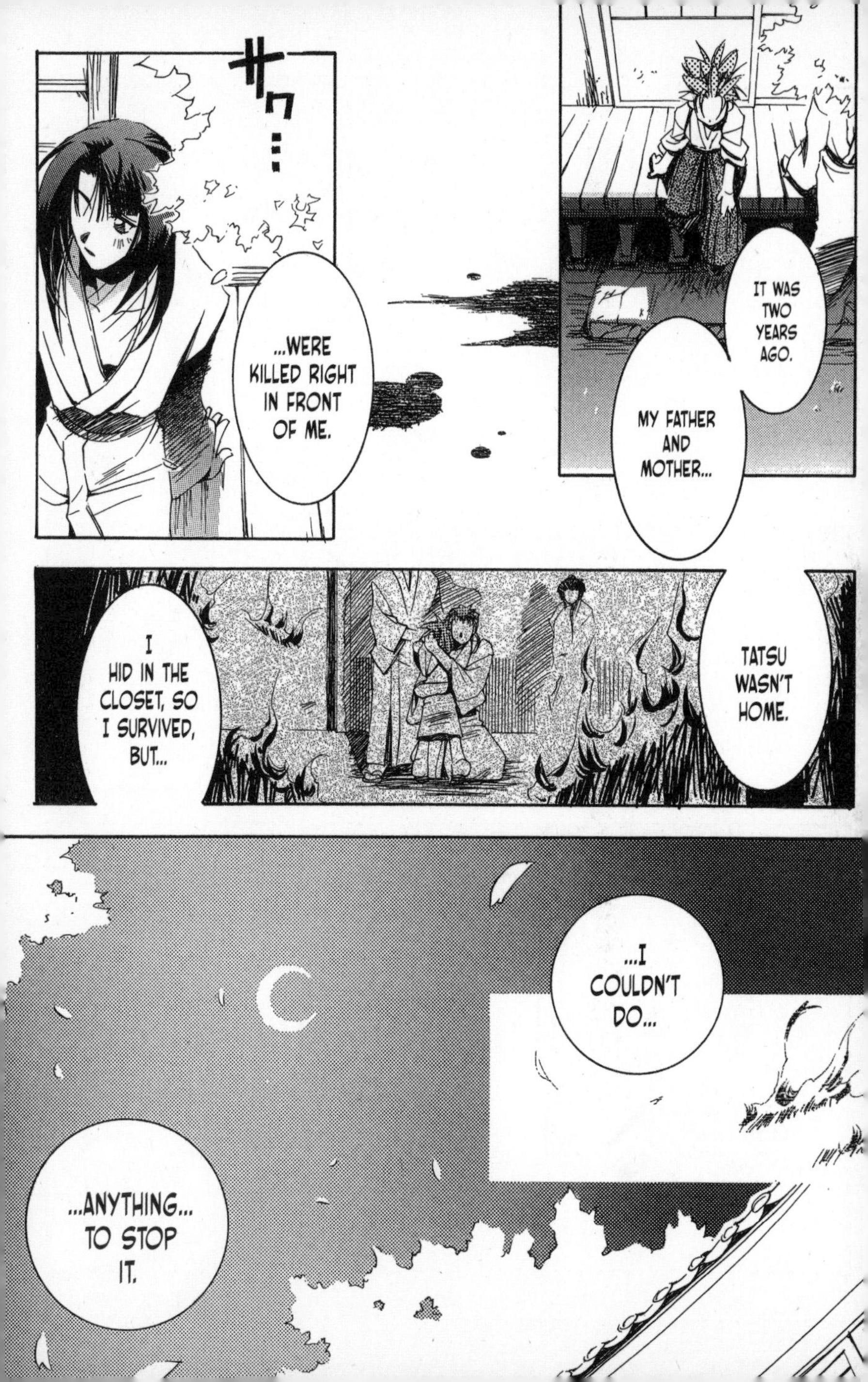
IT WAS TWO YEARS AGO.
MY FATHER AND MOTHER...
サワ…
...WERE KILLED RIGHT IN FRONT OF ME.
TATSU WASN'T HOME.
I HID IN THE CLOSET, SO I SURVIVED, BUT...
...I COULDN'T DO...
...ANYTHING... TO STOP IT.

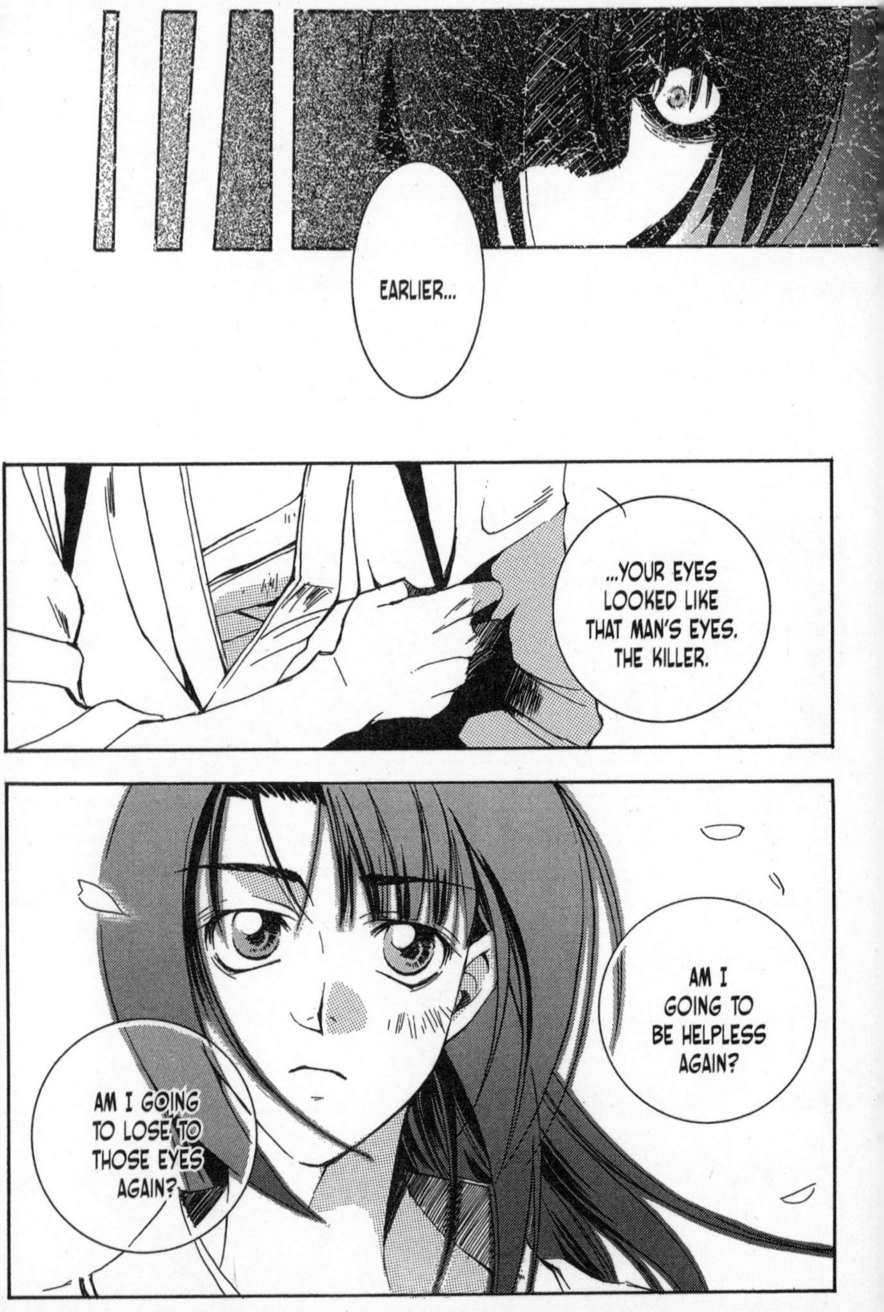
EARLIER...
...YOUR EYES LOOKED LIKE THAT MAN'S EYES. THE KILLER.
AM I GOING TO BE HELPLESS AGAIN?
AM I GOING TO LOSE TO THOSE EYES AGAIN?

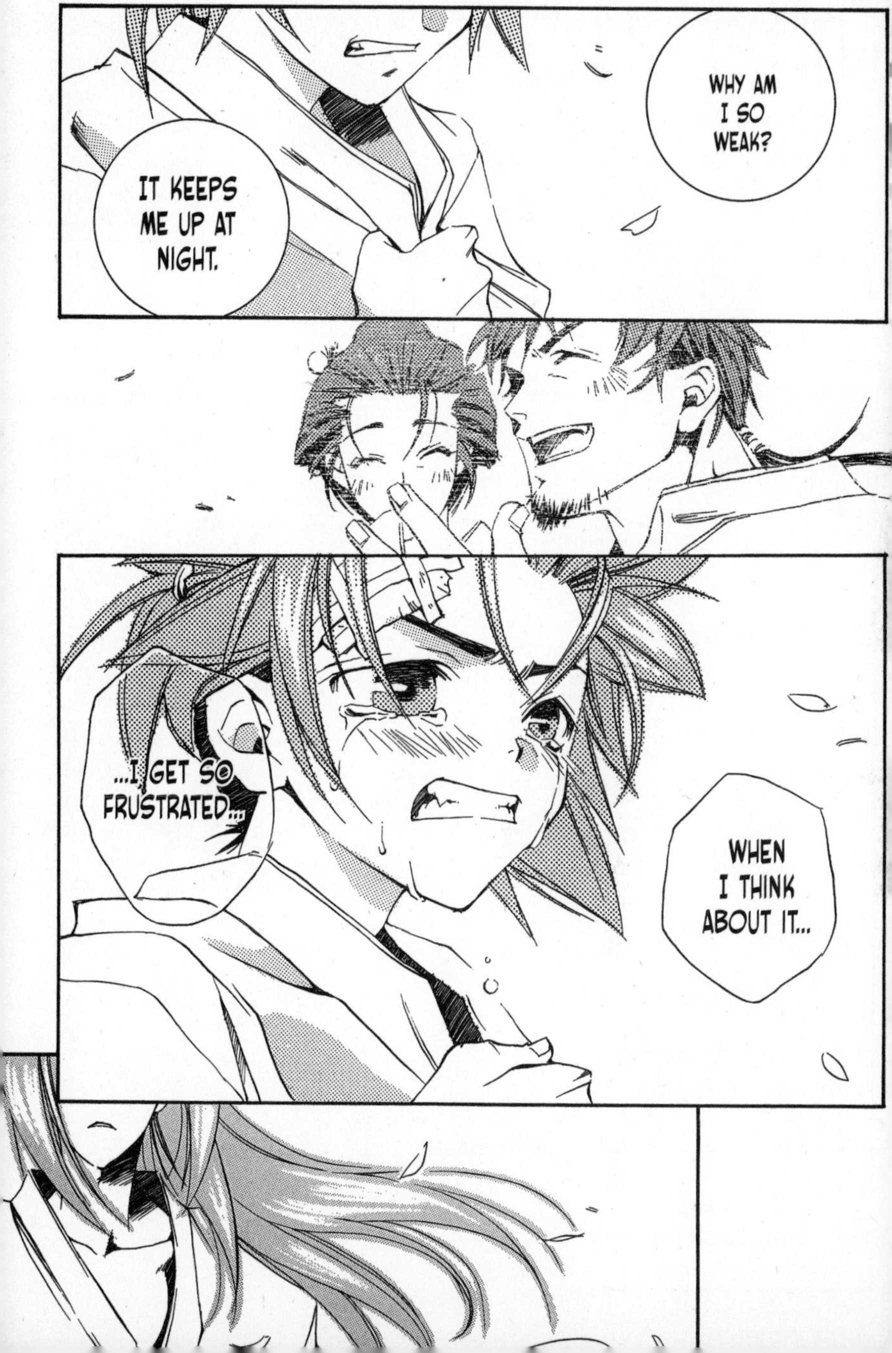
WHY AM I SO WEAK?
IT KEEPS ME UP AT NIGHT.
WHEN I THINK ABOUT IT...
...I GET SO FRUSTRATED...

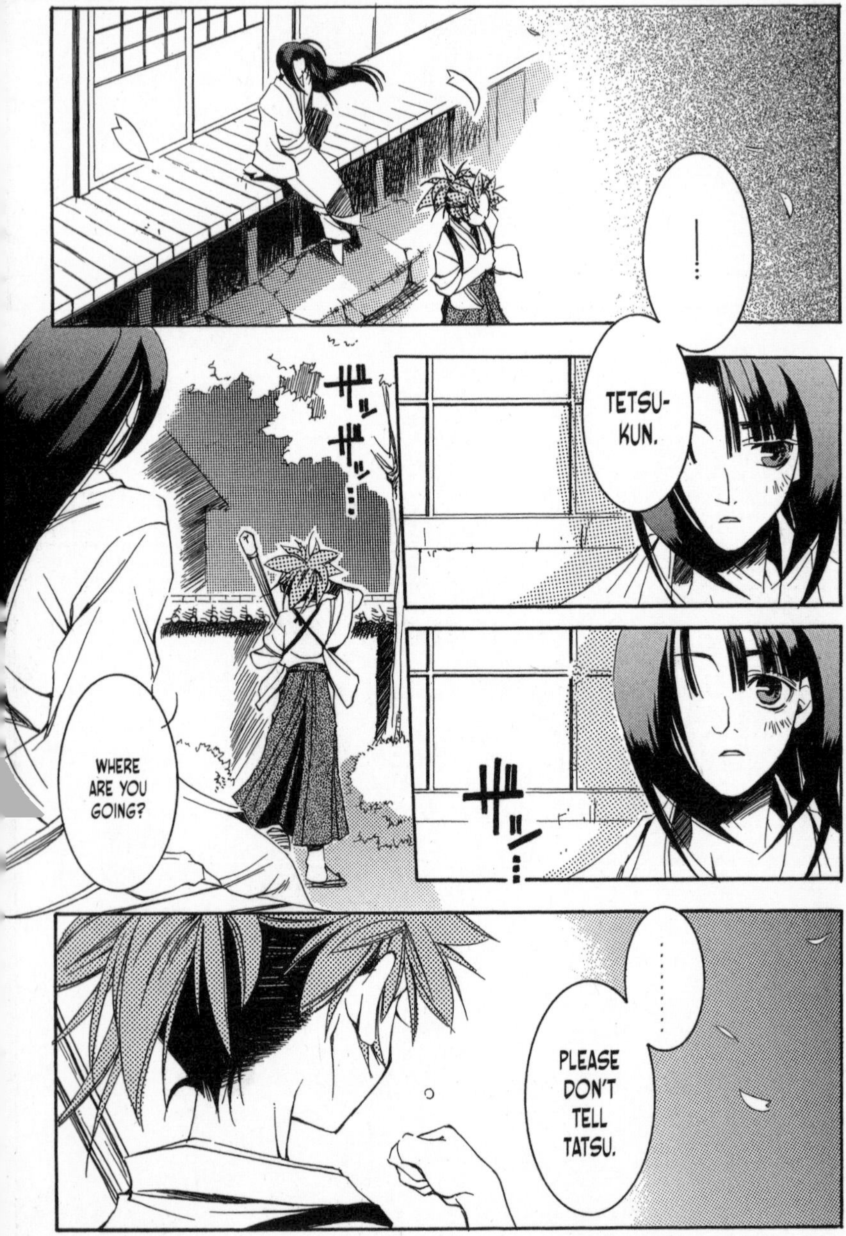
!...
TETSU-KUN.
ザッ…
ザッ ザッ…
WHERE ARE YOU GOING?
......
PLEASE DON'T TELL TATSU.

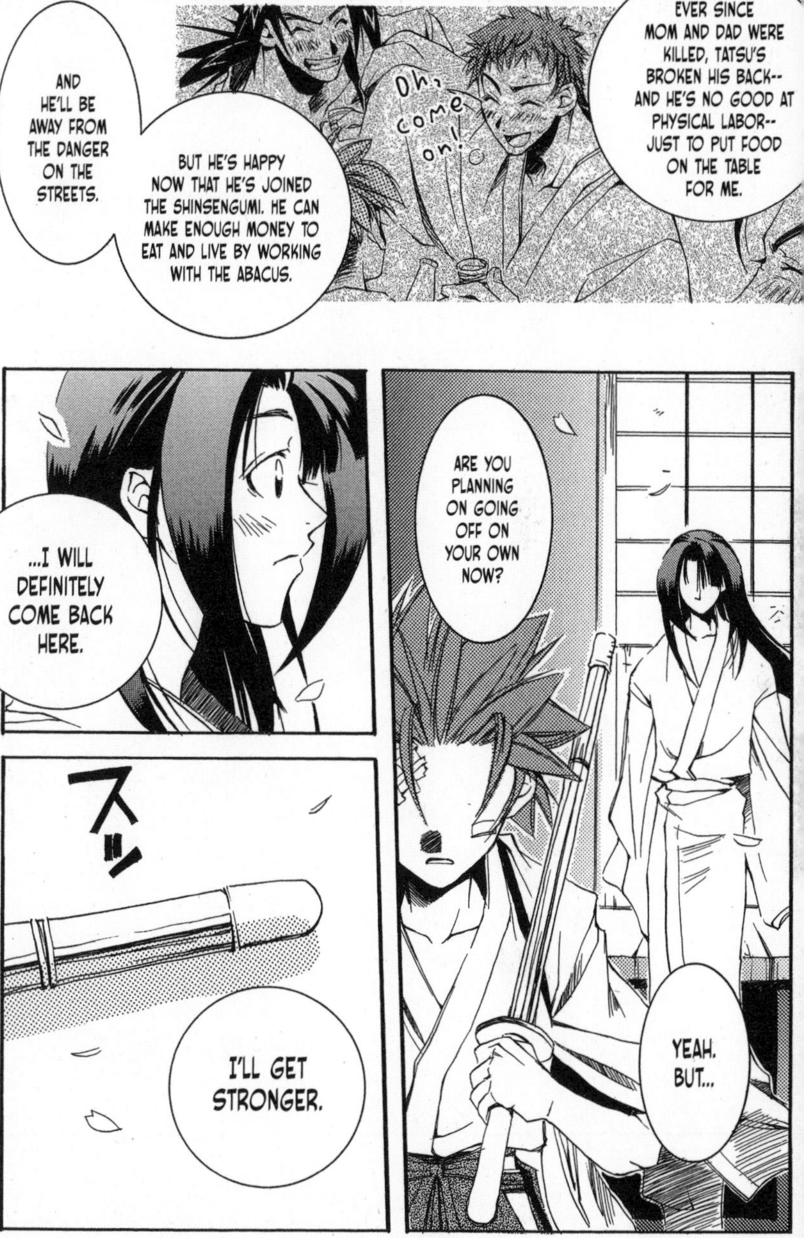
EVER SINCE MOM AND DAD WERE KILLED, TATSU'S BROKEN HIS BACK-- AND HE'S NO GOOD AT PHYSICAL LABOR-- JUST TO PUT FOOD ON THE TABLE FOR ME.
Oh, come on!
BUT HE'S HAPPY NOW THAT HE'S JOINED THE SHINSENGUMI. HE CAN MAKE ENOUGH MONEY TO EAT AND LIVE BY WORKING WITH THE ABACUS.
AND HE'LL BE AWAY FROM THE DANGER ON THE STREETS.
ARE YOU PLANNING ON GOING OFF ON YOUR OWN NOW?
YEAH. BUT...
...I WILL DEFINITELY COME BACK HERE.
スッ
I'LL GET STRONGER.

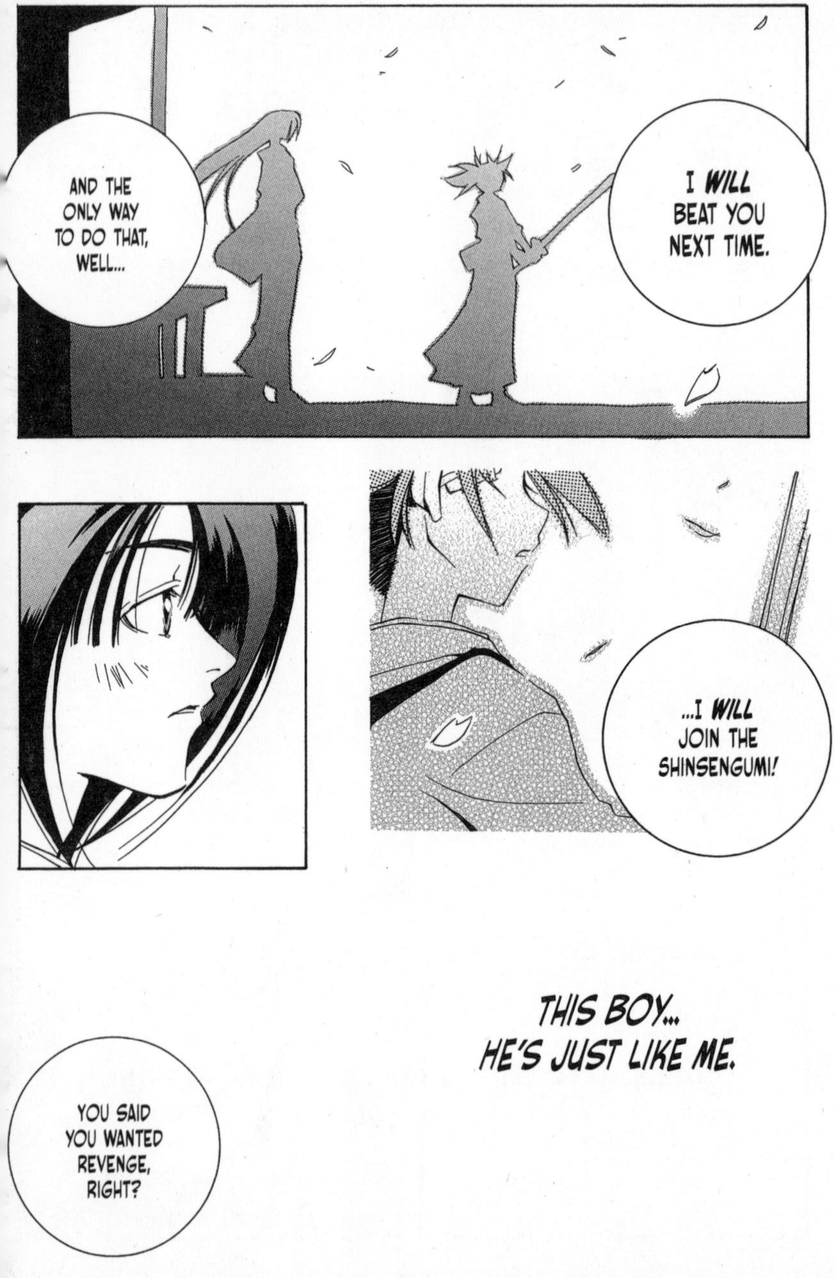
I WILL BEAT YOU NEXT TIME.
AND THE ONLY WAY TO DO THAT, WELL...
...I WILL JOIN THE SHINSENGUMI!
THIS BOY... HE'S JUST LIKE ME.
YOU SAID YOU WANTED REVENGE, RIGHT?

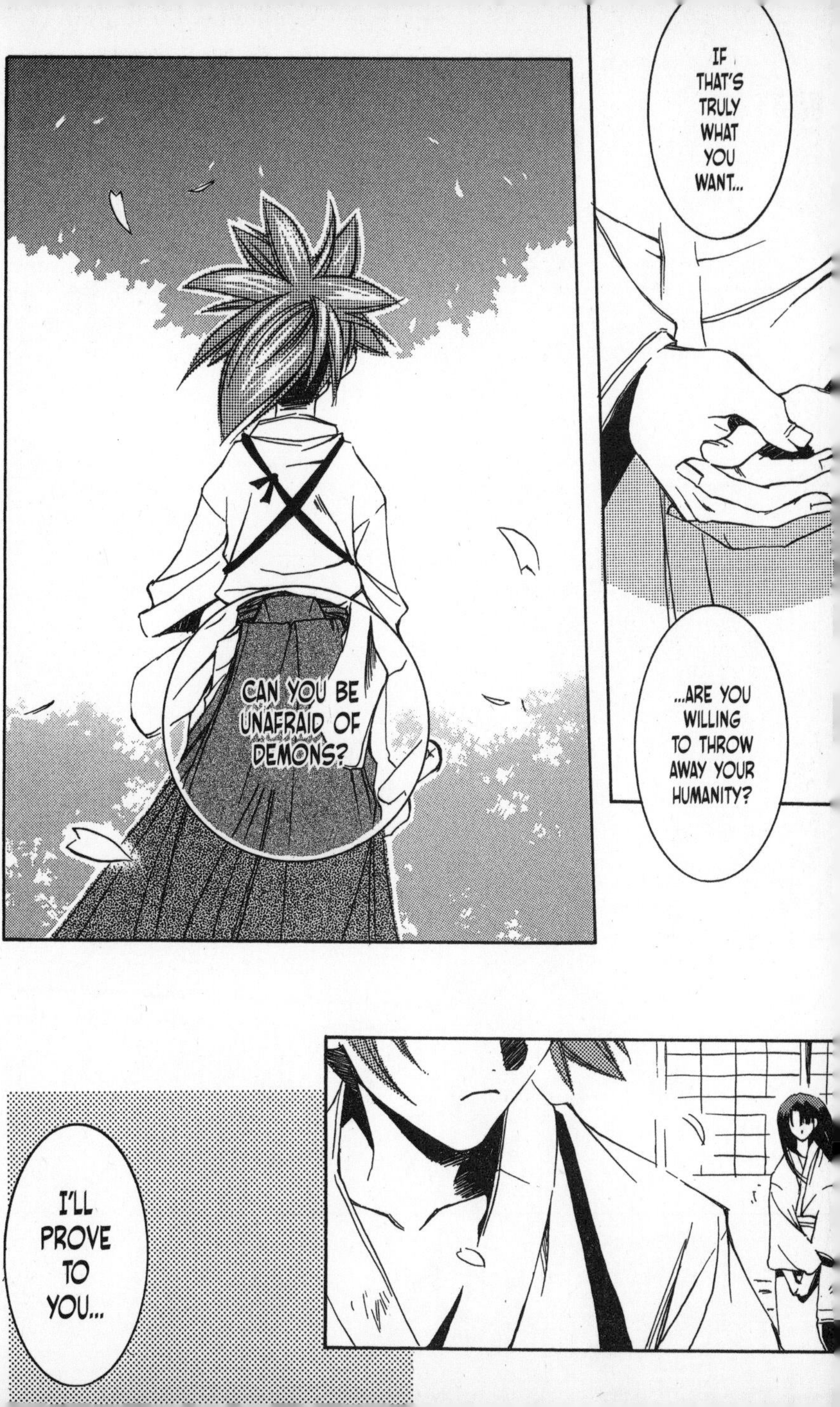
IF THAT'S TRULY WHAT YOU WANT...
...ARE YOU WILLING TO THROW AWAY YOUR HUMANITY?
CAN YOU BE UNAFRAID OF DEMONS?
I'LL PROVE TO YOU...

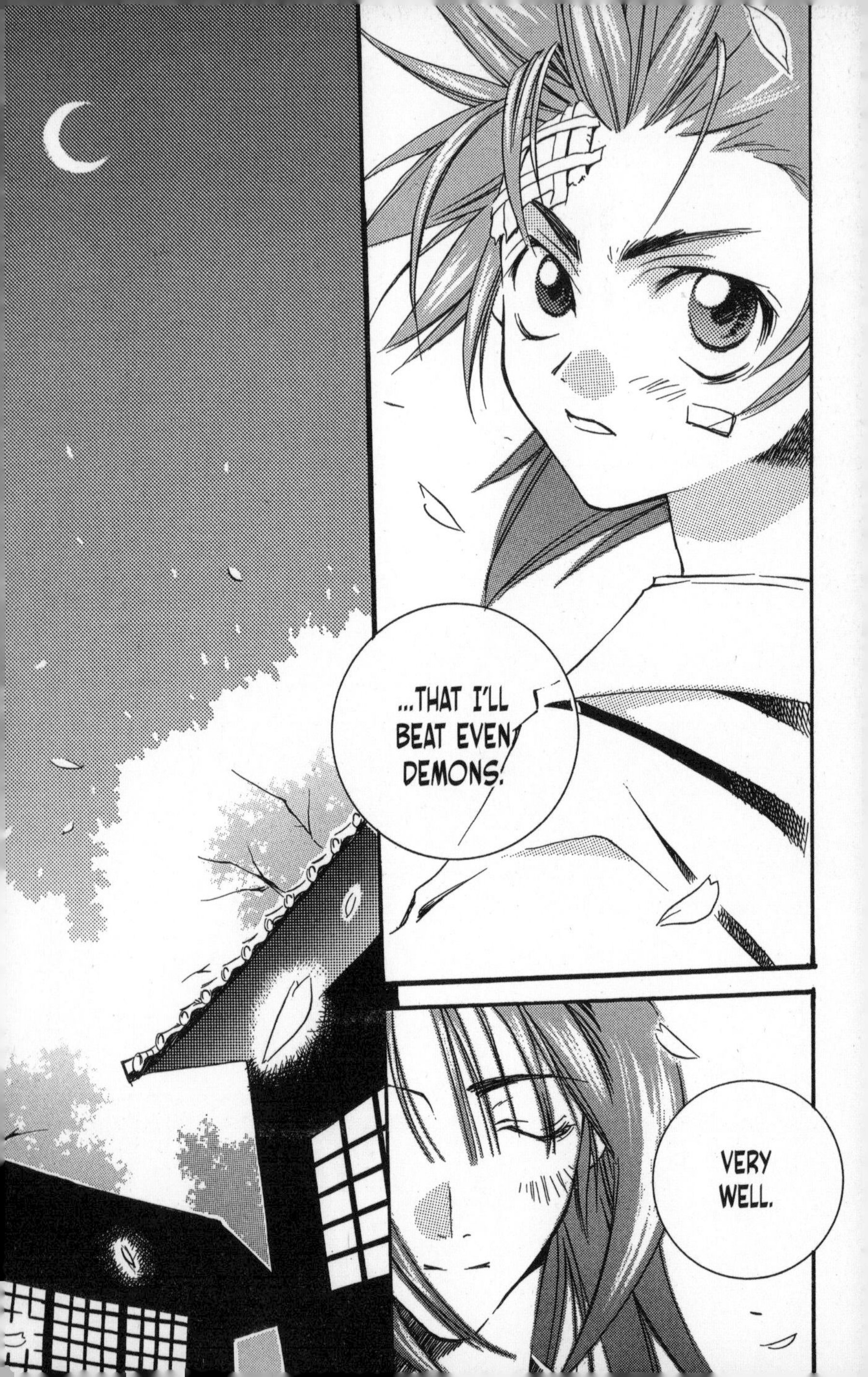
...THAT I'LL BEAT EVEN DEMONS!
VERY WELL.

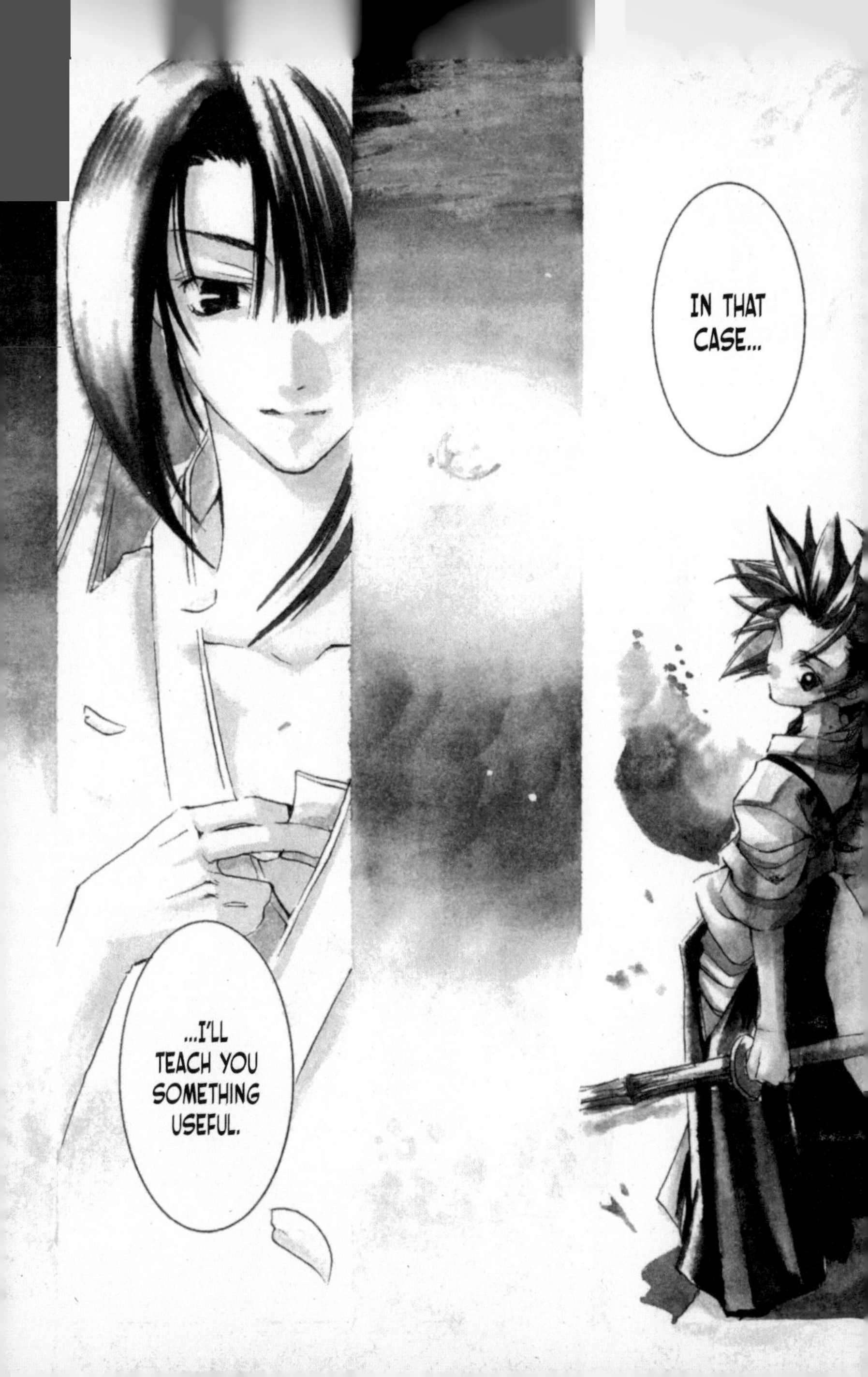
IN THAT CASE...
...I'LL TEACH YOU SOMETHING USEFUL.

Act.2
Things We Said Today

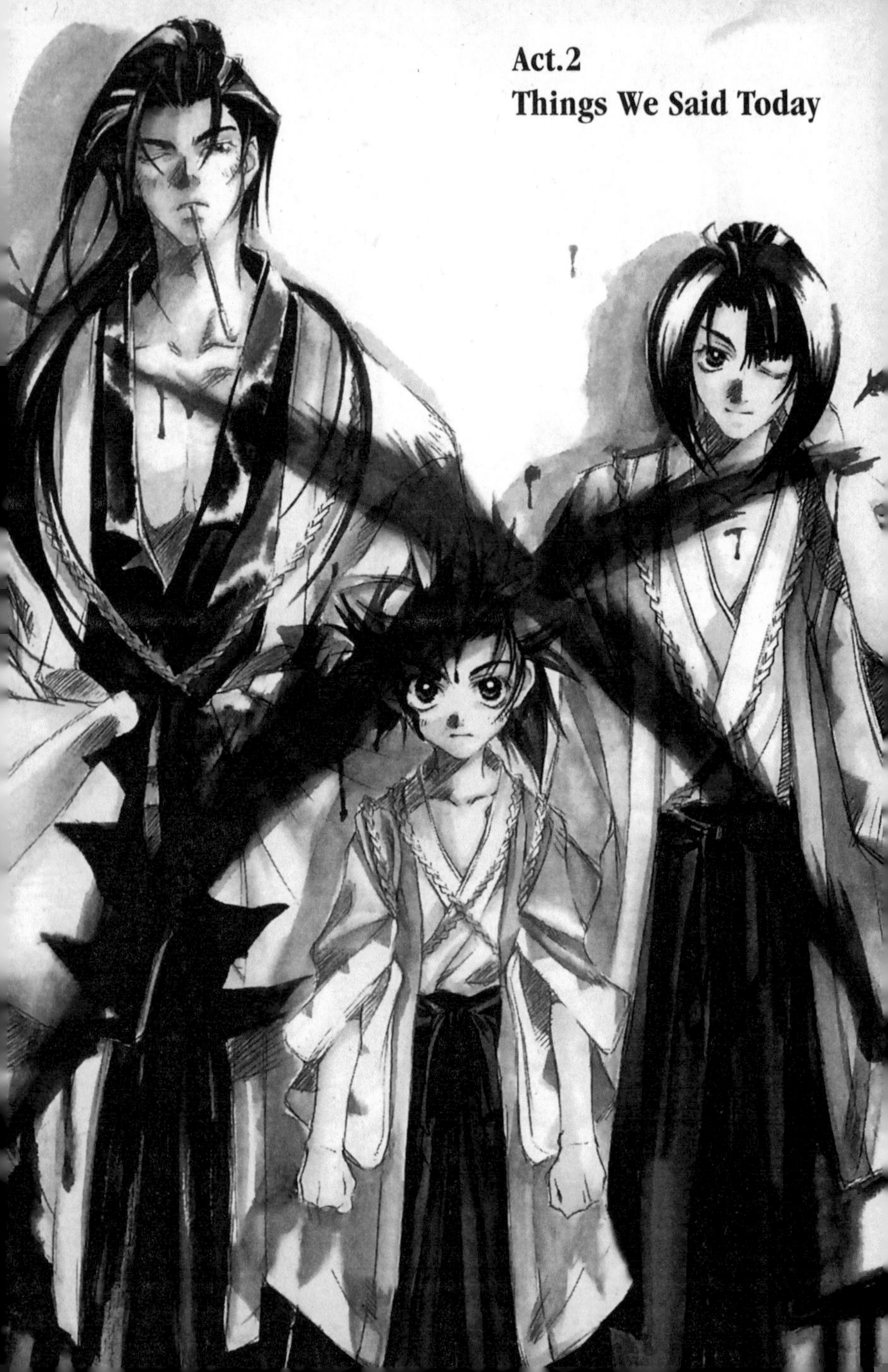

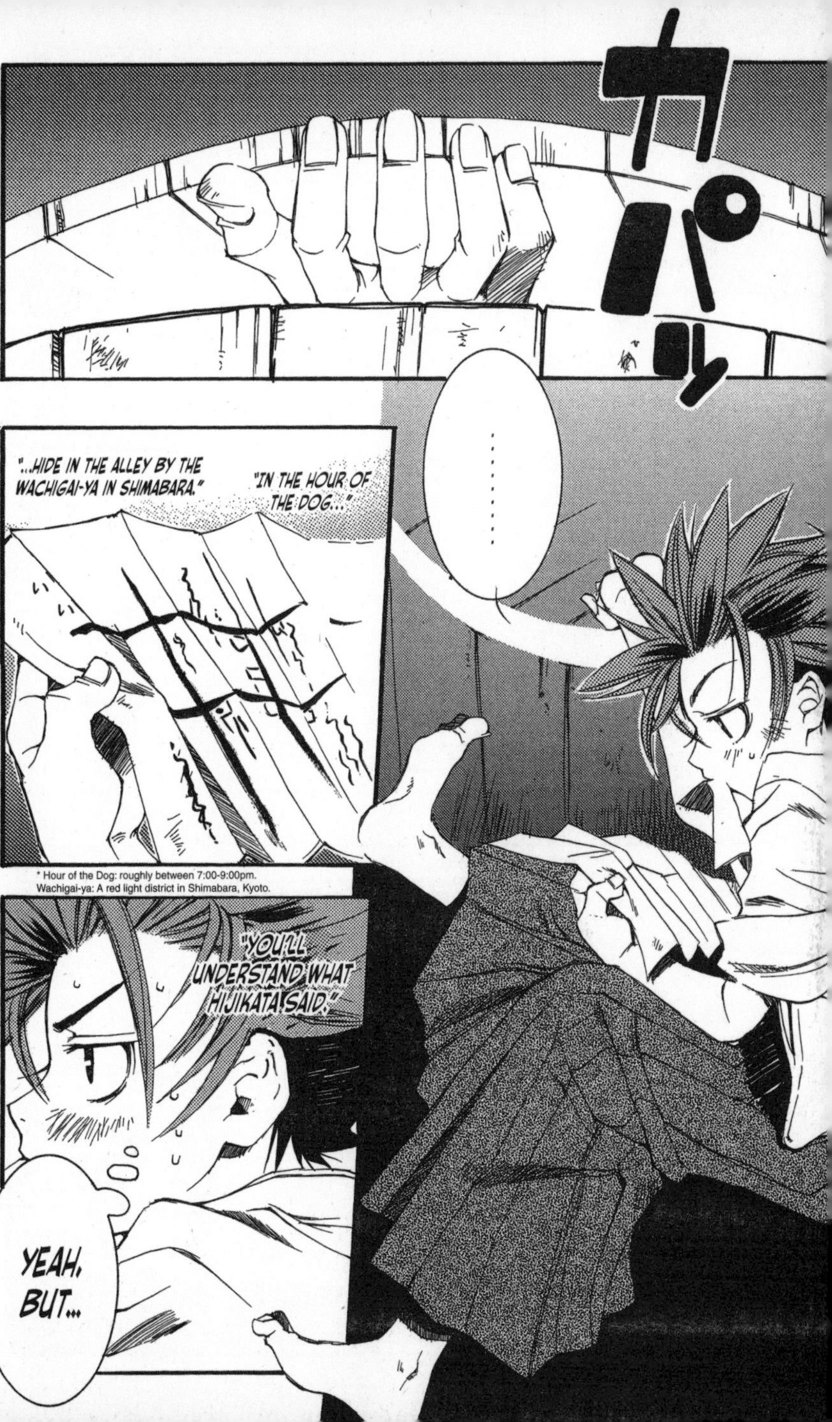
カパッ
......
"IN THE HOUR OF THE DOG..."
"...HIDE IN THE ALLEY BY THE WACHIGAI-YA IN SHIMABARA."
"YOU'LL UNDERSTAND WHAT HIJIKATA SAID."
YEAH. BUT...

* Hour of the Dog: roughly between 7:00-9:00pm.
Wachigai-ya: A red light district in Shimabara, Kyoto.

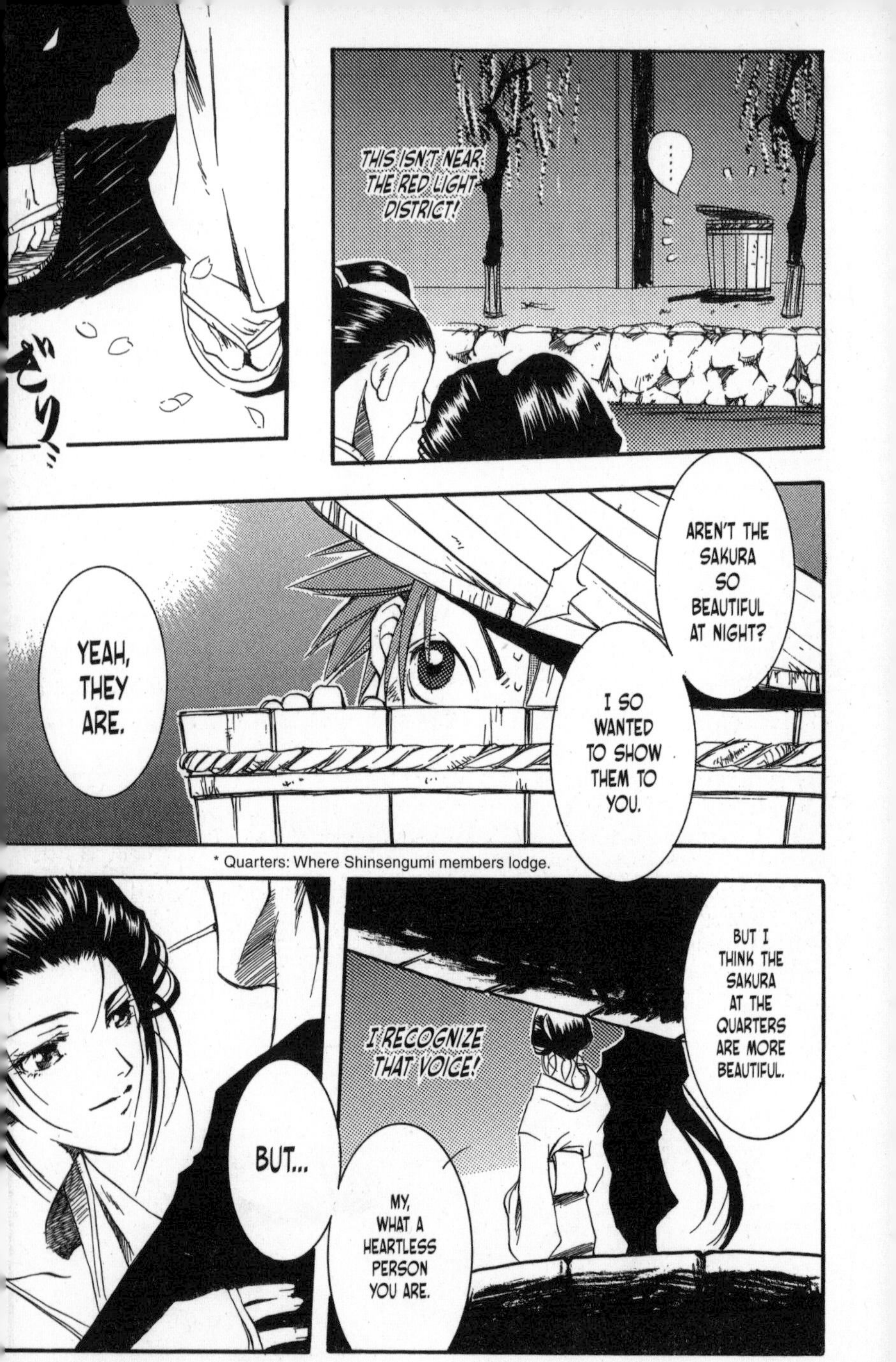
THIS ISN'T NEAR THE RED LIGHT DISTRICT!
......
AREN'T THE SAKURA SO BEAUTIFUL AT NIGHT?
I SO WANTED TO SHOW THEM TO YOU.
YEAH, THEY ARE.
BUT I THINK THE SAKURA AT THE QUARTERS ARE MORE BEAUTIFUL.
I RECOGNIZE THAT VOICE!
MY, WHAT A HEARTLESS PERSON YOU ARE.
BUT...

* Quarters: Where Shinsengumi members lodge.

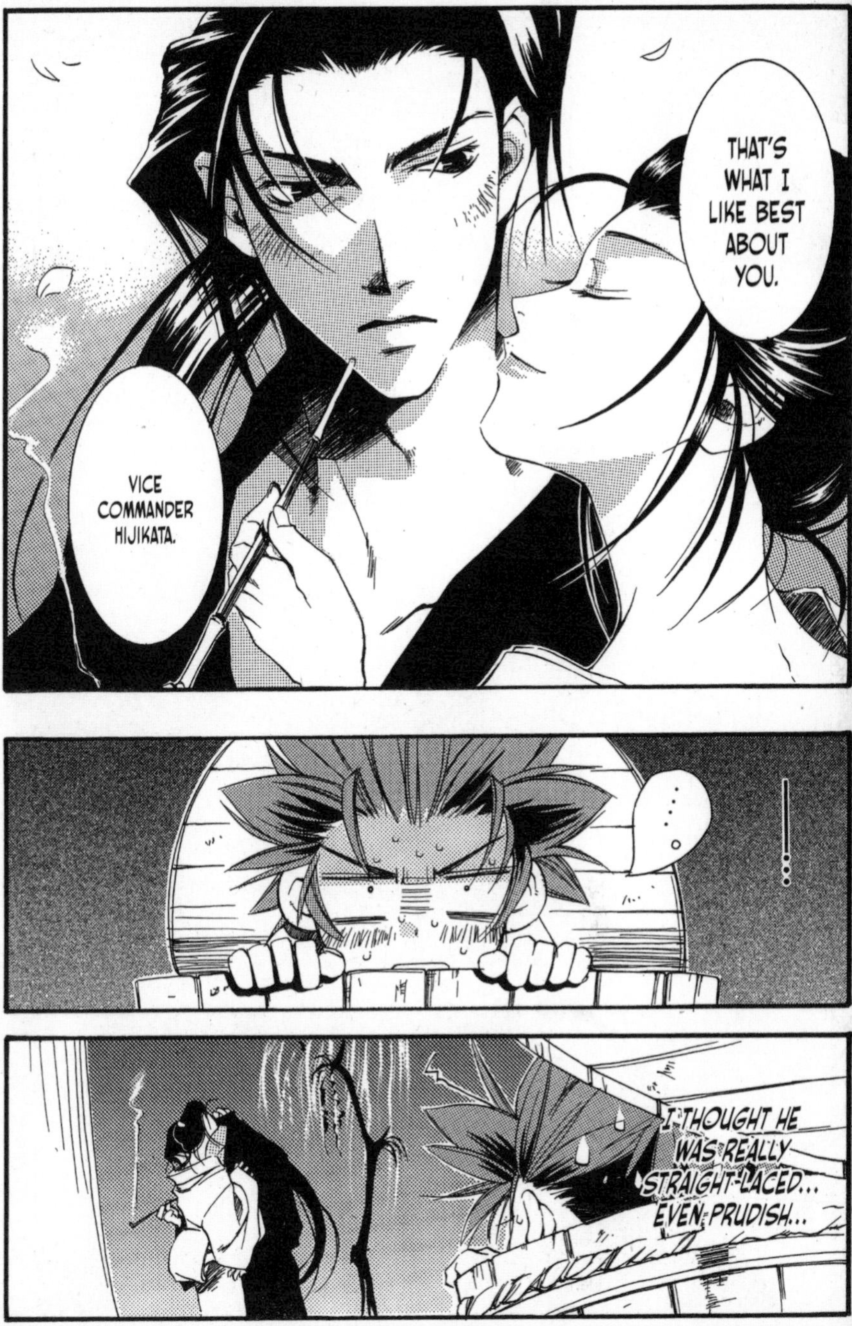
THAT'S WHAT I LIKE BEST ABOUT YOU.
VICE COMMANDER HIJIKATA.
I THOUGHT HE WAS REALLY STRAIGHT-LACED... EVEN PRUDISH...

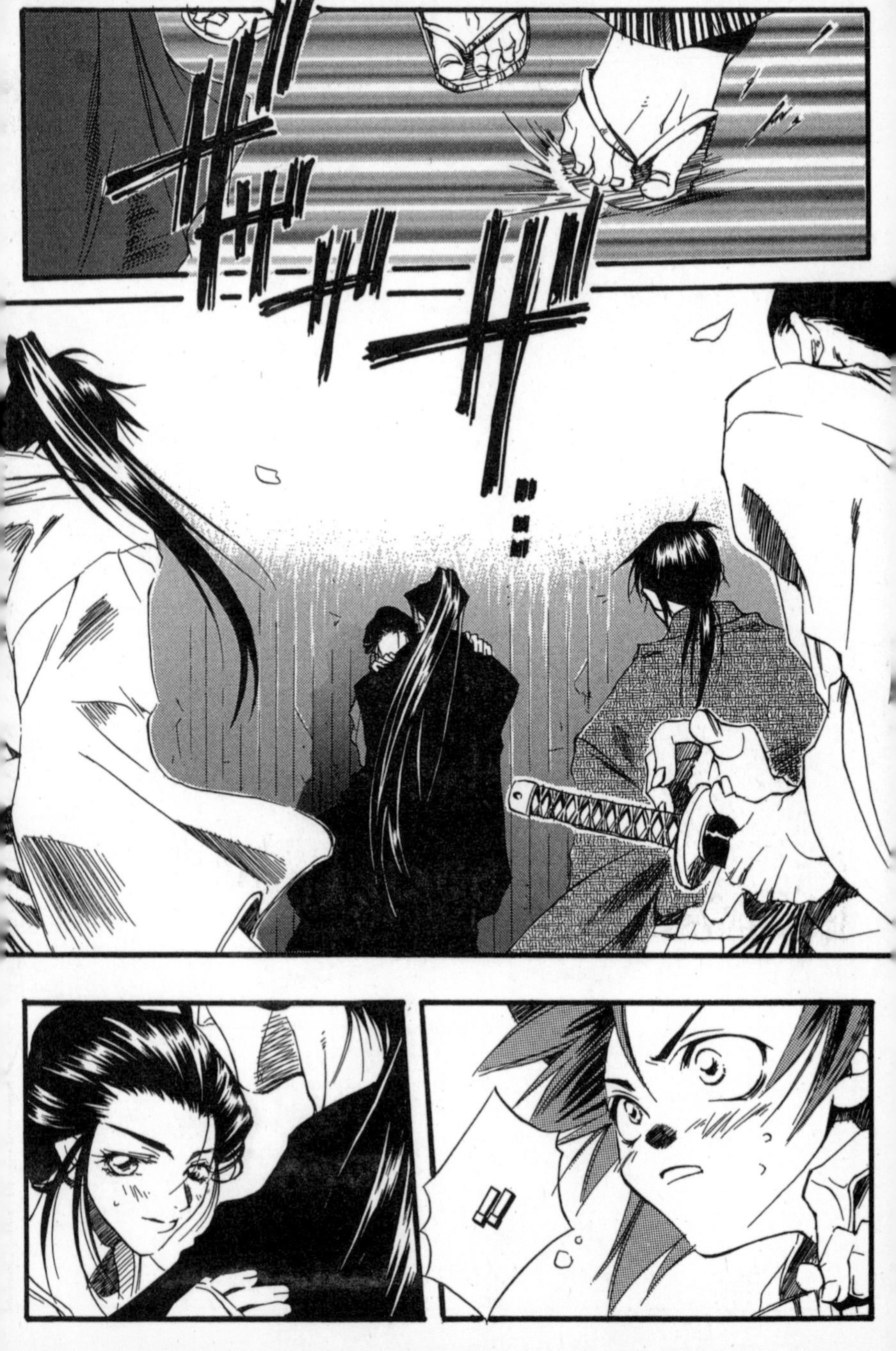
!!

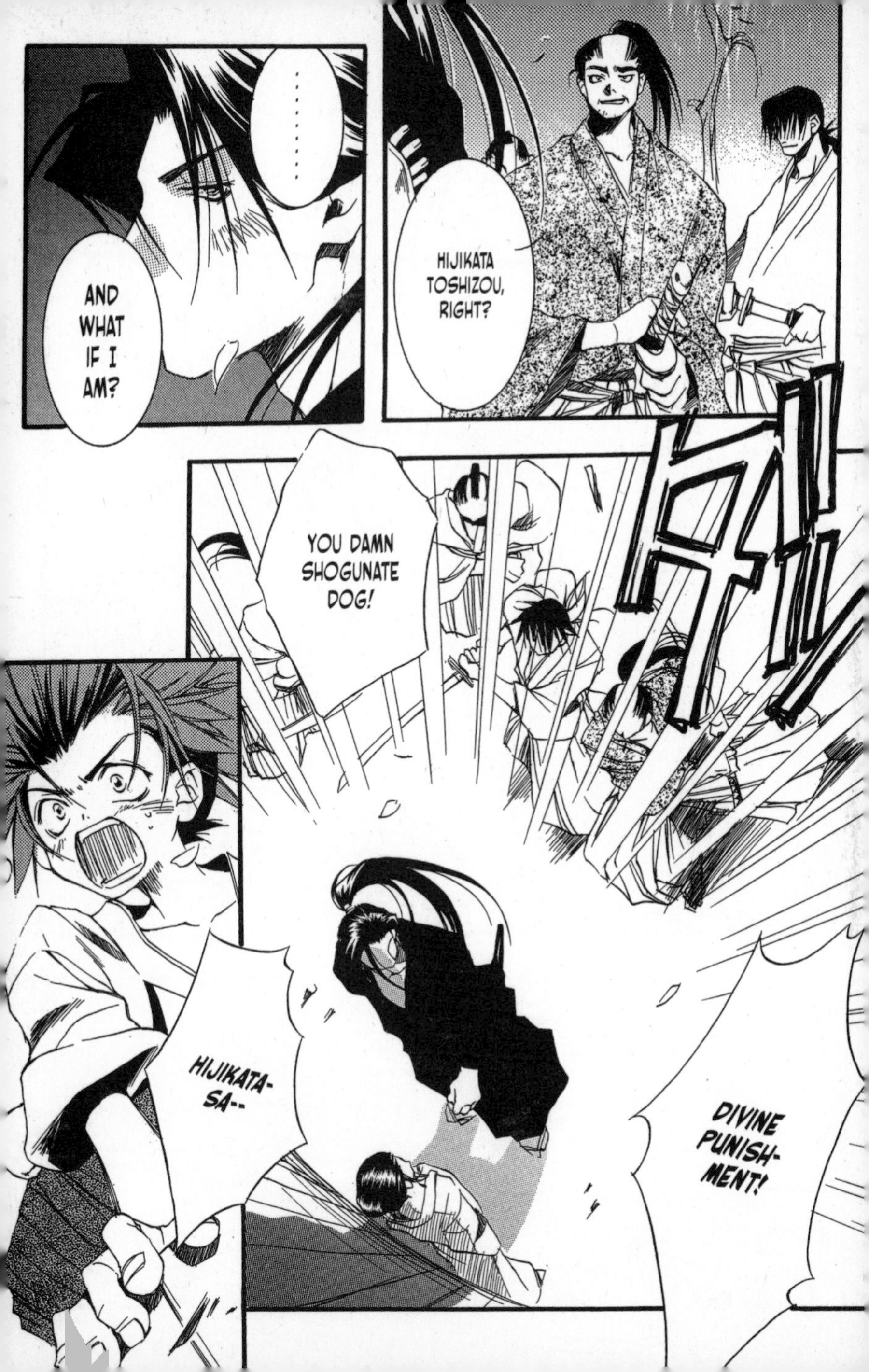
HIJIKATA TOSHIZOU, RIGHT?
......
AND WHAT IF I AM?
YOU DAMN SHOGUNATE DOG!
DIVINE PUNISH-MENT!
HIJIKATA-SA--

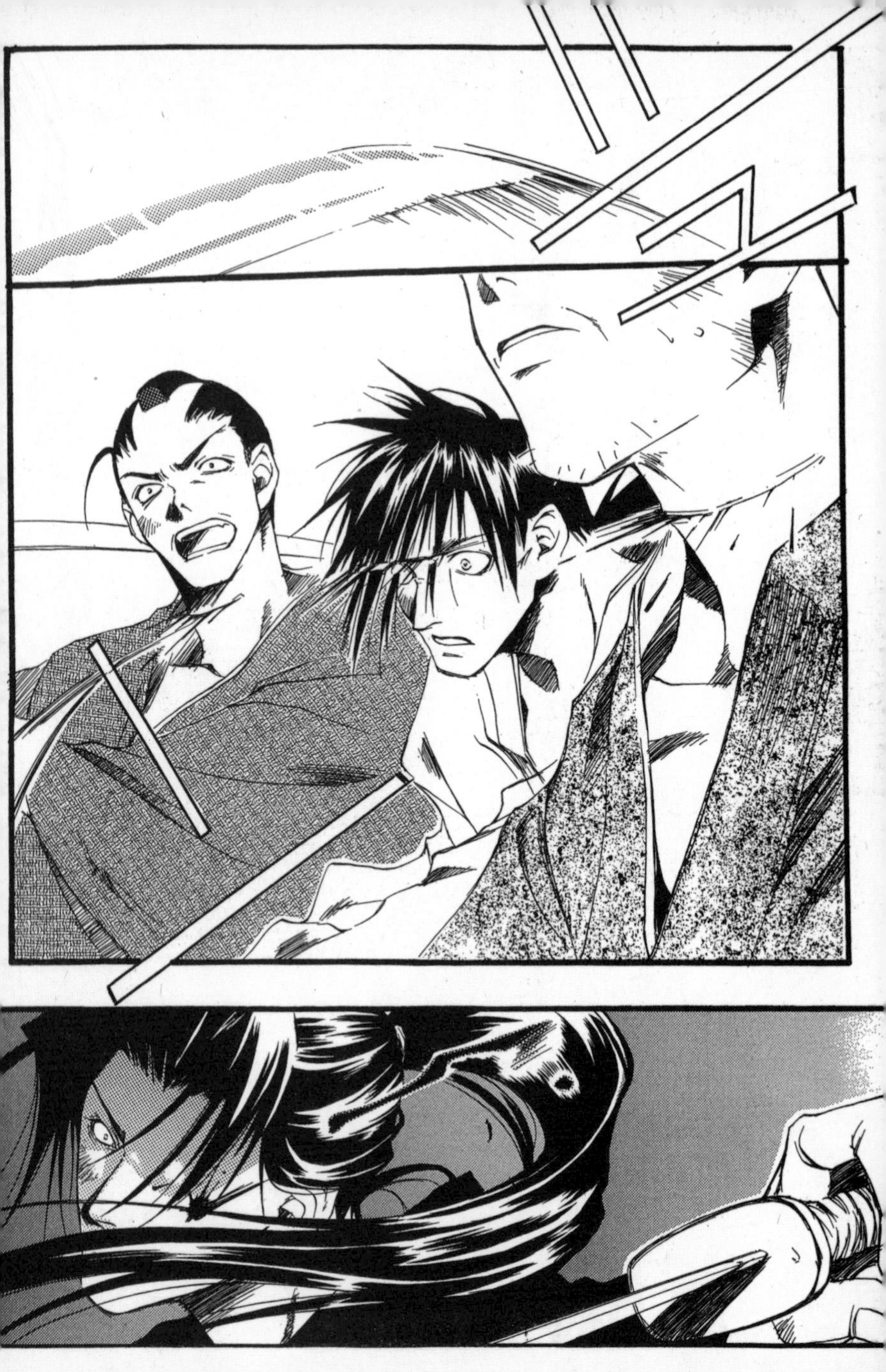

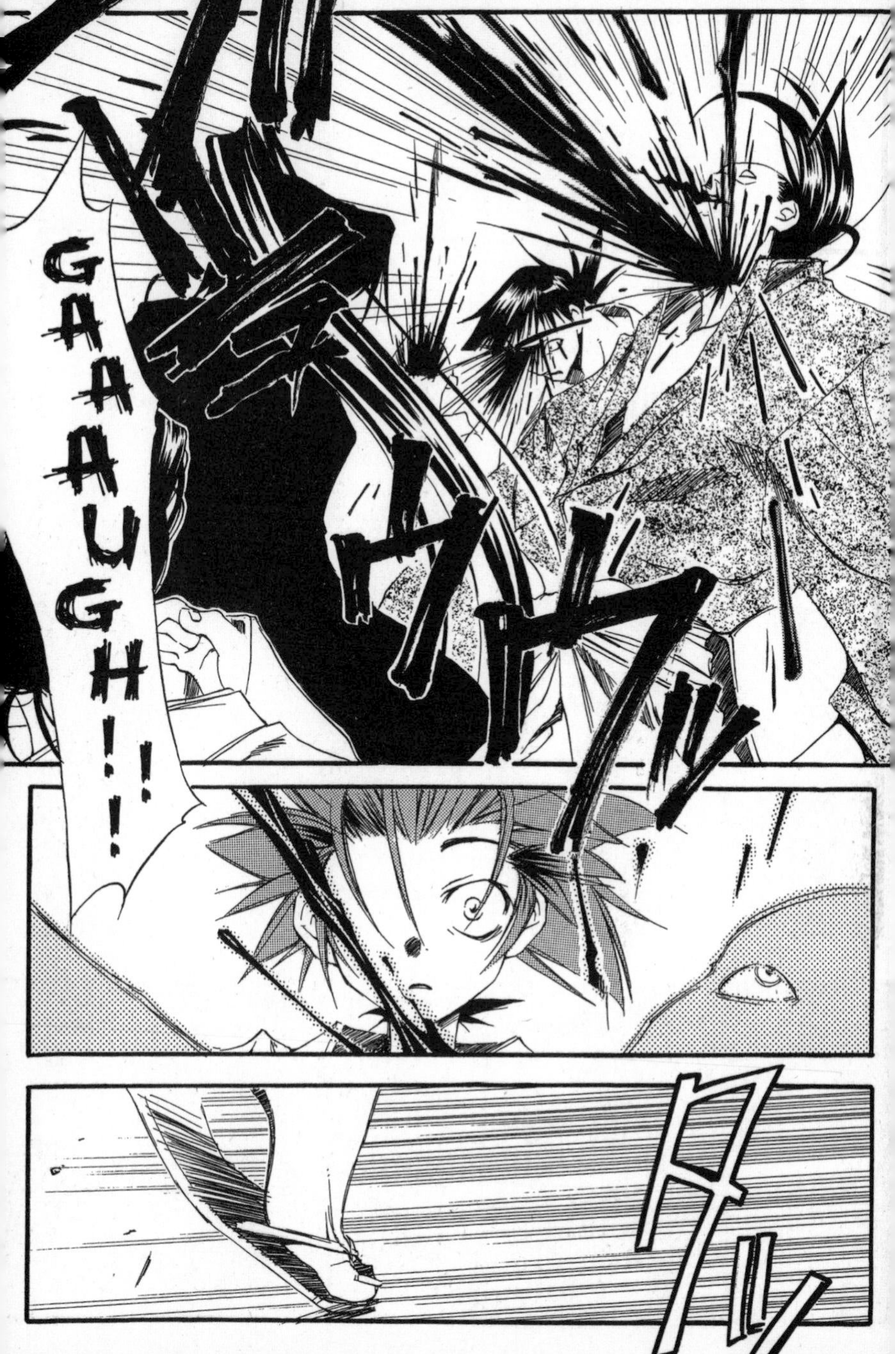
GAAAUGH!!!

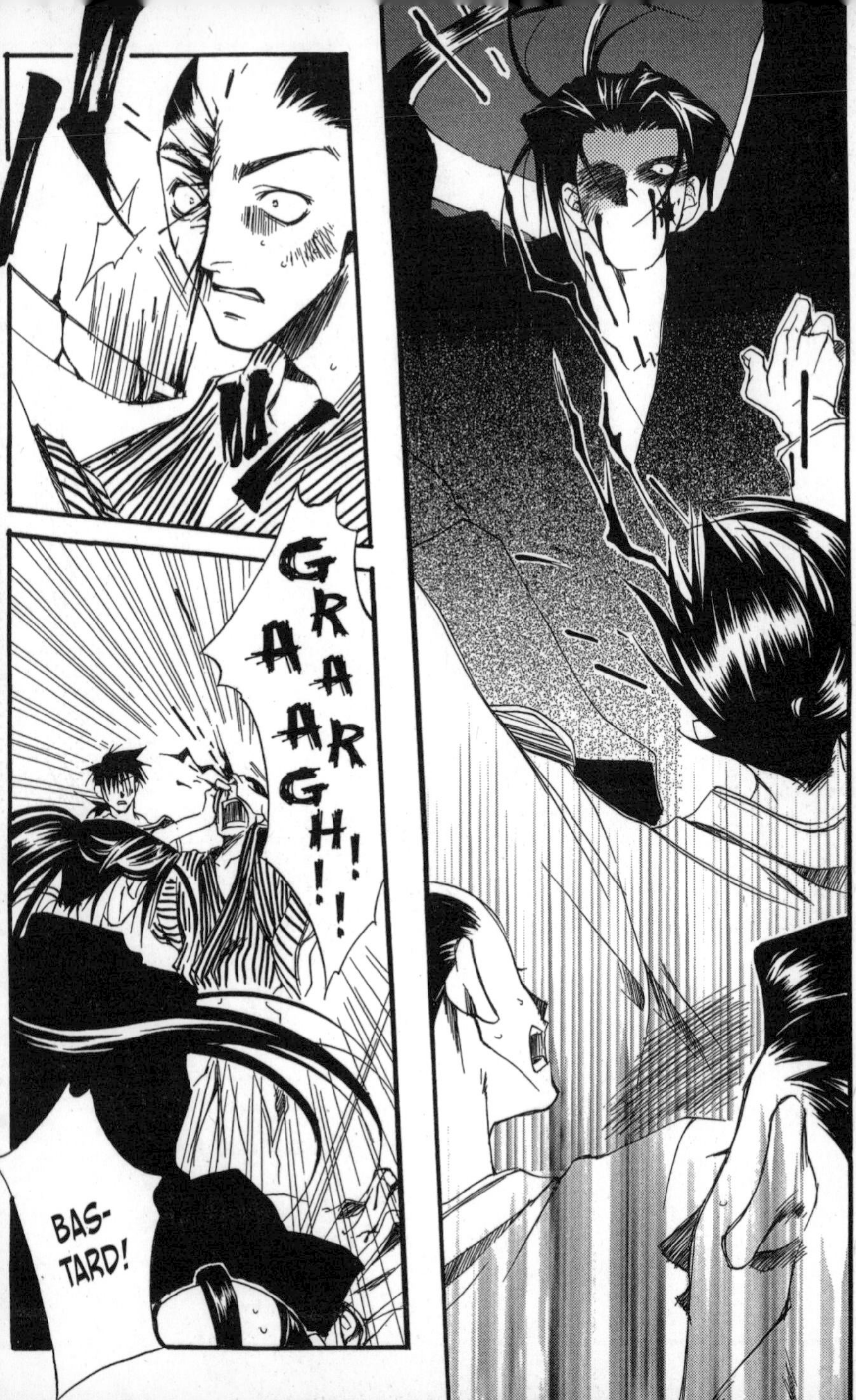
GRAAARGH!!!
BAS-
TARD!

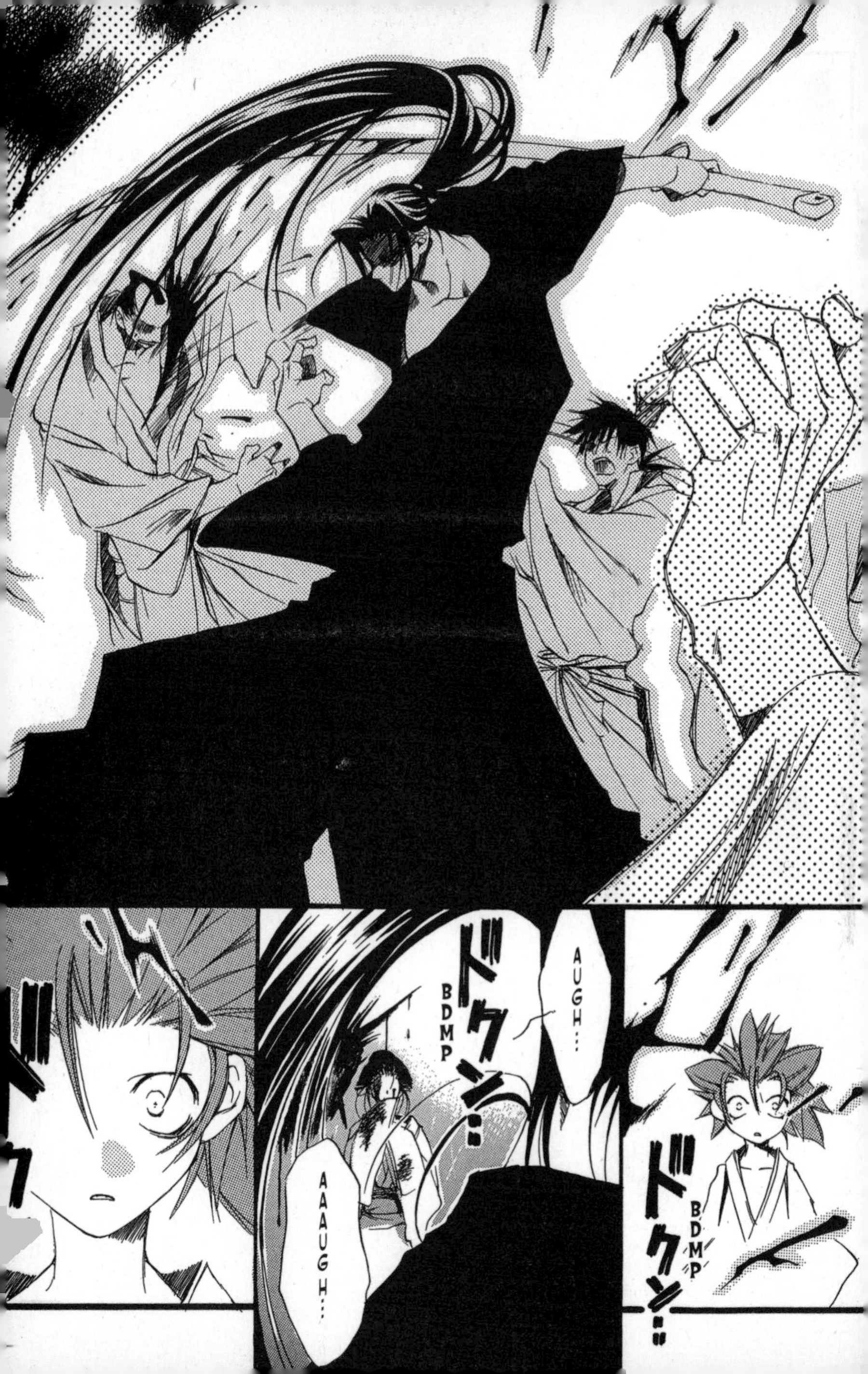
ドクン!!
BDMP
AUGH...
ドクン!!
BDMP
AAAUGH...

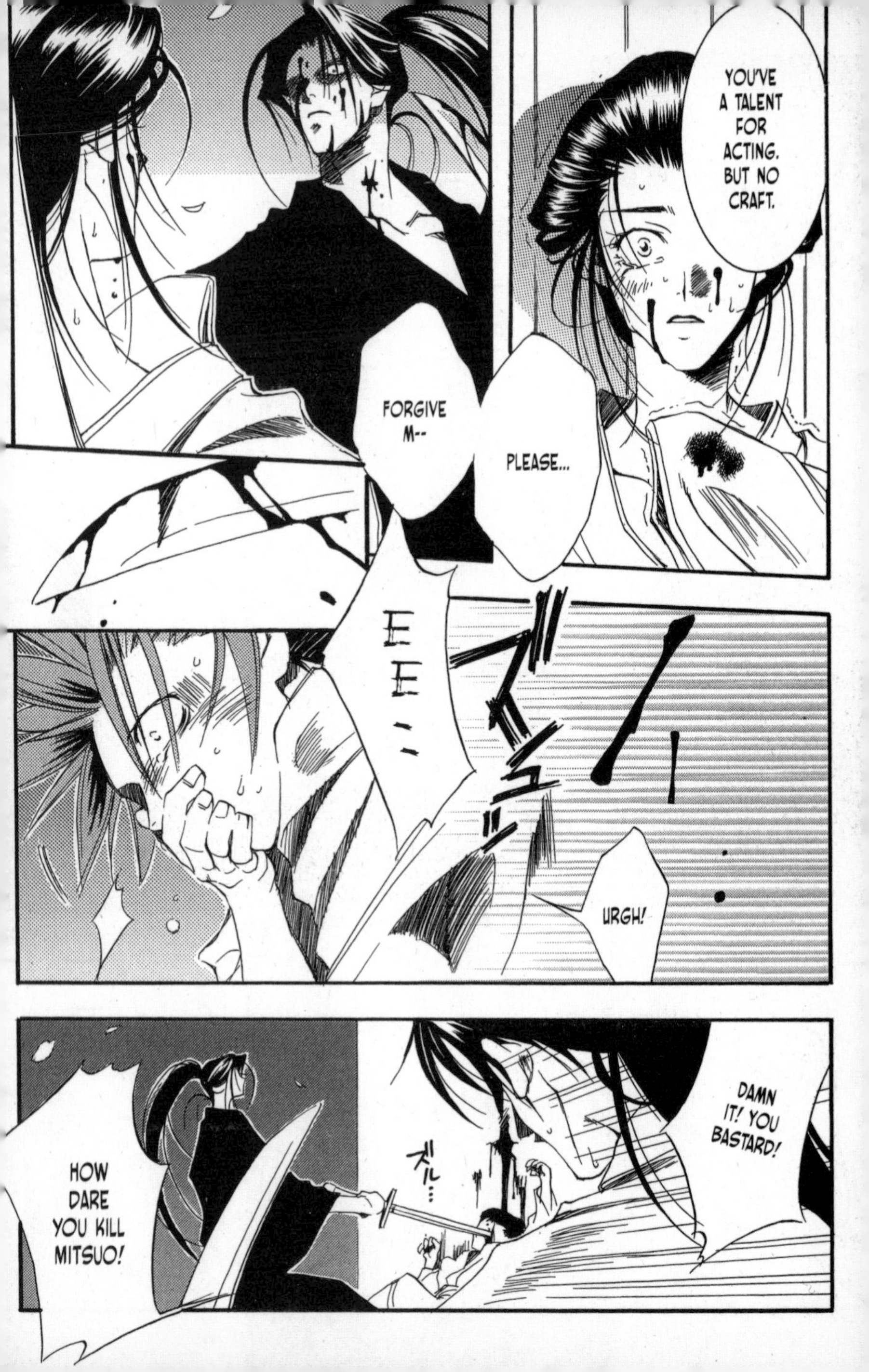
YOU'VE A TALENT FOR ACTING. BUT NO CRAFT.
PLEASE...
FORGIVE M--
URGH!
DAMN IT! YOU BASTARD!
ズル…
HOW DARE YOU KILL MITSUO!

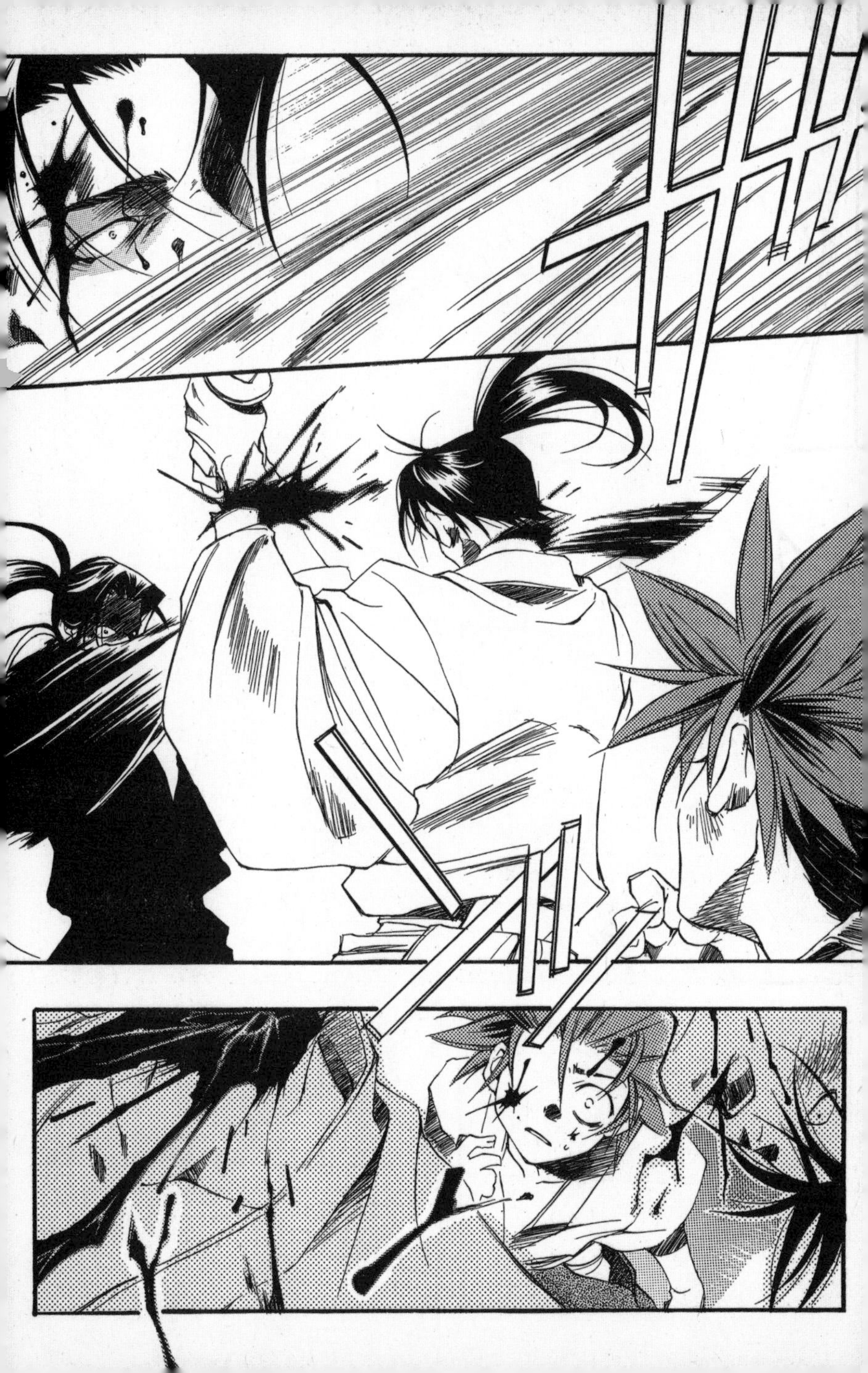

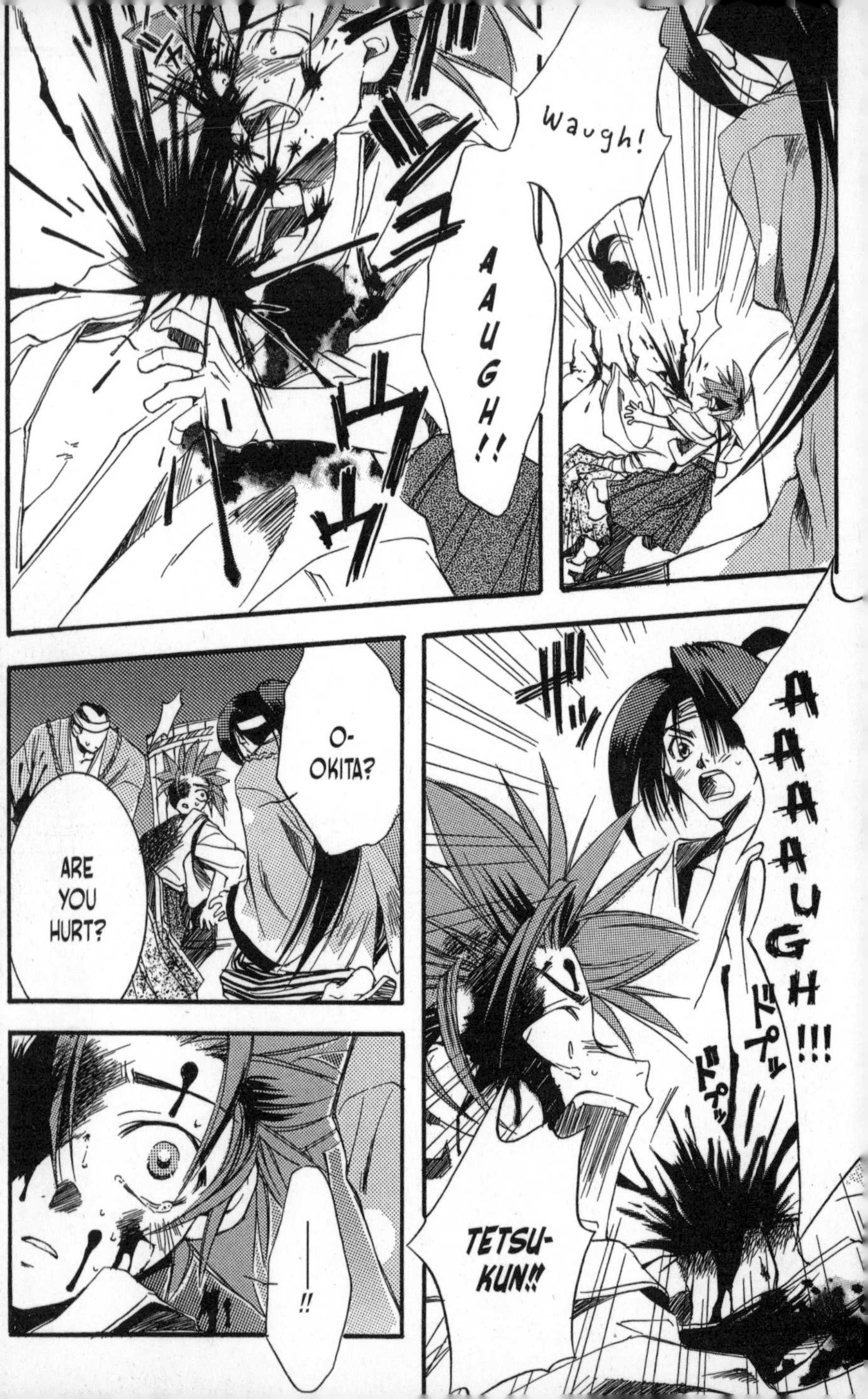
Waugh!
AAAUGH!!
AAAAAUGH!!!
ドパッ
ドパッ
TETSU-KUN!!
O-OKITA?
ARE YOU HURT?
——!!

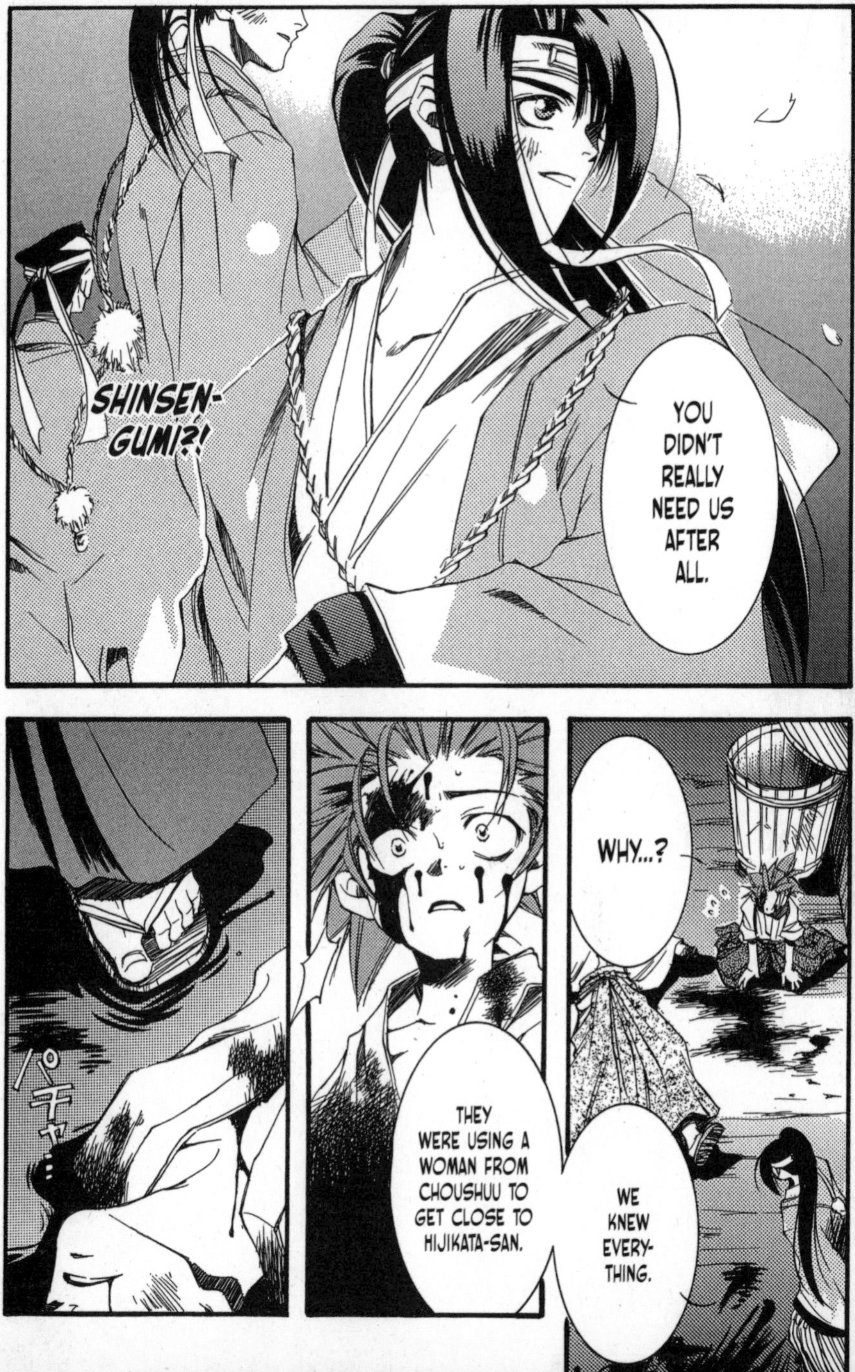
YOU DIDN'T REALLY NEED US AFTER ALL.
SHINSEN-GUMI?!
WHY...?
WE KNEW EVERY-THING.
THEY WERE USING A WOMAN FROM CHOUSHUU TO GET CLOSE TO HIJIKATA-SAN.
パチャ

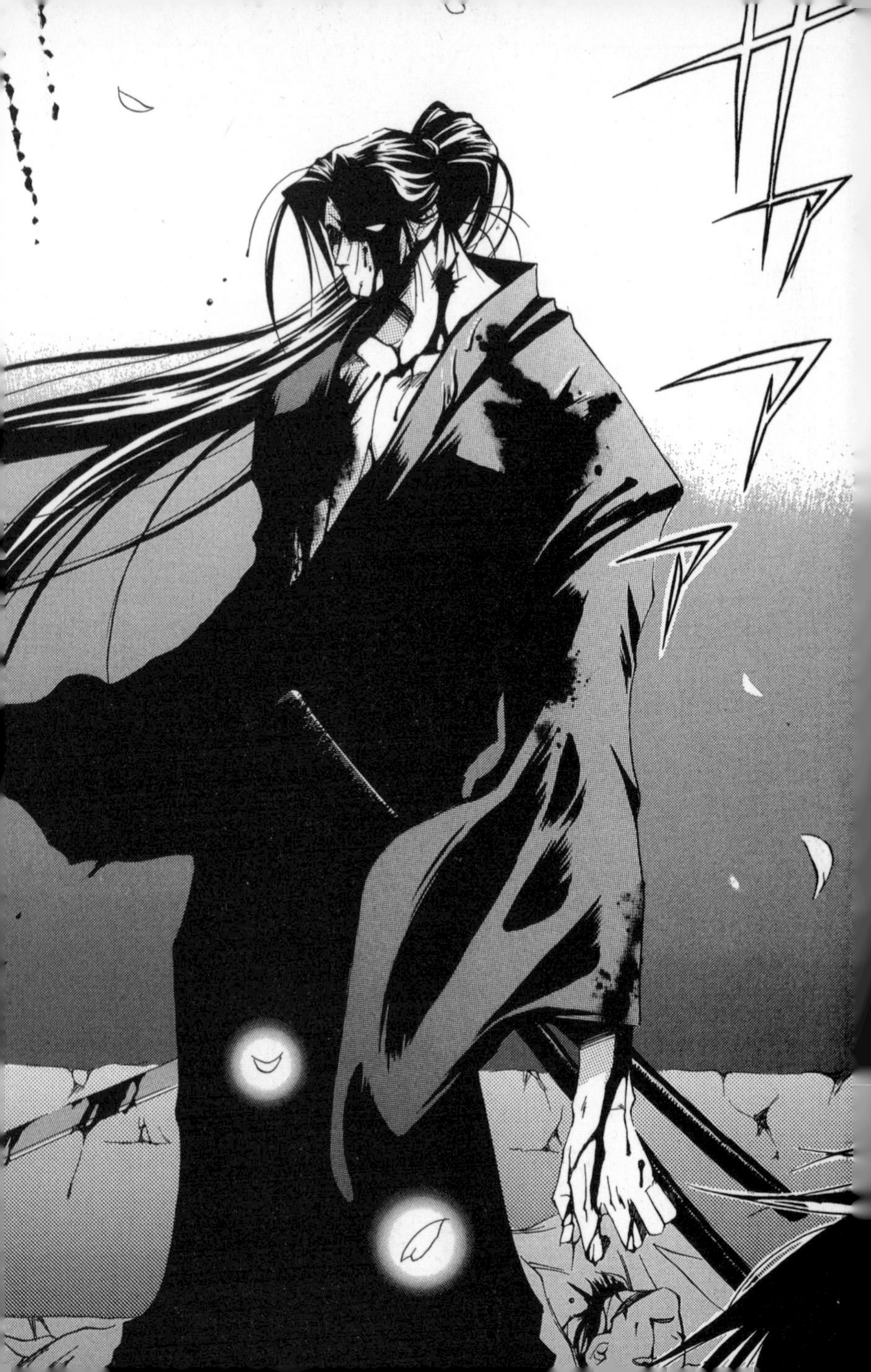
ザァァァ

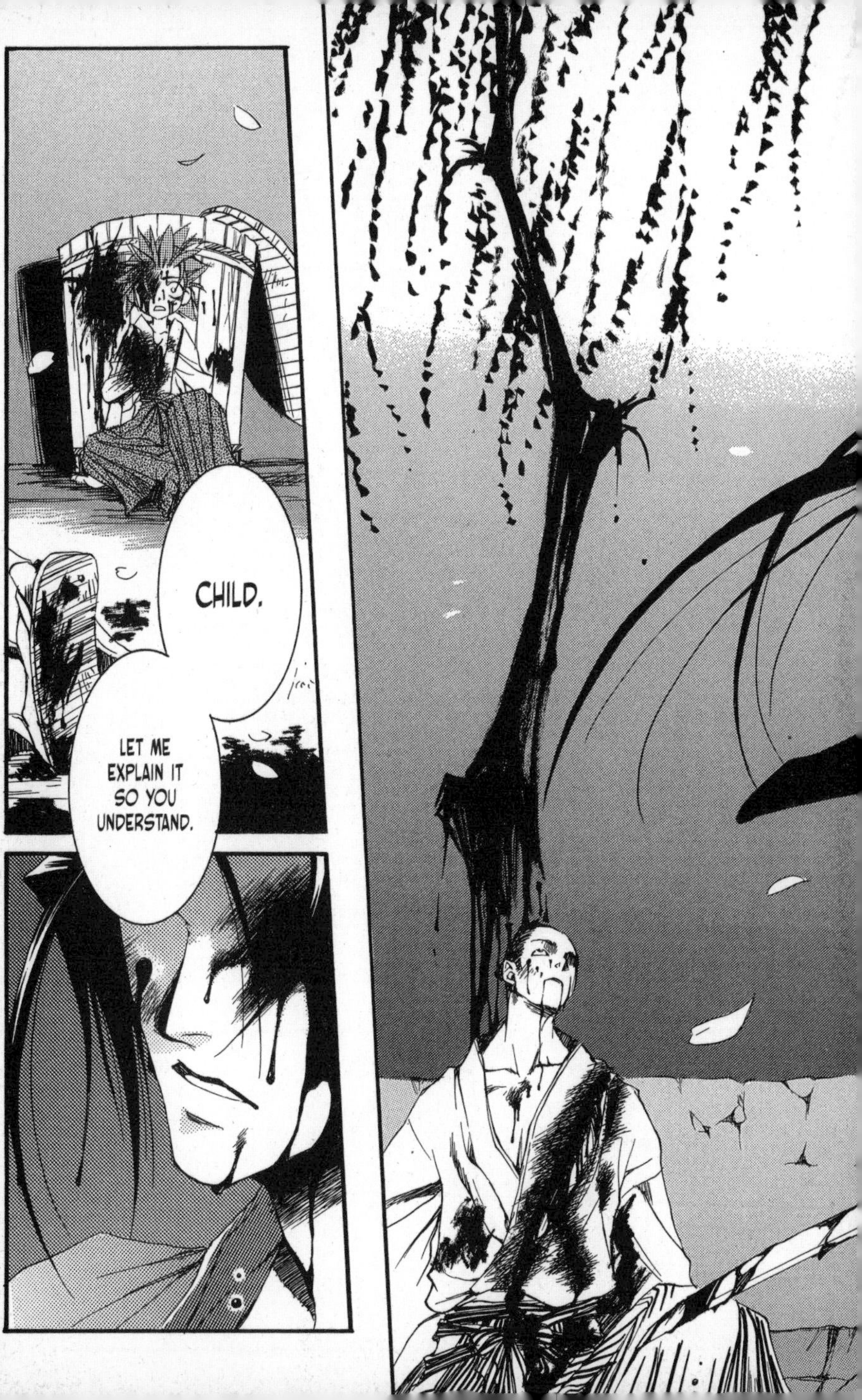
CHILD.
LET ME EXPLAIN IT SO YOU UNDERSTAND.

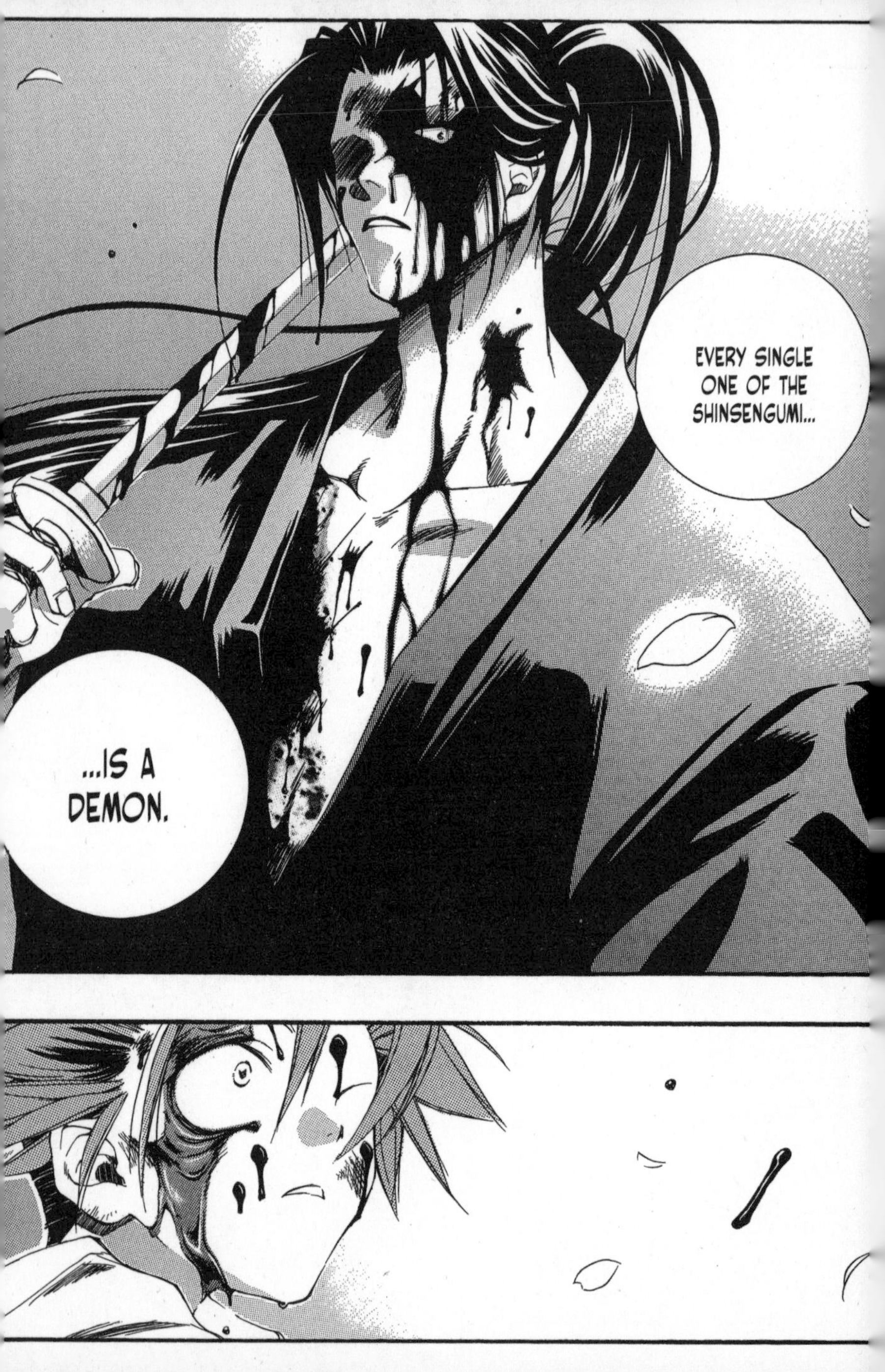
EVERY SINGLE ONE OF THE SHINSENGUMI...
...IS A DEMON.

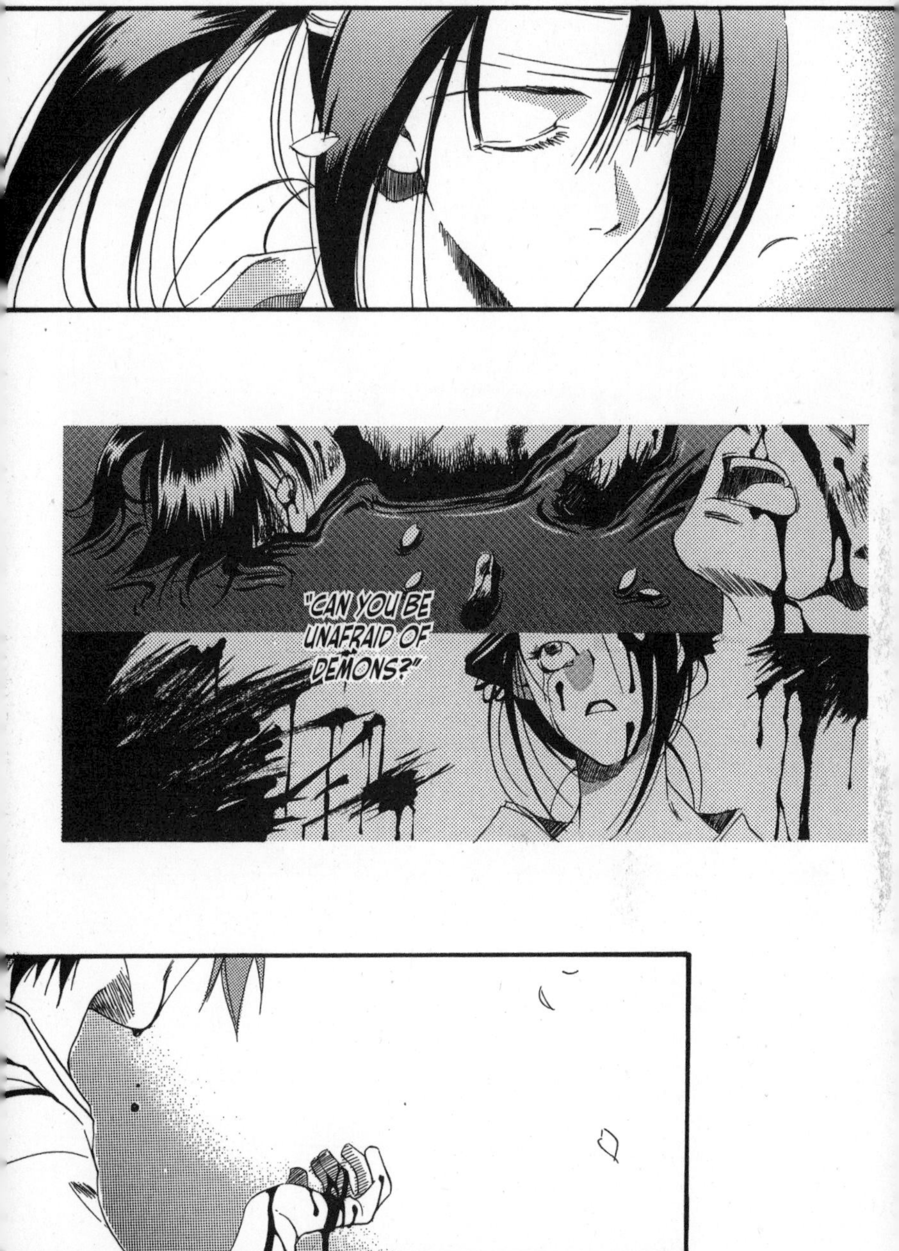
"CAN YOU BE UNAFRAID OF DEMONS?"

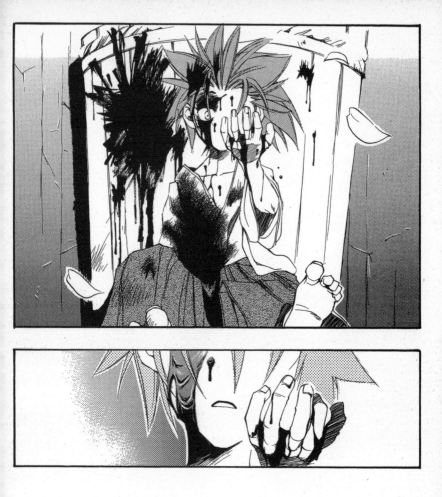

I FEEL
SICK.

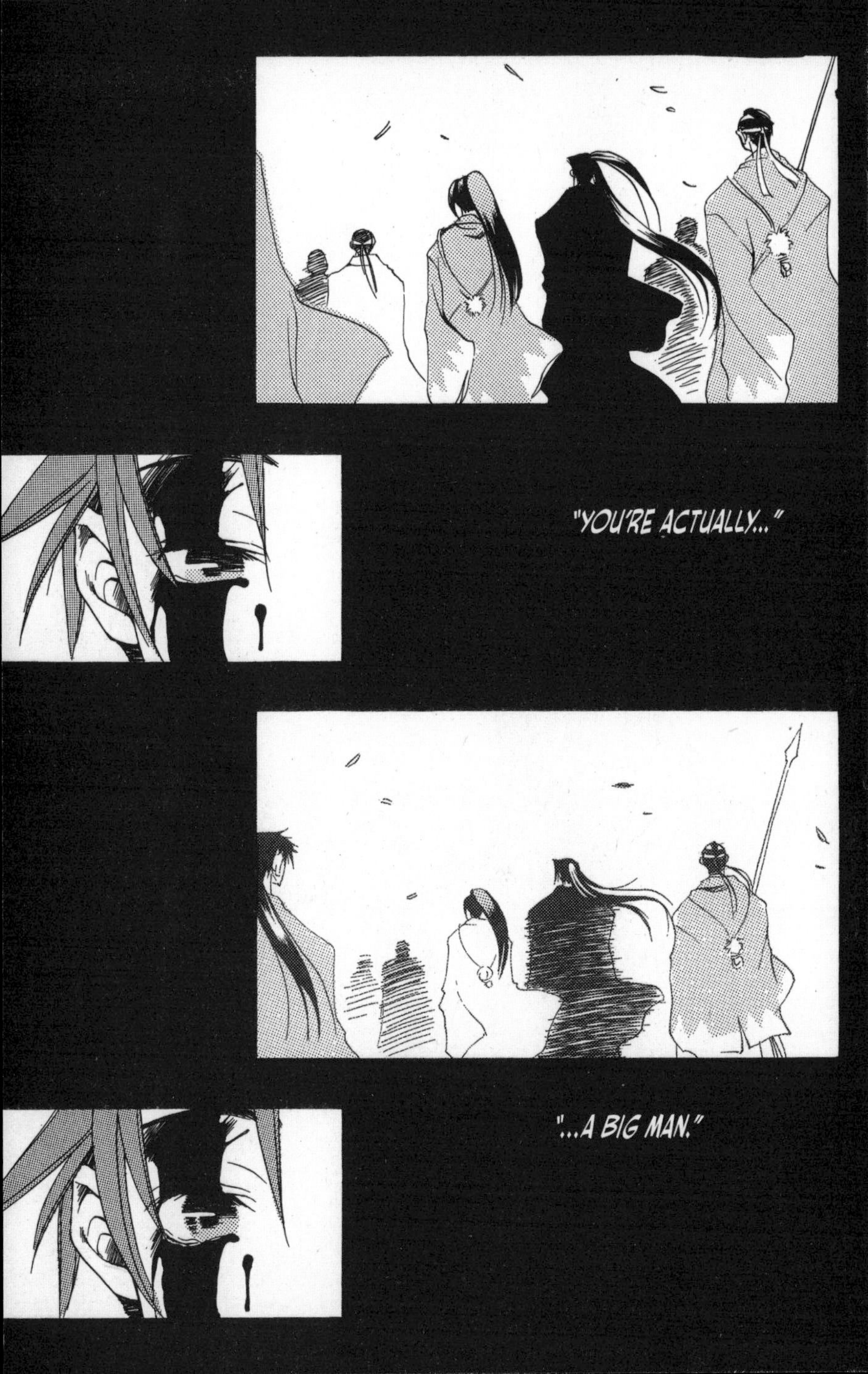
"YOU'RE ACTUALLY..."
"...A BIG MAN."

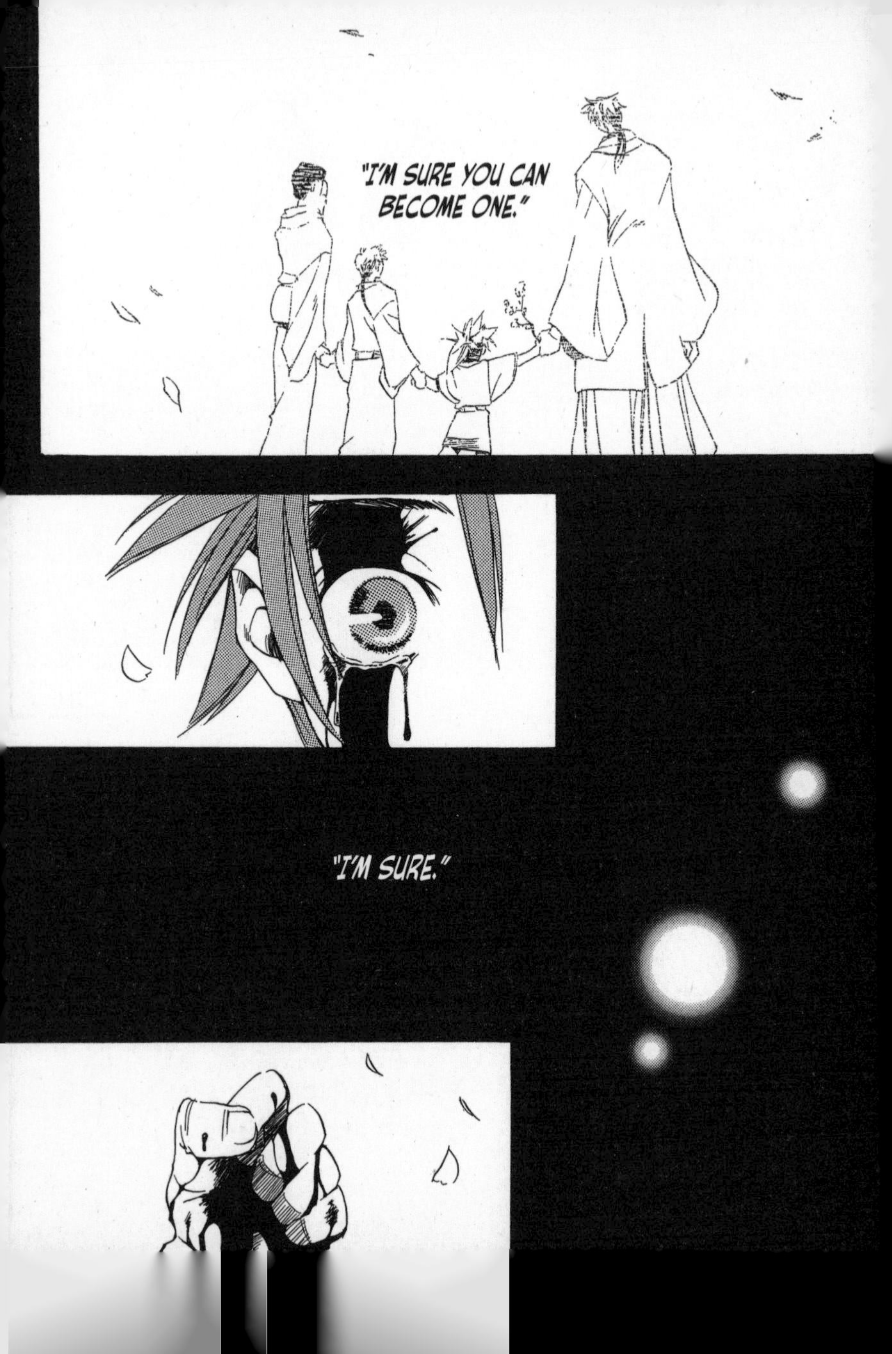
"I'M SURE YOU CAN BECOME ONE."
"I'M SURE."

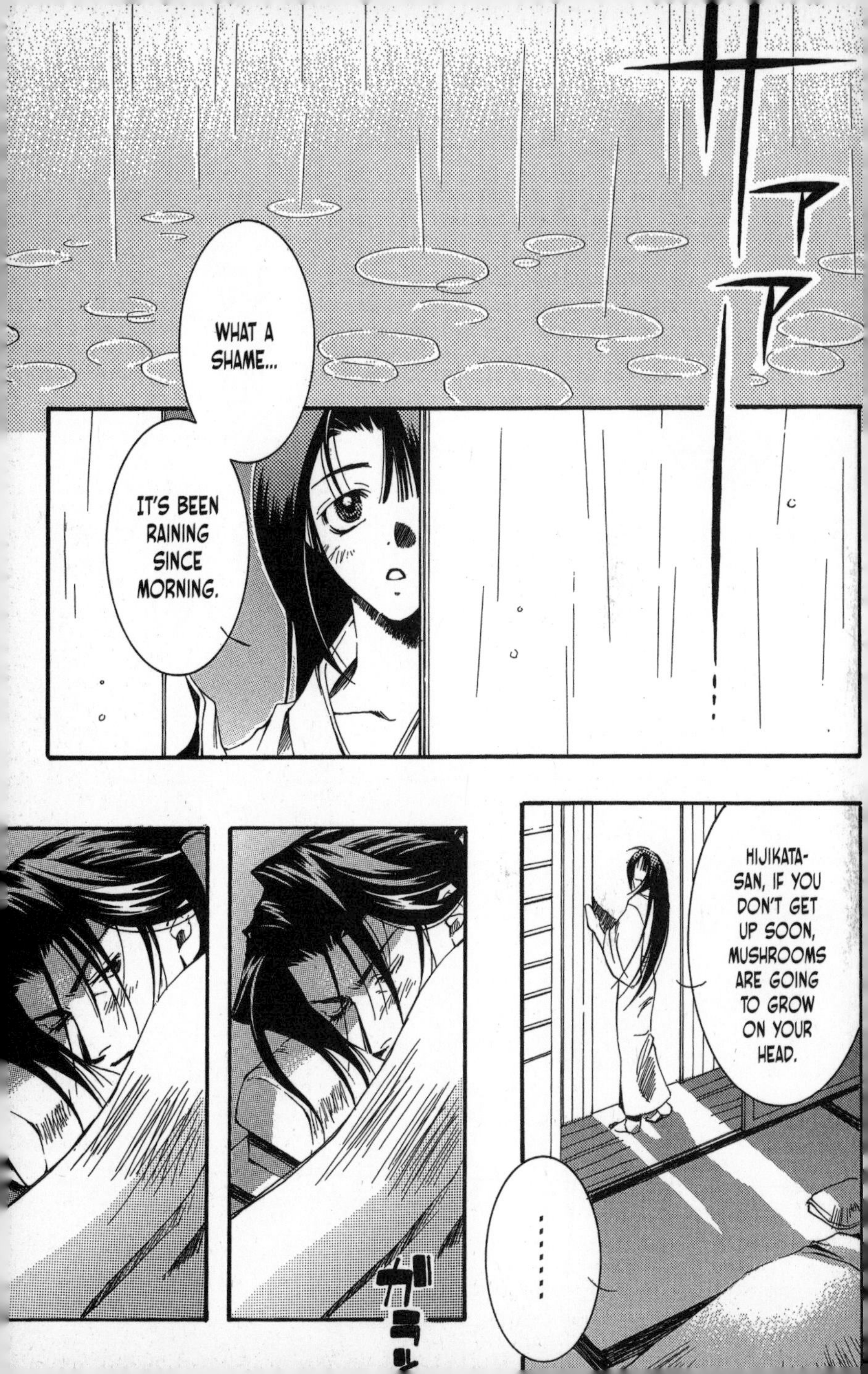
サァァー
WHAT A SHAME...
IT'S BEEN RAINING SINCE MORNING.
HIJIKATA-SAN, IF YOU DON'T GET UP SOON, MUSHROOMS ARE GOING TO GROW ON YOUR HEAD.
......
ガラッ

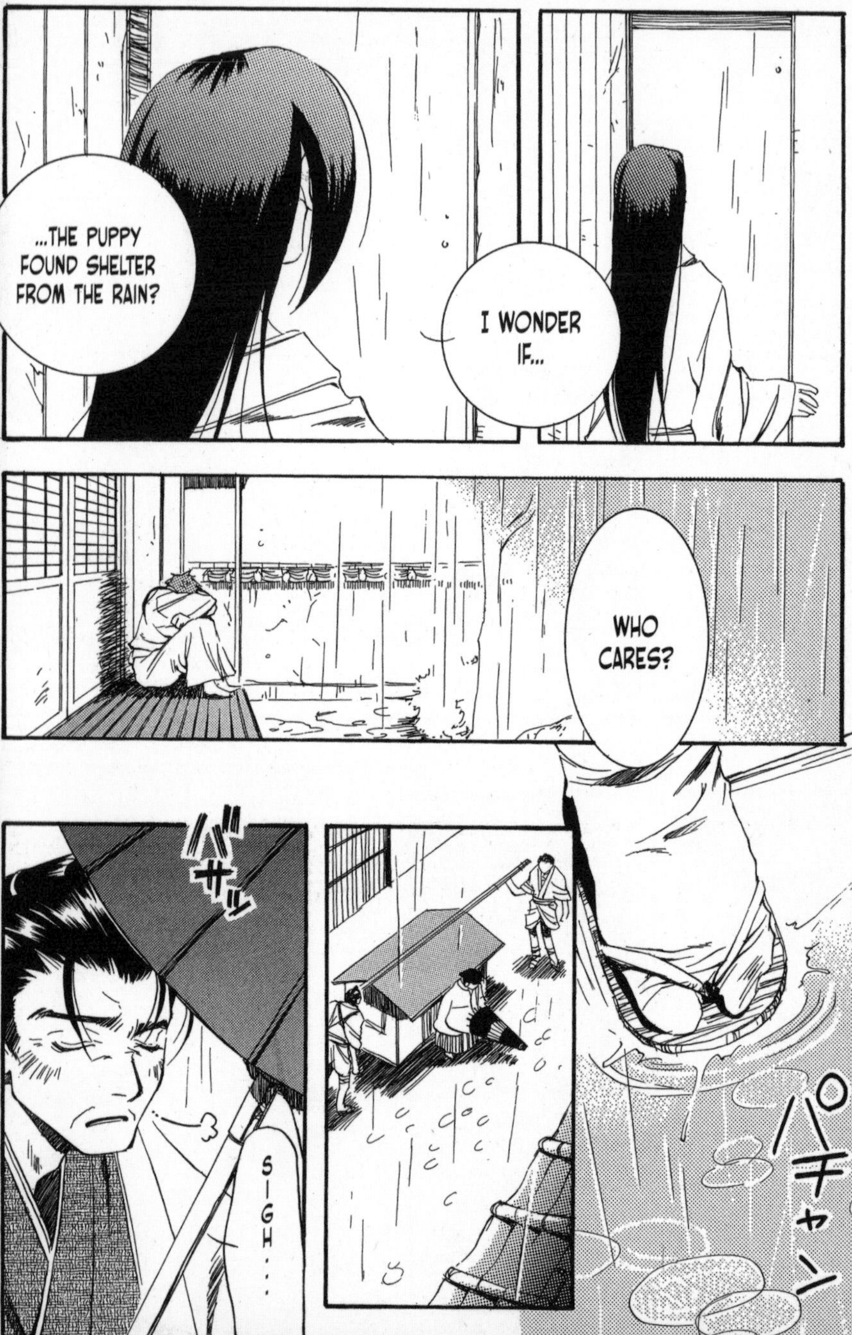
I WONDER IF...
...THE PUPPY FOUND SHELTER FROM THE RAIN?
WHO CARES?
パチャン
バサッ
SIGH...

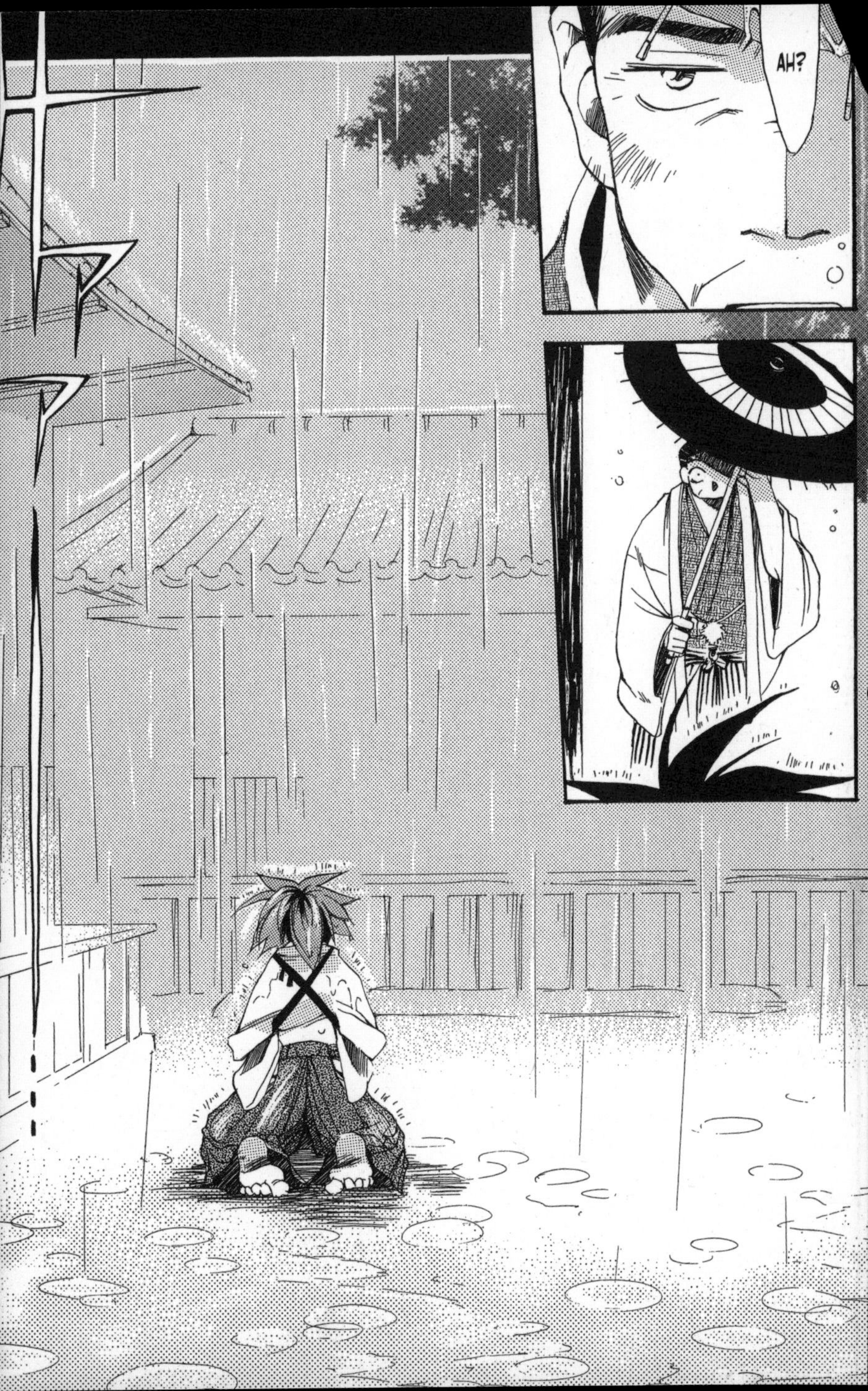
AH?

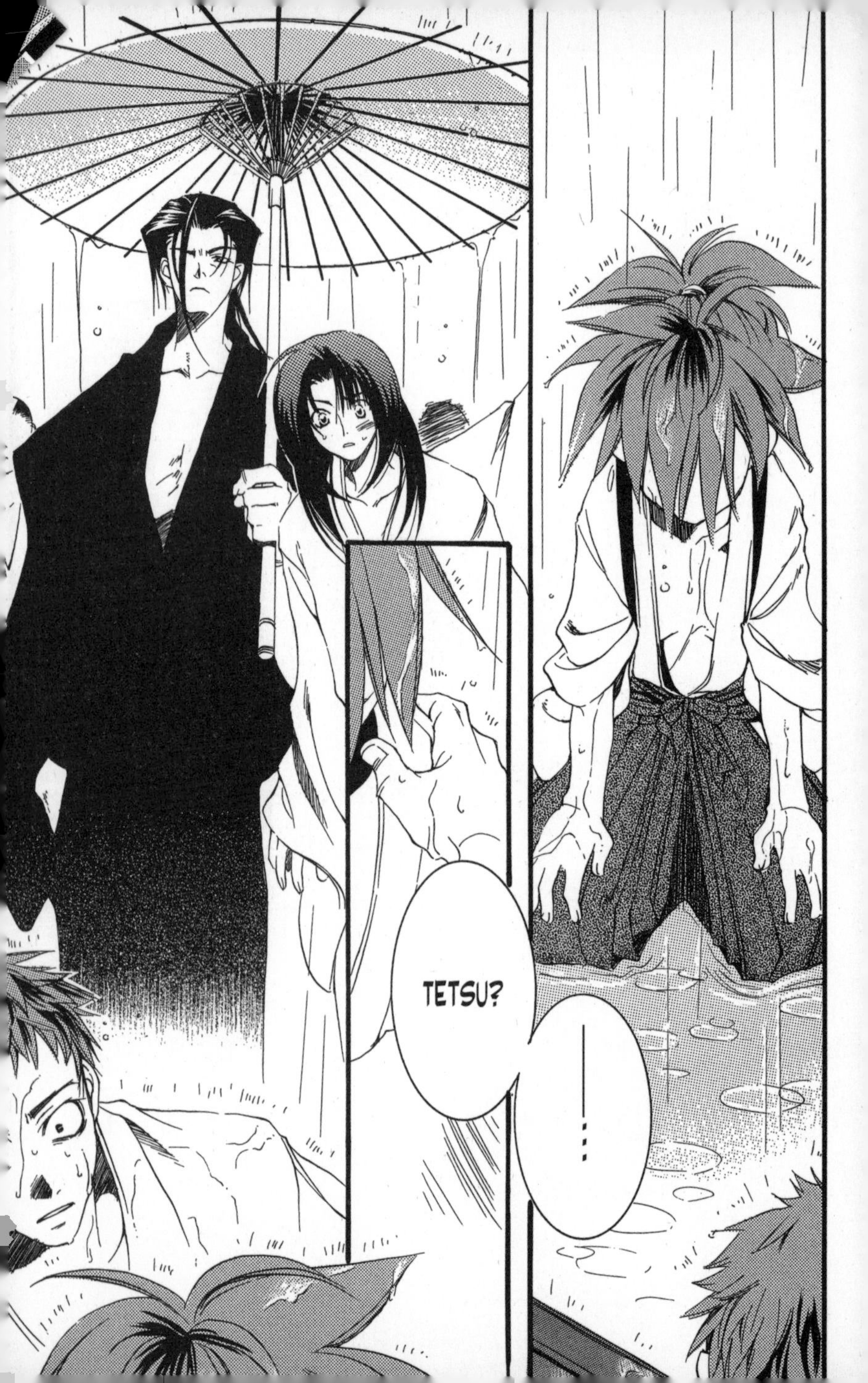
TETSU?
...

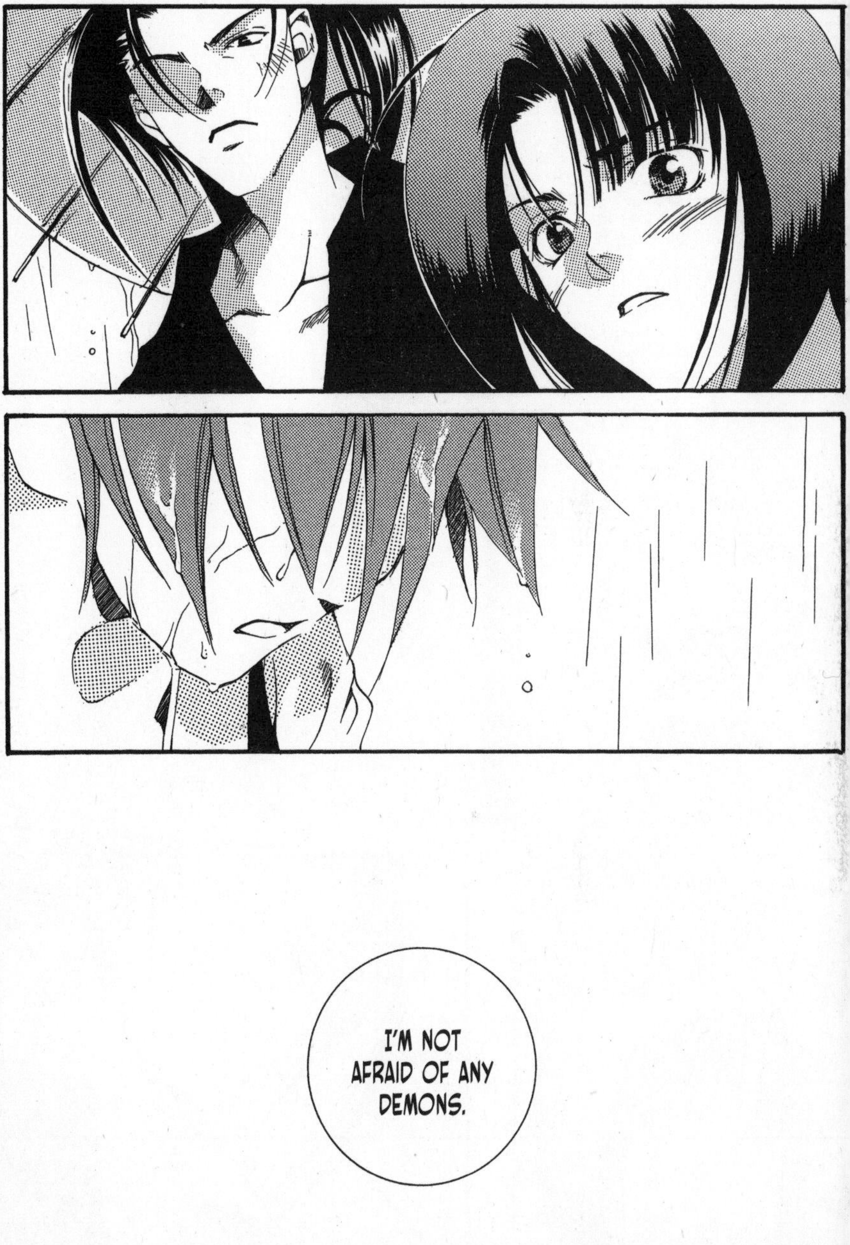
I'M NOT AFRAID OF ANY DEMONS.

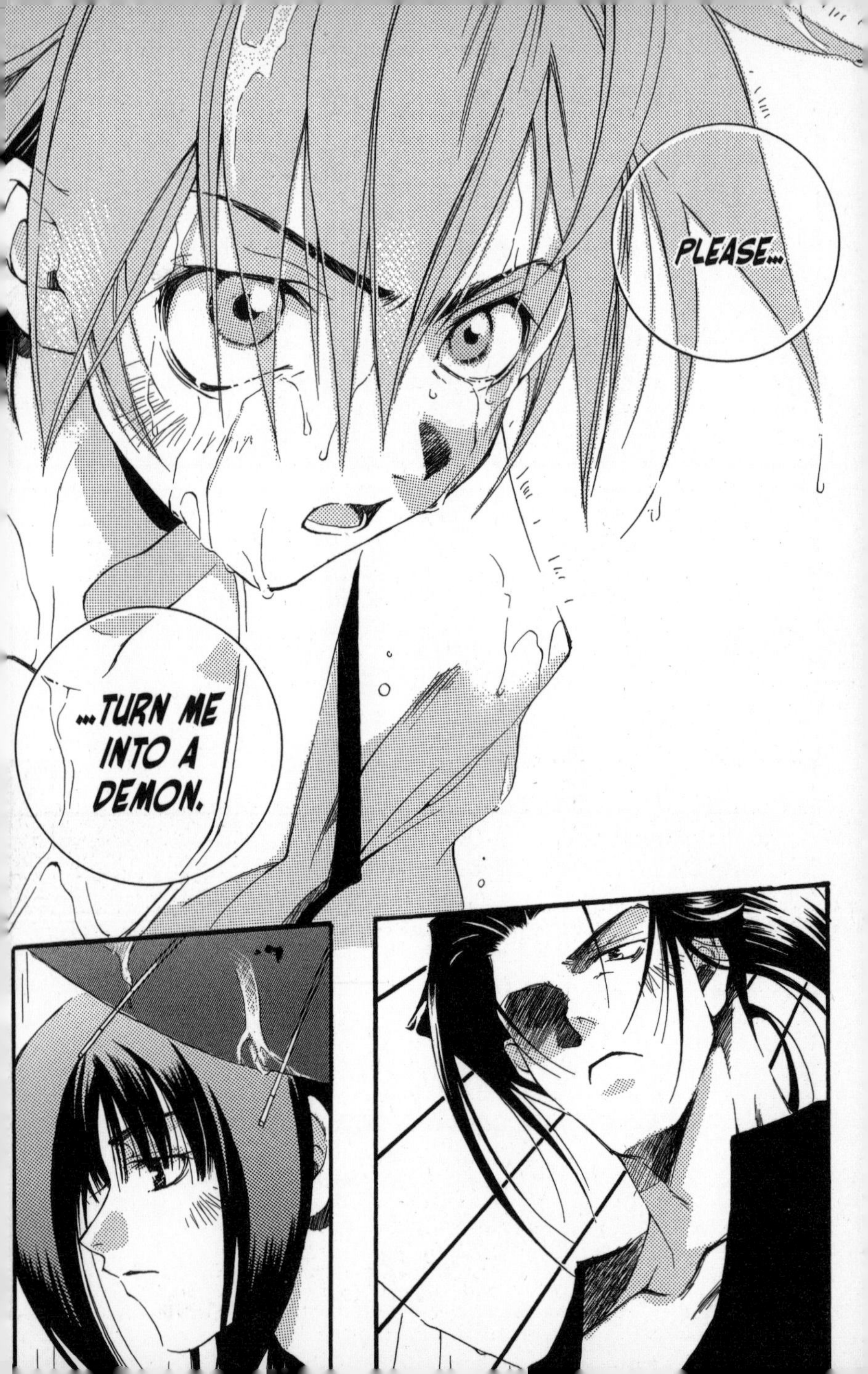
PLEASE...
...TURN ME INTO A DEMON.

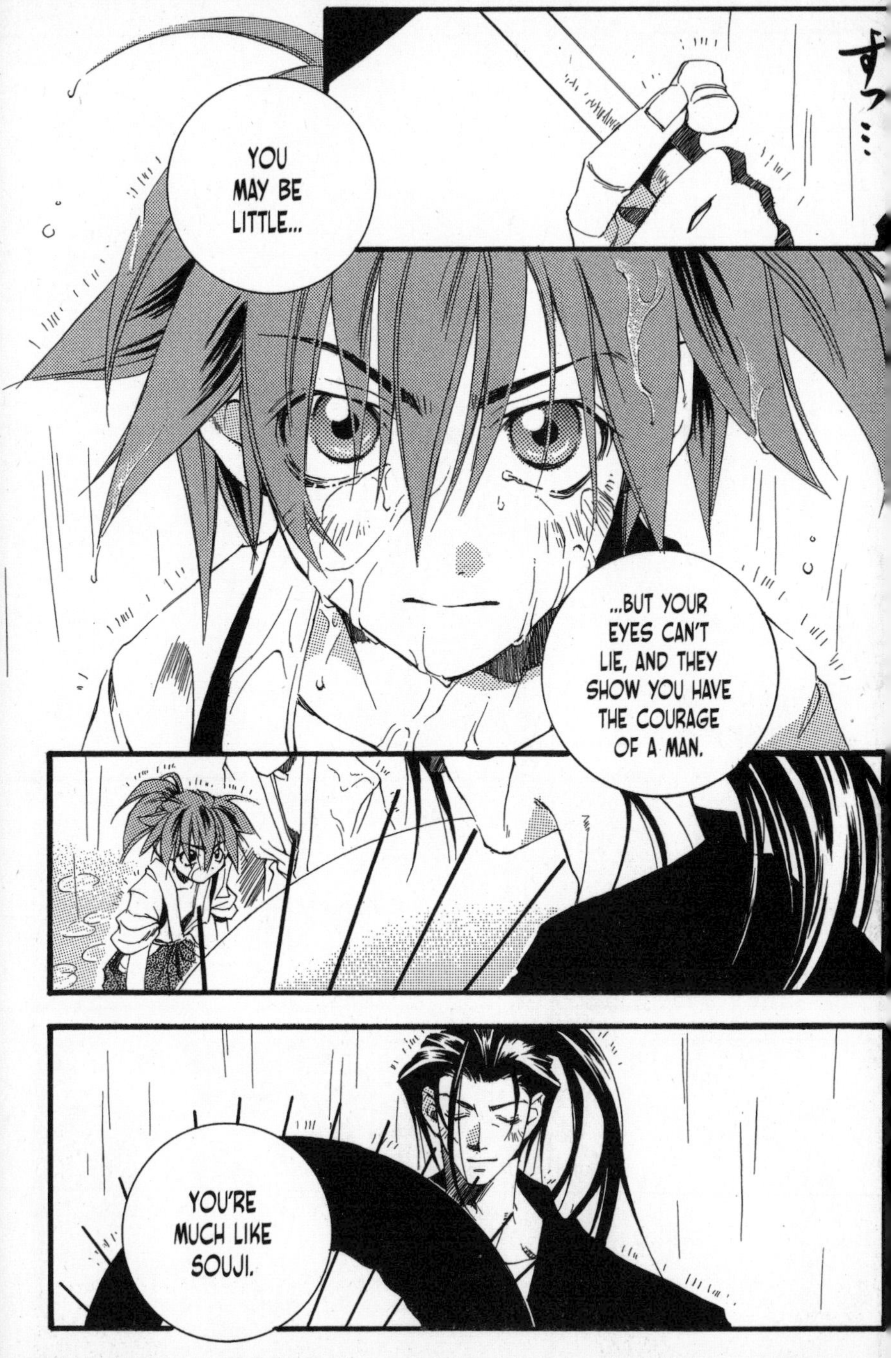
すっ…
YOU MAY BE LITTLE...
...BUT YOUR EYES CAN'T LIE, AND THEY SHOW YOU HAVE THE COURAGE OF A MAN.
YOU'RE MUCH LIKE SOUJI.

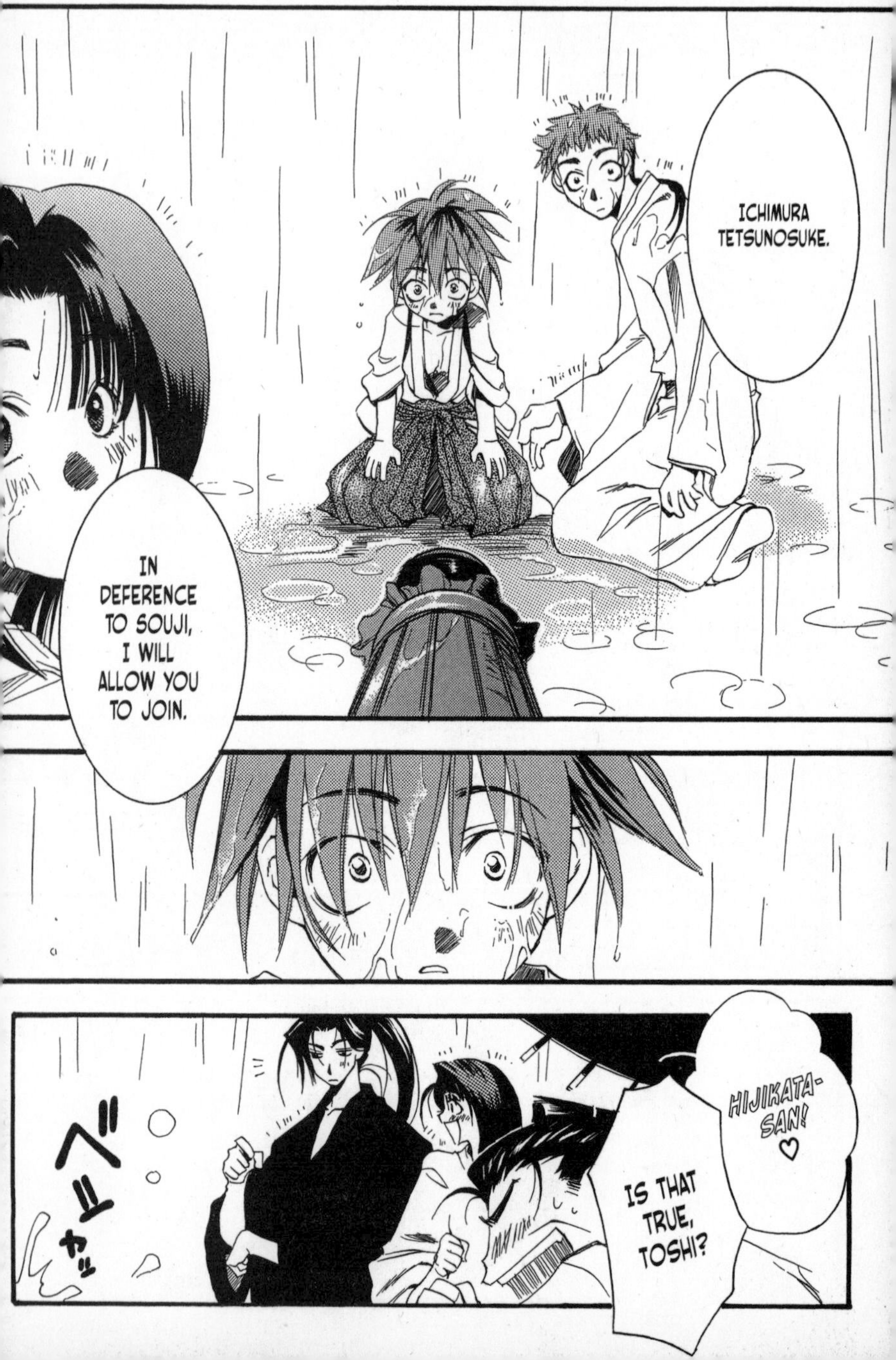
ICHIMURA TETSUNOSUKE.
IN DEFERENCE TO SOUJI, I WILL ALLOW YOU TO JOIN.
HIJIKATA-SAN! ♡
IS THAT TRUE, TOSHI?

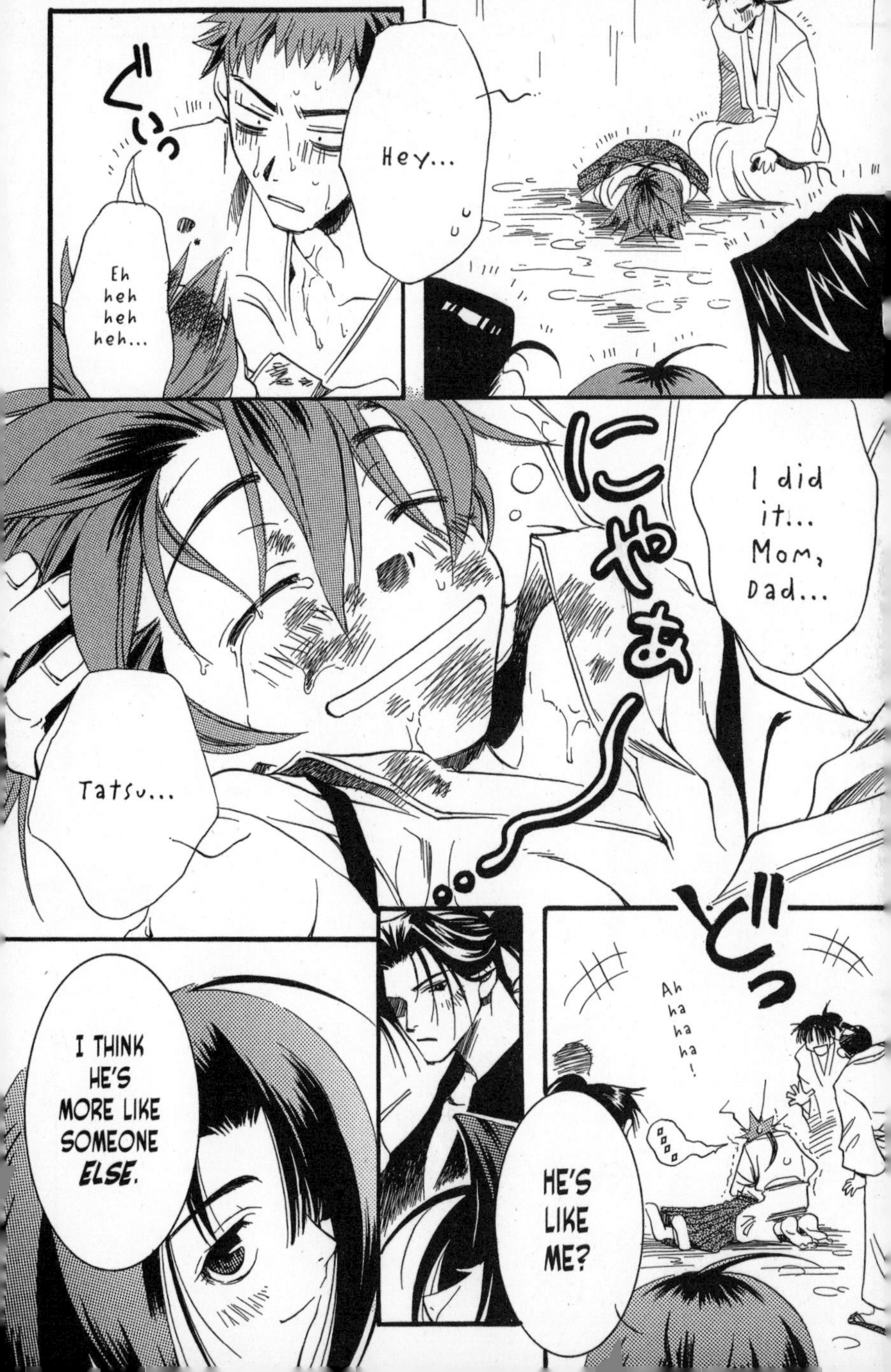
Hey...
ぐいっ
Eh heh heh heh...
I did it... Mom, Dad...
にやぁ〜
Tatsu...
どっ
Ah ha ha ha!
HE'S LIKE ME?
I THINK HE'S MORE LIKE SOMEONE ELSE.

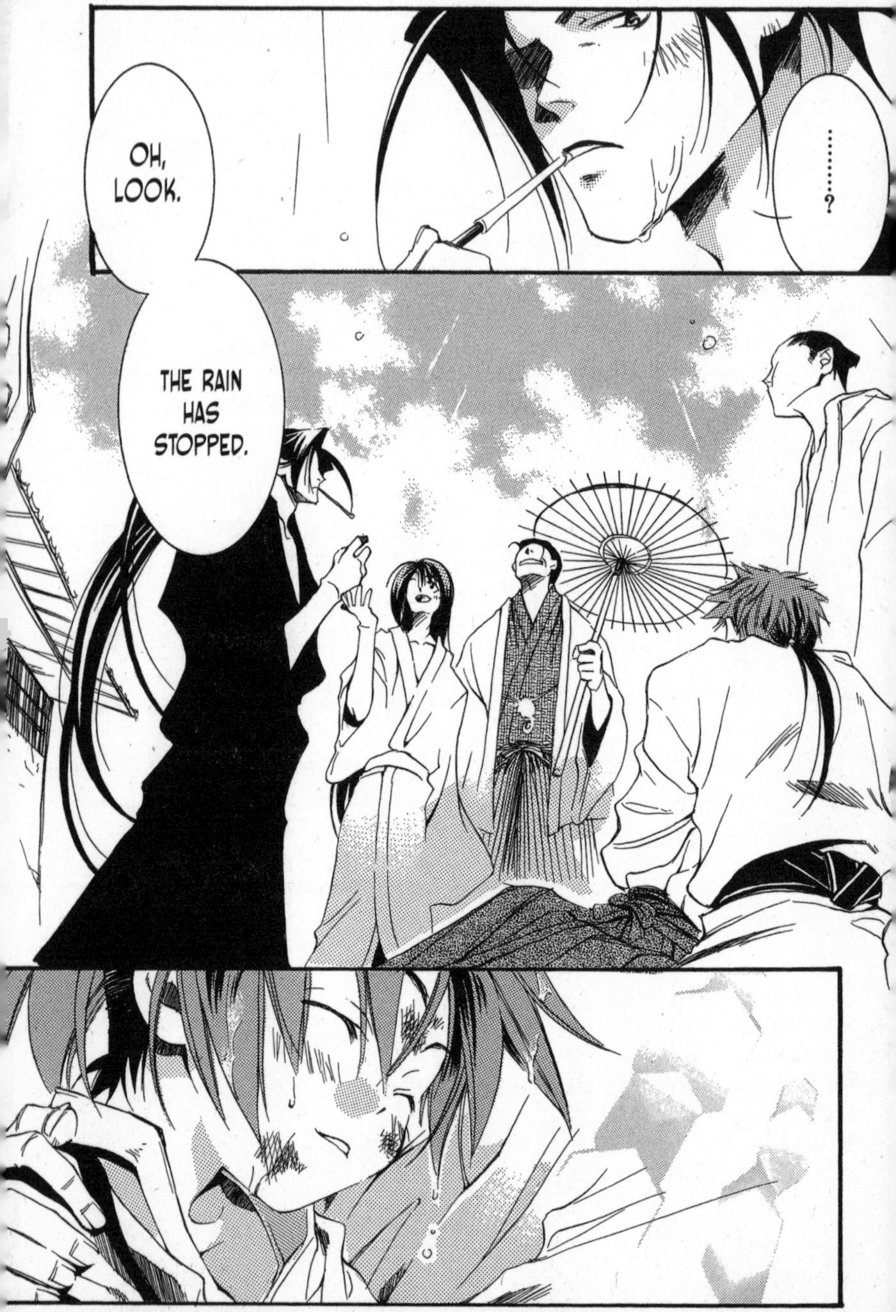
......?
OH, LOOK.
THE RAIN HAS STOPPED.

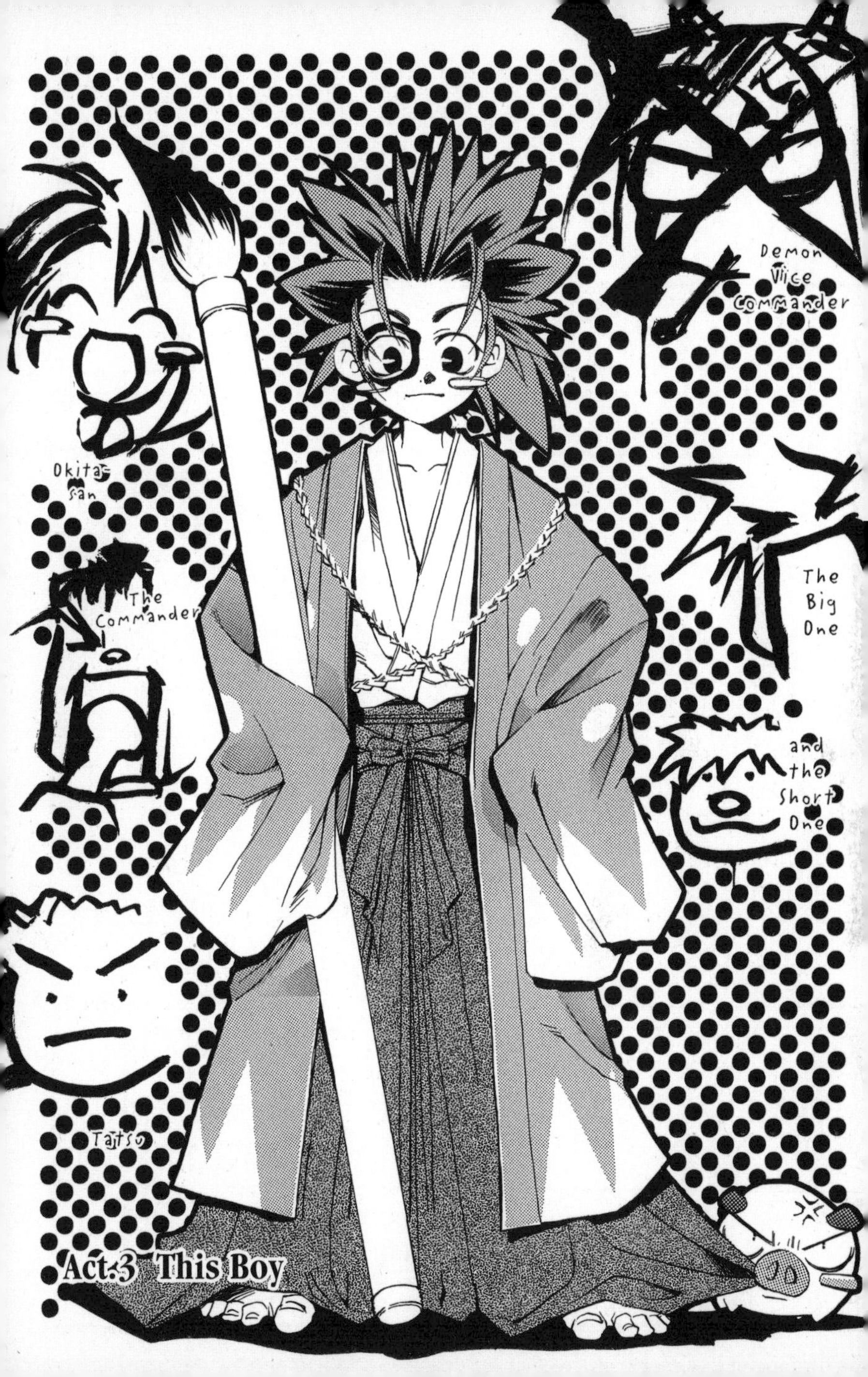
Demon Vice Commander
The Big One
and the Short One
Okita-san
The Commander
Tatsu
Act.3 This Boy

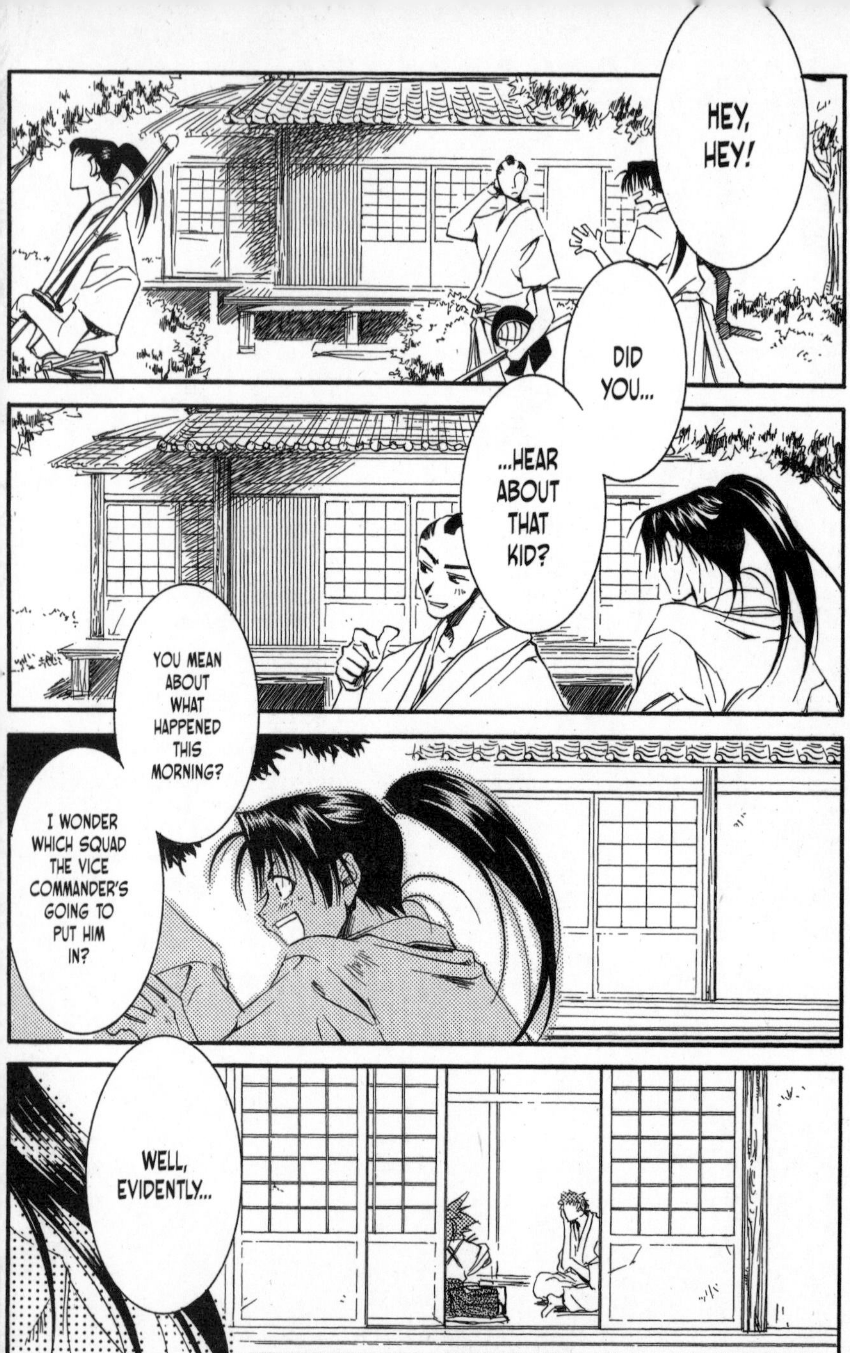
HEY, HEY!
DID YOU...
...HEAR ABOUT THAT KID?
YOU MEAN ABOUT WHAT HAPPENED THIS MORNING?
I WONDER WHICH SQUAD THE VICE COMMANDER'S GOING TO PUT HIM IN?
WELL, EVIDENTLY...

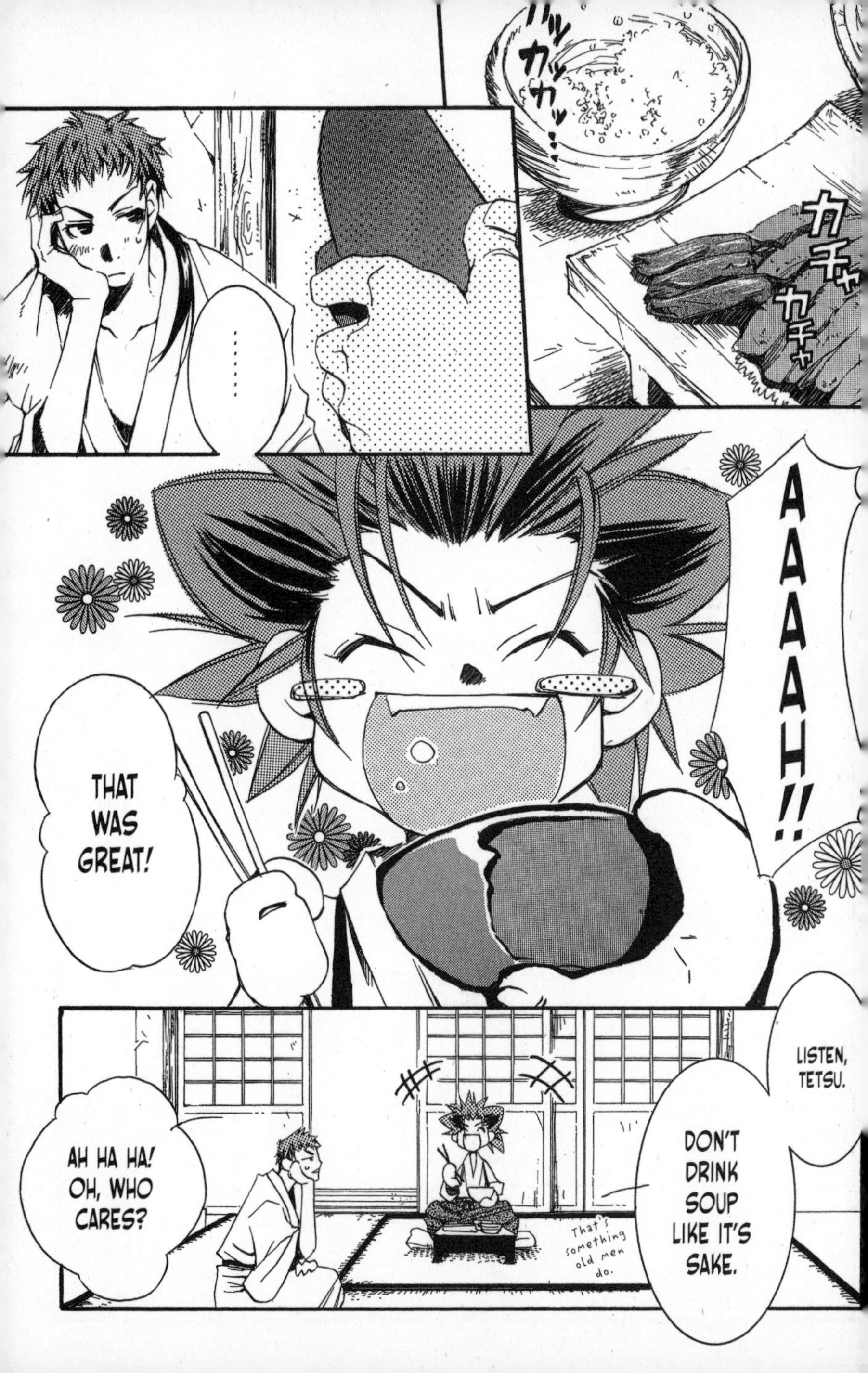
カチャ カチャ
……
AAAAAH!!
THAT WAS GREAT!
LISTEN, TETSU.
DON'T DRINK SOUP LIKE IT'S SAKE.
That's something old men do.
AH HA HA! OH, WHO CARES?

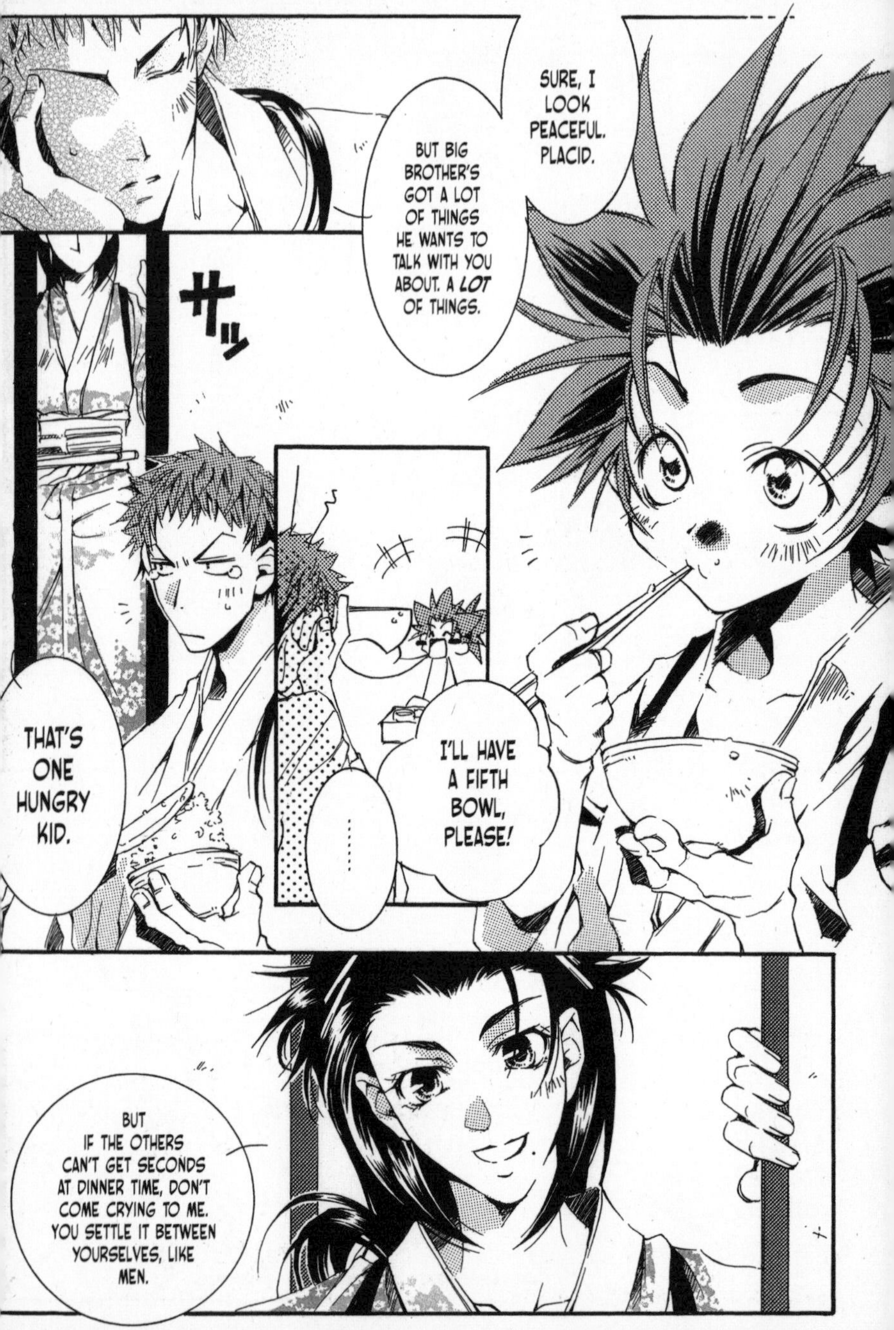
SURE, I LOOK PEACEFUL. PLACID.
BUT BIG BROTHER'S GOT A LOT OF THINGS HE WANTS TO TALK WITH YOU ABOUT. A *LOT* OF THINGS.
サッ
I'LL HAVE A FIFTH BOWL, PLEASE!
……
THAT'S ONE HUNGRY KID.
BUT IF THE OTHERS CAN'T GET SECONDS AT DINNER TIME, DON'T COME CRYING TO ME. YOU SETTLE IT BETWEEN YOURSELVES, LIKE MEN.

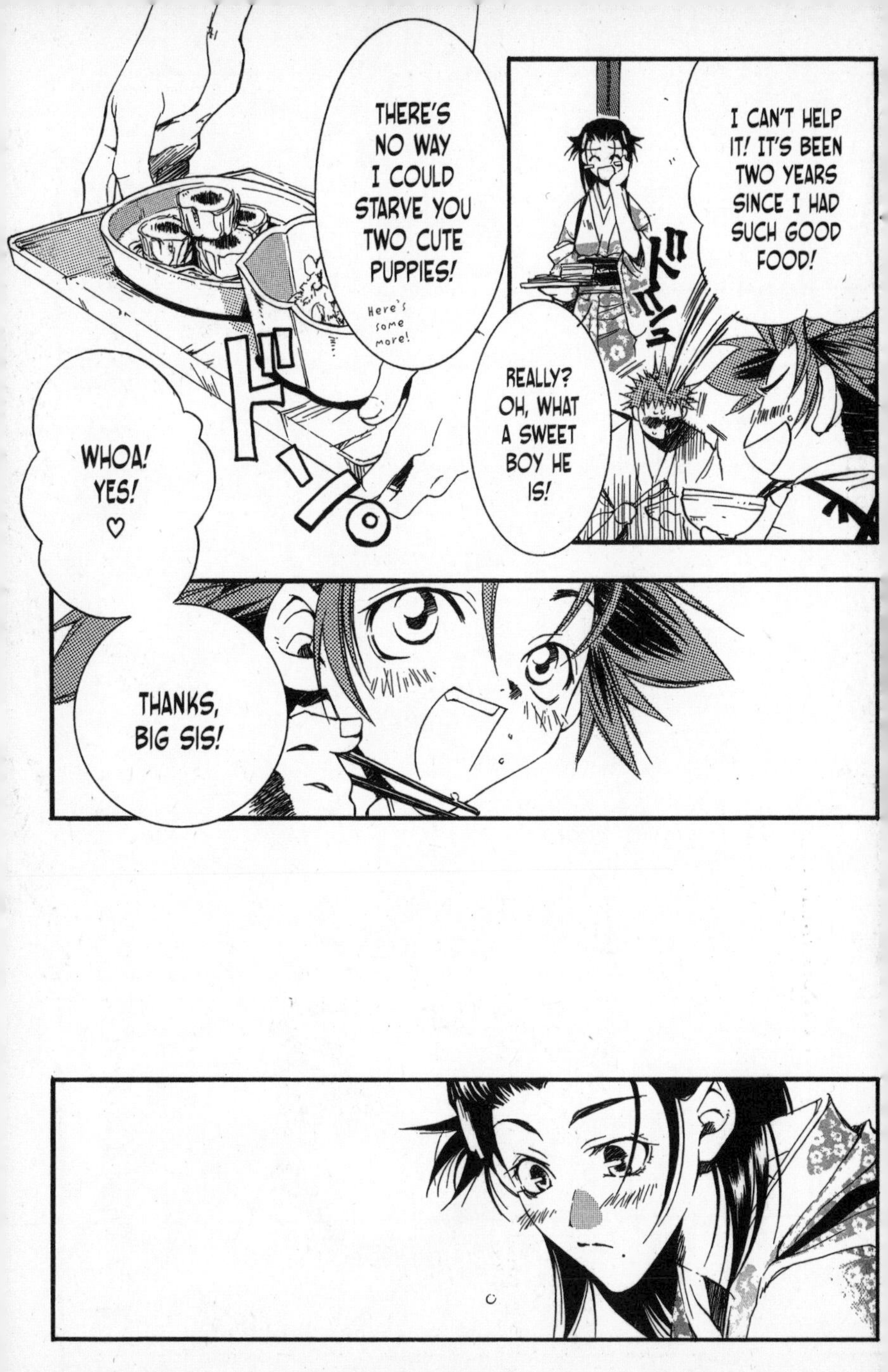
I CAN'T HELP IT! IT'S BEEN TWO YEARS SINCE I HAD SUCH GOOD FOOD!
REALLY? OH, WHAT A SWEET BOY HE IS!
THERE'S NO WAY I COULD STARVE YOU TWO CUTE PUPPIES!
Here's some more!
WHOA! YES! ♡
THANKS, BIG SIS!

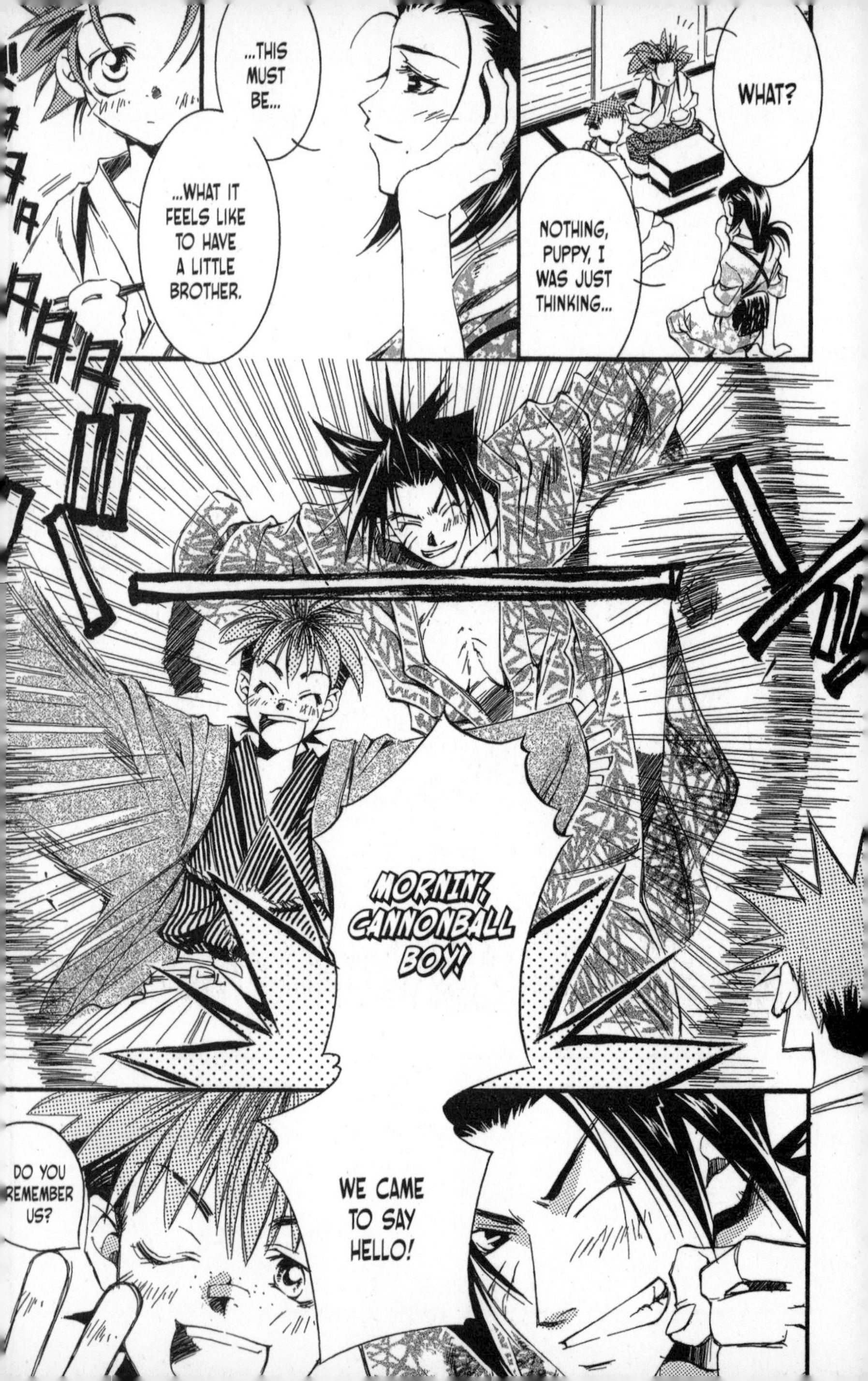
WHAT?
NOTHING, PUPPY, I WAS JUST THINKING...
...THIS MUST BE...
...WHAT IT FEELS LIKE TO HAVE A LITTLE BROTHER.
MORNIN', CANNONBALL BOY!
WE CAME TO SAY HELLO!
DO YOU REMEMBER US?

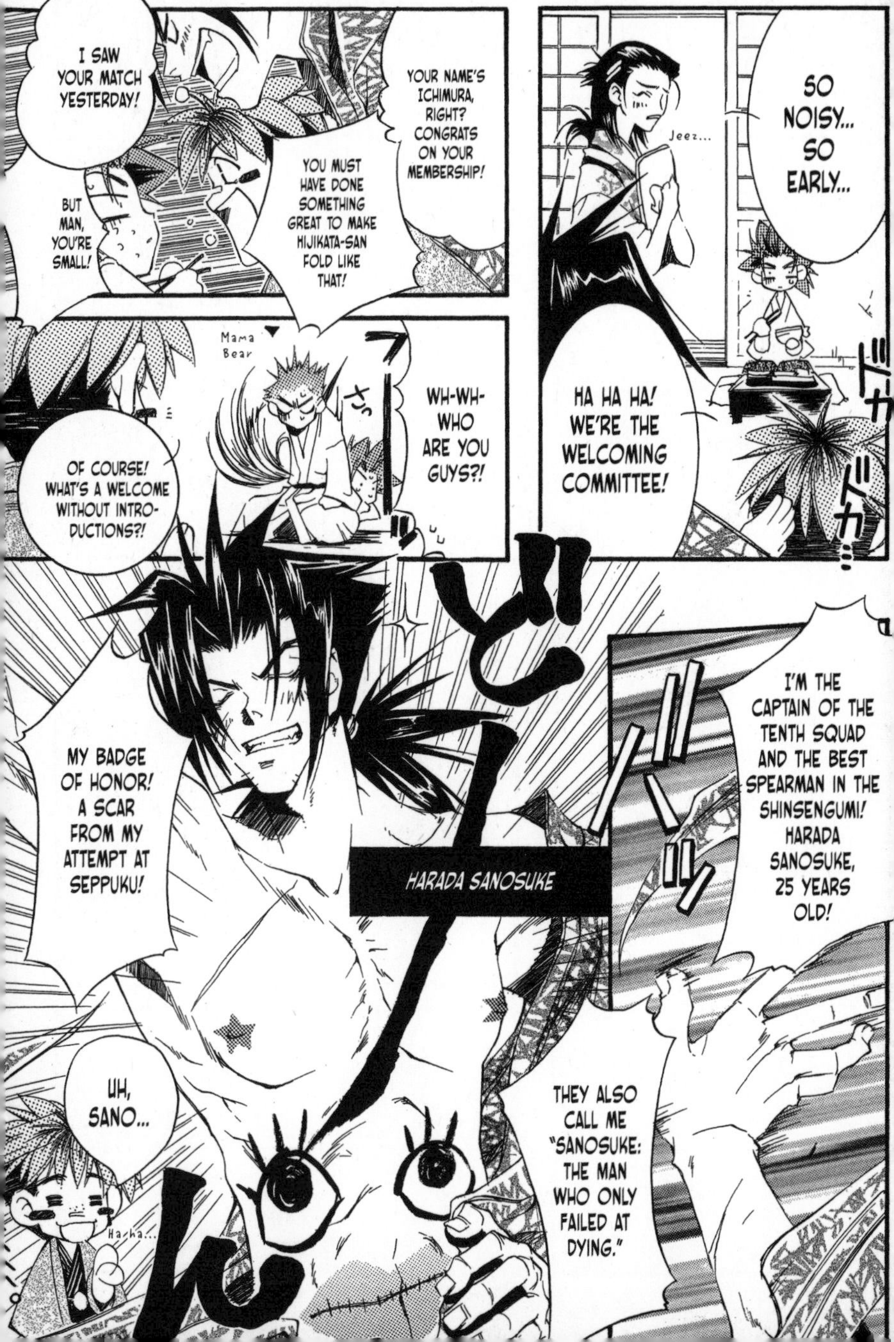
SO NOISY... SO EARLY...
Jeez...
HA HA HA! WE'RE THE WELCOMING COMMITTEE!
YOUR NAME'S ICHIMURA, RIGHT? CONGRATS ON YOUR MEMBERSHIP!
YOU MUST HAVE DONE SOMETHING GREAT TO MAKE HIJIKATA-SAN FOLD LIKE THAT!
I SAW YOUR MATCH YESTERDAY!
BUT MAN, YOU'RE SMALL!
WH-WH-WHO ARE YOU GUYS?!
Mama Bear
OF COURSE! WHAT'S A WELCOME WITHOUT INTRO-DUCTIONS?!
I'M THE CAPTAIN OF THE TENTH SQUAD AND THE BEST SPEARMAN IN THE SHINSENGUMI! HARADA SANOSUKE, 25 YEARS OLD!
HARADA SANOSUKE
MY BADGE OF HONOR! A SCAR FROM MY ATTEMPT AT SEPPUKU!
THEY ALSO CALL ME "SANOSUKE: THE MAN WHO ONLY FAILED AT DYING."
UH, SANO...
Ha-ha...

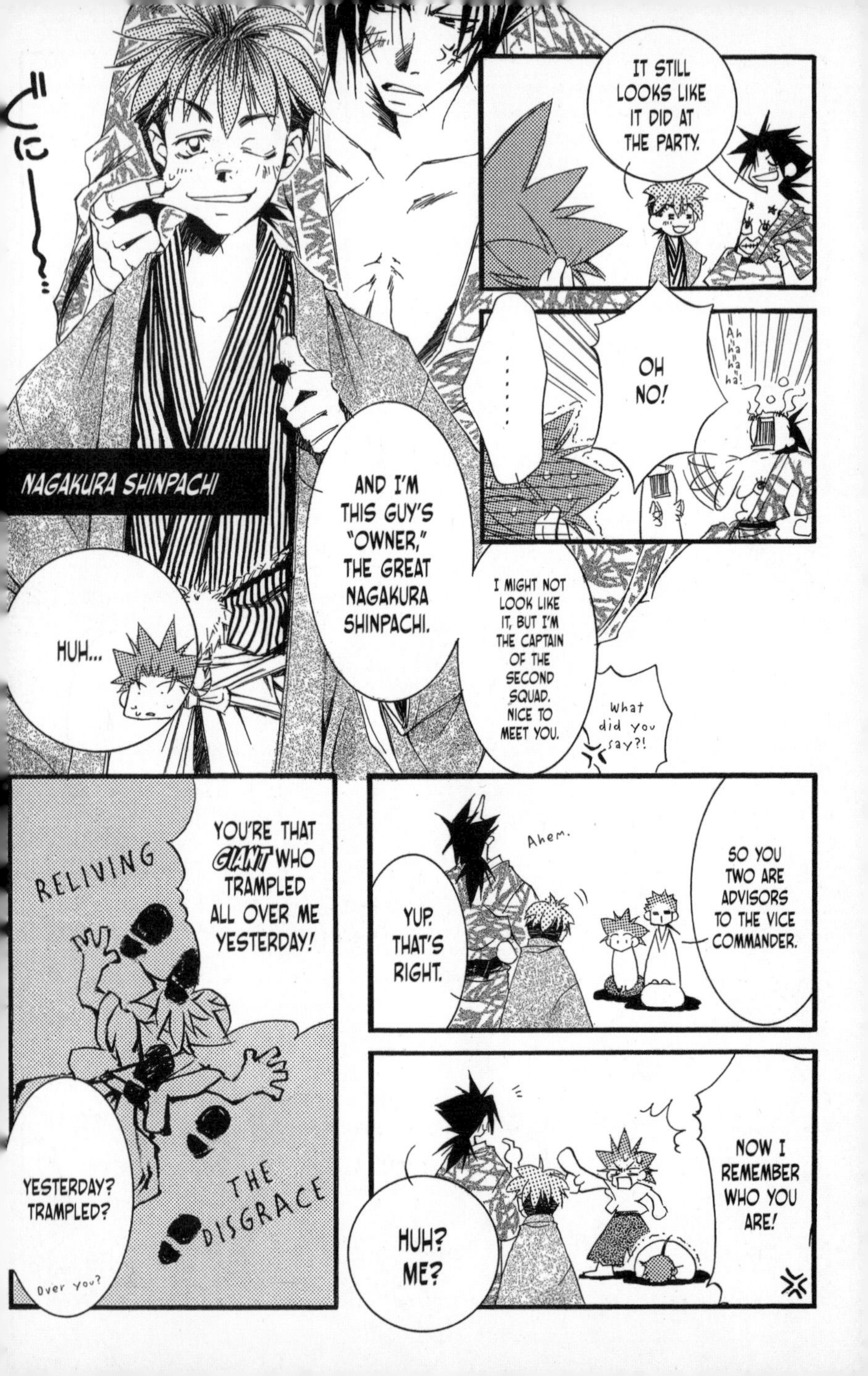
IT STILL LOOKS LIKE IT DID AT THE PARTY.
OH NO!
Ah ha ha ha!
......
AND I'M THIS GUY'S "OWNER," THE GREAT NAGAKURA SHINPACHI.
I MIGHT NOT LOOK LIKE IT, BUT I'M THE CAPTAIN OF THE SECOND SQUAD. NICE TO MEET YOU.
What did you say?!
NAGAKURA SHINPACHI
HUH...
SO YOU TWO ARE ADVISORS TO THE VICE COMMANDER.
Ahem.
YUP. THAT'S RIGHT.
NOW I REMEMBER WHO YOU ARE!
HUH? ME?
YOU'RE THAT GIANT WHO TRAMPLED ALL OVER ME YESTERDAY!
RELIVING THE DISGRACE
YESTERDAY? TRAMPLED?
Over you?

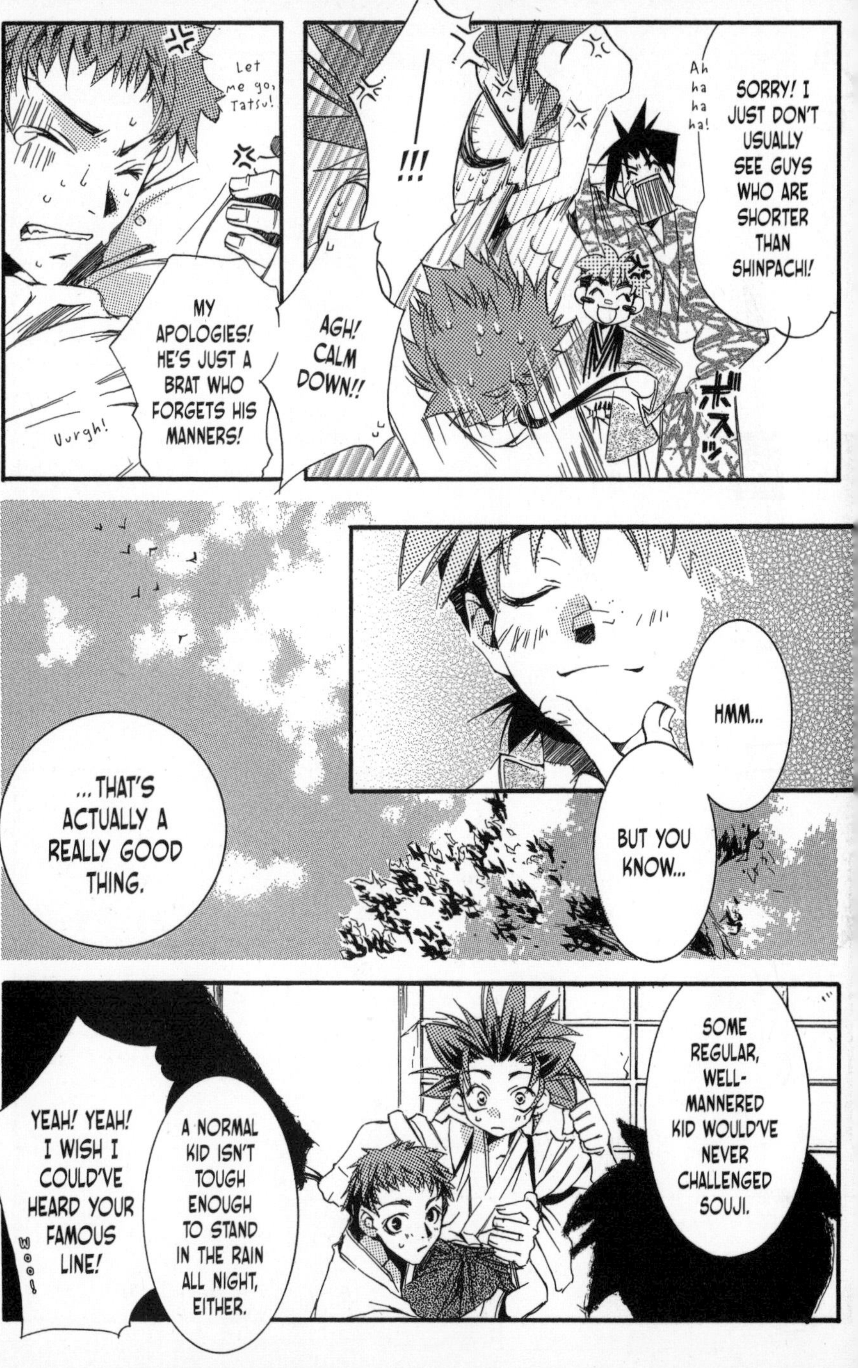
Ah ha ha ha!
SORRY! I JUST DON'T USUALLY SEE GUYS WHO ARE SHORTER THAN SHINPACHI!
!!!
ボスッ
AGH! CALM DOWN!!
Let me go, Tatsu!
MY APOLOGIES! HE'S JUST A BRAT WHO FORGETS HIS MANNERS!
Uurgh!
HMM...
BUT YOU KNOW...
...THAT'S ACTUALLY A REALLY GOOD THING.
SOME REGULAR, WELL-MANNERED KID WOULD'VE NEVER CHALLENGED SOUJI.
A NORMAL KID ISN'T TOUGH ENOUGH TO STAND IN THE RAIN ALL NIGHT, EITHER.
YEAH! YEAH! I WISH I COULD'VE HEARD YOUR FAMOUS LINE!
Wooo!

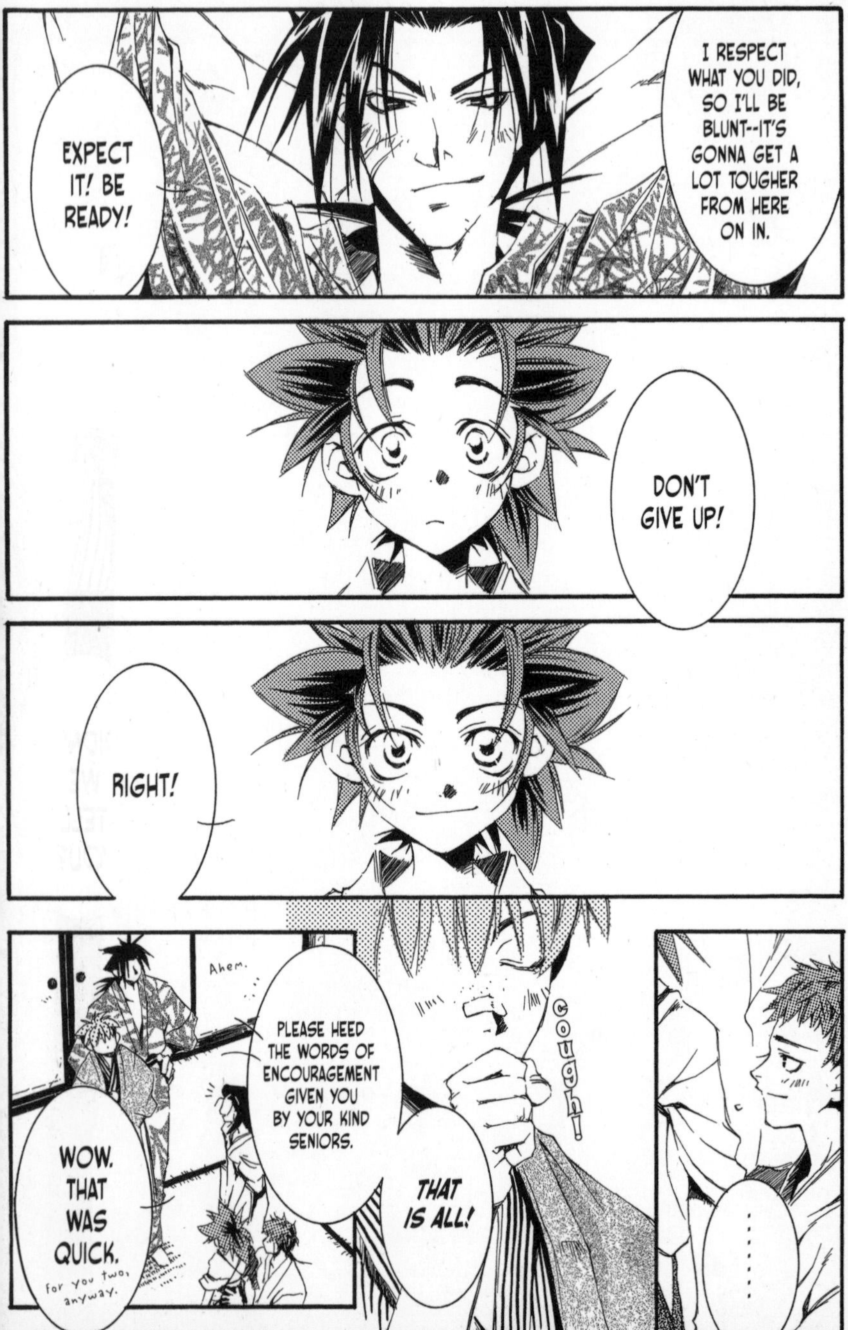
I RESPECT WHAT YOU DID, SO I'LL BE BLUNT--IT'S GONNA GET A LOT TOUGHER FROM HERE ON IN.
EXPECT IT! BE READY!
DON'T GIVE UP!
RIGHT!
......
Cough!
PLEASE HEED THE WORDS OF ENCOURAGEMENT GIVEN YOU BY YOUR KIND SENIORS.
THAT IS ALL!
Ahem.
WOW. THAT WAS QUICK.
for you two, anyway.

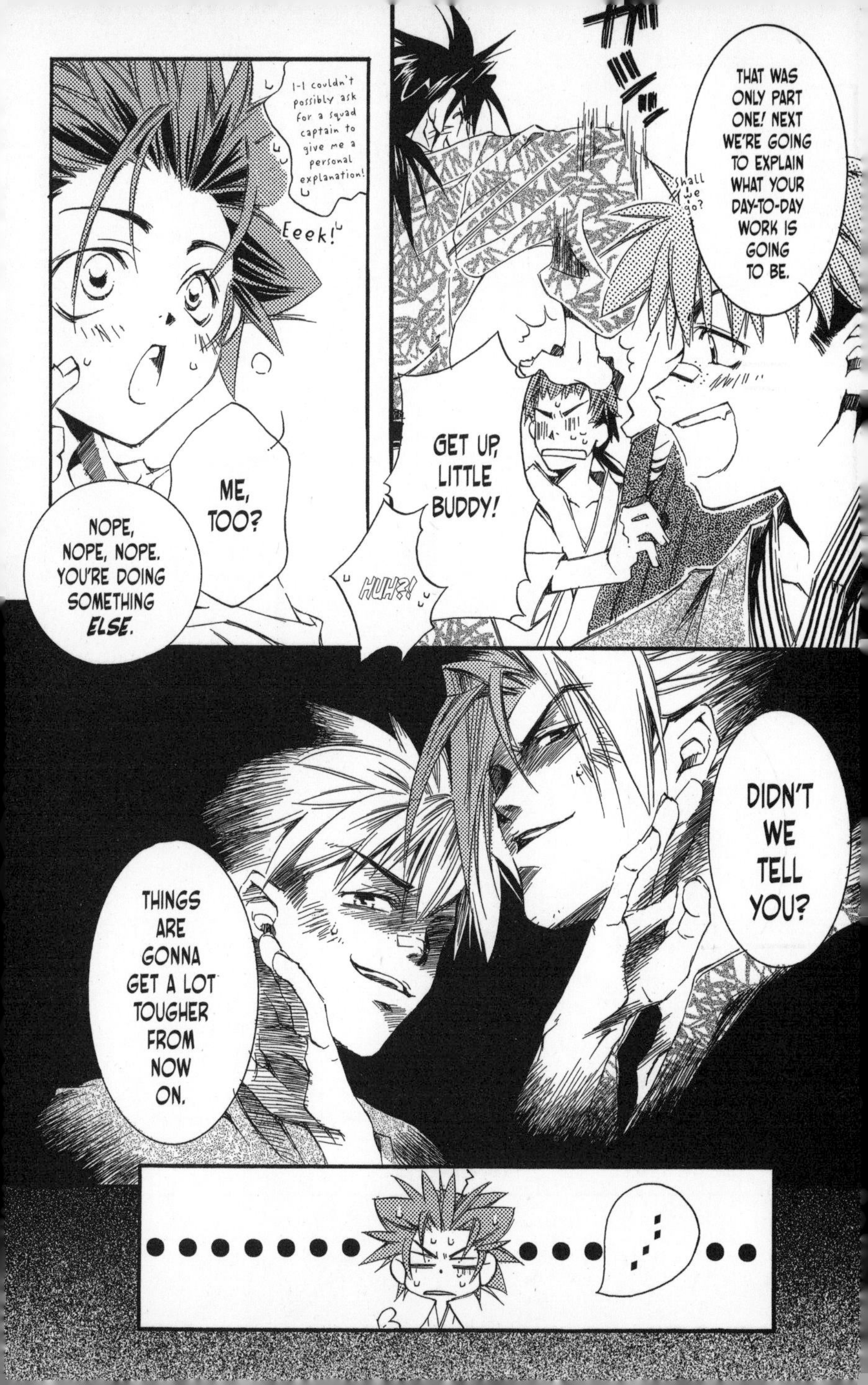
THAT WAS ONLY PART ONE! NEXT WE'RE GOING TO EXPLAIN WHAT YOUR DAY-TO-DAY WORK IS GOING TO BE.
Shall we go?
GET UP, LITTLE BUDDY!
HUH?!
I-I couldn't possibly ask for a squad captain to give me a personal explanation!
Eeek!
ME, TOO?
NOPE, NOPE, NOPE. YOU'RE DOING SOMETHING ELSE.
DIDN'T WE TELL YOU?
THINGS ARE GONNA GET A LOT TOUGHER FROM NOW ON.

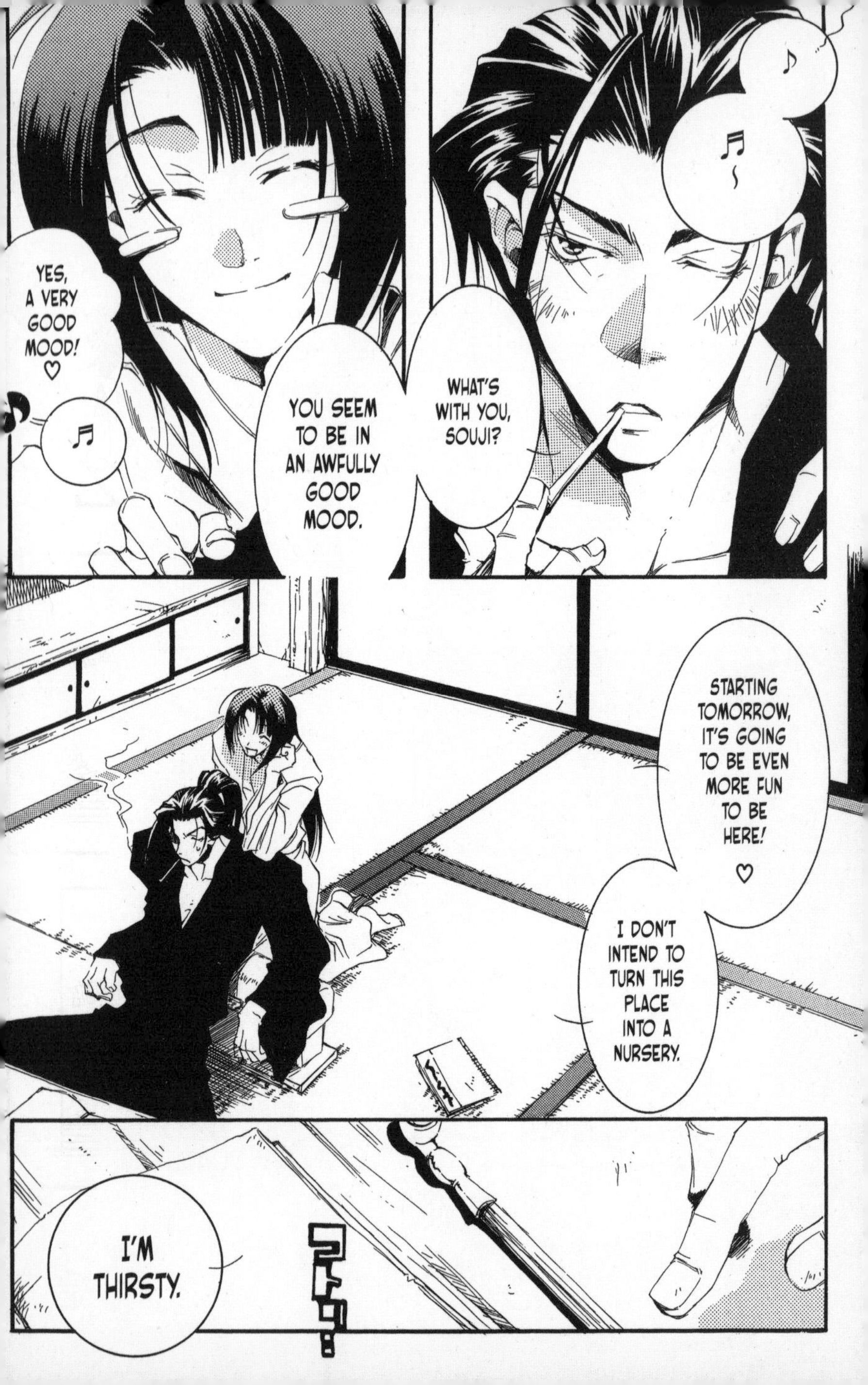
♪
♬
WHAT'S WITH YOU, SOUJI?
YOU SEEM TO BE IN AN AWFULLY GOOD MOOD.
YES, A VERY GOOD MOOD! ♡
♬
STARTING TOMORROW, IT'S GOING TO BE EVEN MORE FUN TO BE HERE! ♡
I DON'T INTEND TO TURN THIS PLACE INTO A NURSERY.
I'M THIRSTY.

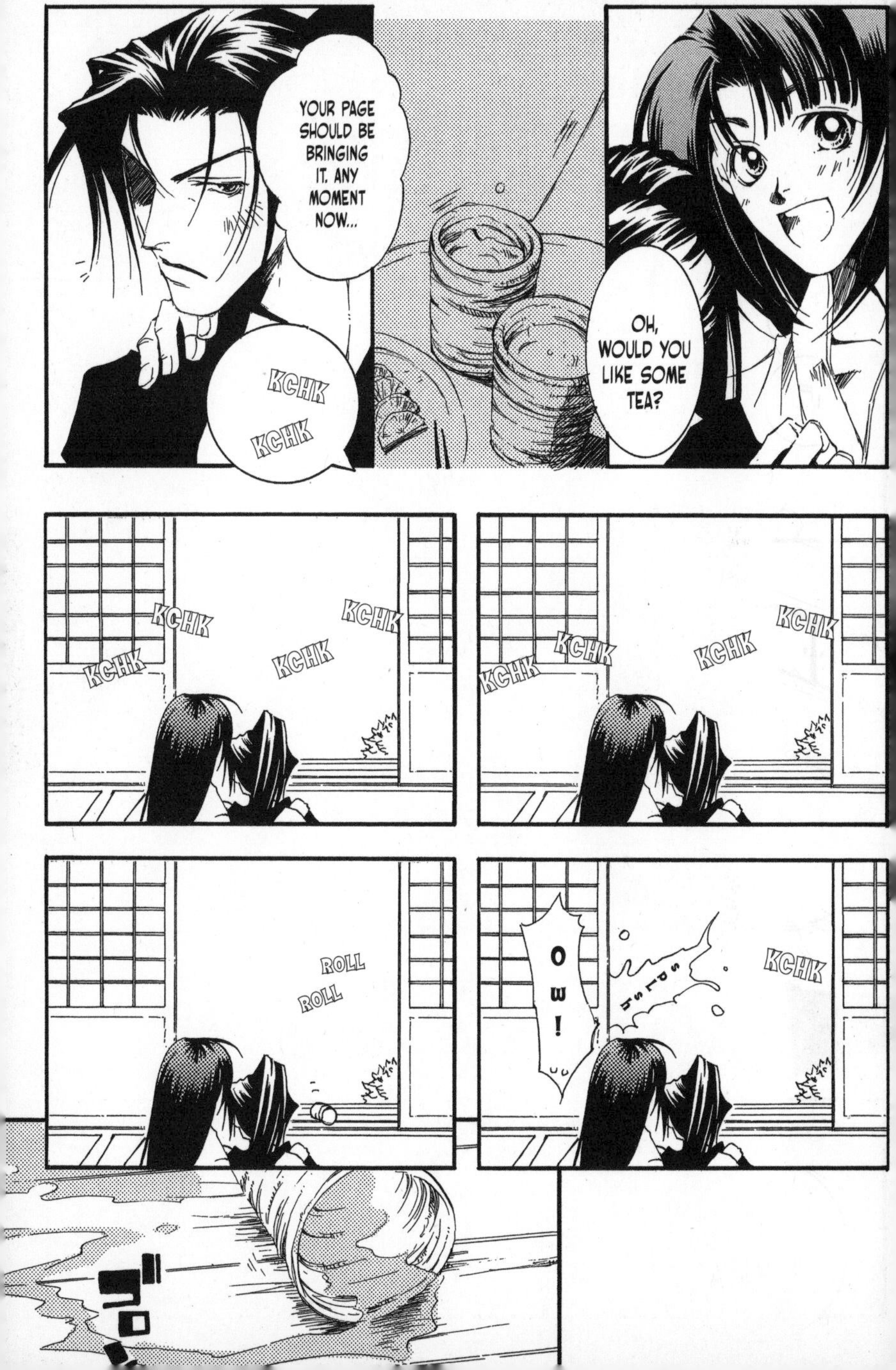
OH, WOULD YOU LIKE SOME TEA?
YOUR PAGE SHOULD BE BRINGING IT. ANY MOMENT NOW...
KCHK KCHK
KCHK
KCHK
KCHK
KCHK
KCHK
KCHK
KCHK
KCHK
KCHK
SPLSH
OW!
ROLL
ROLL
ゴロ

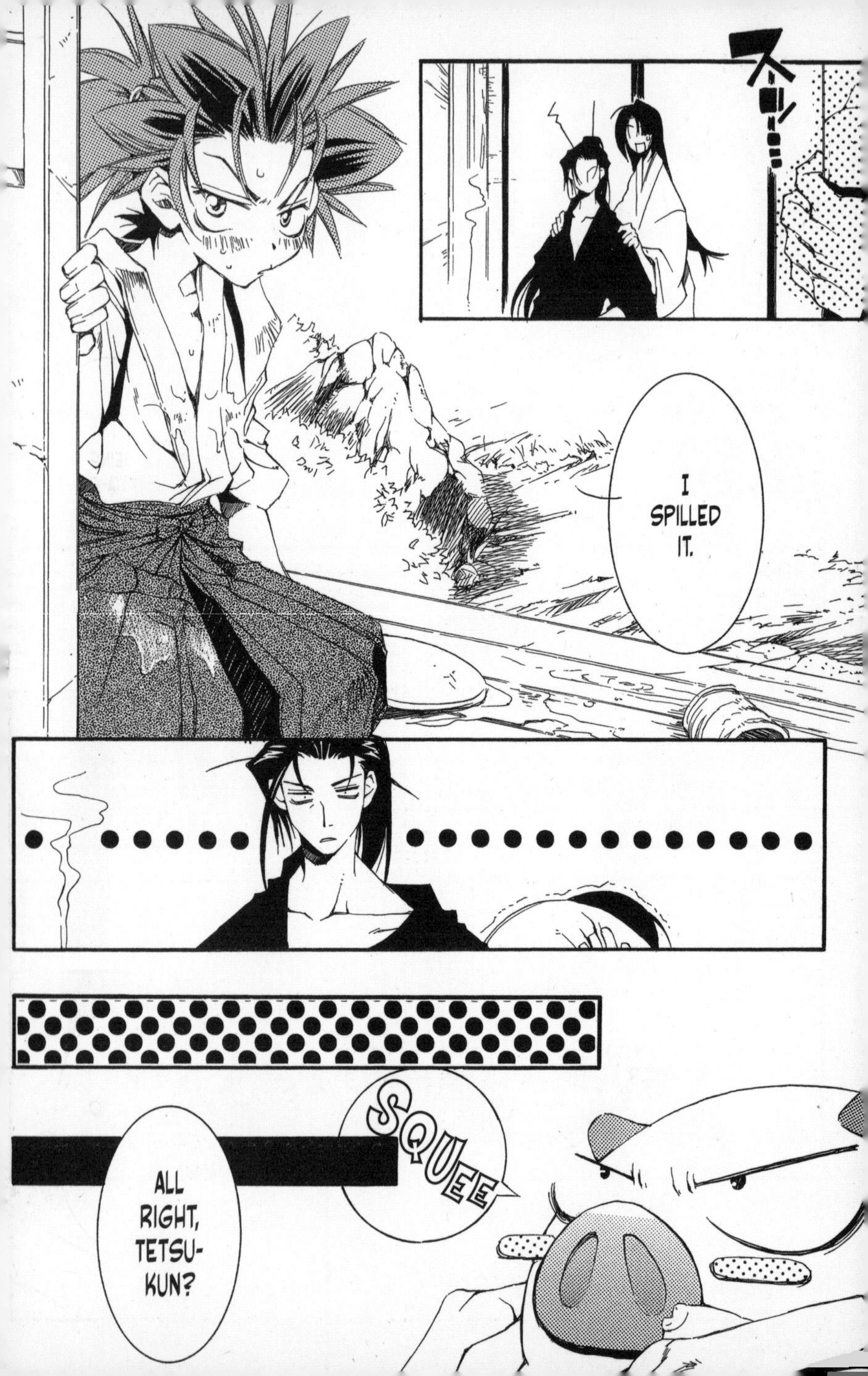
I SPILLED IT.
SQUEE
ALL RIGHT, TETSU-KUN?

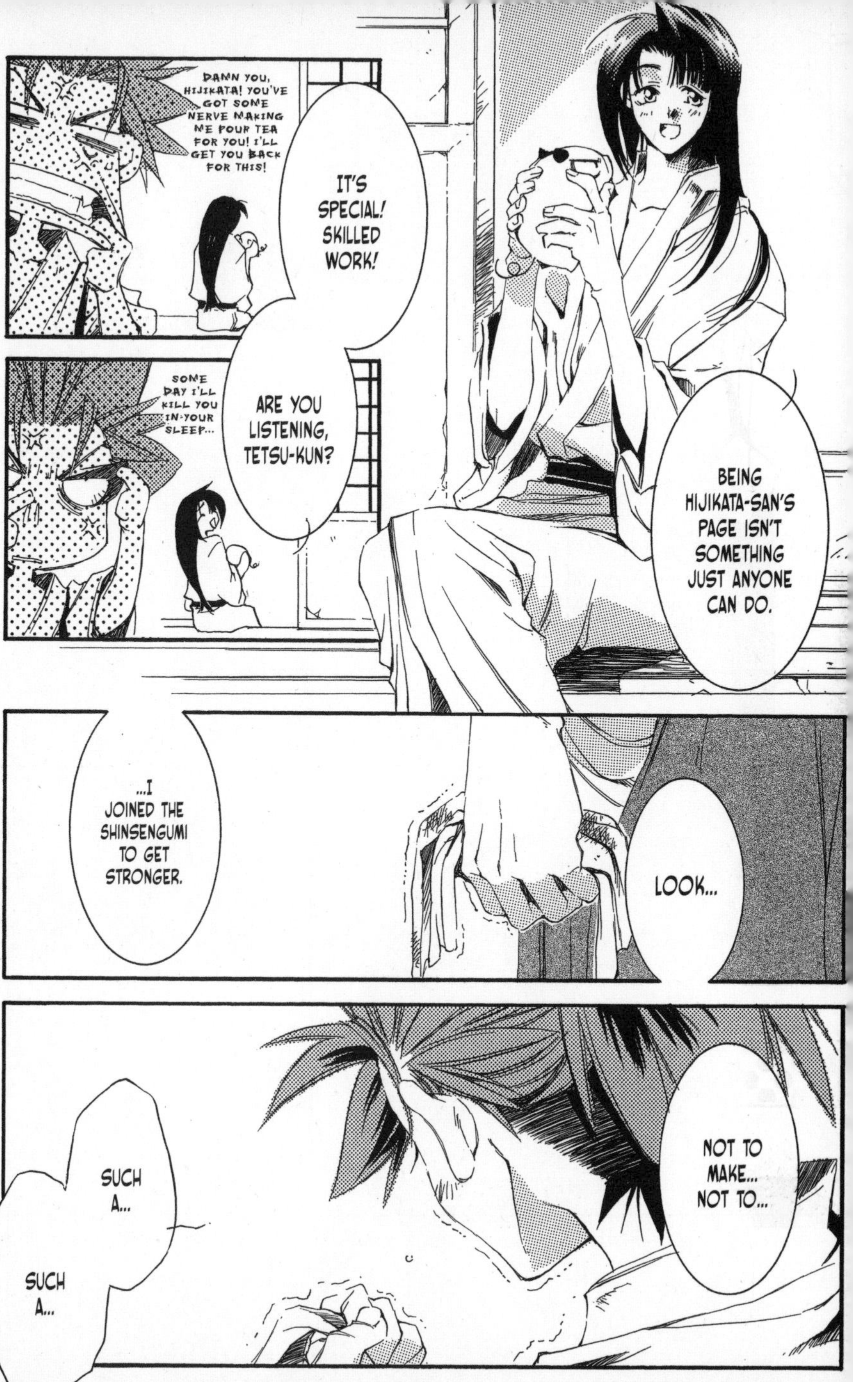
BEING HIJIKATA-SAN'S PAGE ISN'T SOMETHING JUST ANYONE CAN DO.
IT'S SPECIAL! SKILLED WORK!
ARE YOU LISTENING, TETSU-KUN?
DAMN YOU, HIJIKATA! YOU'VE GOT SOME NERVE MAKING ME POUR TEA FOR YOU! I'LL GET YOU BACK FOR THIS!
SOME DAY I'LL KILL YOU IN YOUR SLEEP...
LOOK...
...I JOINED THE SHINSENGUMI TO GET STRONGER.
NOT TO MAKE... NOT TO...
SUCH A...
SUCH A...

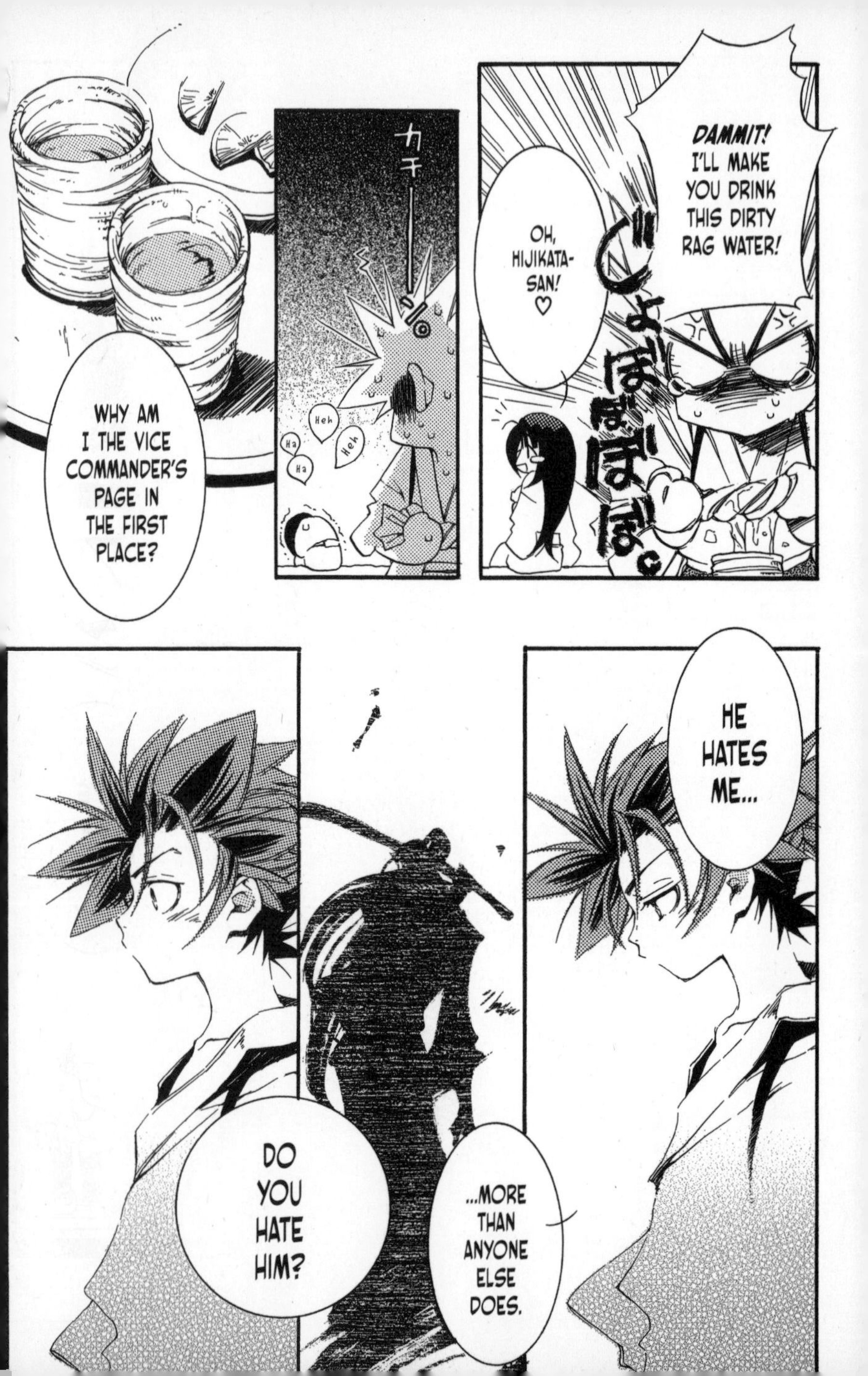
DAMMIT! I'LL MAKE YOU DRINK THIS DIRTY RAG WATER!
OH, HIJIKATA-SAN! ♡
じょぼぼぼぼ
カチーン
Heh
Heh
Ha
Ha
WHY AM I THE VICE COMMANDER'S PAGE IN THE FIRST PLACE?
HE HATES ME...
...MORE THAN ANYONE ELSE DOES.
DO YOU HATE HIM?

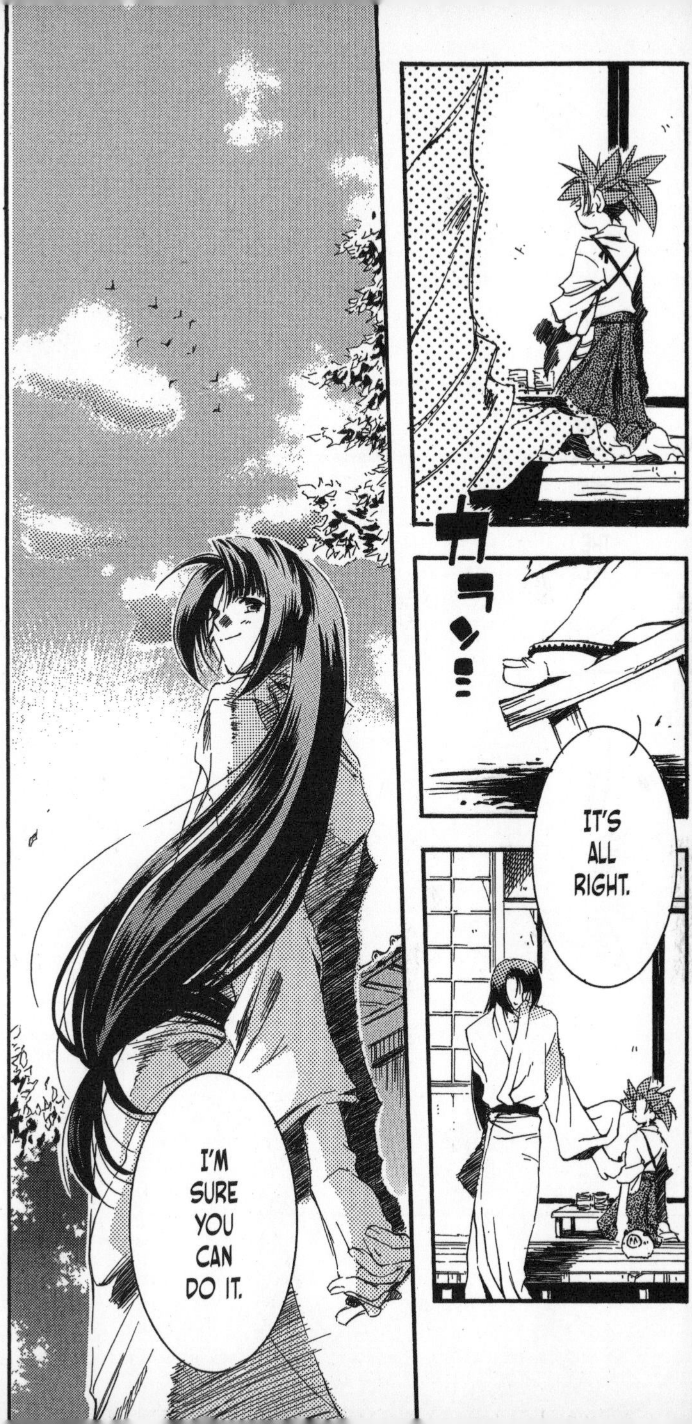
カラン!!
IT'S ALL RIGHT.
I'M SURE YOU CAN DO IT.

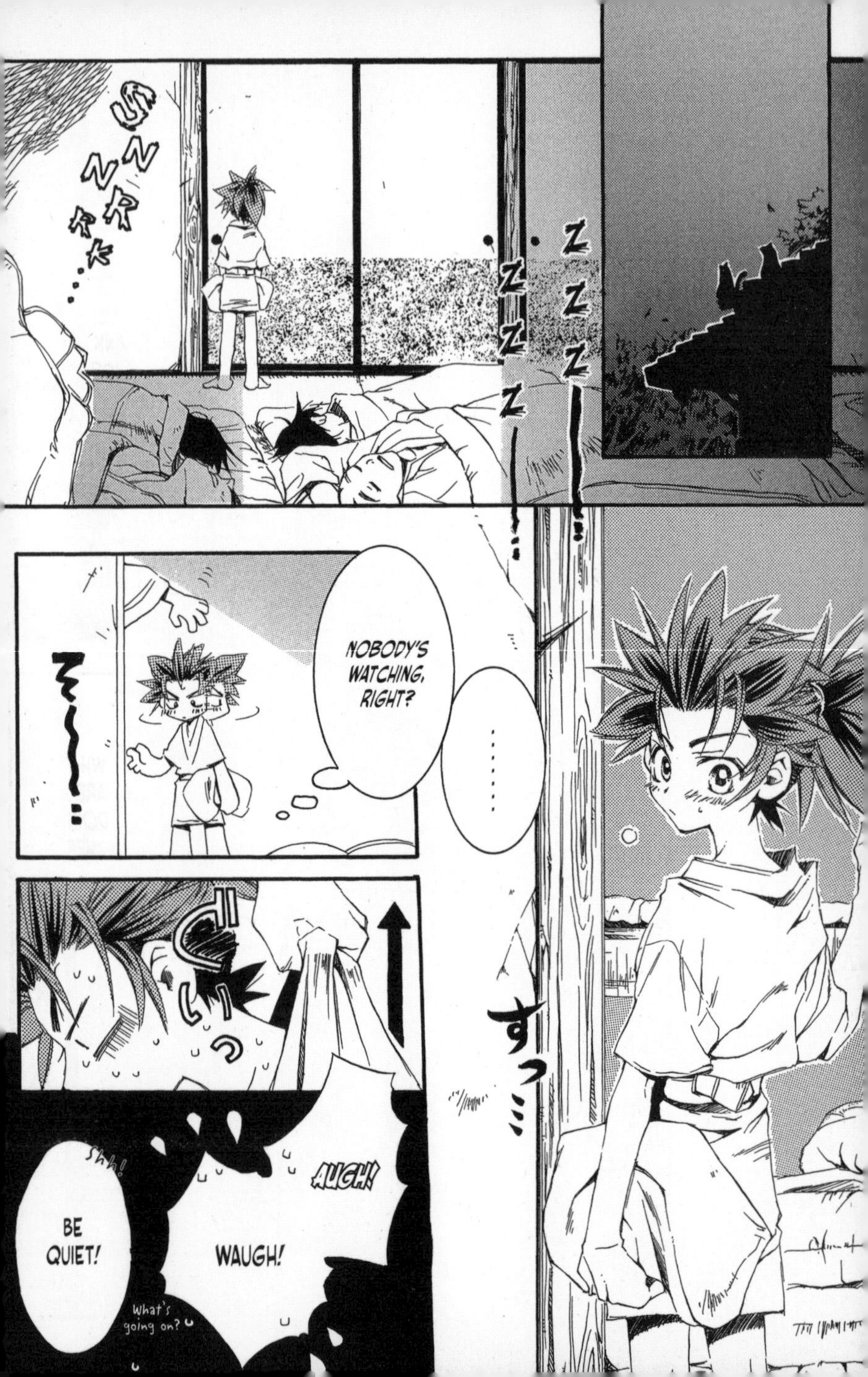

ZZZ—!
ZZZ—!
SNNRRK...
......
すっ
NOBODY'S WATCHING, RIGHT?
そ〜〜〜!
じーっ
AUGH!
WAUGH!
Shh!
BE QUIET!
What's going on?

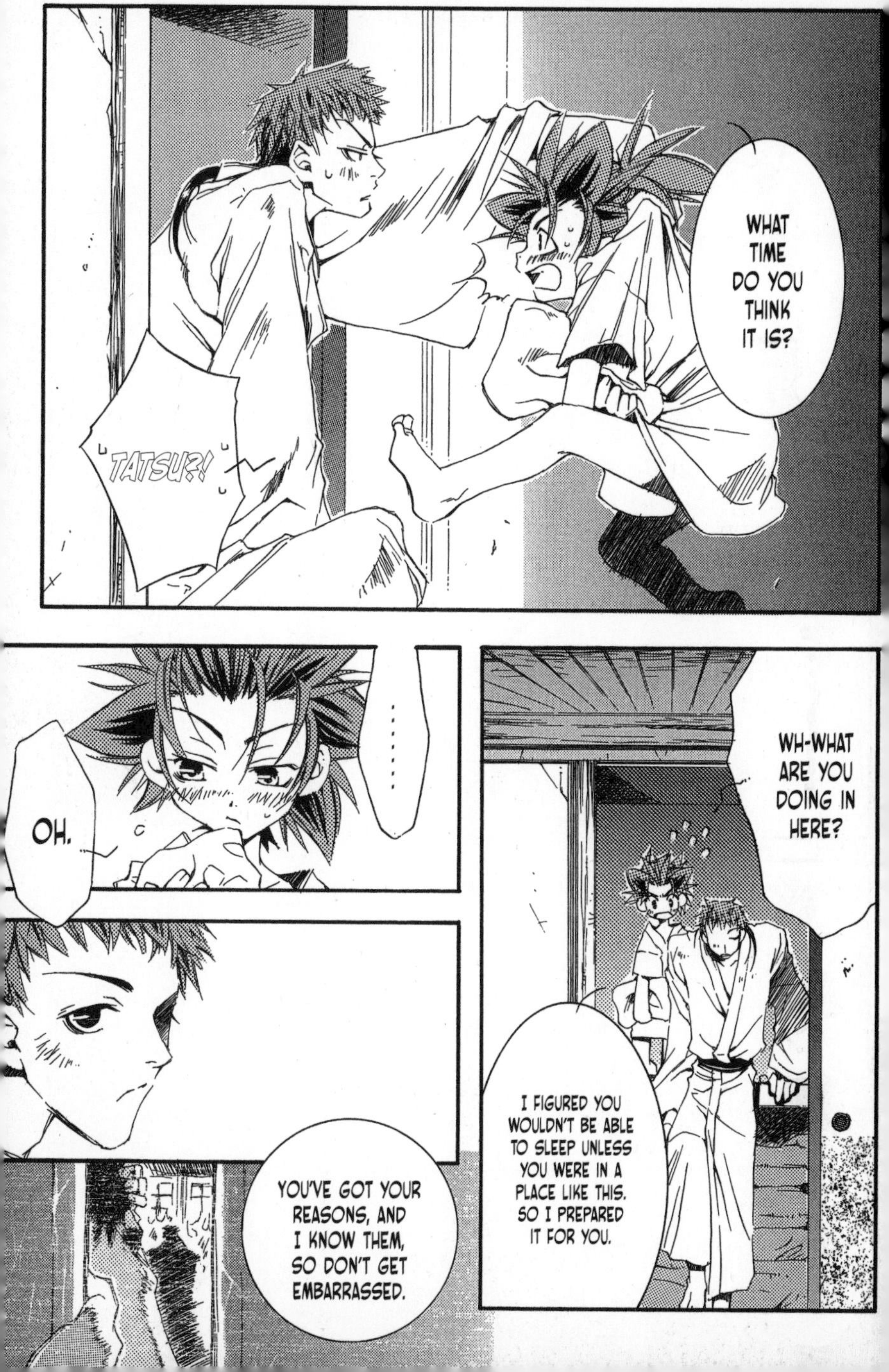
WHAT TIME DO YOU THINK IT IS?
TATSU?!
WH-WHAT ARE YOU DOING IN HERE?
I FIGURED YOU WOULDN'T BE ABLE TO SLEEP UNLESS YOU WERE IN A PLACE LIKE THIS. SO I PREPARED IT FOR YOU.
......
OH.
YOU'VE GOT YOUR REASONS, AND I KNOW THEM, SO DON'T GET EMBARRASSED.

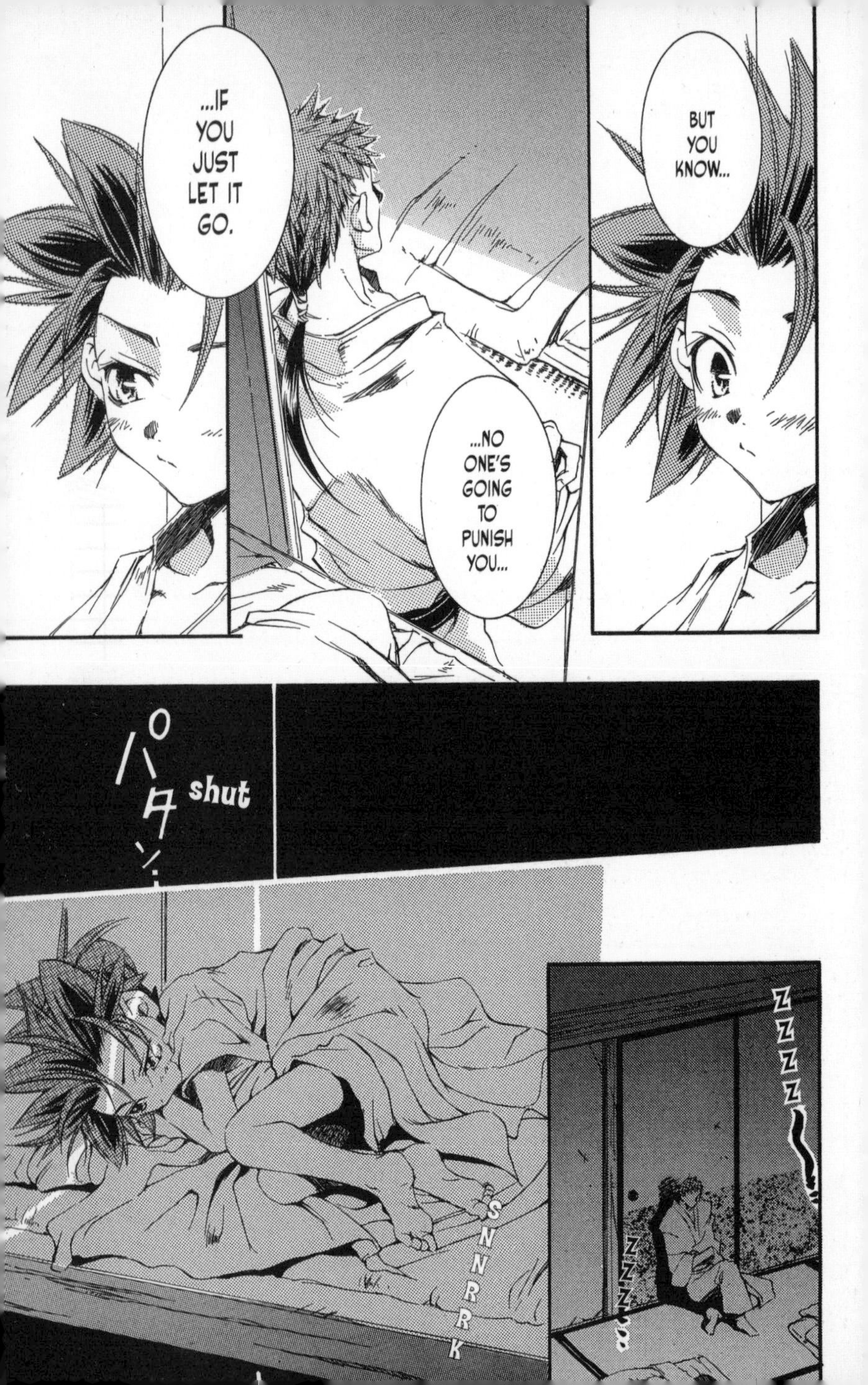
BUT YOU KNOW...
...NO ONE'S GOING TO PUNISH YOU...
...IF YOU JUST LET IT GO.
パタン
shut
ZZZZ~
ZZZ...
SNNRRK

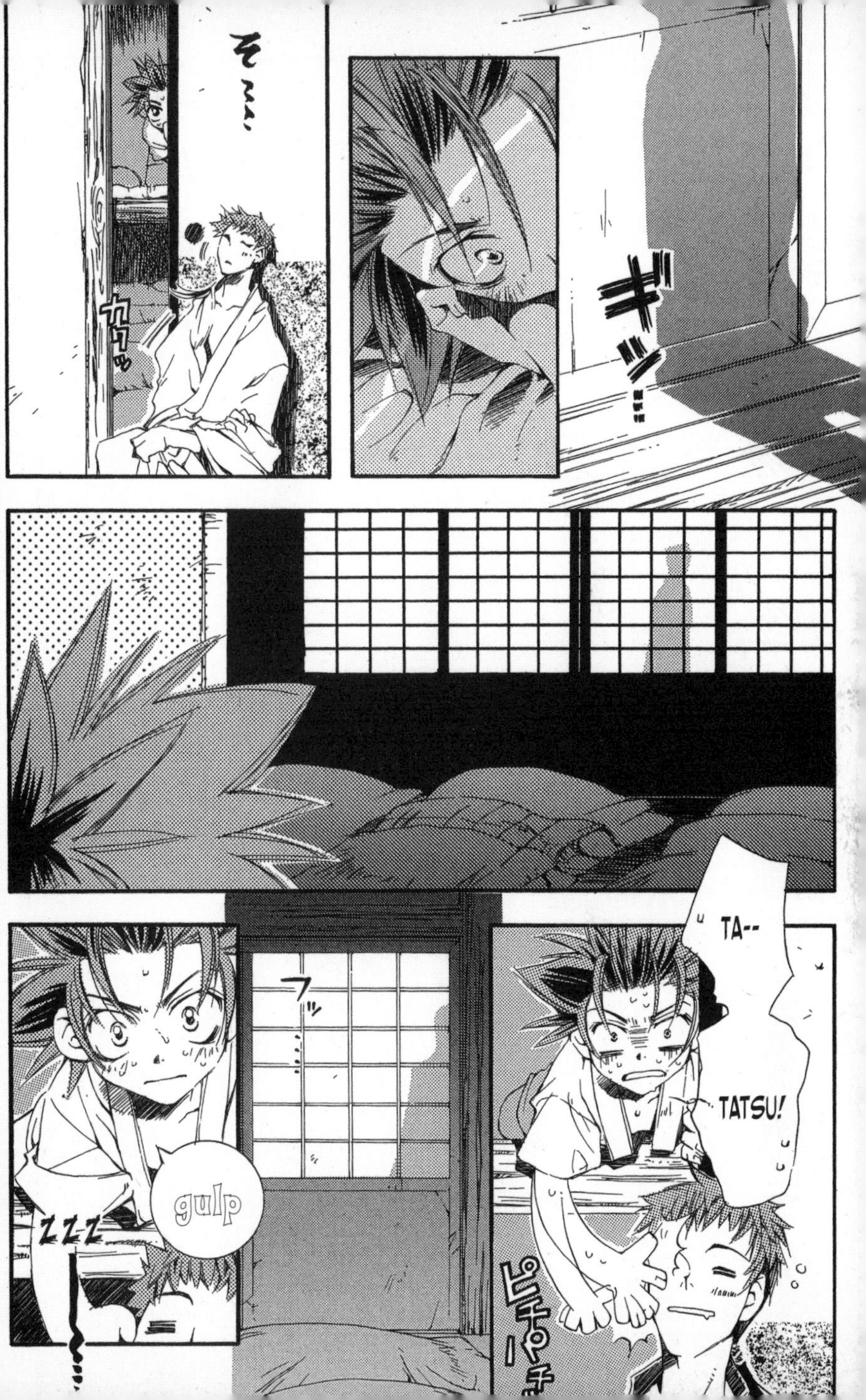
TA--
TATSU!
gulp
ZZZ

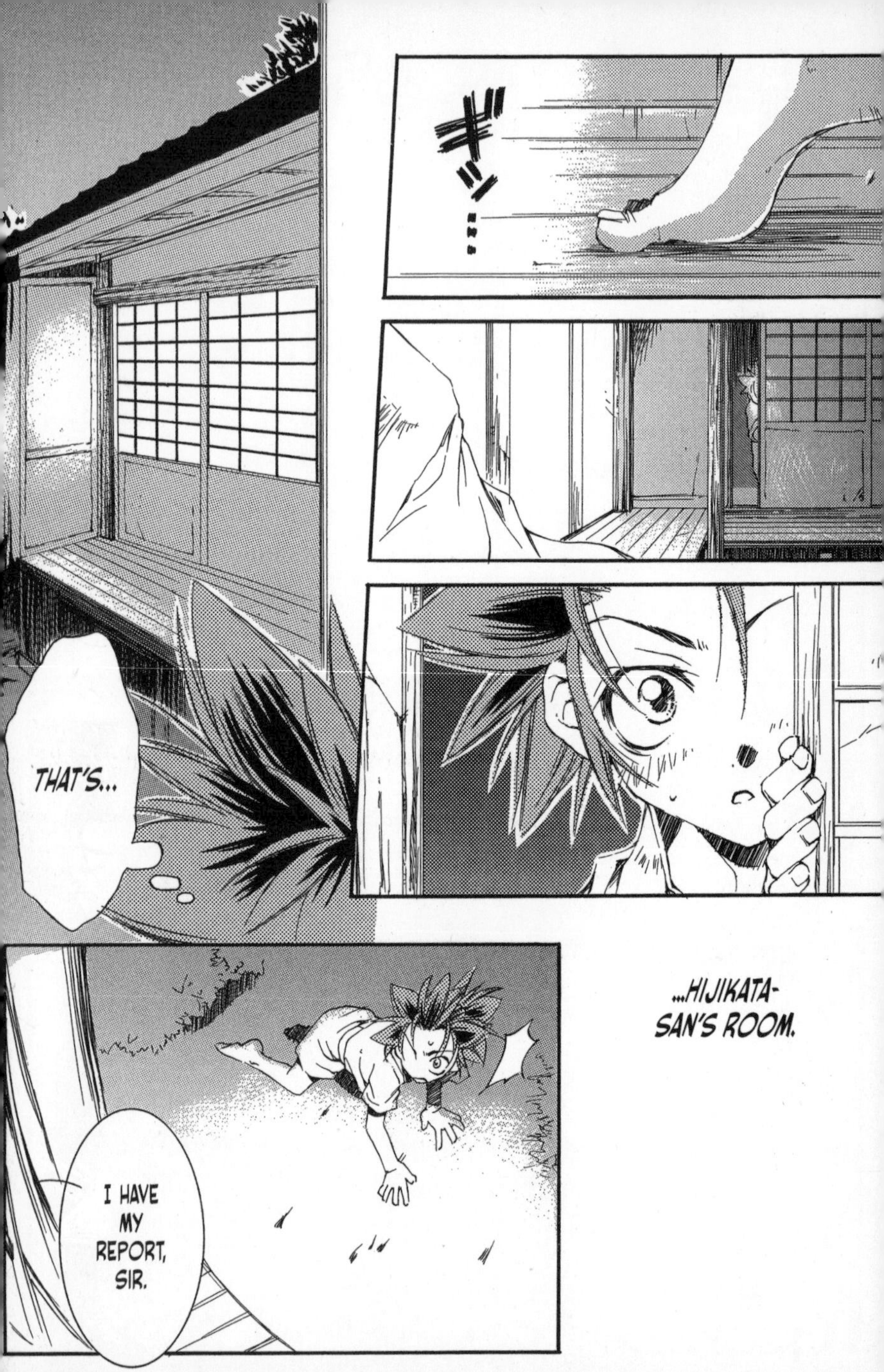
ギシ…
THAT'S...
...HIJIKATA-SAN'S ROOM.
I HAVE MY REPORT, SIR.

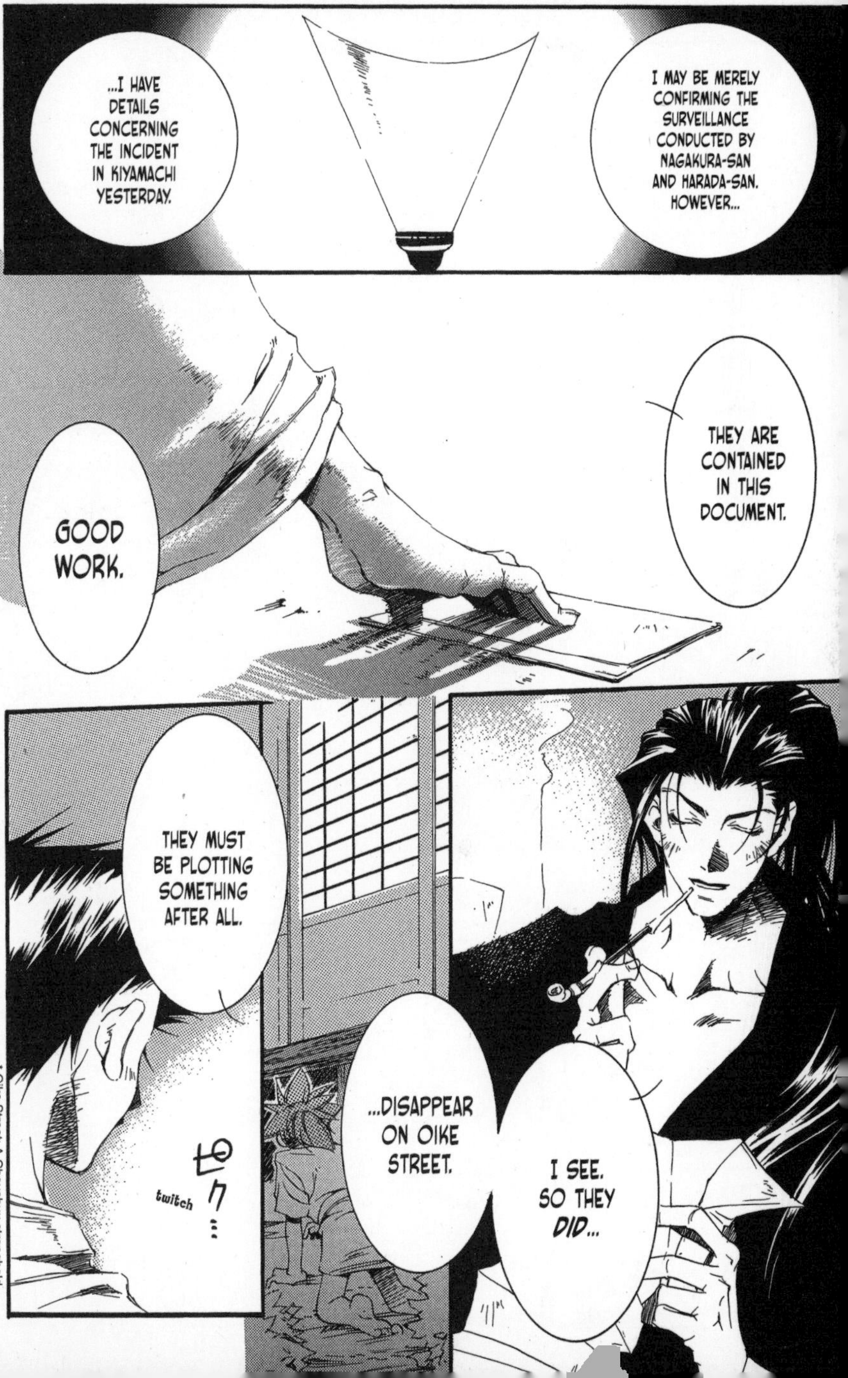
I MAY BE MERELY CONFIRMING THE SURVEILLANCE CONDUCTED BY NAGAKURA-SAN AND HARADA-SAN. HOWEVER...
...I HAVE DETAILS CONCERNING THE INCIDENT IN KIYAMACHI YESTERDAY.
THEY ARE CONTAINED IN THIS DOCUMENT.
GOOD WORK.
...DISAPPEAR ON OIKE STREET.
I SEE. SO THEY *DID*...
THEY MUST BE PLOTTING SOMETHING AFTER ALL.
ピク…
twitch

* Oike Street: A Choushu stronghold.

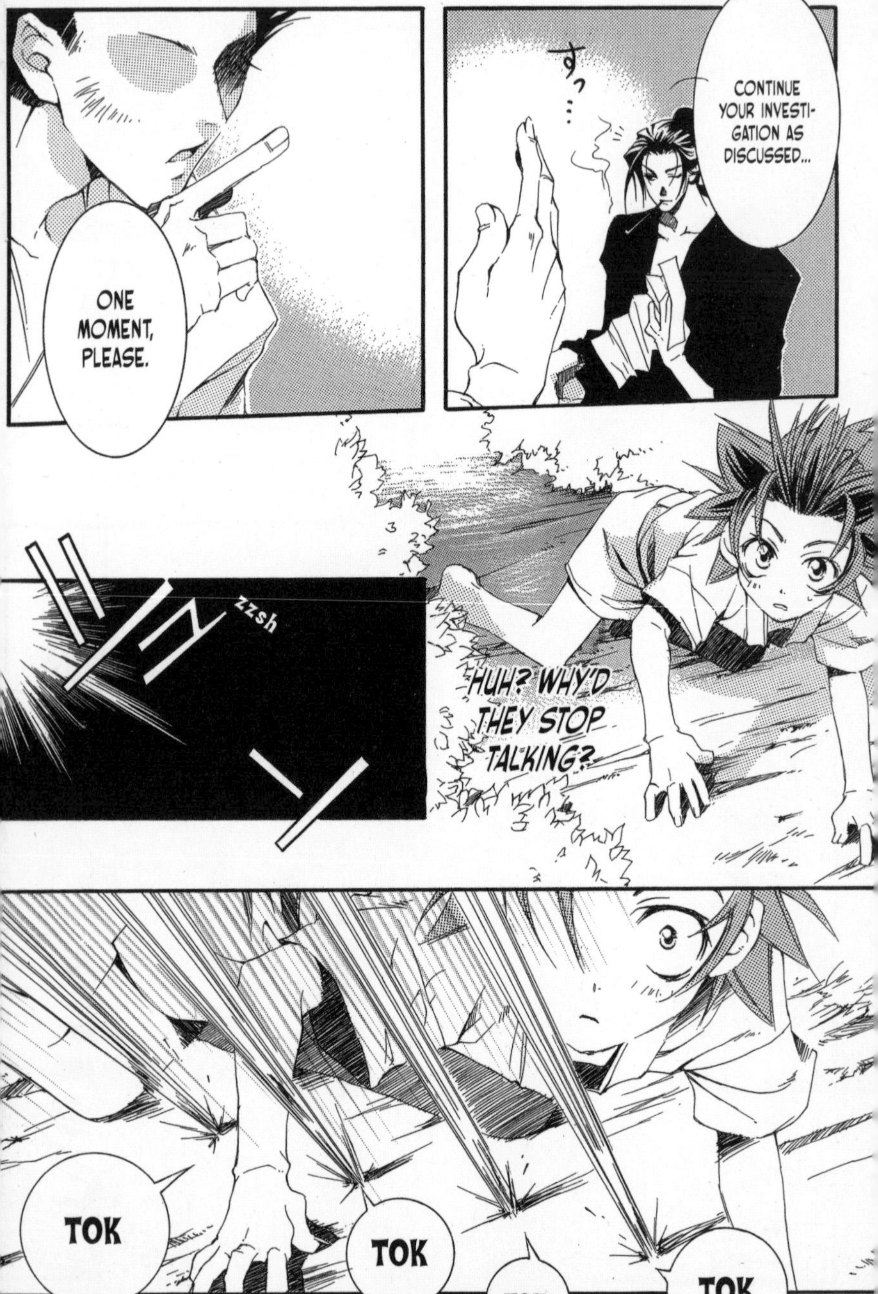
すっ…
CONTINUE YOUR INVESTI-GATION AS DISCUSSED...
ONE MOMENT, PLEASE.
HUH? WHY'D THEY STOP TALKING?
zzsh
TOK
TOK
TOK
TOK

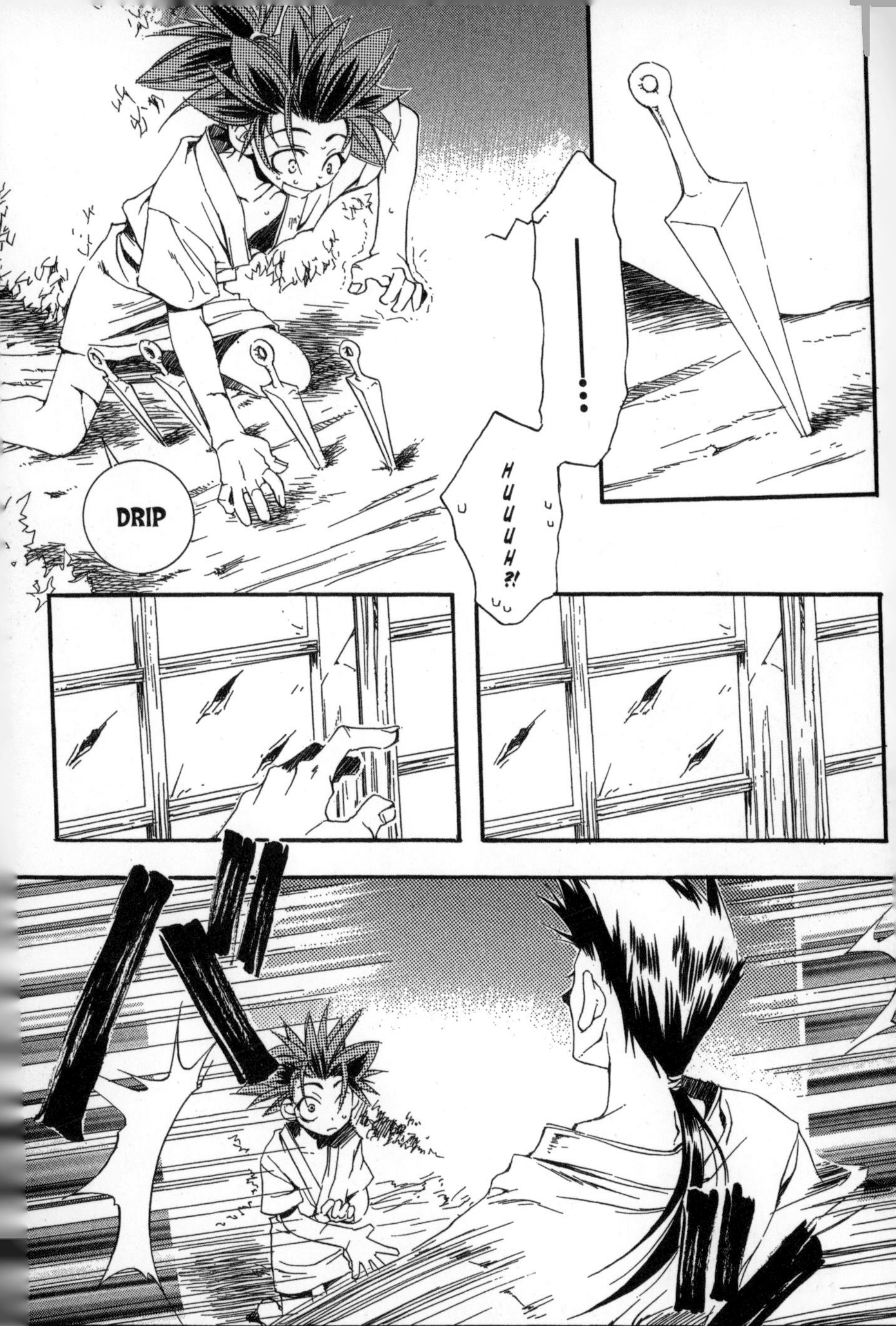
—...
HUUUH?!
DRIP

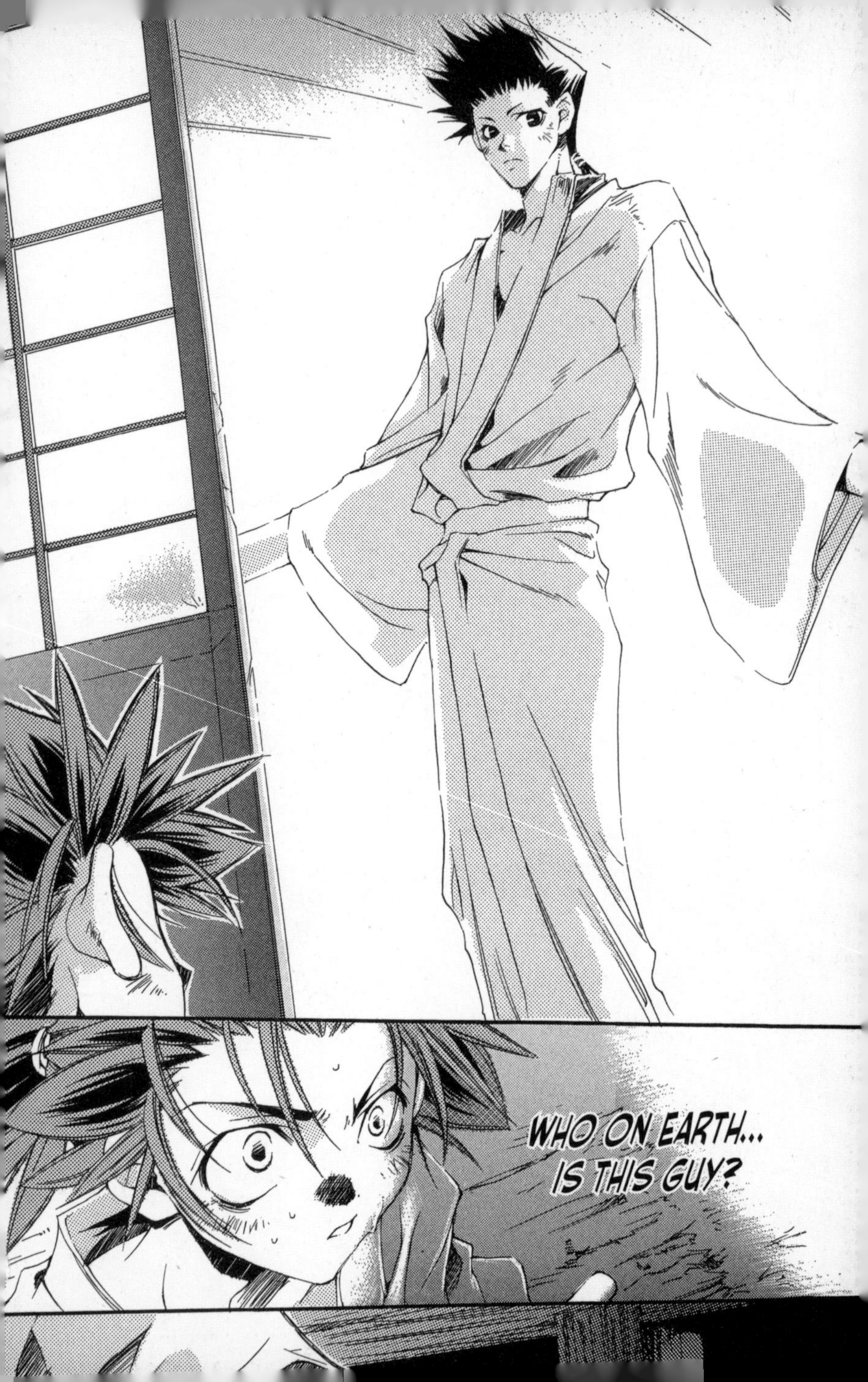
WHO ON EARTH... IS THIS GUY?

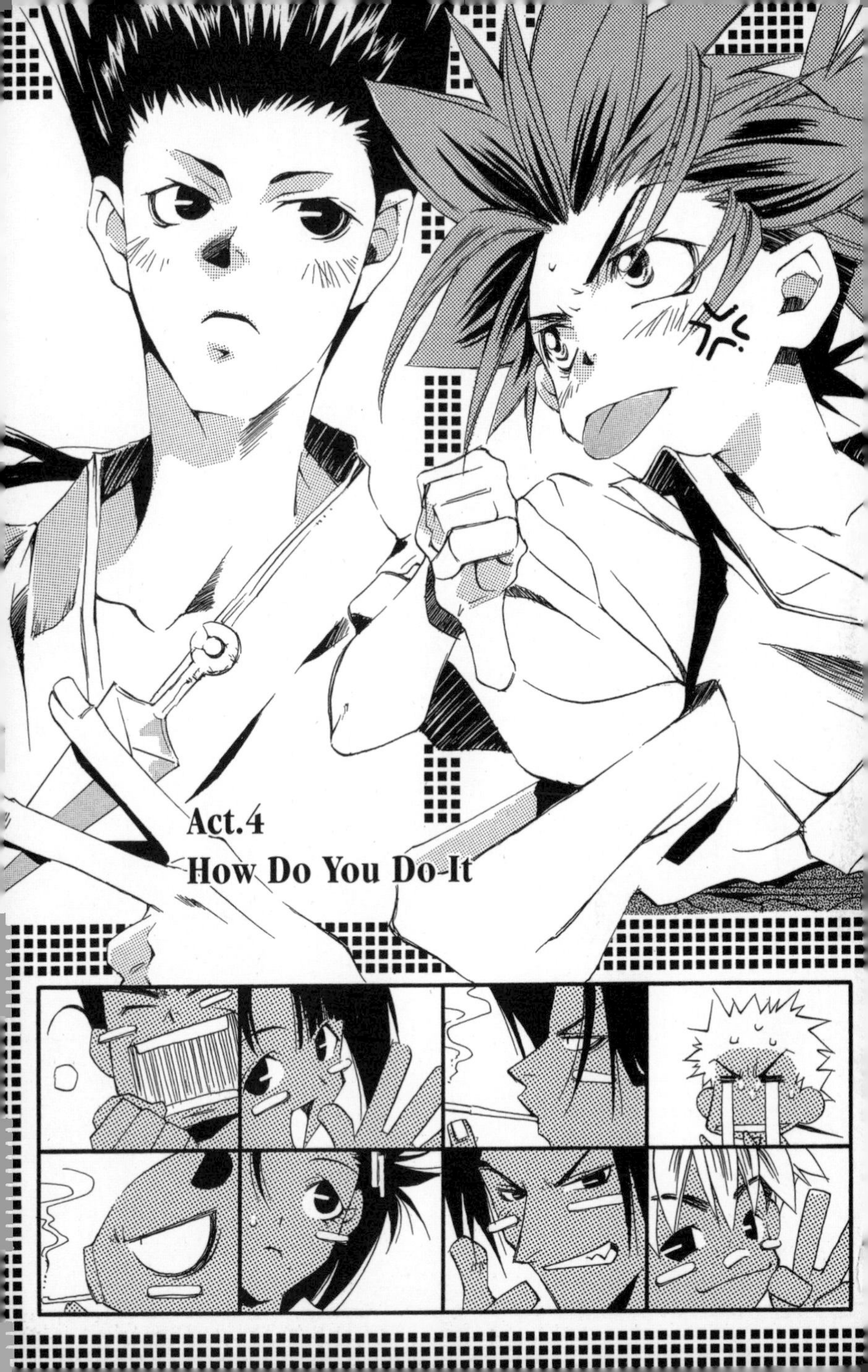
Act.4
How Do You Do-It

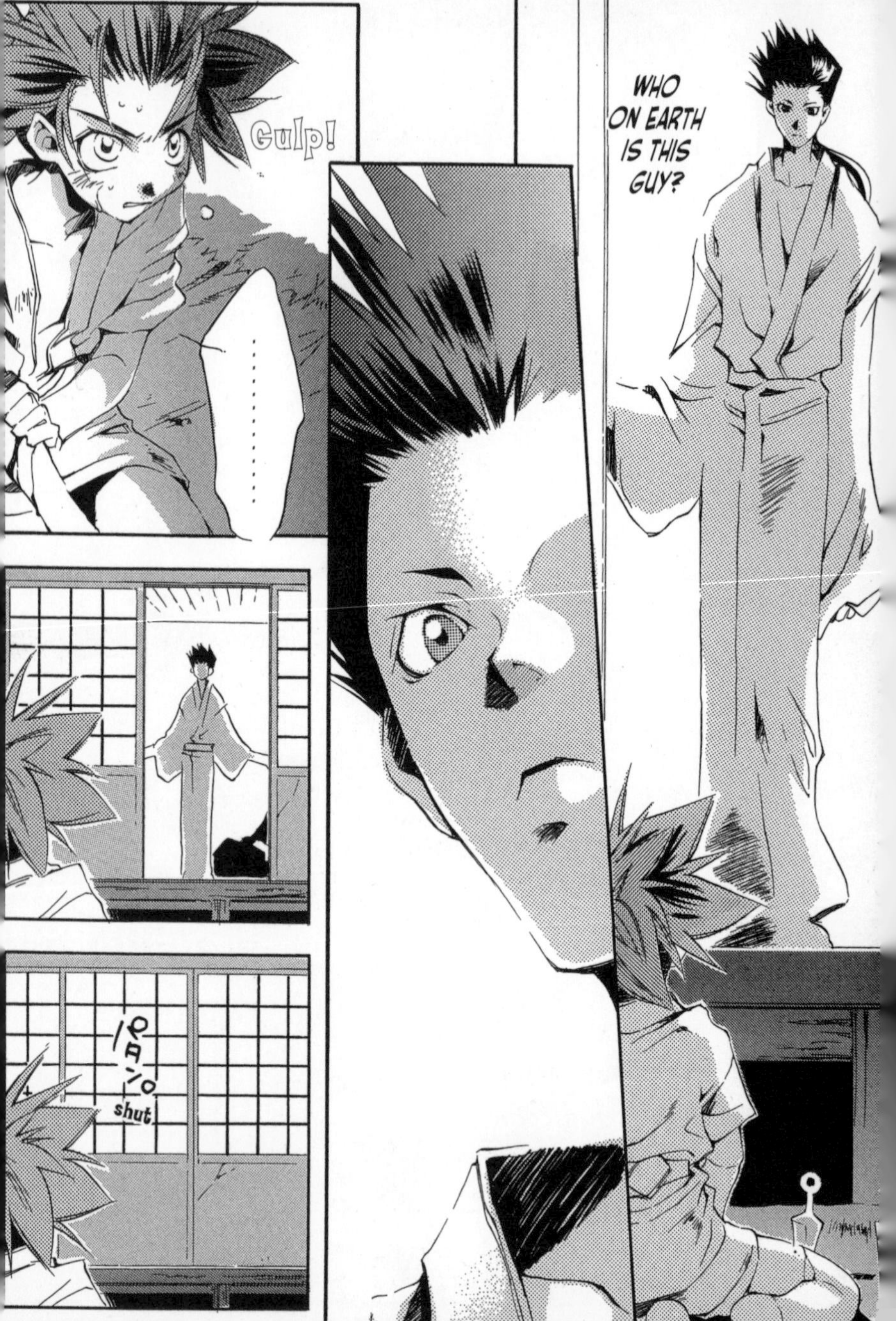
WHO ON EARTH IS THIS GUY?
Gulp!
パタン
shut

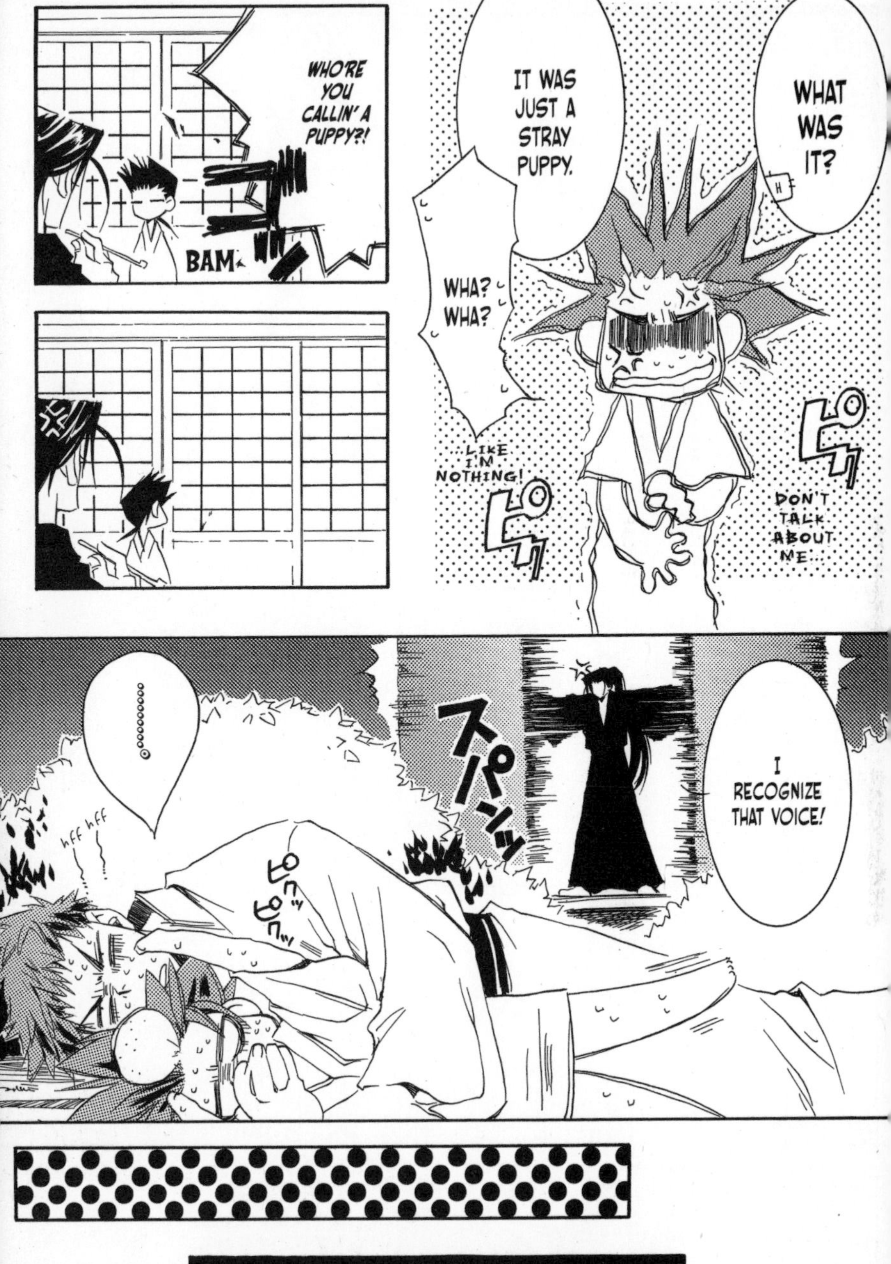
WHAT WAS IT?
IT WAS JUST A STRAY PUPPY.
WHA? WHA?
LIKE I'M NOTHING!
DON'T TALK ABOUT ME...
WHO'RE YOU CALLIN' A PUPPY?!
BAM
I RECOGNIZE THAT VOICE!
スパーンッ
..........!
hff hff

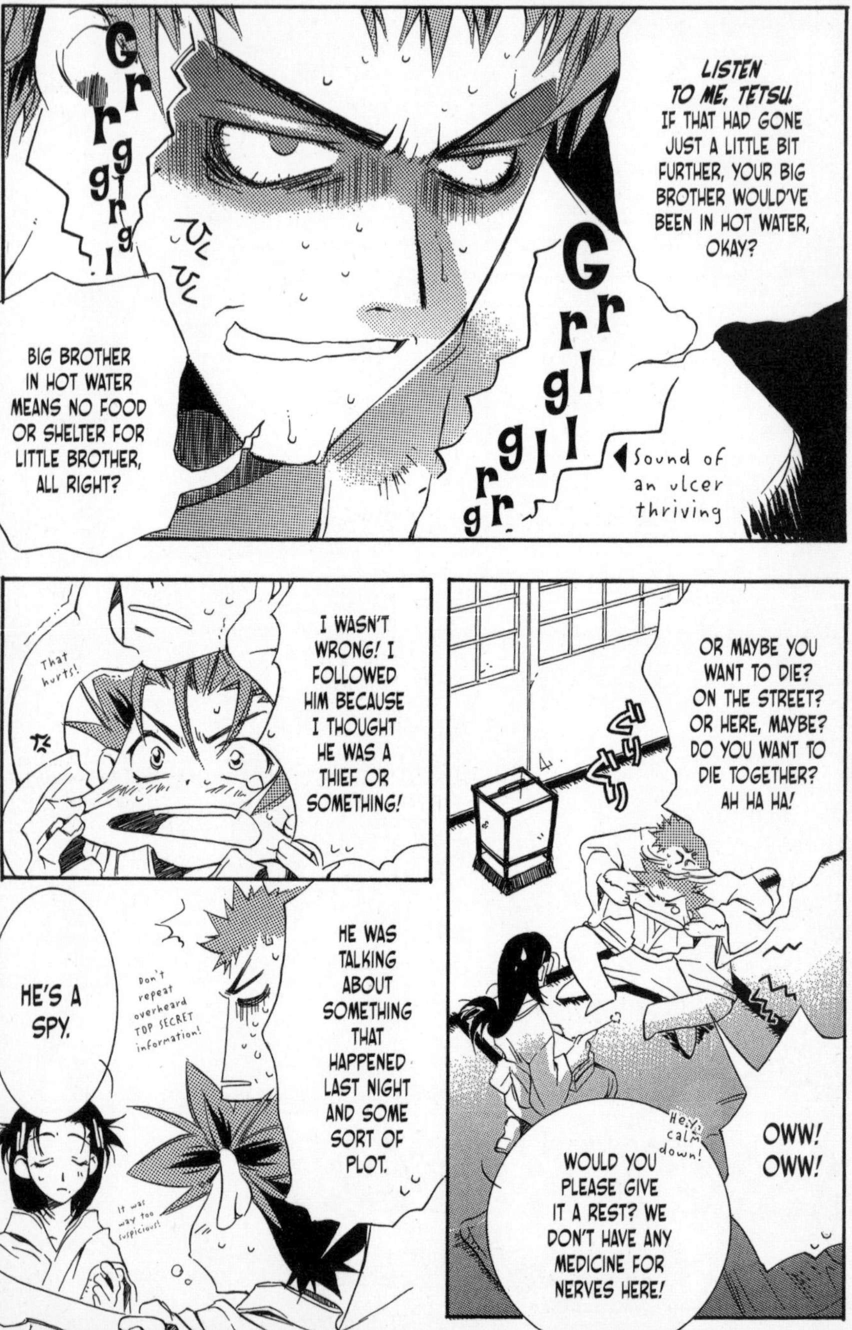
LISTEN TO ME, TETSU. IF THAT HAD GONE JUST A LITTLE BIT FURTHER, YOUR BIG BROTHER WOULD'VE BEEN IN HOT WATER, OKAY?
Grrglll
Grrrgglll
BIG BROTHER IN HOT WATER MEANS NO FOOD OR SHELTER FOR LITTLE BROTHER, ALL RIGHT?
Sound of an ulcer thriving
OR MAYBE YOU WANT TO DIE? ON THE STREET? OR HERE, MAYBE? DO YOU WANT TO DIE TOGETHER? AH HA HA!
OWW! OWW!
Hey, calm down!
WOULD YOU PLEASE GIVE IT A REST? WE DON'T HAVE ANY MEDICINE FOR NERVES HERE!
I WASN'T WRONG! I FOLLOWED HIM BECAUSE I THOUGHT HE WAS A THIEF OR SOMETHING!
That hurts!
HE WAS TALKING ABOUT SOMETHING THAT HAPPENED LAST NIGHT AND SOME SORT OF PLOT.
Don't repeat overheard TOP SECRET information!
HE'S A SPY.
It was way too suspicious!

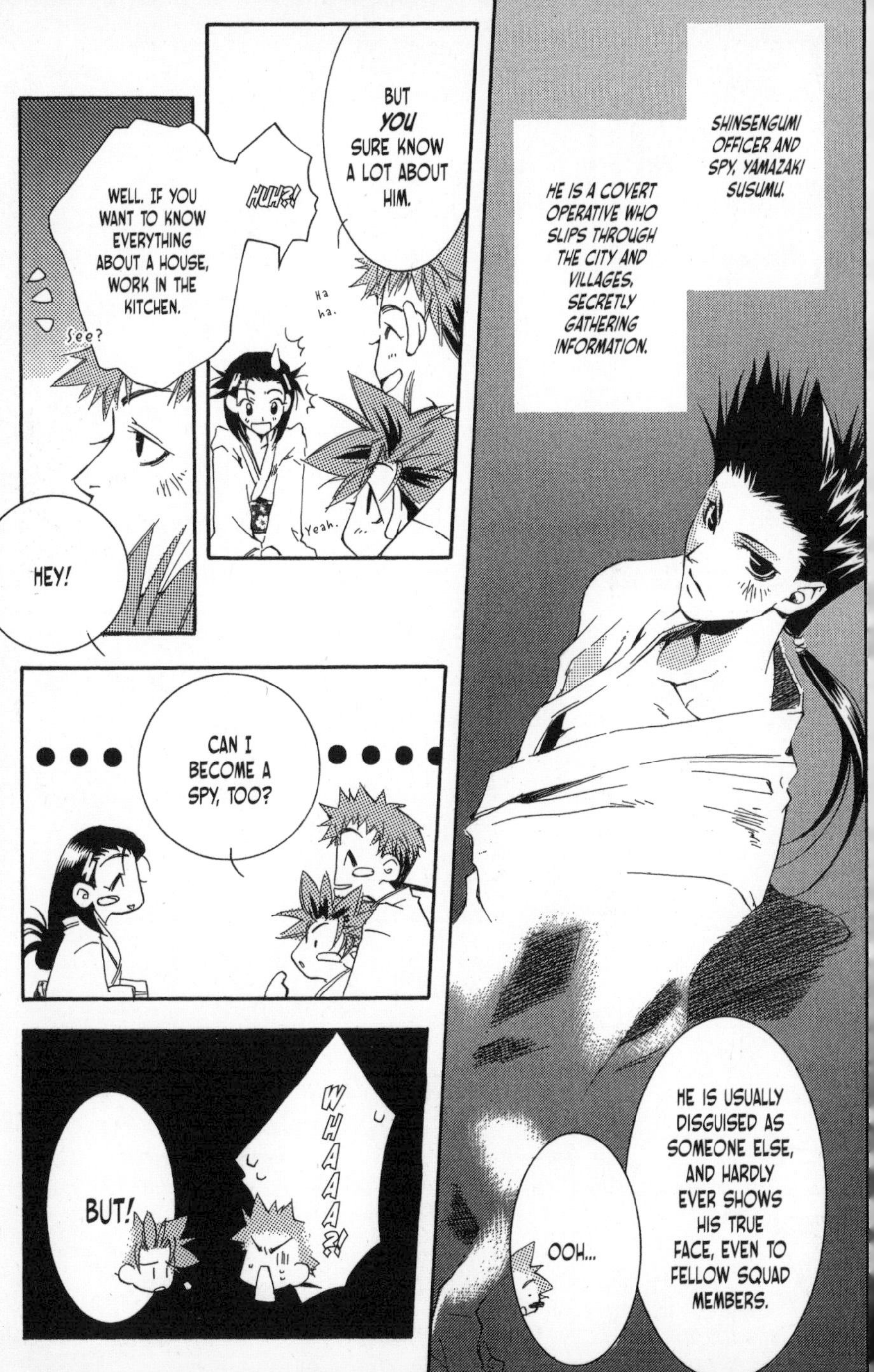

SHINSENGUMI OFFICER AND SPY, YAMAZAKI SUSUMU.
HE IS A COVERT OPERATIVE WHO SLIPS THROUGH THE CITY AND VILLAGES, SECRETLY GATHERING INFORMATION.
HE IS USUALLY DISGUISED AS SOMEONE ELSE, AND HARDLY EVER SHOWS HIS TRUE FACE, EVEN TO FELLOW SQUAD MEMBERS.
OOH...
BUT YOU SURE KNOW A LOT ABOUT HIM.
HUH?!
Ha ha.
Yeah.
WELL. IF YOU WANT TO KNOW EVERYTHING ABOUT A HOUSE, WORK IN THE KITCHEN.
See?
HEY!
•••
CAN I BECOME A SPY, TOO?
••••
WHAAAA?!
BUT!

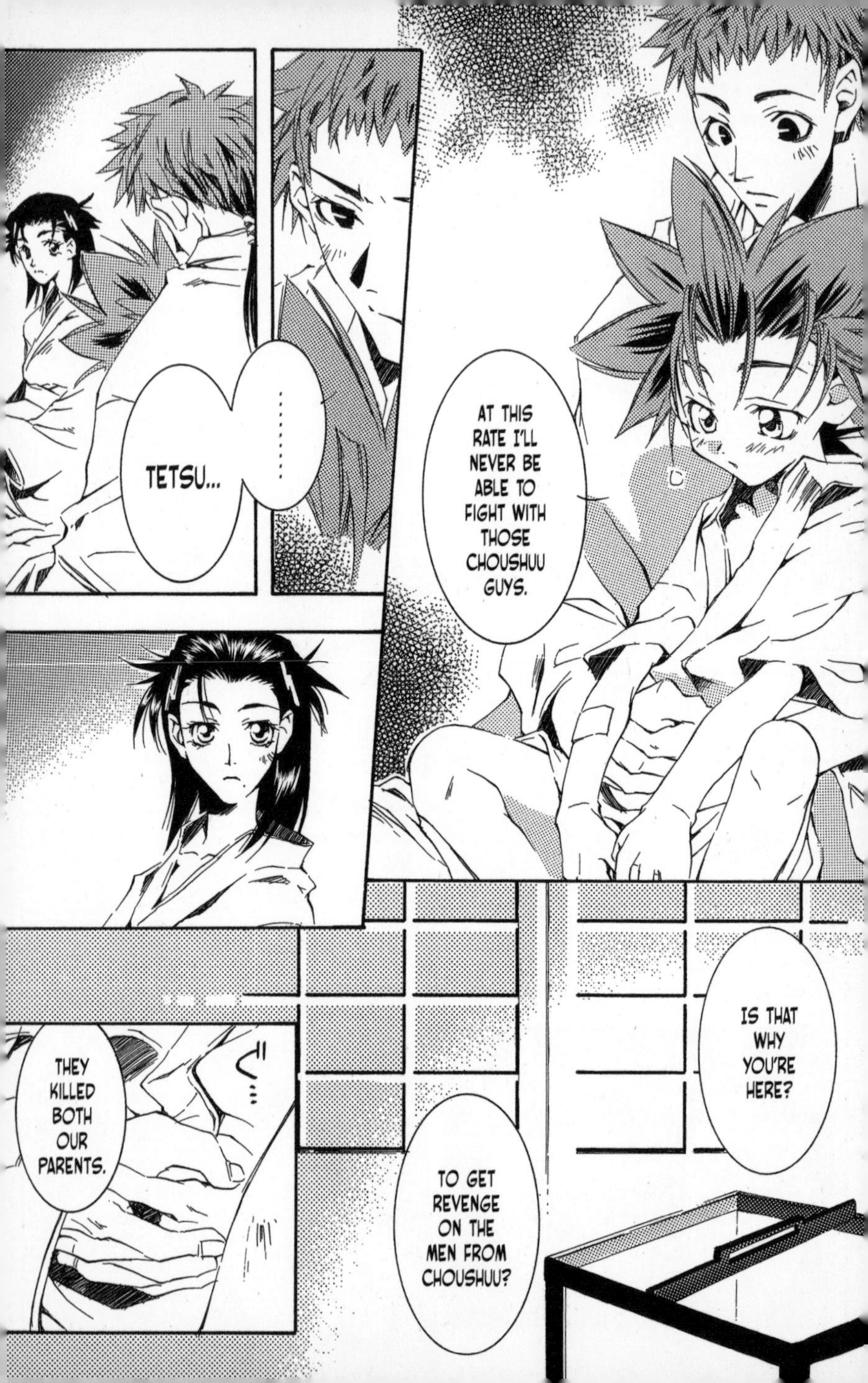

AT THIS RATE I'LL NEVER BE ABLE TO FIGHT WITH THOSE CHOUSHUU GUYS.
......
TETSU...
IS THAT WHY YOU'RE HERE?
TO GET REVENGE ON THE MEN FROM CHOUSHUU?
THEY KILLED BOTH OUR PARENTS.

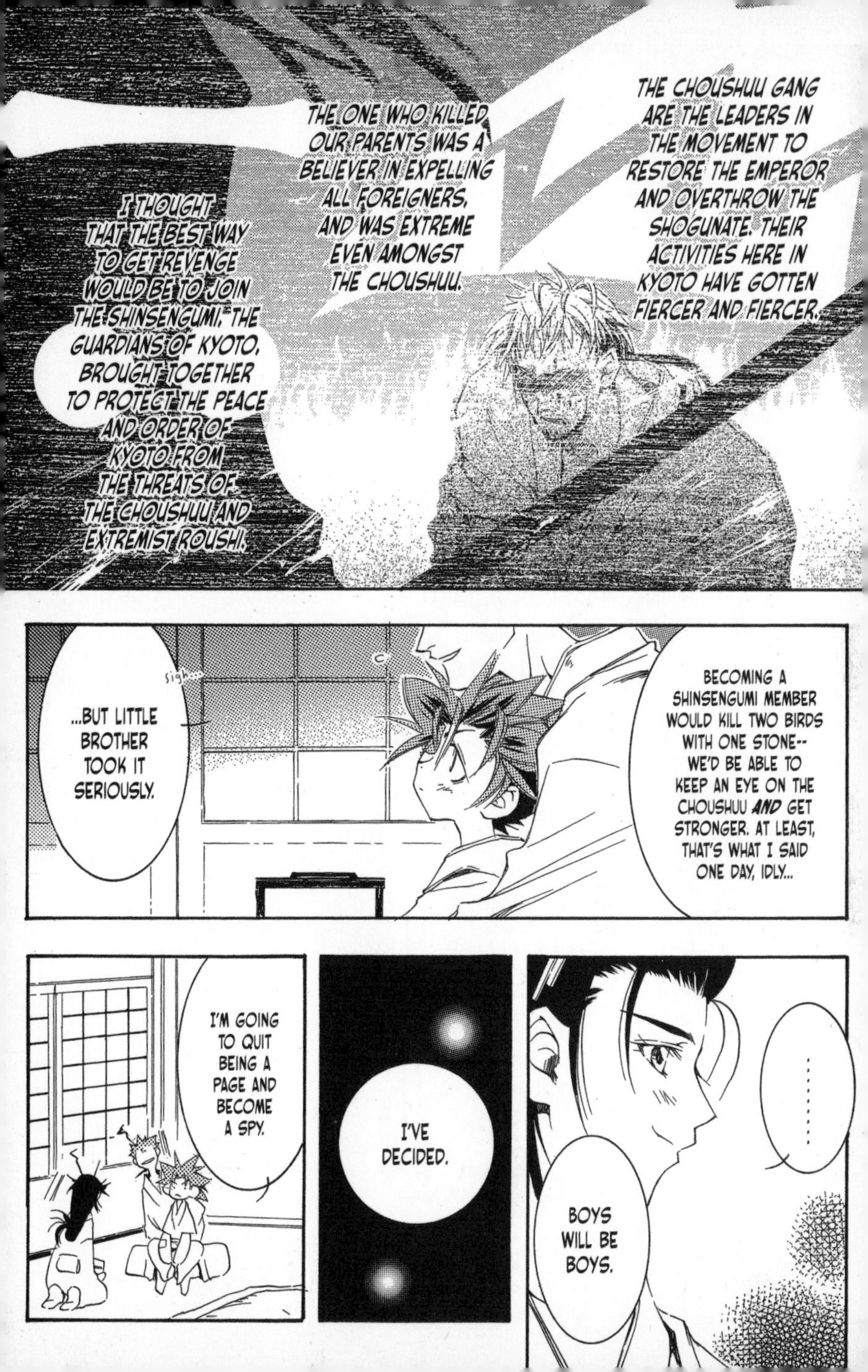
THE CHOUSHUU GANG ARE THE LEADERS IN THE MOVEMENT TO RESTORE THE EMPEROR AND OVERTHROW THE SHOGUNATE. THEIR ACTIVITIES HERE IN KYOTO HAVE GOTTEN FIERCER AND FIERCER.
THE ONE WHO KILLED OUR PARENTS WAS A BELIEVER IN EXPELLING ALL FOREIGNERS, AND WAS EXTREME EVEN AMONGST THE CHOUSHUU.
I THOUGHT THAT THE BEST WAY TO GET REVENGE WOULD BE TO JOIN THE SHINSENGUMI, THE GUARDIANS OF KYOTO, BROUGHT TOGETHER TO PROTECT THE PEACE AND ORDER OF KYOTO FROM THE THREATS OF THE CHOUSHUU AND EXTREMIST ROUSHI.
BECOMING A SHINSENGUMI MEMBER WOULD KILL TWO BIRDS WITH ONE STONE-- WE'D BE ABLE TO KEEP AN EYE ON THE CHOUSHUU AND GET STRONGER. AT LEAST, THAT'S WHAT I SAID ONE DAY, IDLY...
sigh...
...BUT LITTLE BROTHER TOOK IT SERIOUSLY.
......
BOYS WILL BE BOYS.
I'VE DECIDED.
I'M GOING TO QUIT BEING A PAGE AND BECOME A SPY.

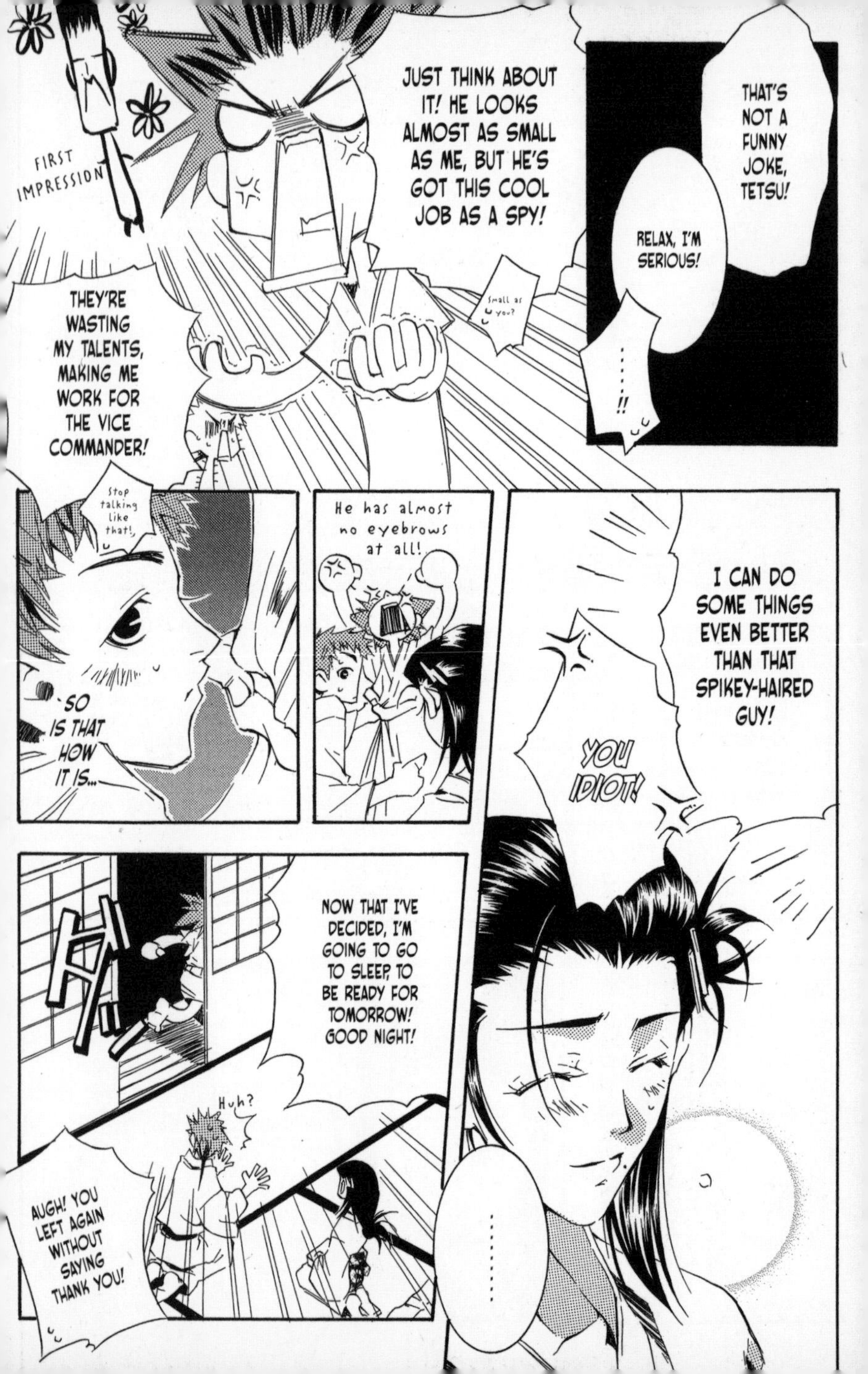
FIRST IMPRESSION
JUST THINK ABOUT IT! HE LOOKS ALMOST AS SMALL AS ME, BUT HE'S GOT THIS COOL JOB AS A SPY!
THEY'RE WASTING MY TALENTS, MAKING ME WORK FOR THE VICE COMMANDER!
Small as you?
THAT'S NOT A FUNNY JOKE, TETSU!
RELAX, I'M SERIOUS!
......!!
I CAN DO SOME THINGS EVEN BETTER THAN THAT SPIKEY-HAIRED GUY!
YOU IDIOT!
......
He has almost no eyebrows at all!
Stop talking like that!
SO IS THAT HOW IT IS...
NOW THAT I'VE DECIDED, I'M GOING TO GO TO SLEEP, TO BE READY FOR TOMORROW! GOOD NIGHT!
Huh?
AUGH! YOU LEFT AGAIN WITHOUT SAYING THANK YOU!

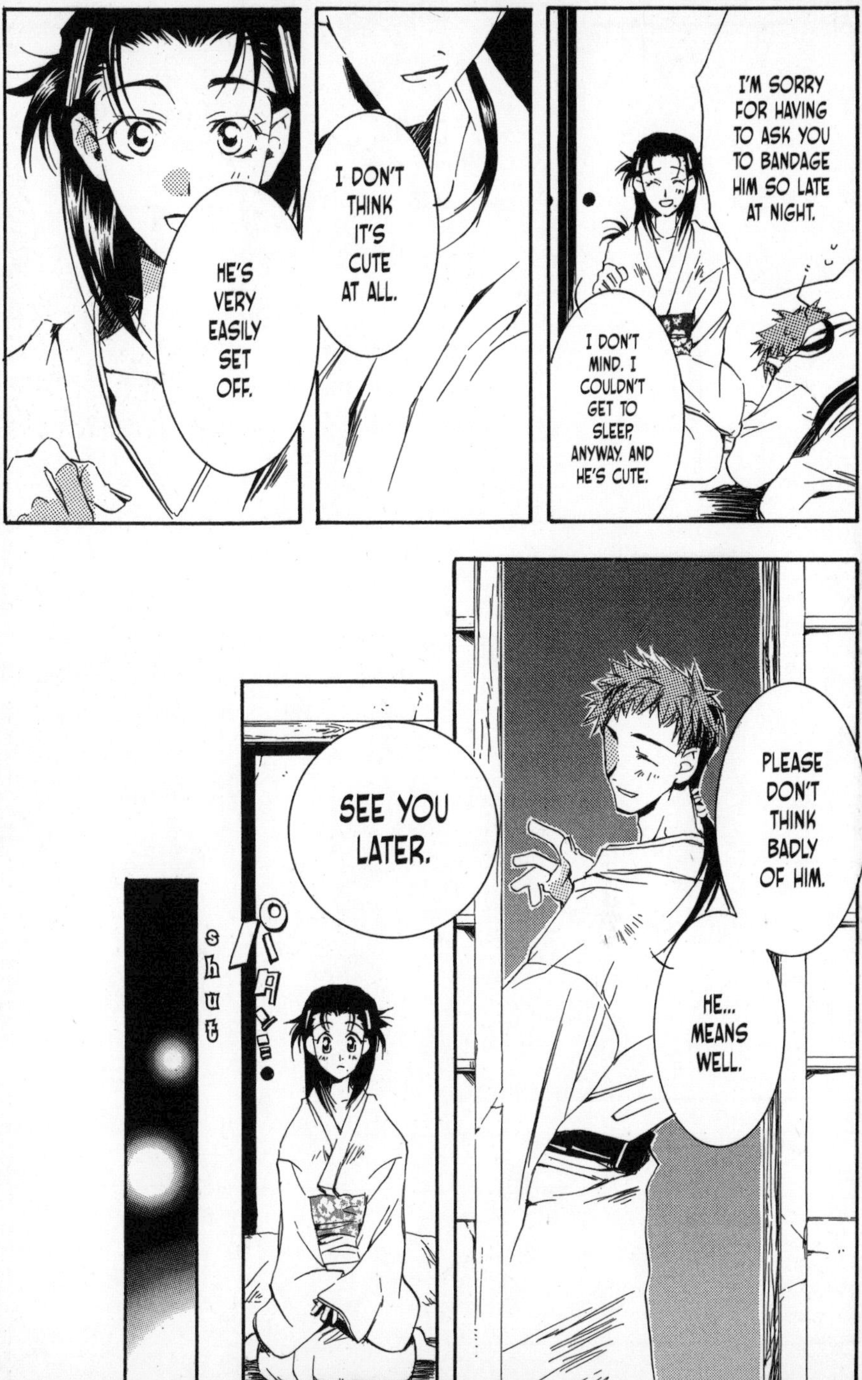
I'M SORRY FOR HAVING TO ASK YOU TO BANDAGE HIM SO LATE AT NIGHT.
I DON'T MIND. I COULDN'T GET TO SLEEP, ANYWAY. AND HE'S CUTE.
I DON'T THINK IT'S CUTE AT ALL.
HE'S VERY EASILY SET OFF.
PLEASE DON'T THINK BADLY OF HIM.
HE... MEANS WELL.
SEE YOU LATER.
shut

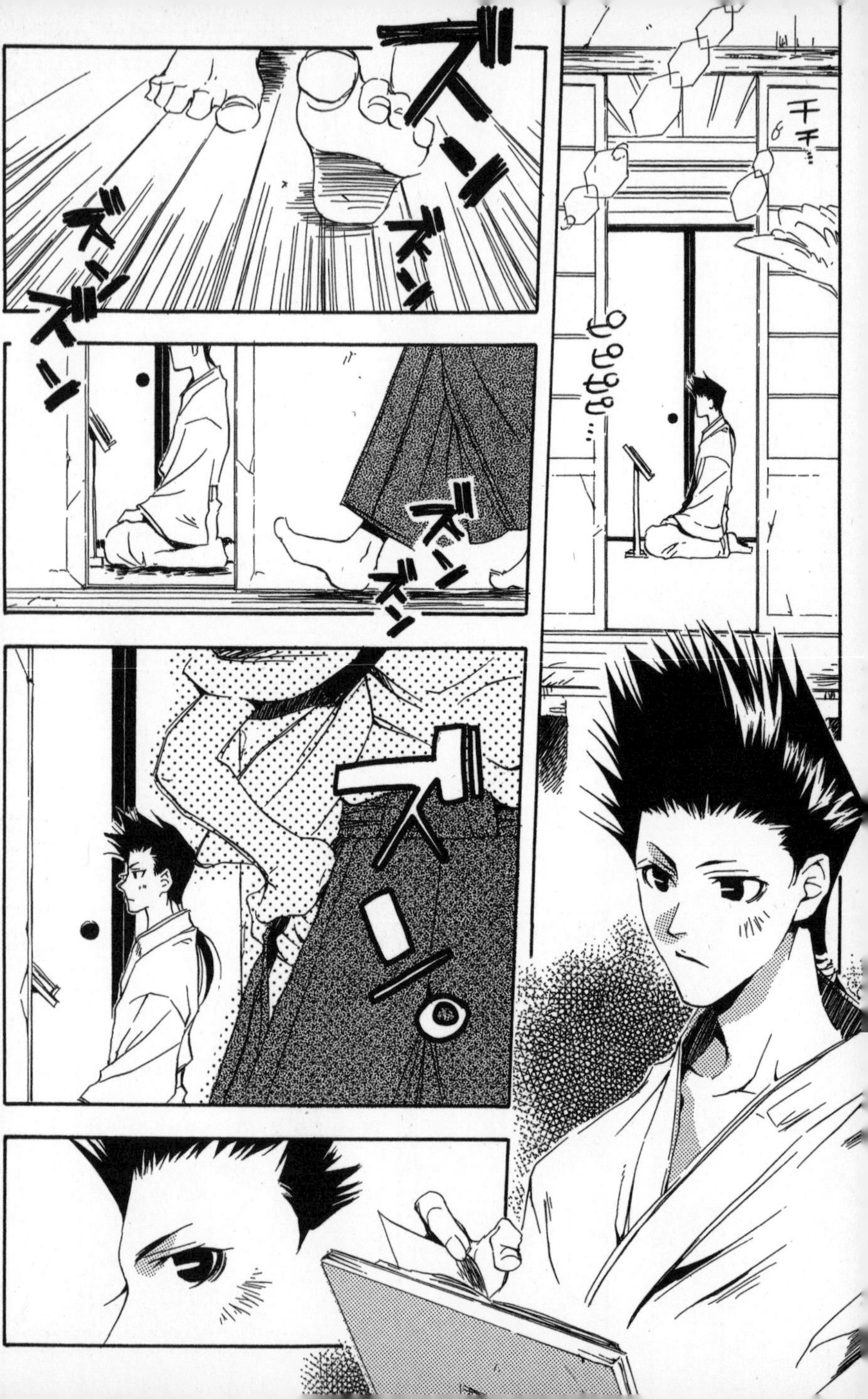
チチ…
ズシーン
ズシン
ズシン
ズシン
ズシン
ズシン
ズーン。

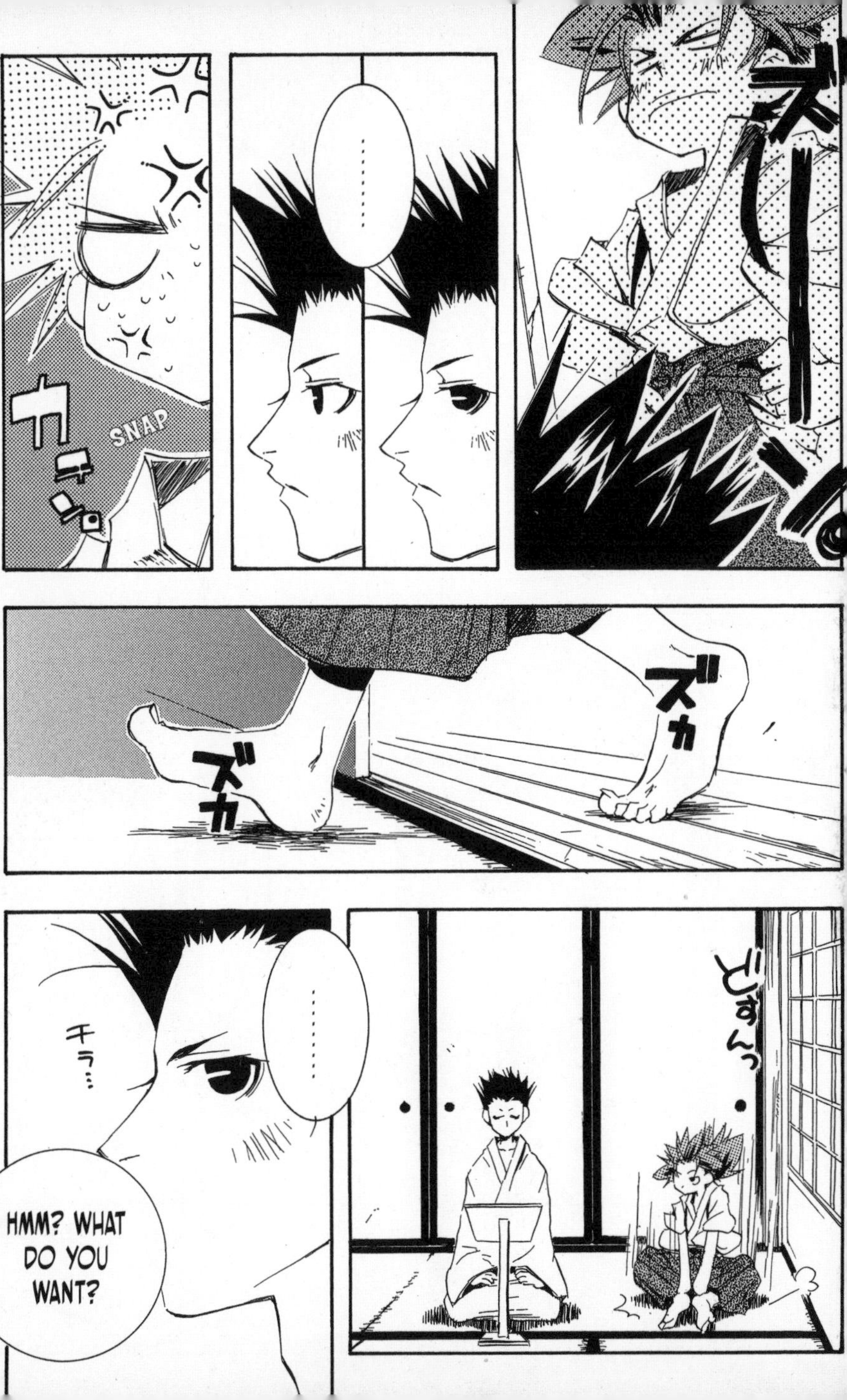
……
SNAP
ズカ
ズカ
どすんっ
……
キラ…
HMM? WHAT DO YOU WANT?

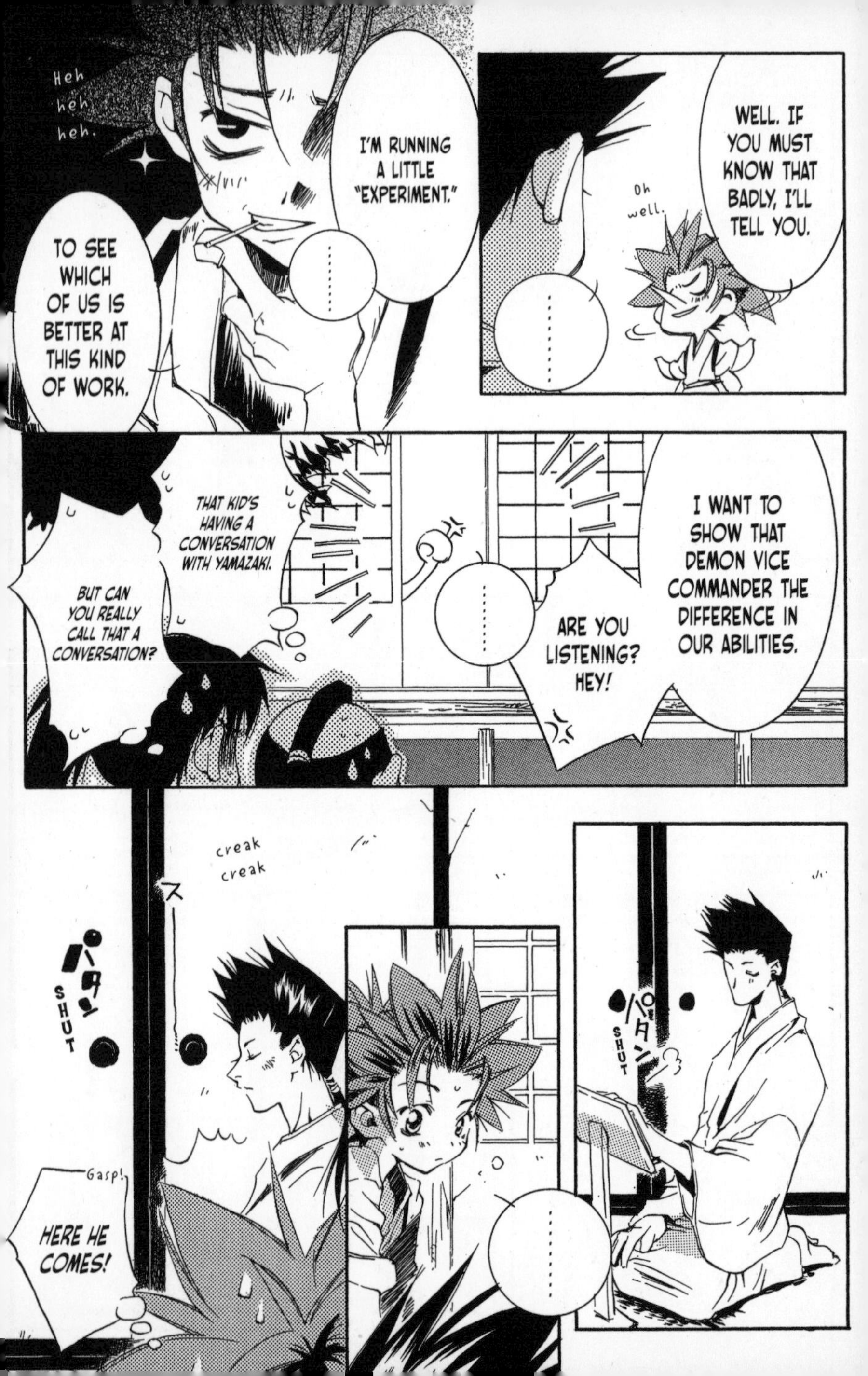

WELL. IF YOU MUST KNOW THAT BADLY, I'LL TELL YOU.
Oh well.
......
I'M RUNNING A LITTLE "EXPERIMENT."
......
Heh heh heh.
TO SEE WHICH OF US IS BETTER AT THIS KIND OF WORK.
I WANT TO SHOW THAT DEMON VICE COMMANDER THE DIFFERENCE IN OUR ABILITIES.
ARE YOU LISTENING? HEY!
......
THAT KID'S HAVING A CONVERSATION WITH YAMAZAKI.
BUT CAN YOU REALLY CALL THAT A CONVERSATION?
SHUT
......
creak creak
SHUT
Gasp!
HERE HE COMES!

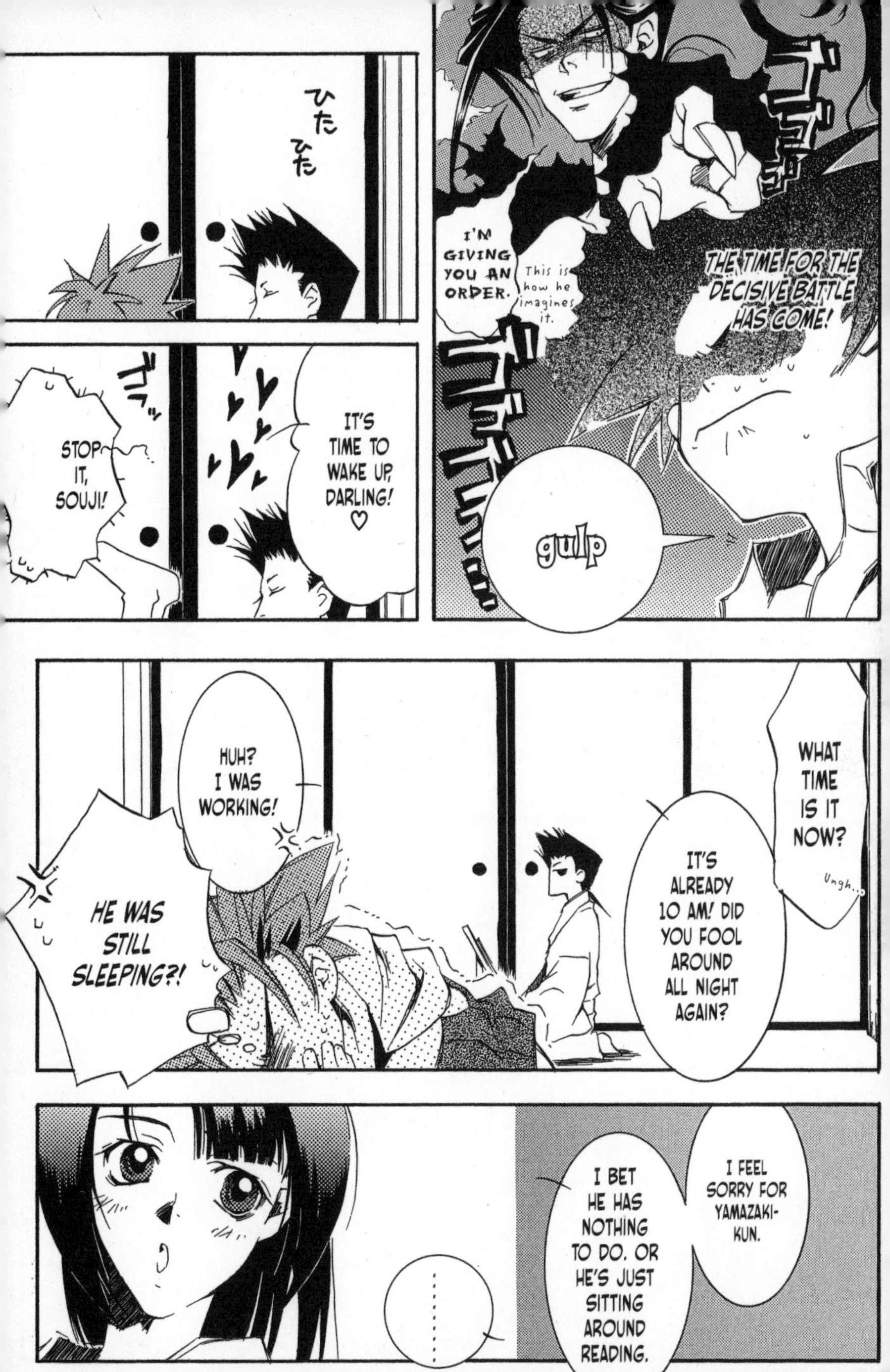
THE TIME FOR THE DECISIVE BATTLE HAS COME!
I'M GIVING YOU AN ORDER.
This is how he imagines it.
gulp
ひたひた
IT'S TIME TO WAKE UP, DARLING! ♡
STOP IT, SOUJI!
WHAT TIME IS IT NOW?
Ungh...
IT'S ALREADY 10 AM! DID YOU FOOL AROUND ALL NIGHT AGAIN?
HUH? I WAS WORKING!
HE WAS STILL SLEEPING?!
I FEEL SORRY FOR YAMAZAKI-KUN.
I BET HE HAS NOTHING TO DO. OR HE'S JUST SITTING AROUND READING.
......

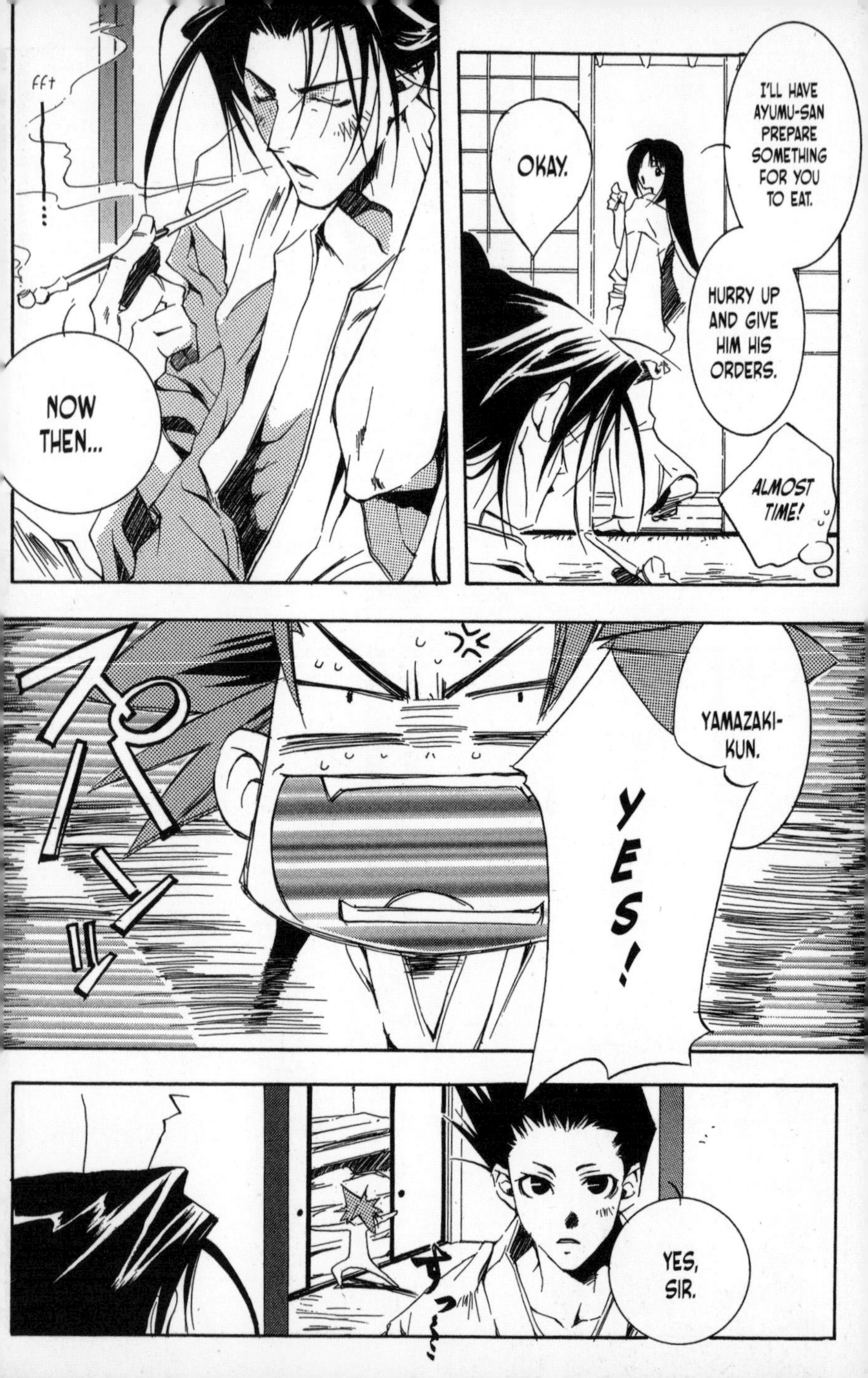
I'LL HAVE AYUMU-SAN PREPARE SOMETHING FOR YOU TO EAT.
OKAY.
HURRY UP AND GIVE HIM HIS ORDERS.
ALMOST TIME!
fft
NOW THEN...
YAMAZAKI-KUN.
YES!
YES, SIR.

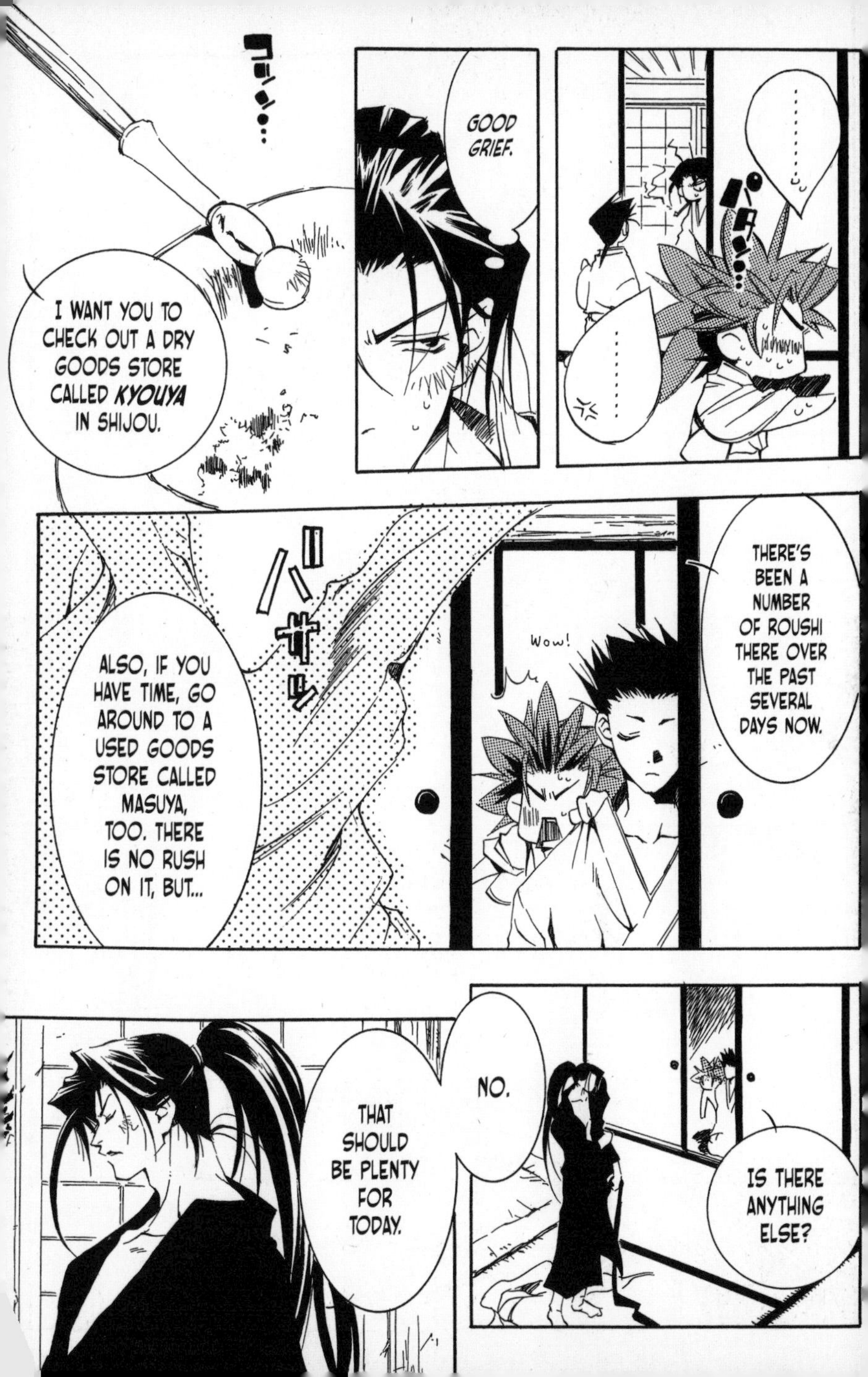
......
......
GOOD GRIEF.
I WANT YOU TO CHECK OUT A DRY GOODS STORE CALLED KYOUYA IN SHIJOU.
THERE'S BEEN A NUMBER OF ROUSHI THERE OVER THE PAST SEVERAL DAYS NOW.
Wow!
ALSO, IF YOU HAVE TIME, GO AROUND TO A USED GOODS STORE CALLED MASUYA, TOO. THERE IS NO RUSH ON IT, BUT...
IS THERE ANYTHING ELSE?
NO.
THAT SHOULD BE PLENTY FOR TODAY.

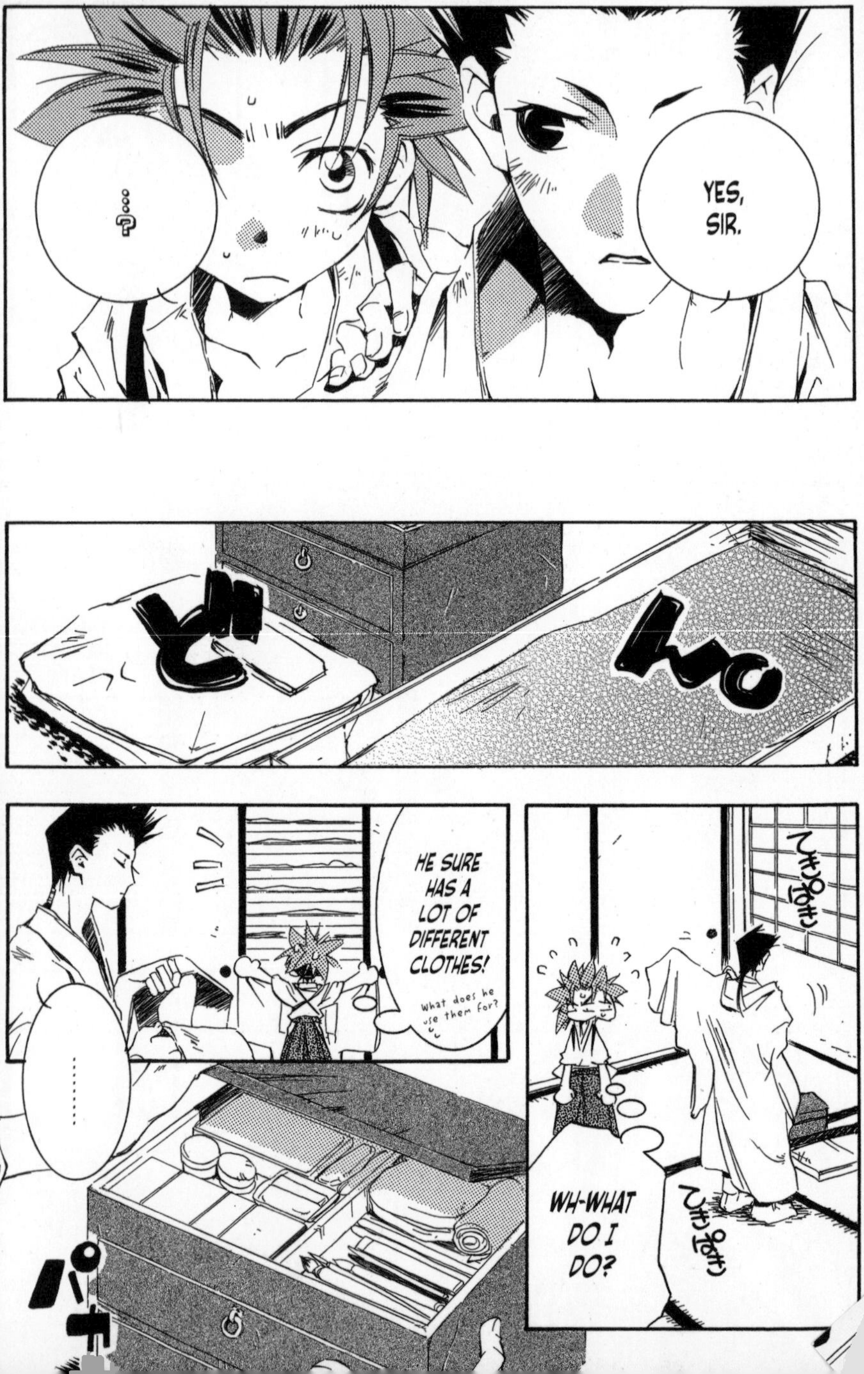
YES, SIR.
?...
てきぱき
てきぱき
WH-WHAT DO I DO?
HE SURE HAS A LOT OF DIFFERENT CLOTHES!
What does he use them for?
......

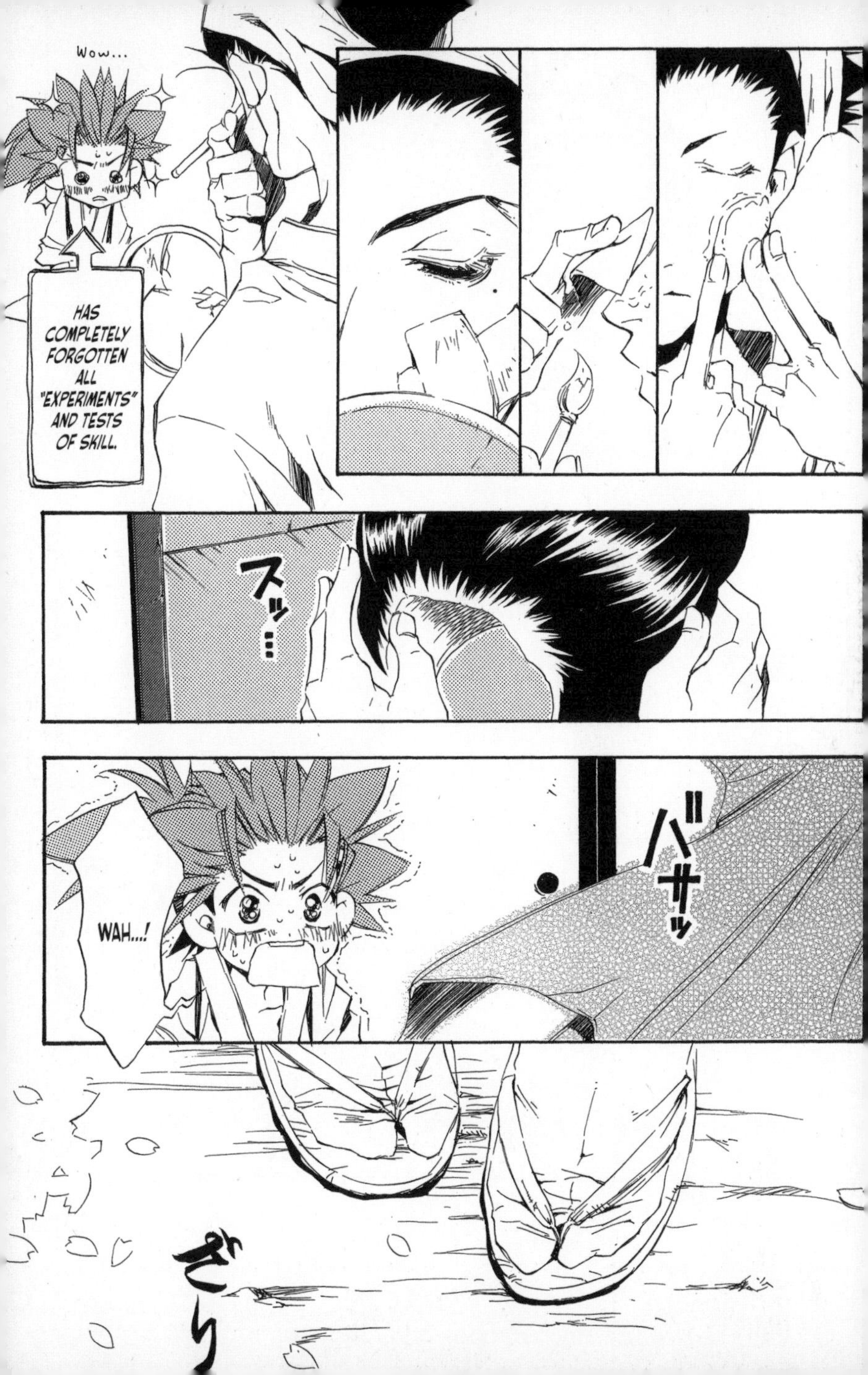
Wow...
HAS COMPLETELY FORGOTTEN ALL "EXPERIMENTS" AND TESTS OF SKILL.
スッ...
バサッ
WAH...!
ざり

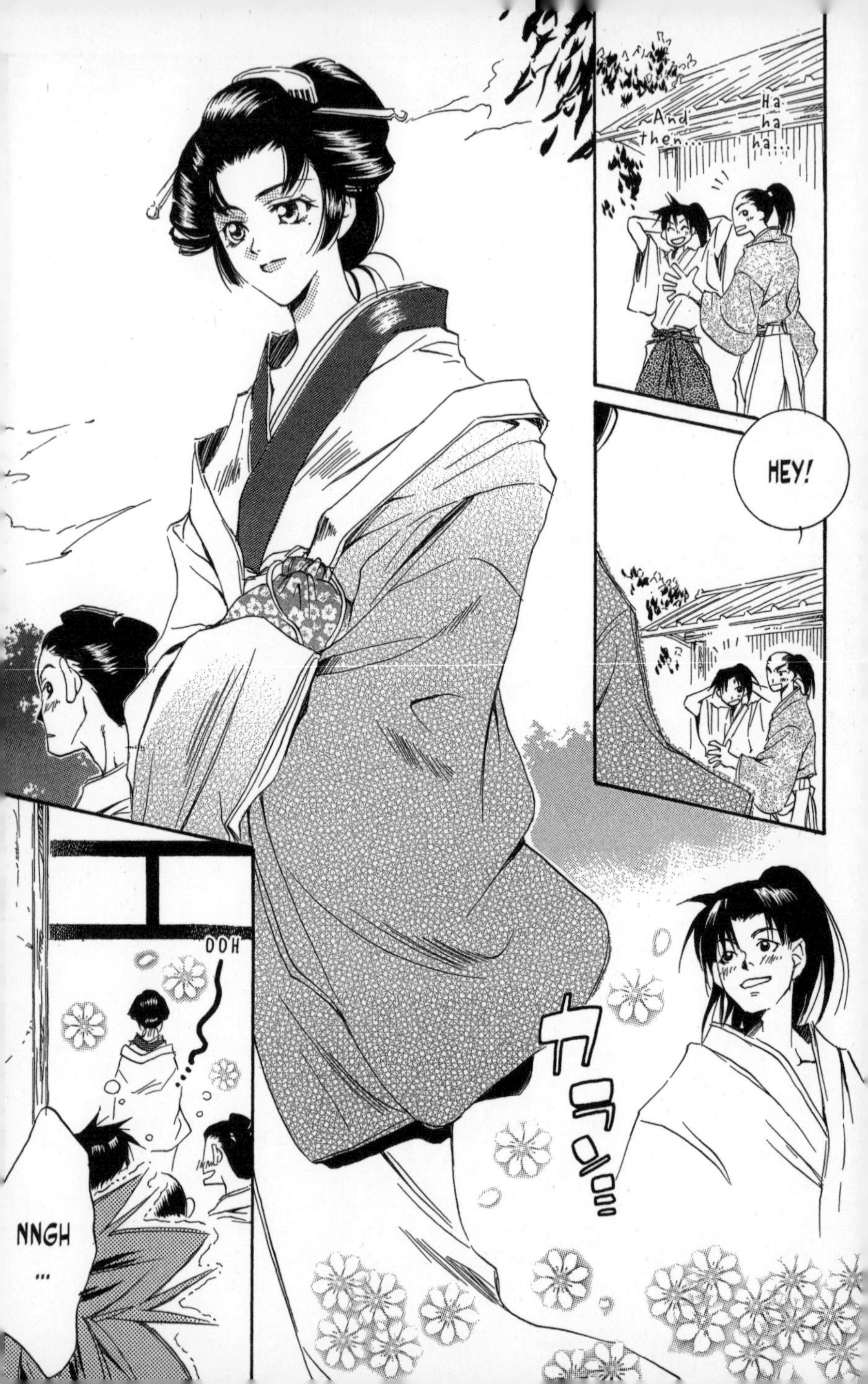
Ha ha ha...
~And then...
HEY!
OOH
NNGH ...

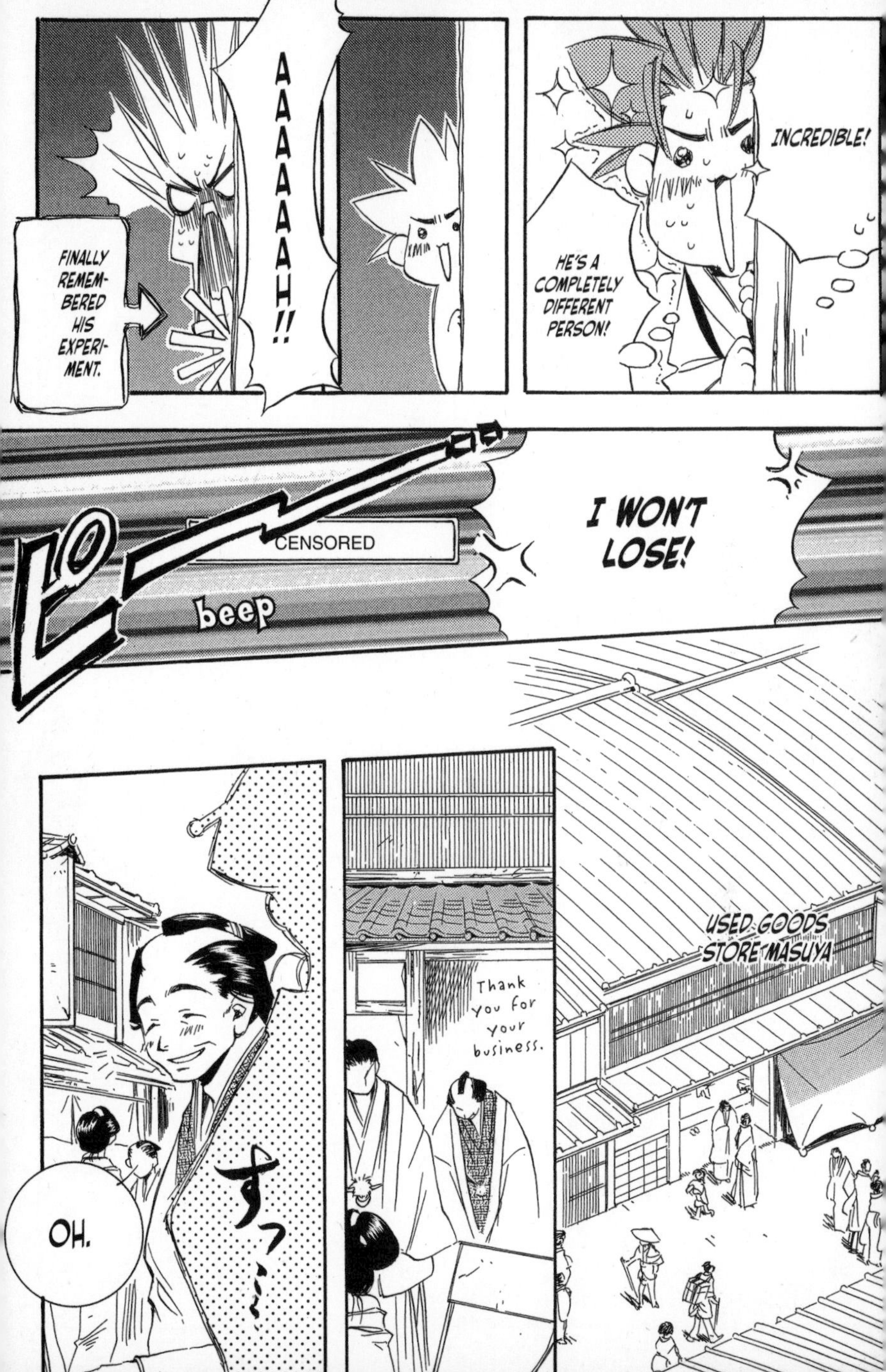
INCREDIBLE!
HE'S A COMPLETELY DIFFERENT PERSON!
AAAAAAAH!!
FINALLY REMEMBERED HIS EXPERIMENT.
I WON'T LOSE!
CENSORED
beep
USED GOODS STORE MASUYA
Thank you for your business.
すっ
OH.

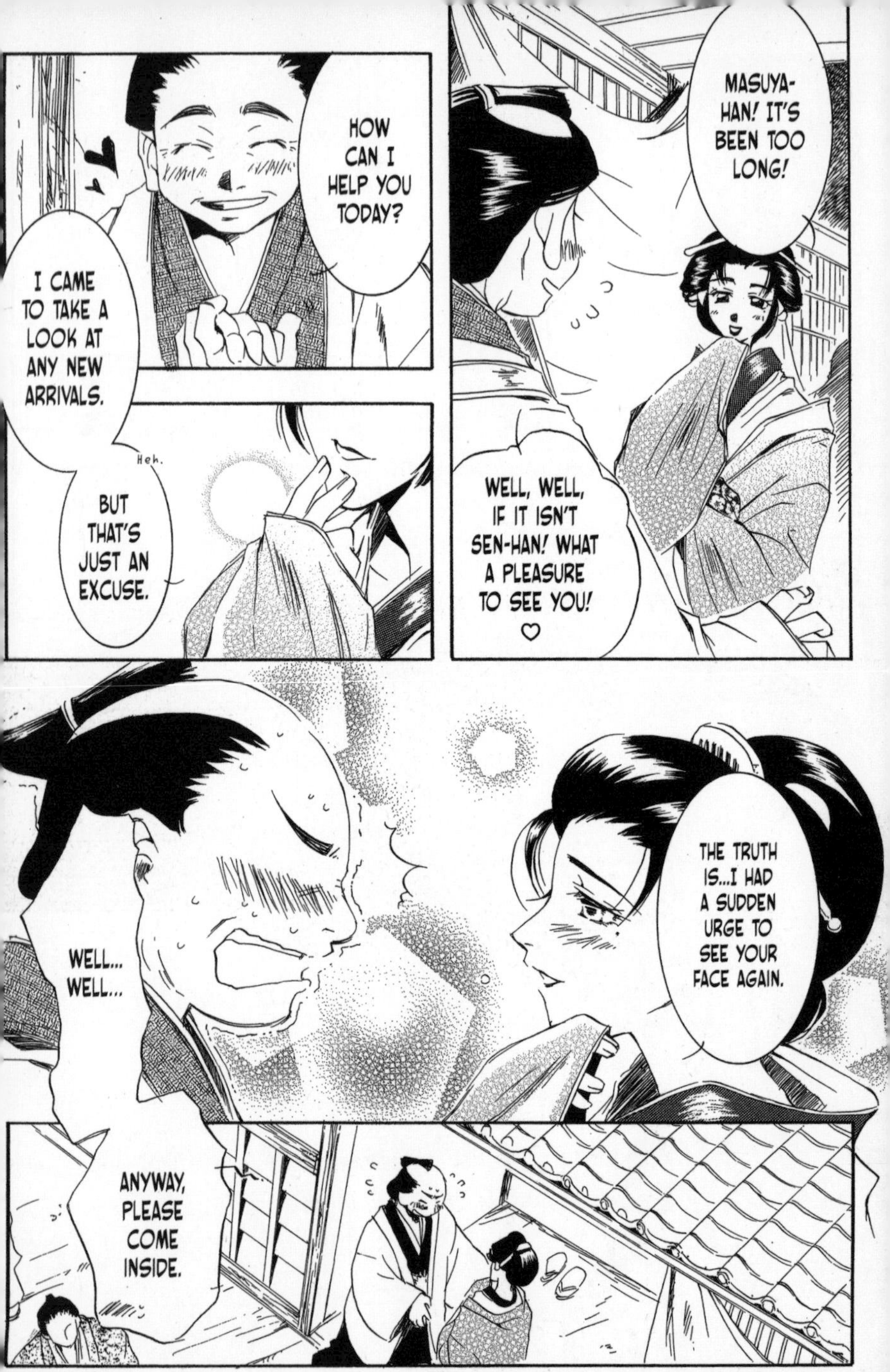
MASUYA-HAN! IT'S BEEN TOO LONG!
WELL, WELL, IF IT ISN'T SEN-HAN! WHAT A PLEASURE TO SEE YOU! ♡
HOW CAN I HELP YOU TODAY?
I CAME TO TAKE A LOOK AT ANY NEW ARRIVALS.
Heh.
BUT THAT'S JUST AN EXCUSE.
THE TRUTH IS...I HAD A SUDDEN URGE TO SEE YOUR FACE AGAIN.
WELL... WELL...
ANYWAY, PLEASE COME INSIDE.

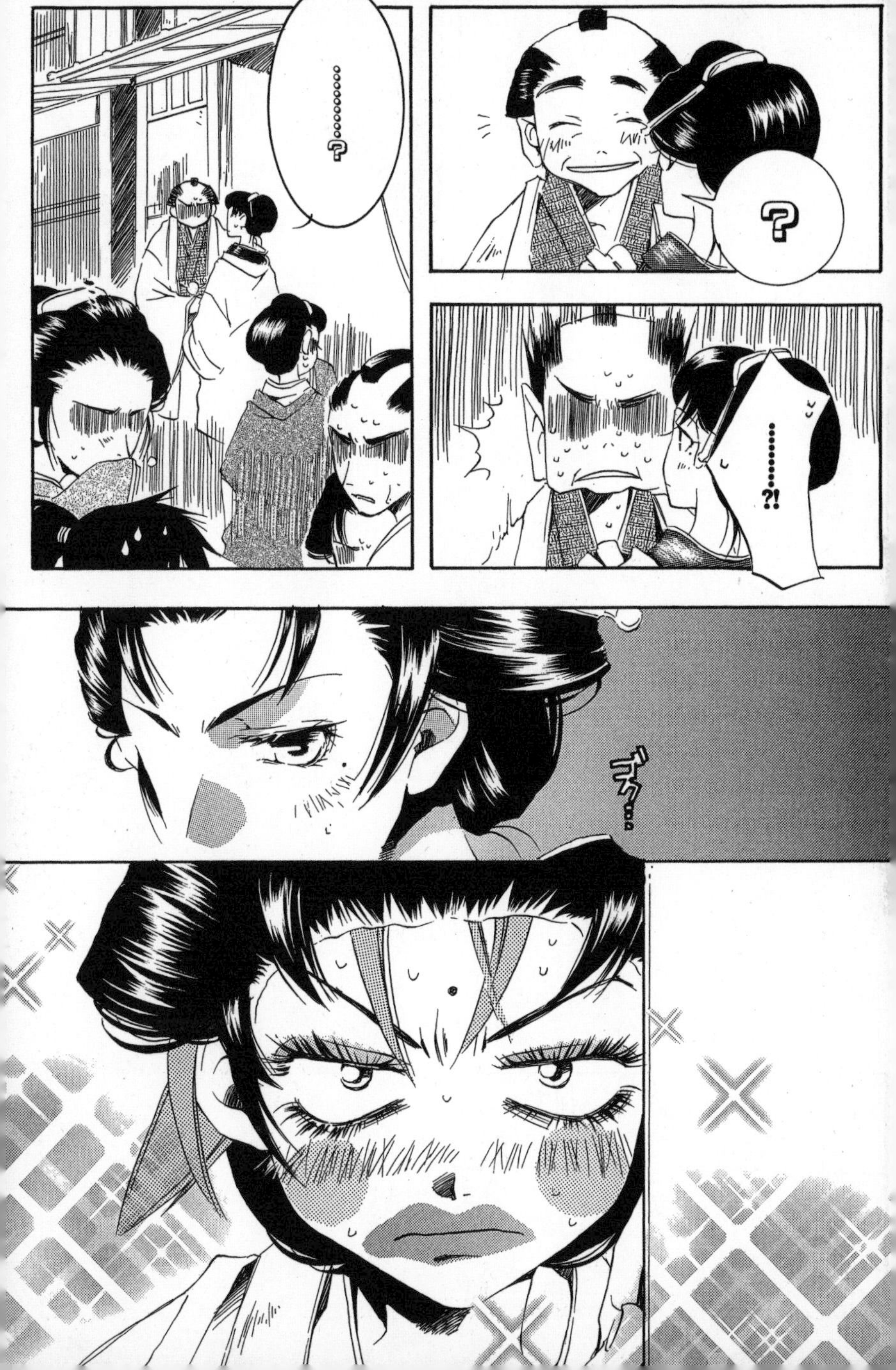
?
........?!
..........?
ズク...

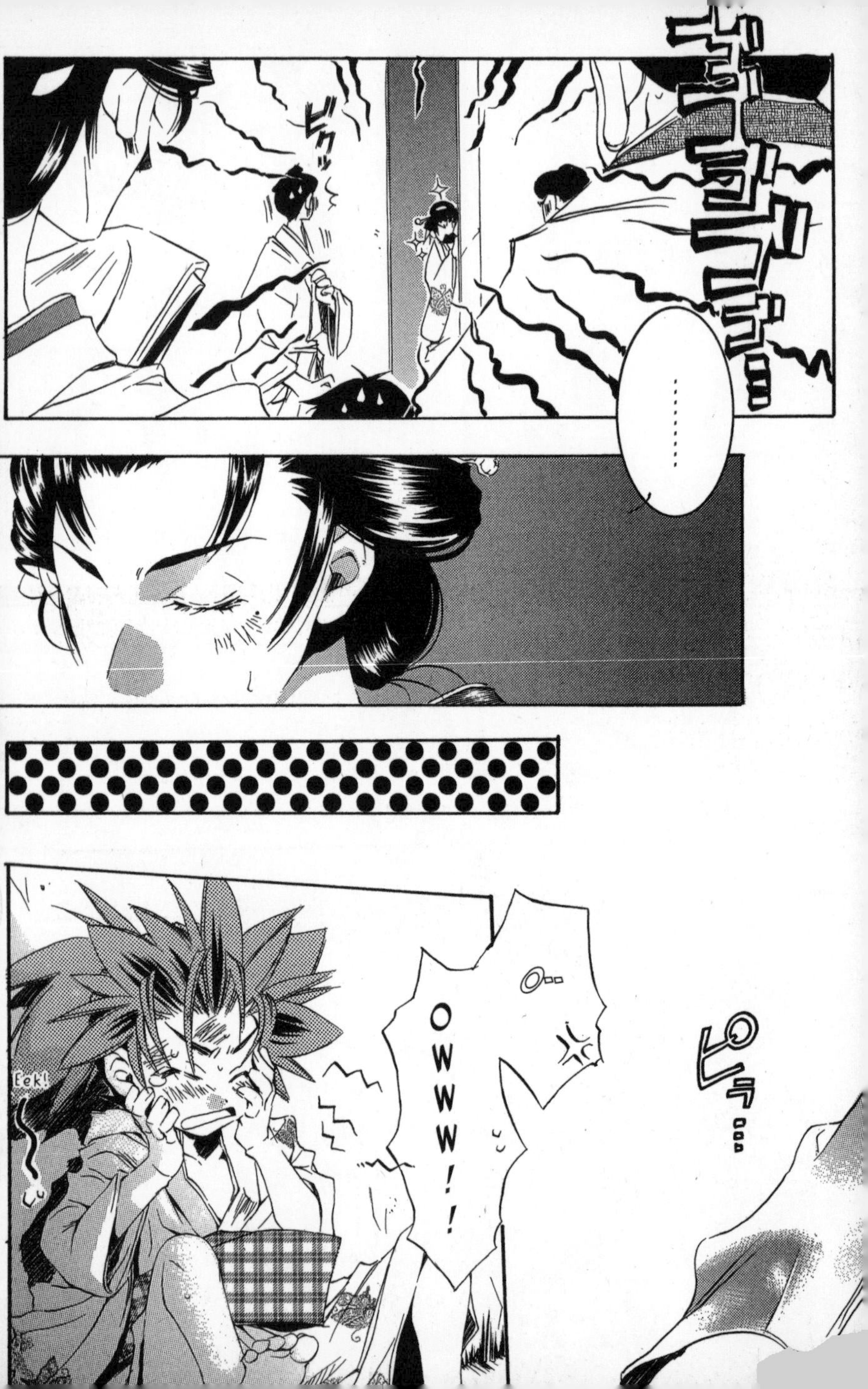

ゴゴゴゴゴ…
......
ビクッ
ピク…
O...
OWWW!!
Eek!

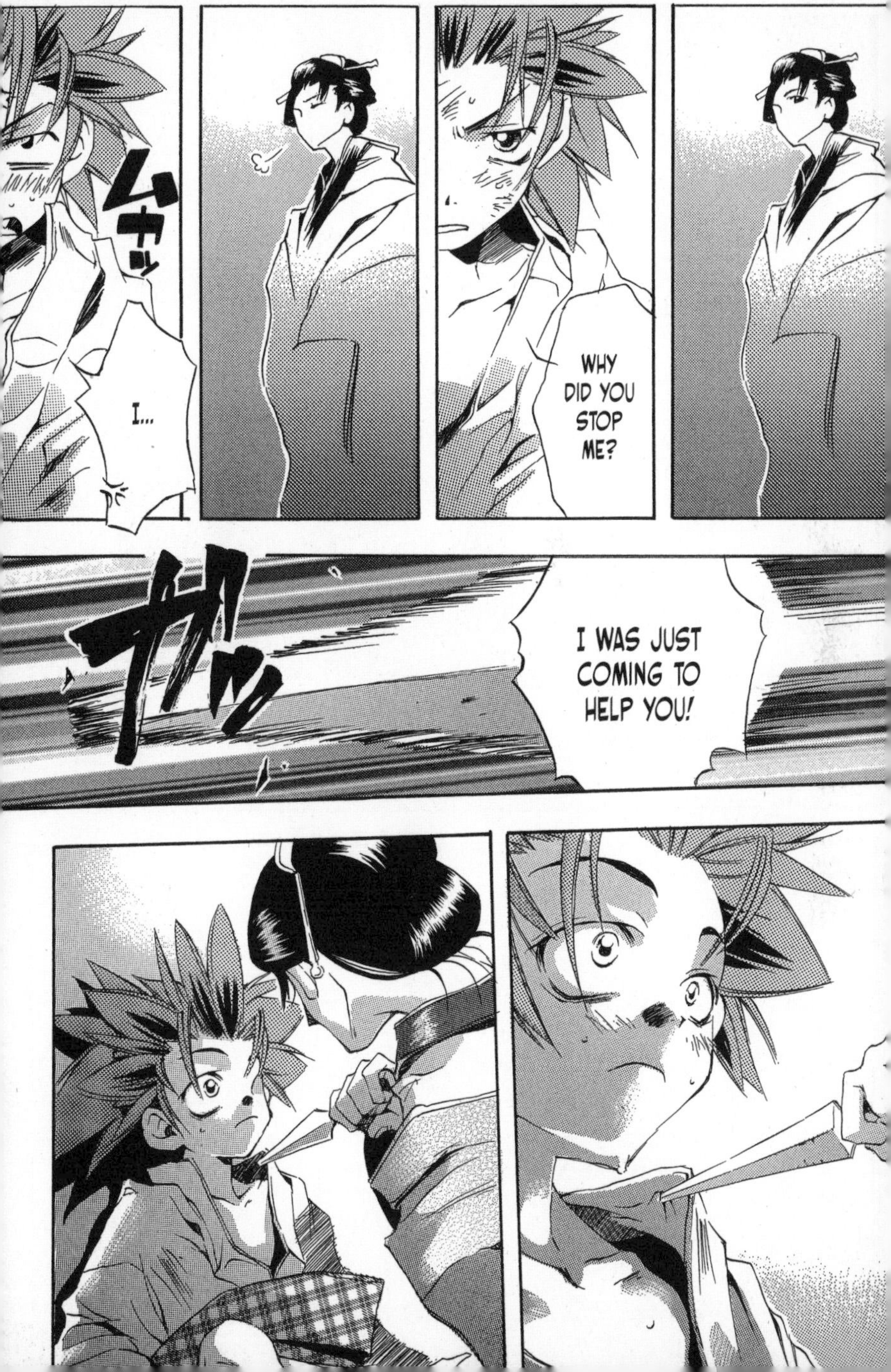
WHY DID YOU STOP ME?
ムカッ
I...
I WAS JUST COMING TO HELP YOU!

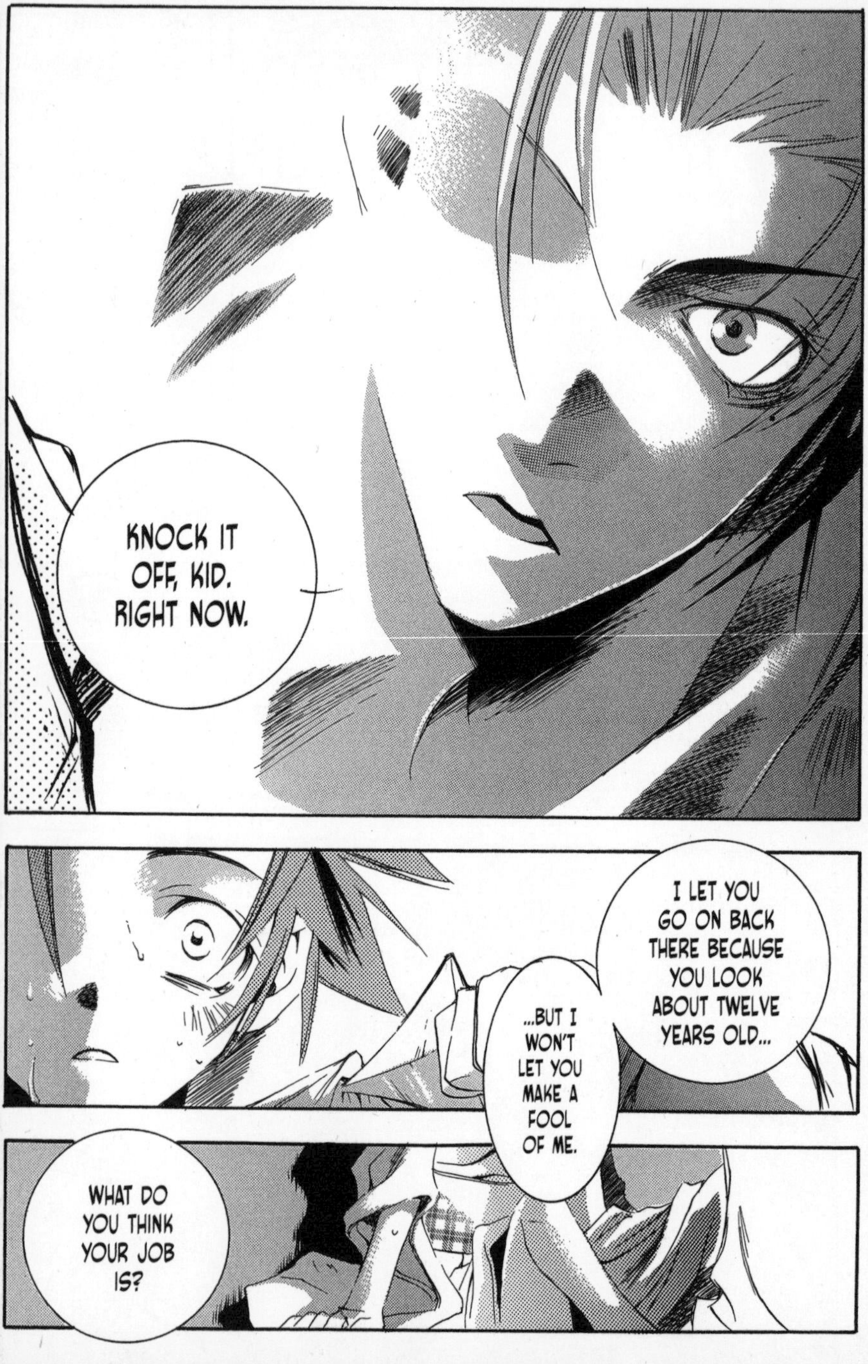
KNOCK IT OFF, KID. RIGHT NOW.
I LET YOU GO ON BACK THERE BECAUSE YOU LOOK ABOUT TWELVE YEARS OLD...
...BUT I WON'T LET YOU MAKE A FOOL OF ME.
WHAT DO YOU THINK YOUR JOB IS?

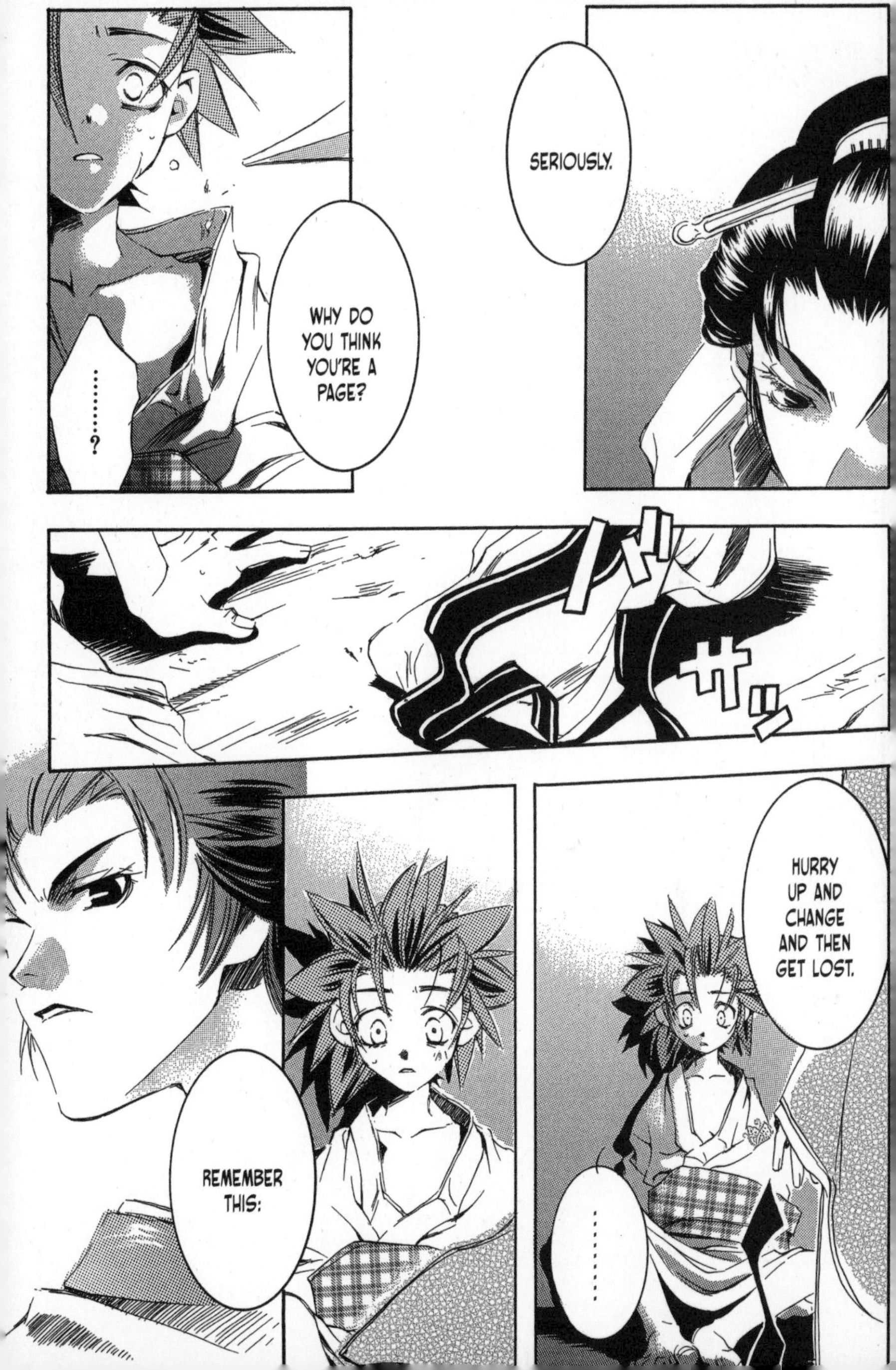
SERIOUSLY.
WHY DO YOU THINK YOU'RE A PAGE?
......?
サッ
HURRY UP AND CHANGE AND THEN GET LOST.
......
REMEMBER THIS:

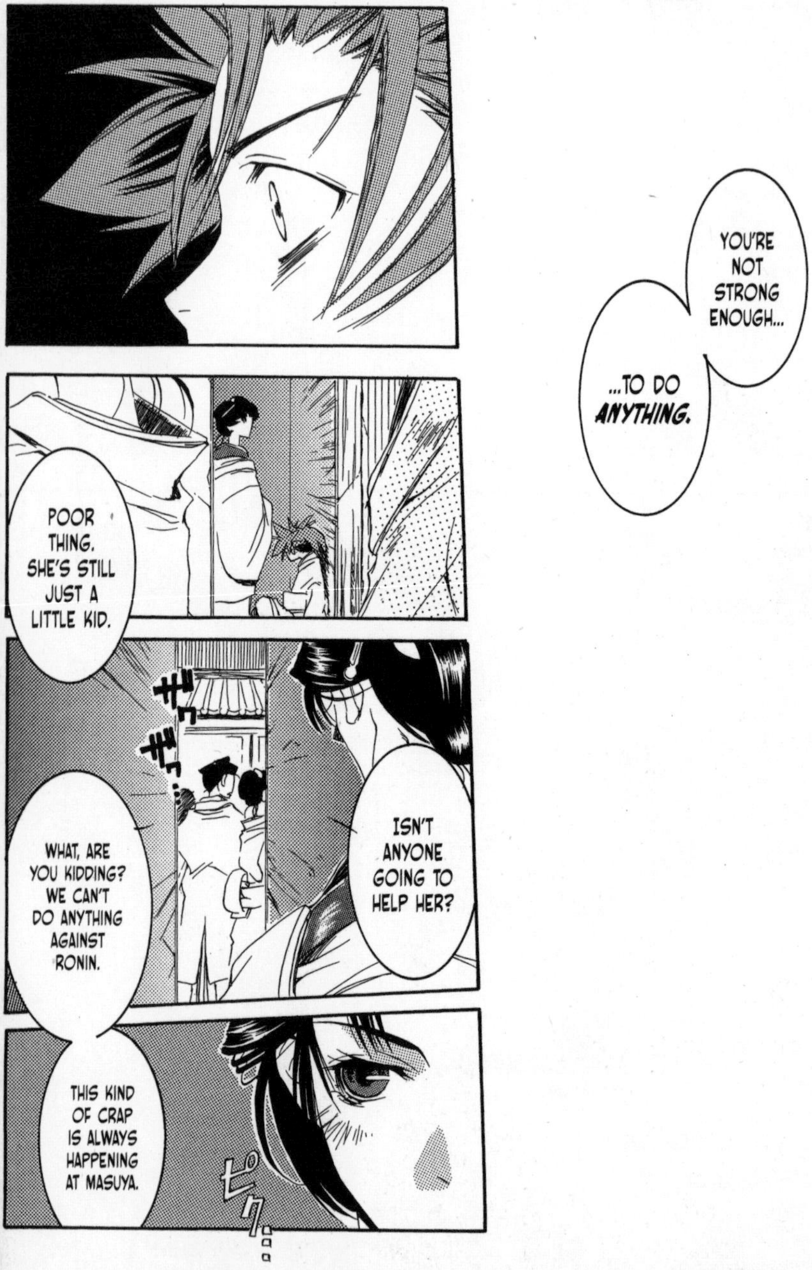
YOU'RE NOT STRONG ENOUGH...
...TO DO *ANYTHING.*
POOR THING. SHE'S STILL JUST A LITTLE KID.
ISN'T ANYONE GOING TO HELP HER?
WHAT, ARE YOU KIDDING? WE CAN'T DO ANYTHING AGAINST RONIN.
THIS KIND OF CRAP IS ALWAYS HAPPENING AT MASUYA.

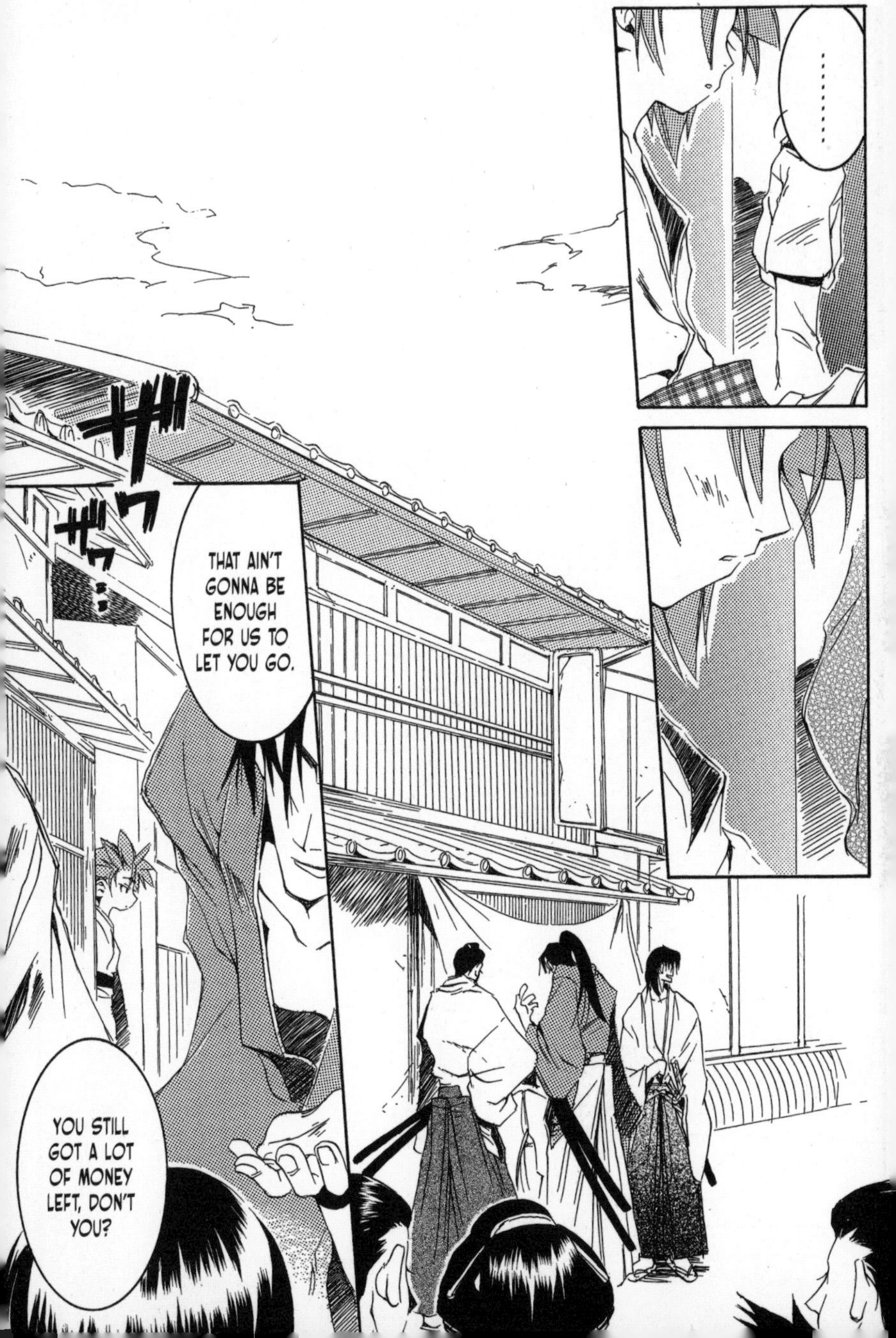
......
ザワ
ザワ…
THAT AIN'T GONNA BE ENOUGH FOR US TO LET YOU GO.
YOU STILL GOT A LOT OF MONEY LEFT, DON'T YOU?

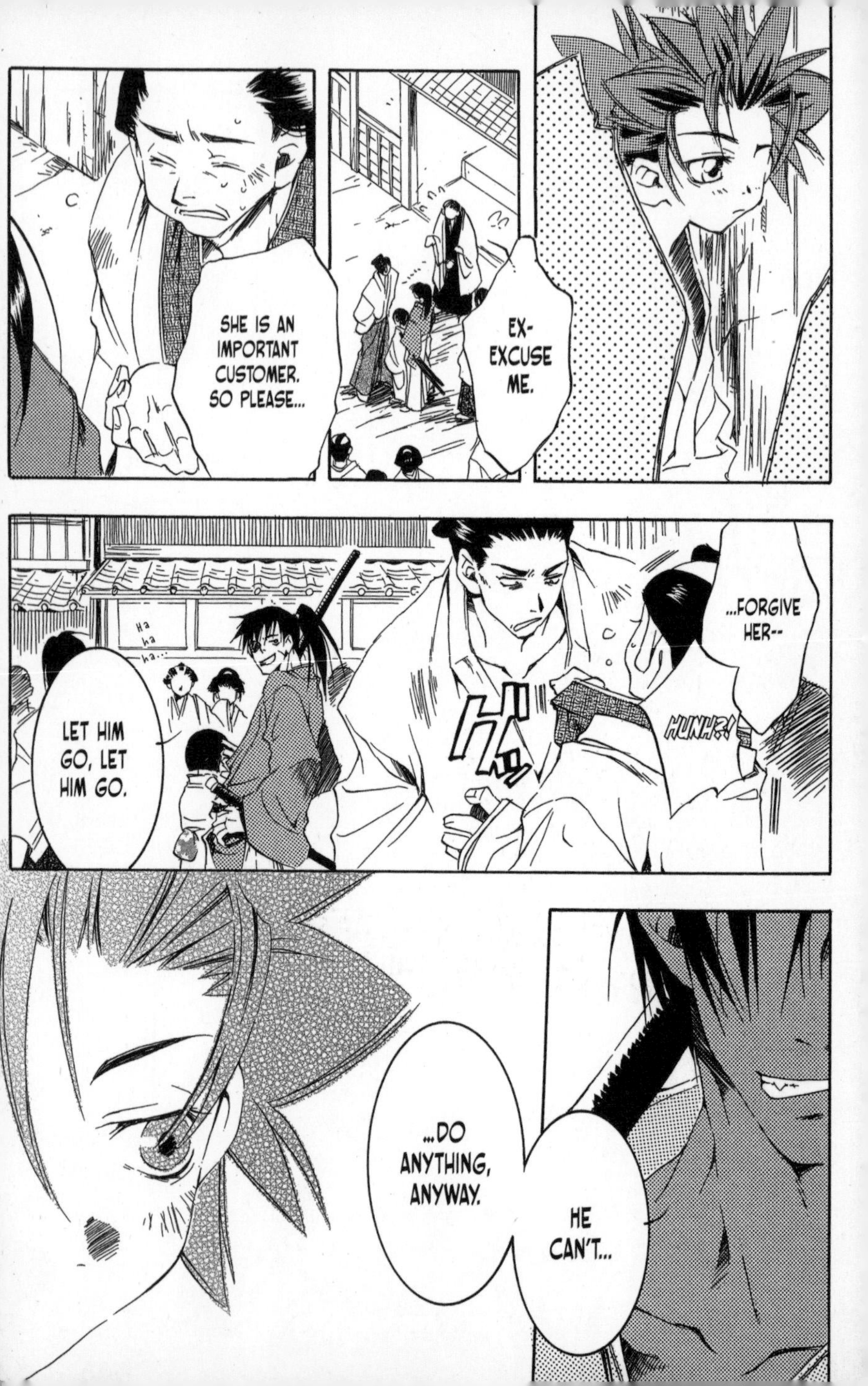
EX-
EXCUSE ME.
SHE IS AN IMPORTANT CUSTOMER. SO PLEASE...
...FORGIVE HER--
HUNH?!
Ha ha ha...
LET HIM GO, LET HIM GO.
HE CAN'T...
...DO ANYTHING, ANYWAY.

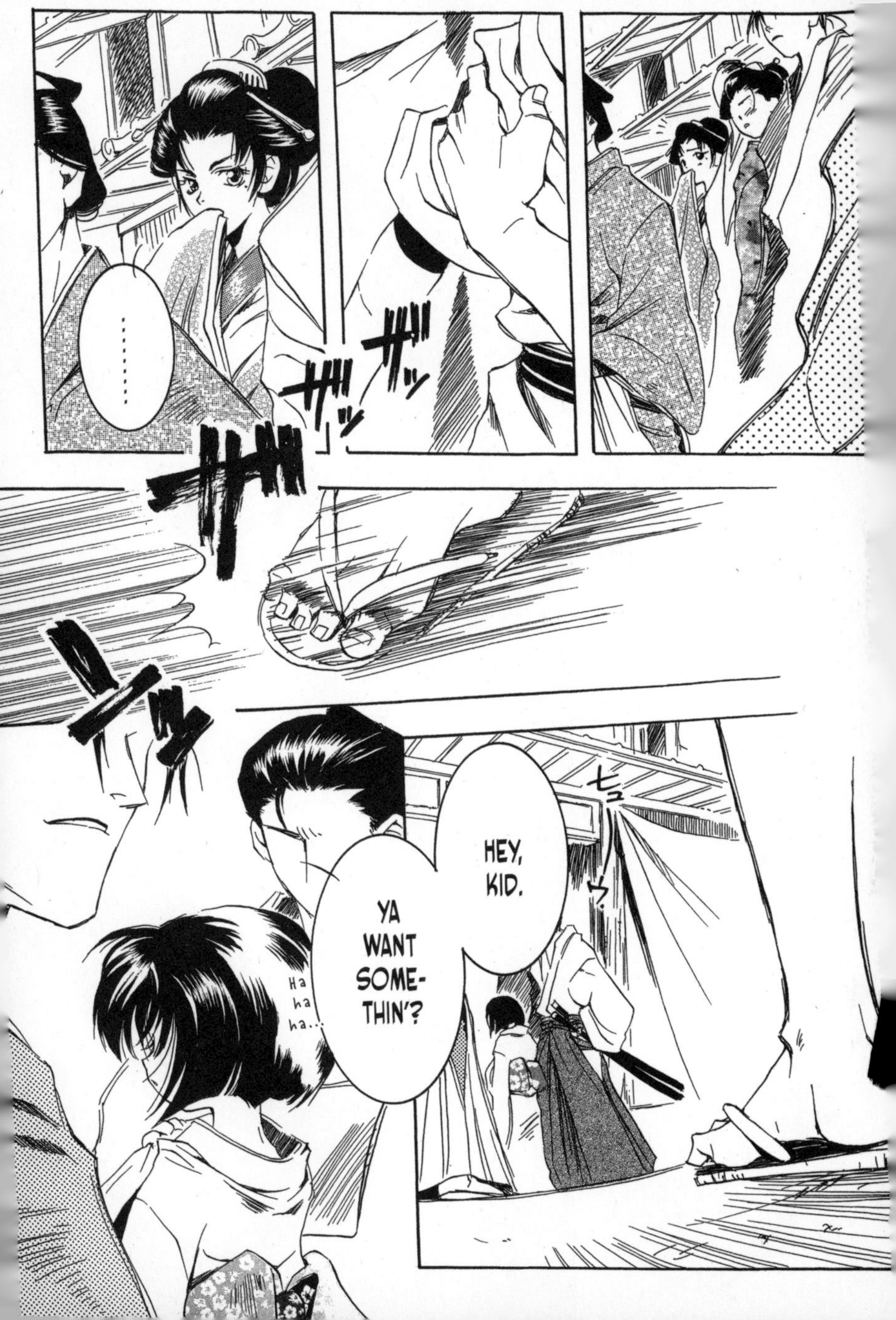
ザッ
ザッ
……
ヒュッ
HEY, KID.
YA WANT SOME-THIN'?
Ha ha ha...

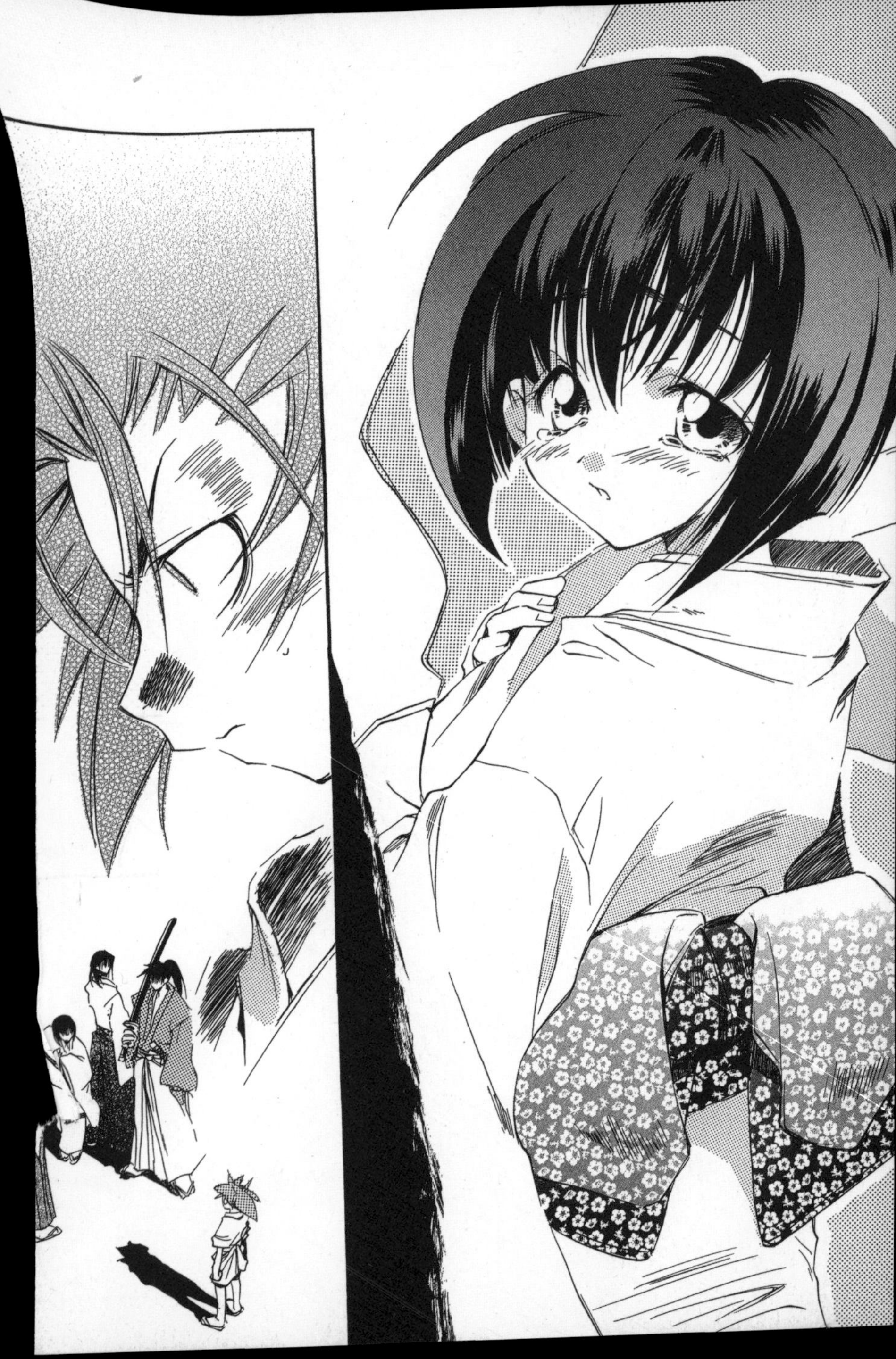

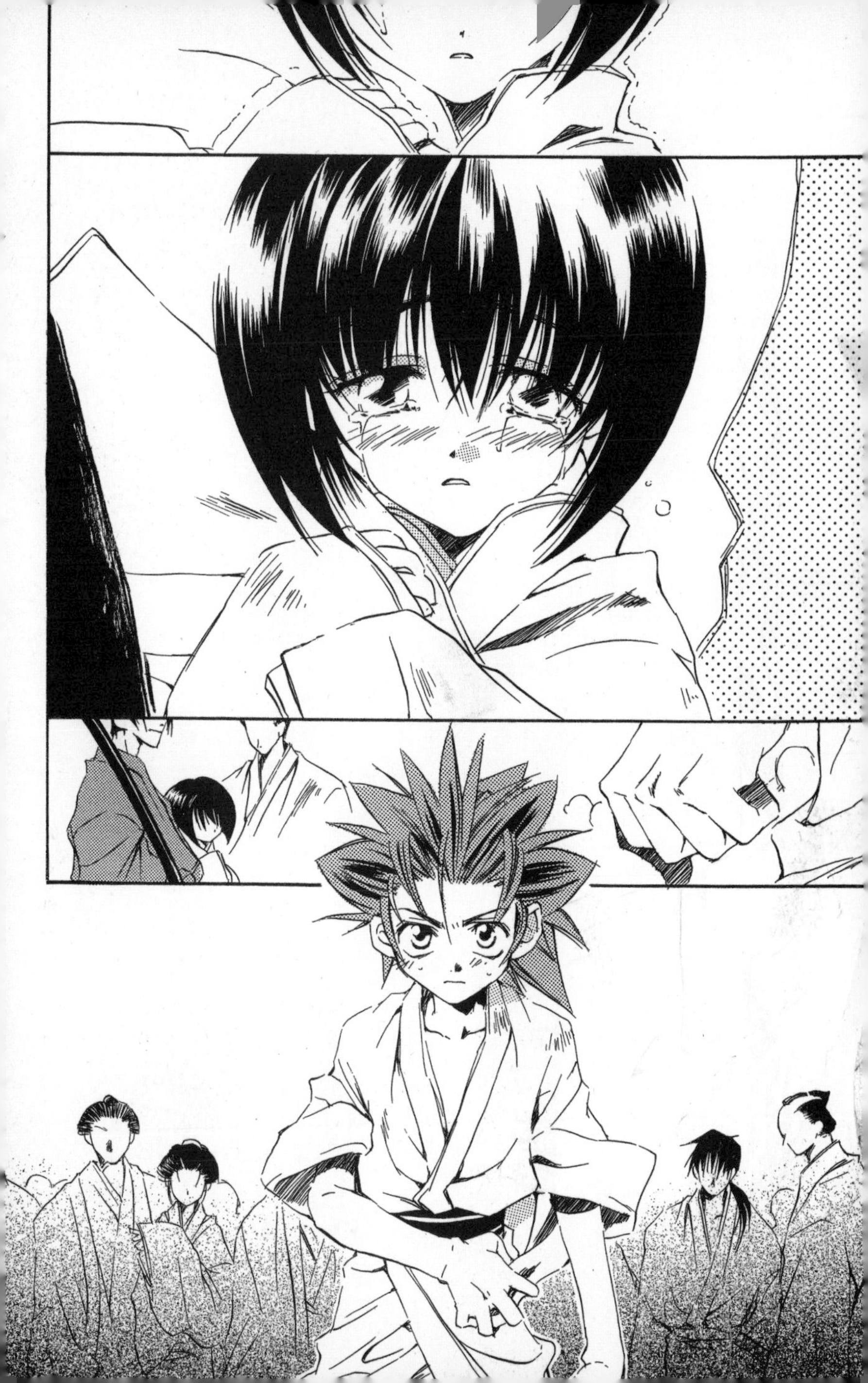

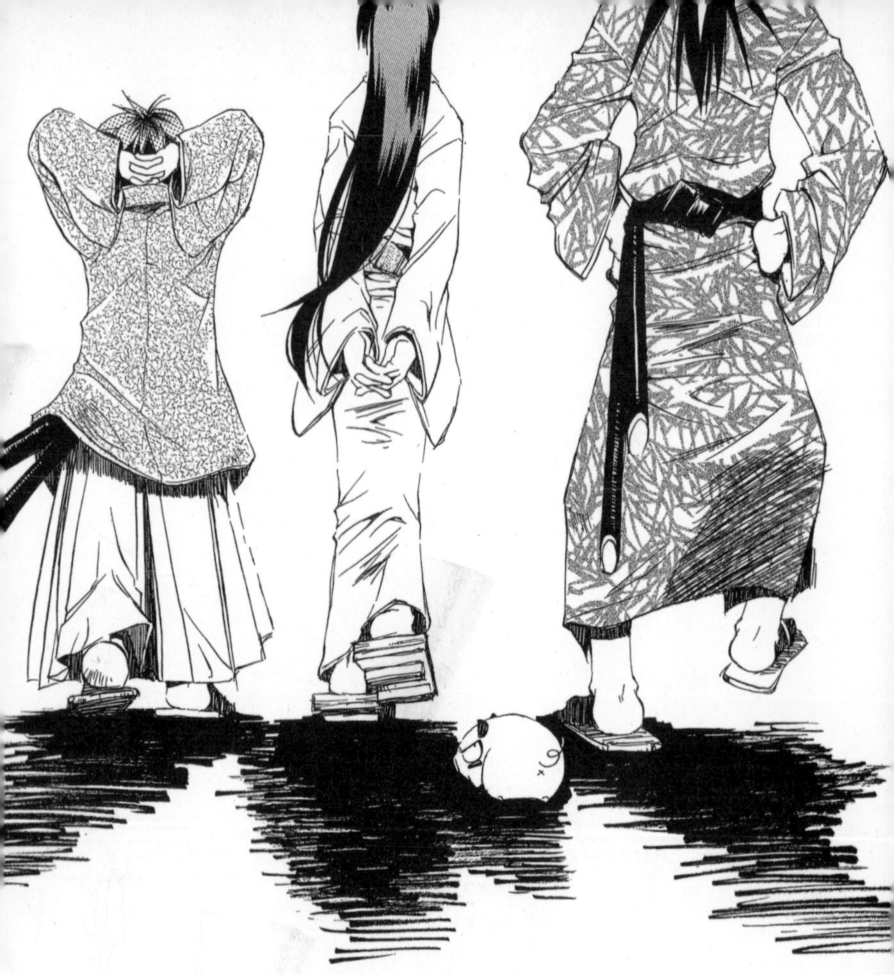

Act.5
Act Naturally

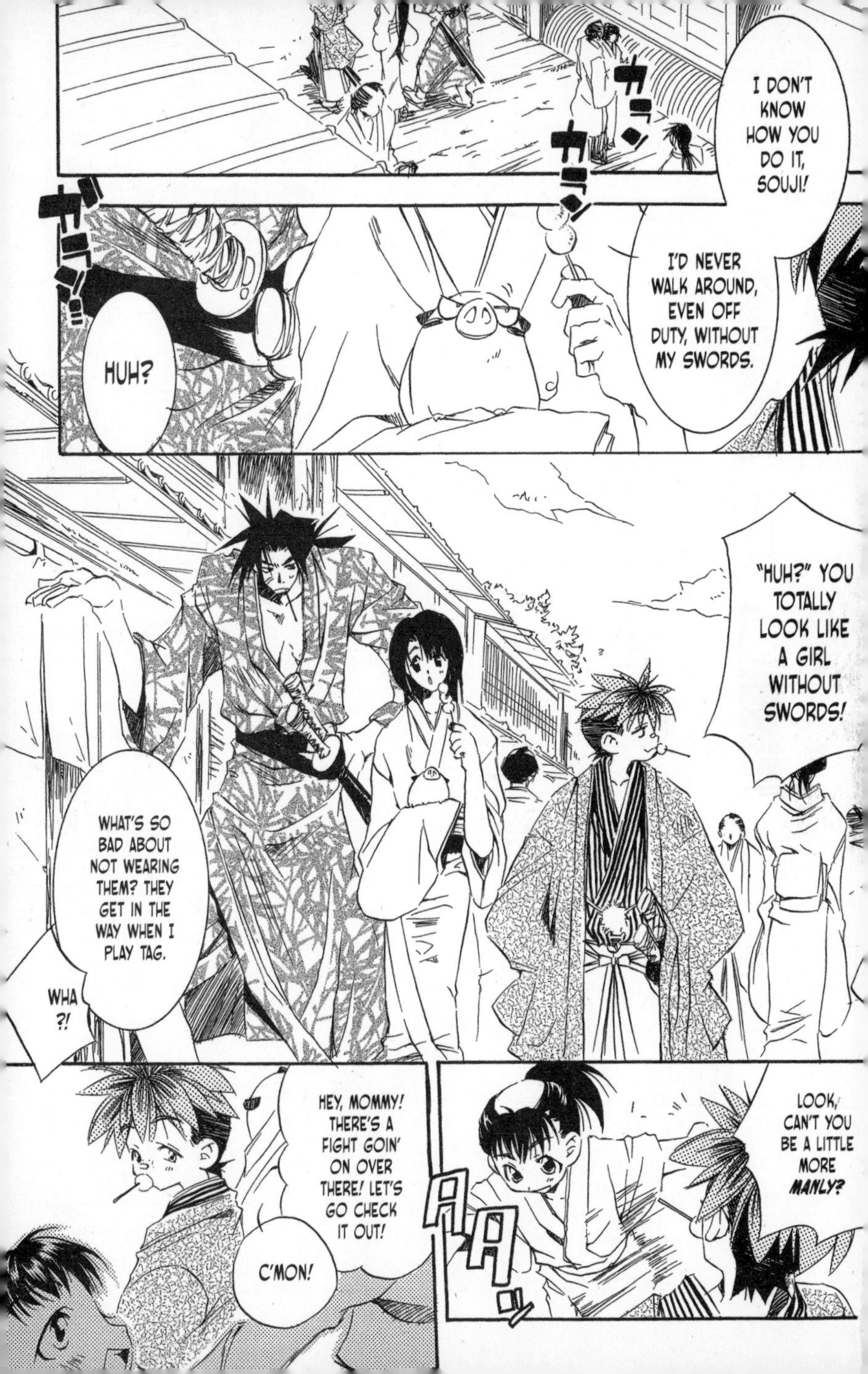
I DON'T KNOW HOW YOU DO IT, SOUJI!
I'D NEVER WALK AROUND, EVEN OFF DUTY, WITHOUT MY SWORDS.
HUH?
"HUH?" YOU TOTALLY LOOK LIKE A GIRL WITHOUT SWORDS!
WHAT'S SO BAD ABOUT NOT WEARING THEM? THEY GET IN THE WAY WHEN I PLAY TAG.
WHA ?!
LOOK, CAN'T YOU BE A LITTLE MORE *MANLY?*
AAA
HEY, MOMMY! THERE'S A FIGHT GOIN' ON OVER THERE! LET'S GO CHECK IT OUT!
C'MON!

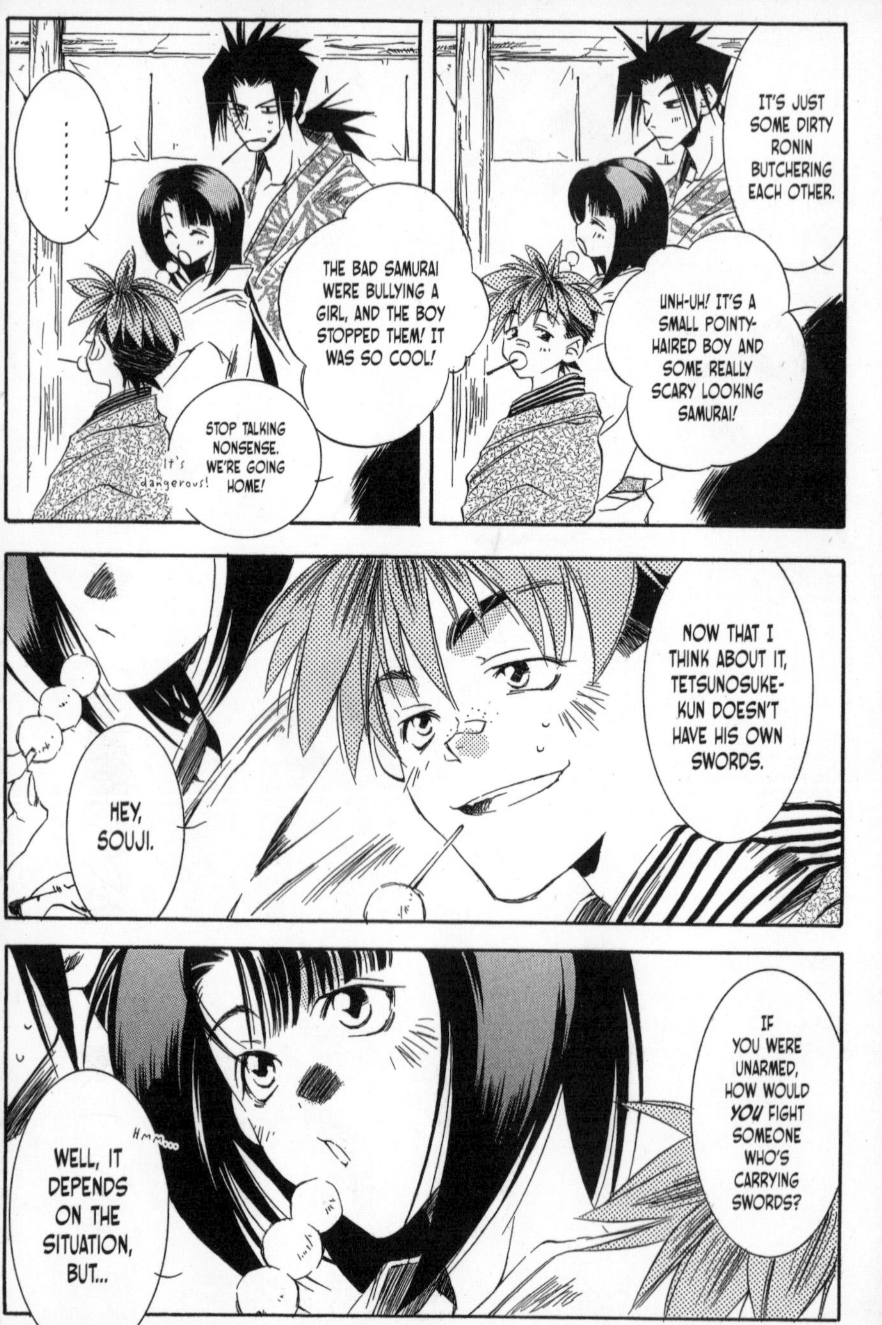
IT'S JUST SOME DIRTY RONIN BUTCHERING EACH OTHER.
UNH-UH! IT'S A SMALL POINTY-HAIRED BOY AND SOME REALLY SCARY LOOKING SAMURAI!
......
THE BAD SAMURAI WERE BULLYING A GIRL, AND THE BOY STOPPED THEM! IT WAS SO COOL!
STOP TALKING NONSENSE. WE'RE GOING HOME!
It's dangerous!
NOW THAT I THINK ABOUT IT, TETSUNOSUKE-KUN DOESN'T HAVE HIS OWN SWORDS.
HEY, SOUJI.
IF YOU WERE UNARMED, HOW WOULD *YOU* FIGHT SOMEONE WHO'S CARRYING SWORDS?
HMMooo
WELL, IT DEPENDS ON THE SITUATION, BUT...

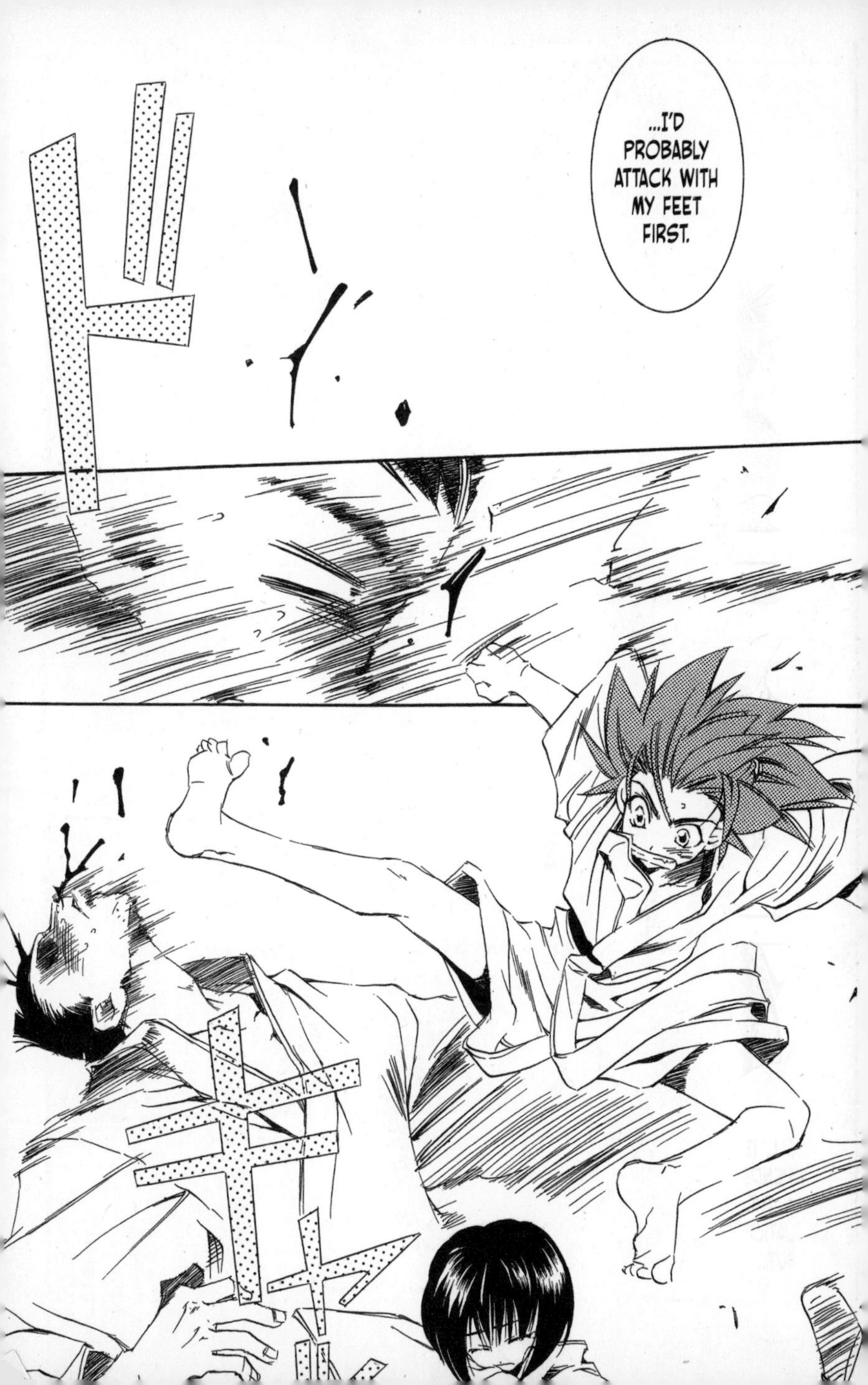
...I'D PROBABLY ATTACK WITH MY FEET FIRST.

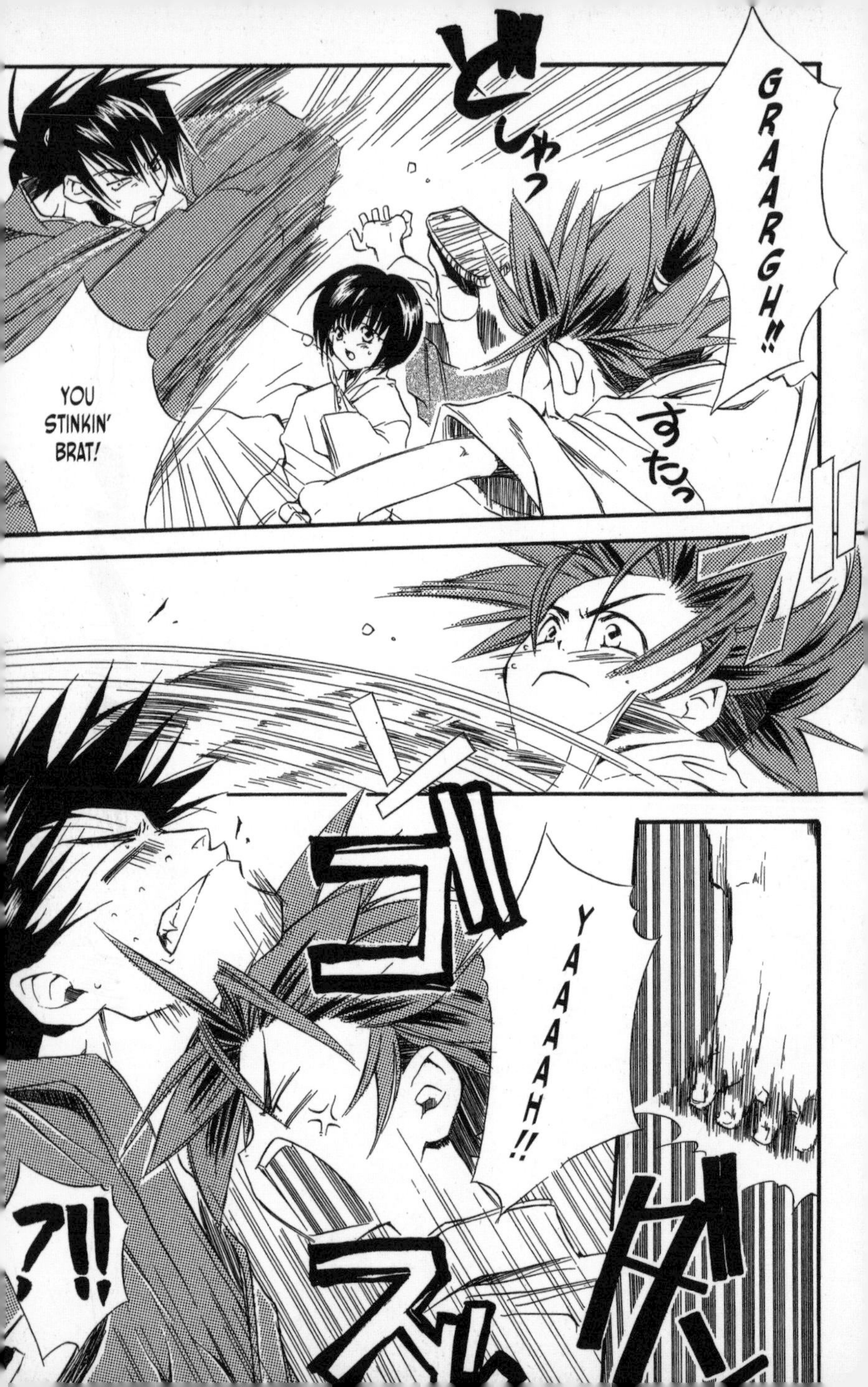
GRAARGH!!
どしゃっ
すたっ
YOU STINKIN' BRAT!
YAAAAAAH!!

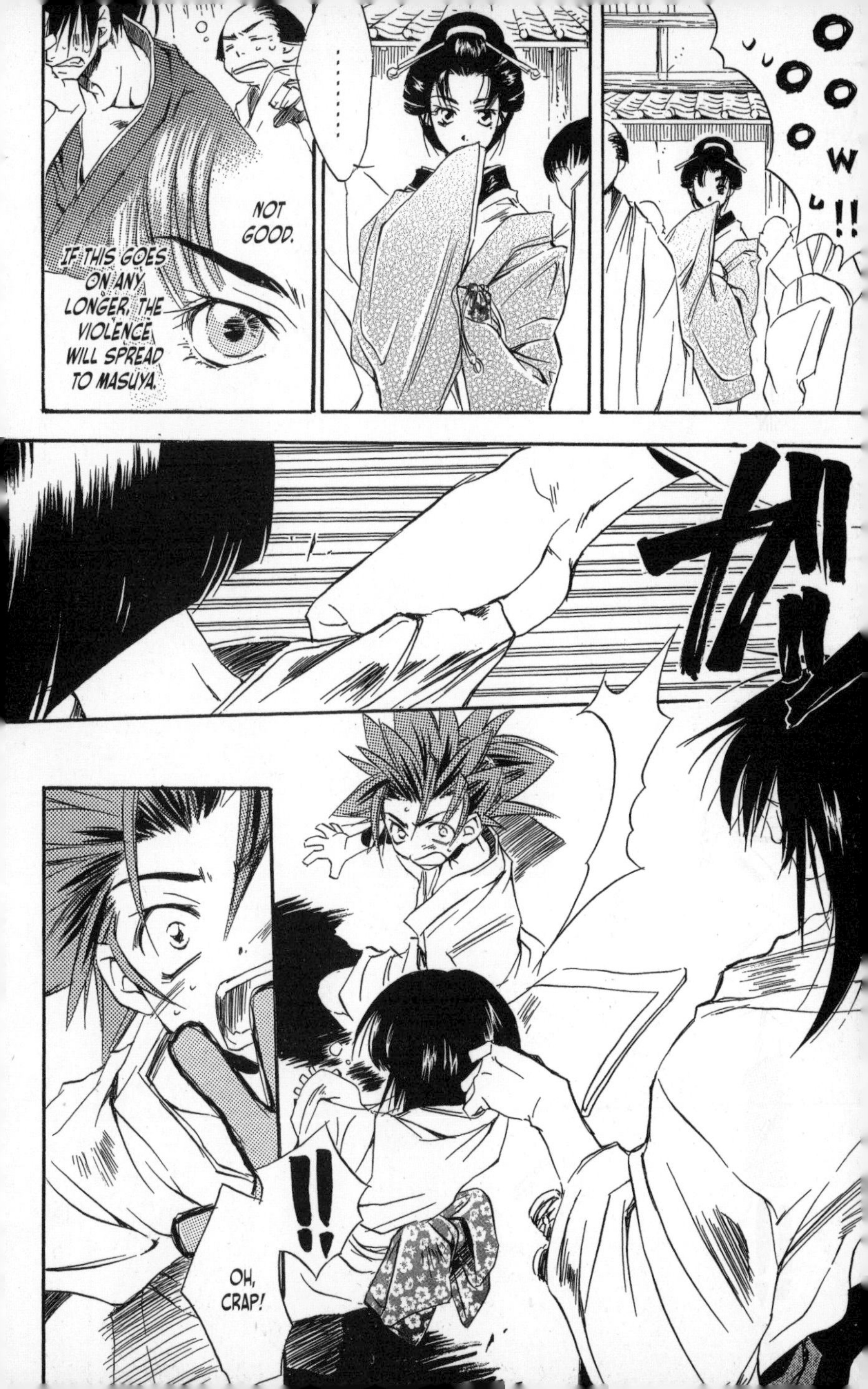
OOOOOOW!!
......
NOT GOOD.
IF THIS GOES ON ANY LONGER, THE VIOLENCE WILL SPREAD TO MASUYA.
!!
OH, CRAP!

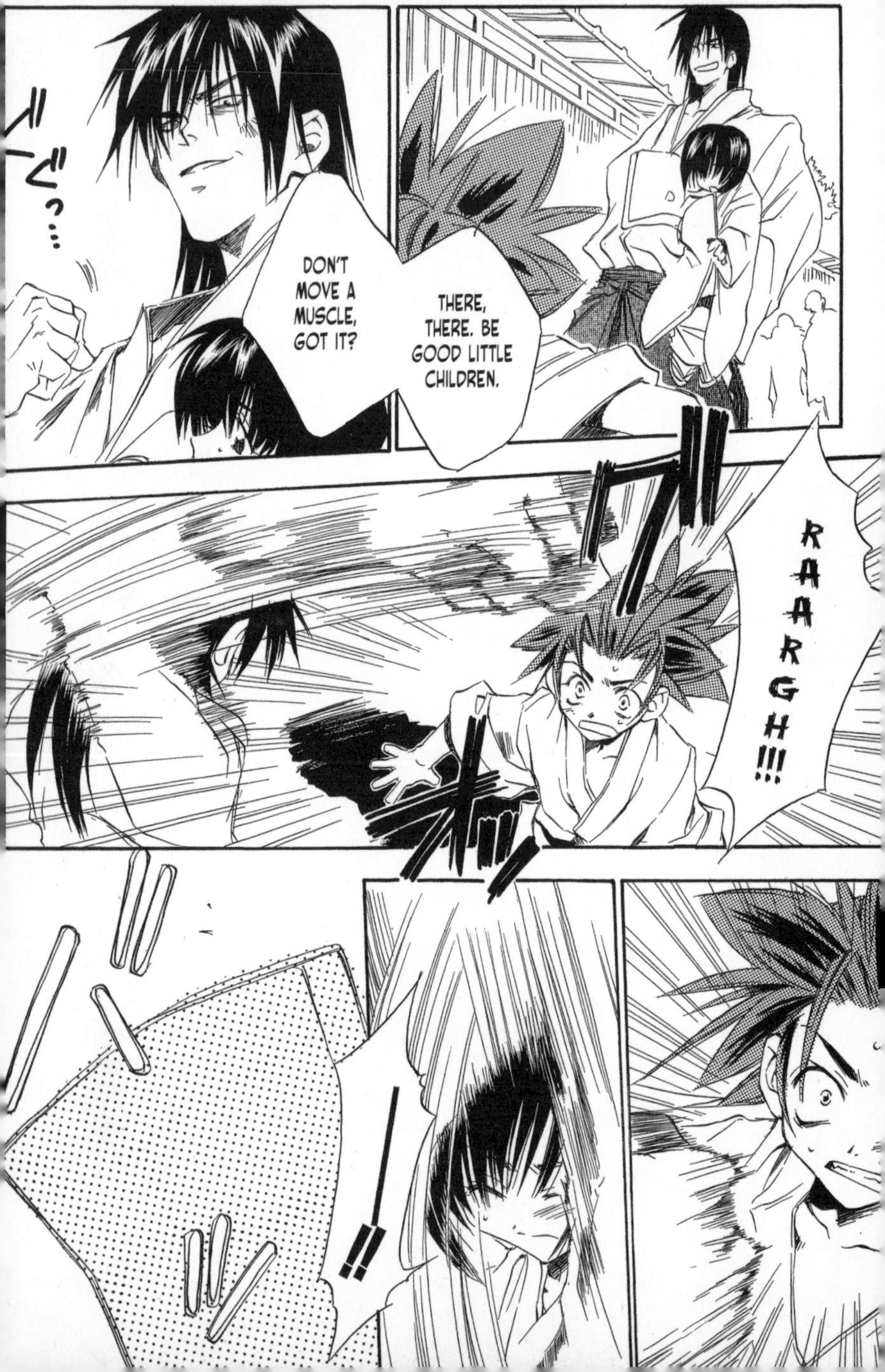
THERE, THERE. BE GOOD LITTLE CHILDREN.
DON'T MOVE A MUSCLE, GOT IT?
ぐっ…
RAAARGH!!!

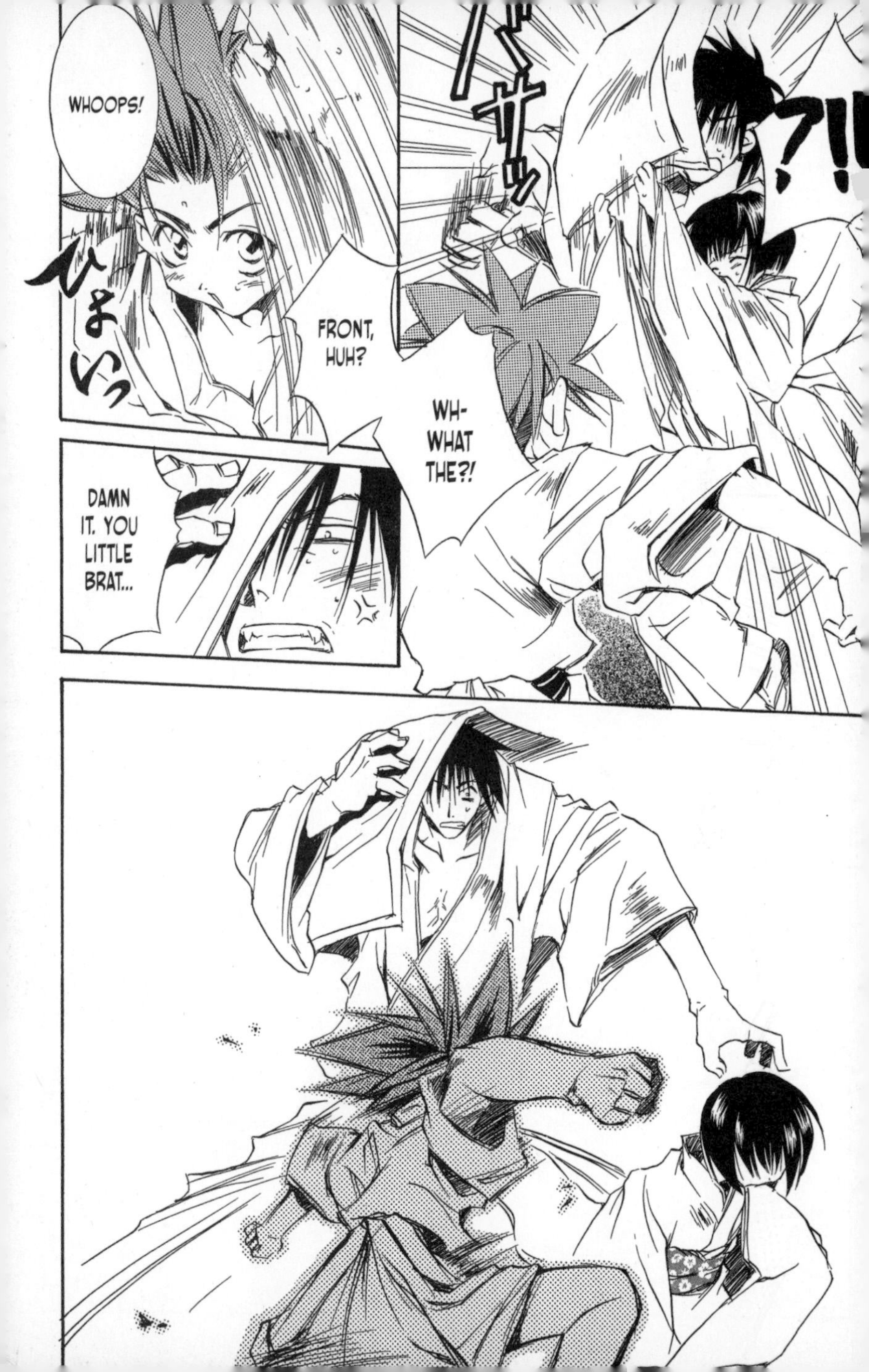

バサッ
?!!
WH- WHAT THE?!
WHOOPS!
ひょいっ
FRONT, HUH?
DAMN IT. YOU LITTLE BRAT...

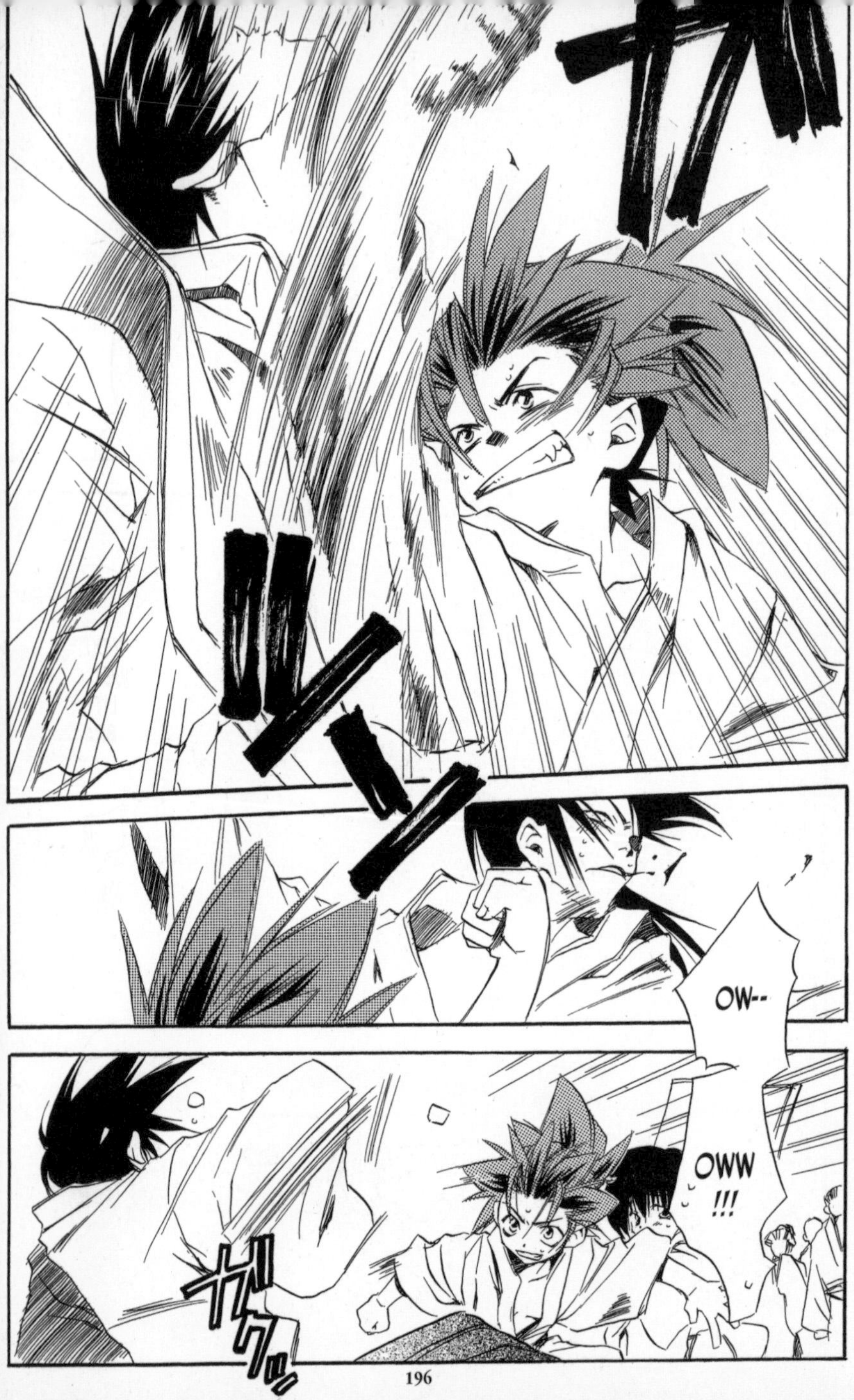
OW--
OWW !!!

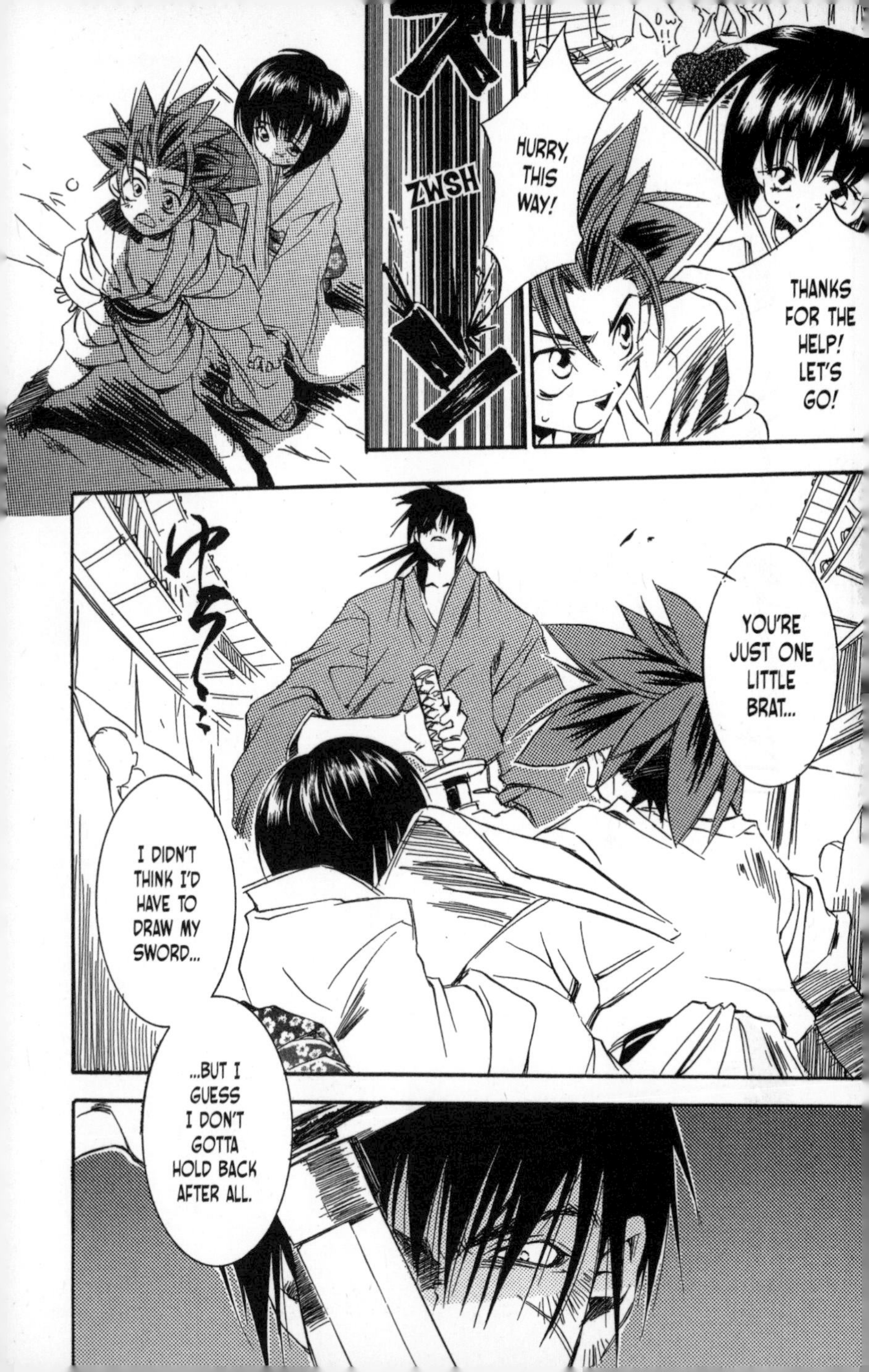
Ow!!
HURRY, THIS WAY!
THANKS FOR THE HELP! LET'S GO!
ZWSH
YOU'RE JUST ONE LITTLE BRAT...
I DIDN'T THINK I'D HAVE TO DRAW MY SWORD...
...BUT I GUESS I DON'T GOTTA HOLD BACK AFTER ALL.

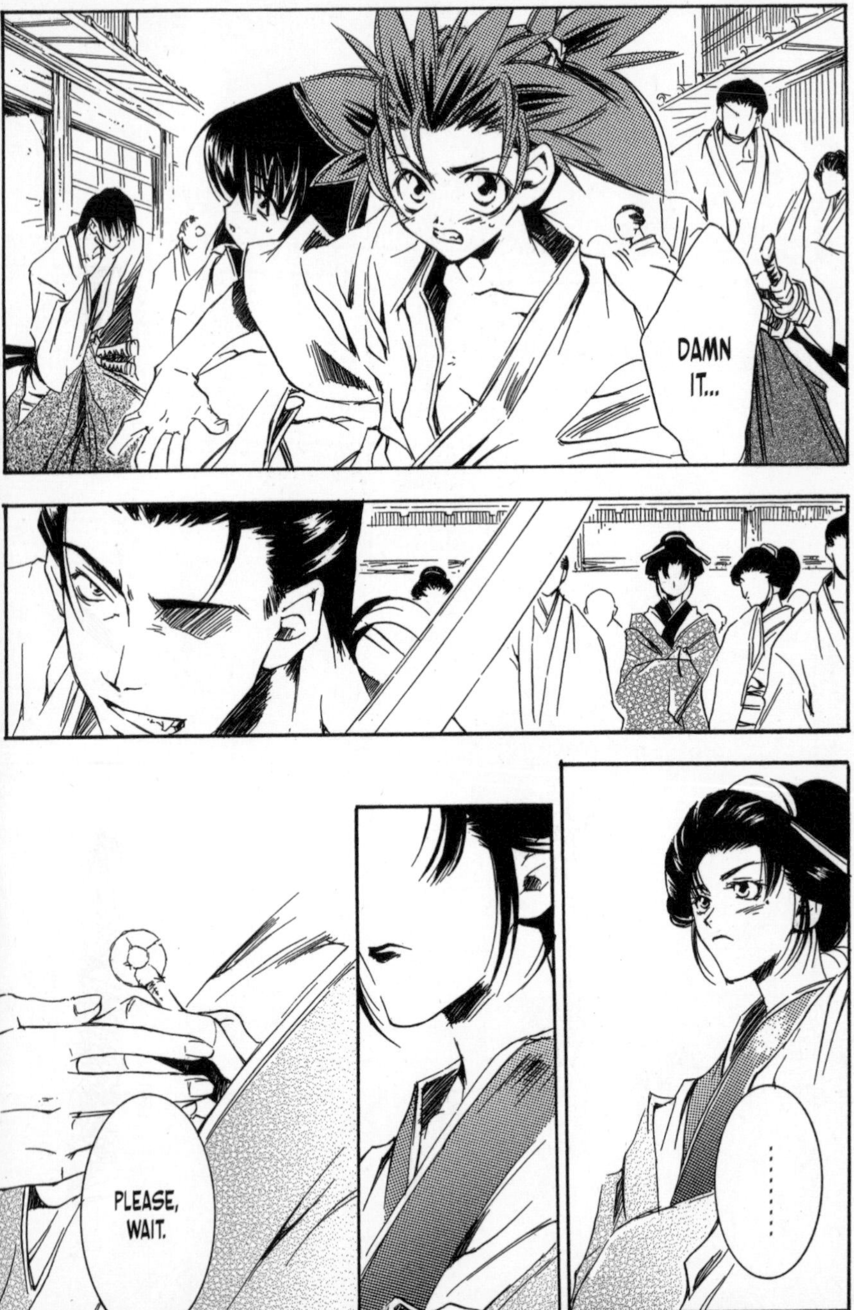
DAMN IT...
......
PLEASE, WAIT.

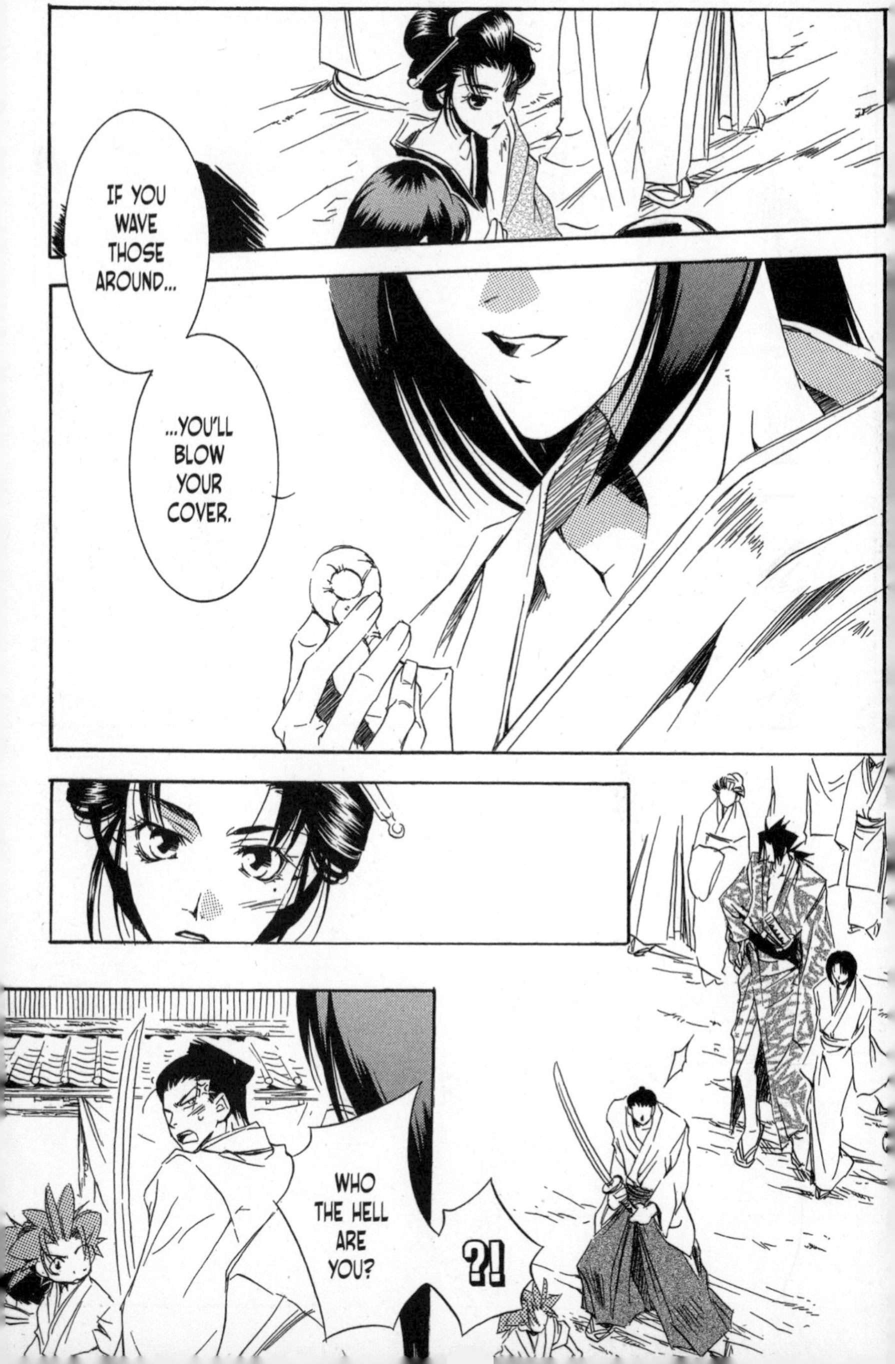
IF YOU WAVE THOSE AROUND...
...YOU'LL BLOW YOUR COVER.
?!
WHO THE HELL ARE YOU?

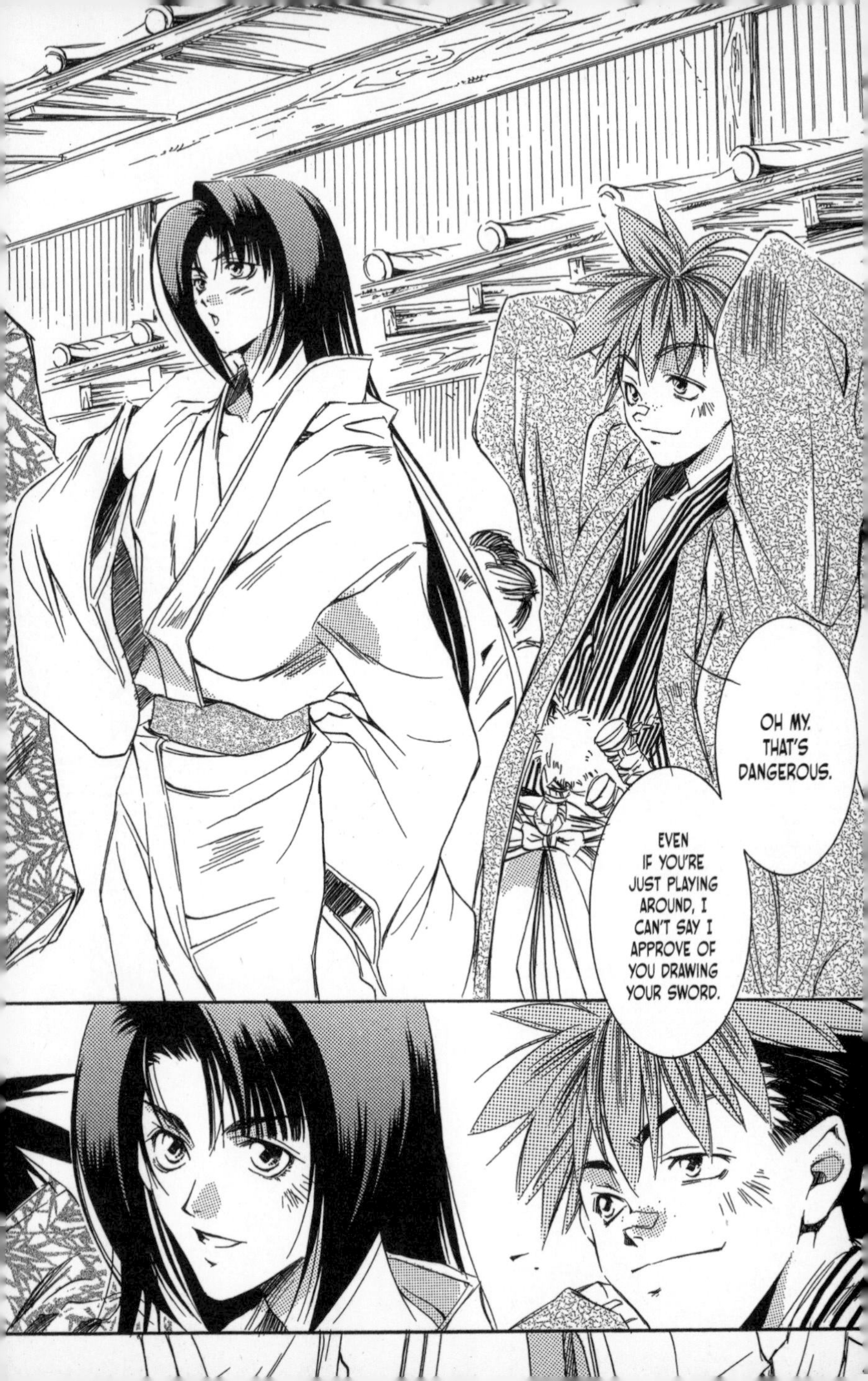
OH MY. THAT'S DANGEROUS.
EVEN IF YOU'RE JUST PLAYING AROUND, I CAN'T SAY I APPROVE OF YOU DRAWING YOUR SWORD.

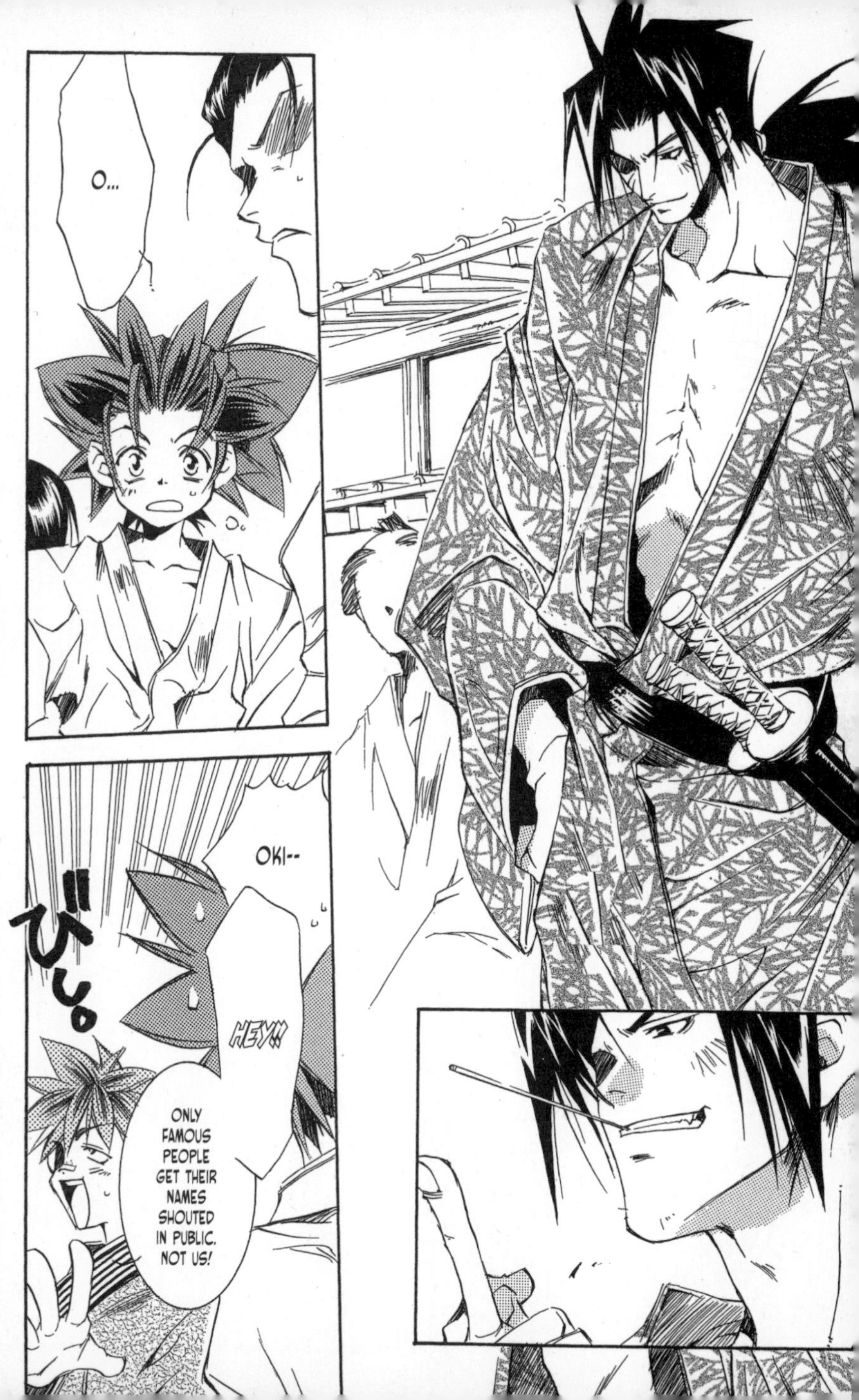
O...
OKI--
HEY!!
びし。
ONLY FAMOUS PEOPLE GET THEIR NAMES SHOUTED IN PUBLIC. NOT US!

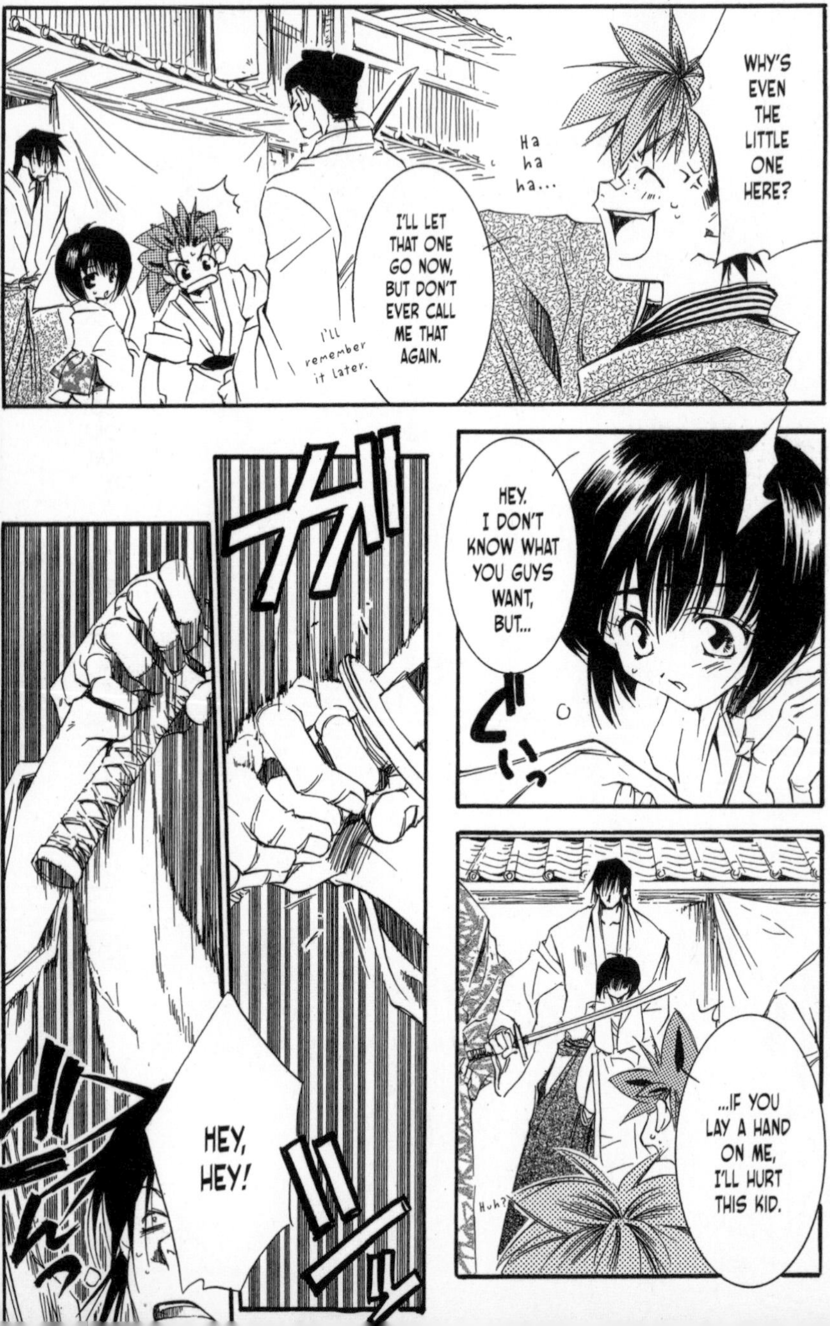
WHY'S EVEN THE LITTLE ONE HERE?
Ha ha ha...
I'LL LET THAT ONE GO NOW, BUT DON'T EVER CALL ME THAT AGAIN.
I'll remember it later.
HEY. I DON'T KNOW WHAT YOU GUYS WANT, BUT...
ぐいっ
...IF YOU LAY A HAND ON ME, I'LL HURT THIS KID.
Huh?
HEY, HEY!

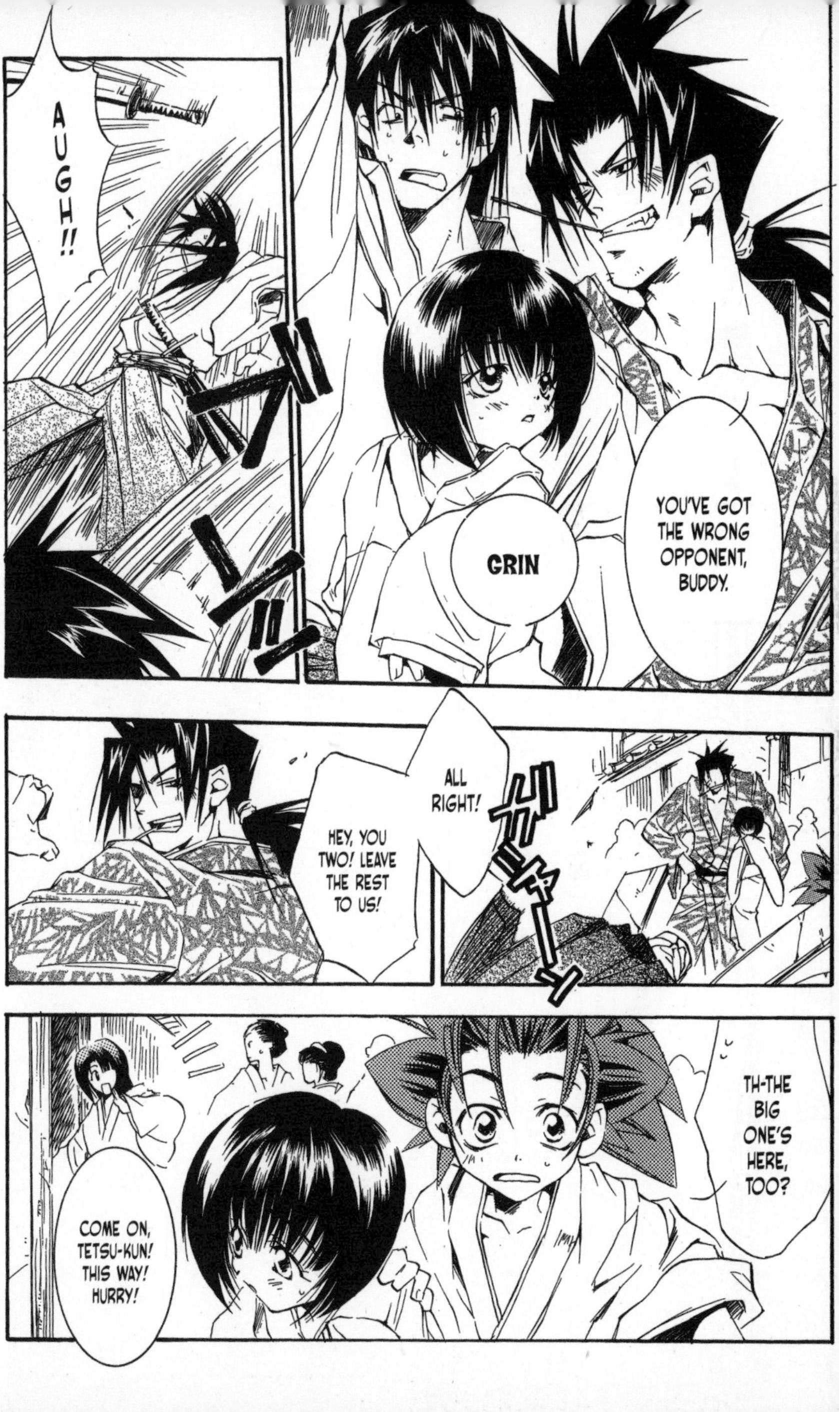
YOU'VE GOT THE WRONG OPPONENT, BUDDY.
GRIN
AUGH!!
ALL RIGHT!
HEY, YOU TWO! LEAVE THE REST TO US!
TH-THE BIG ONE'S HERE, TOO?
COME ON, TETSU-KUN! THIS WAY! HURRY!

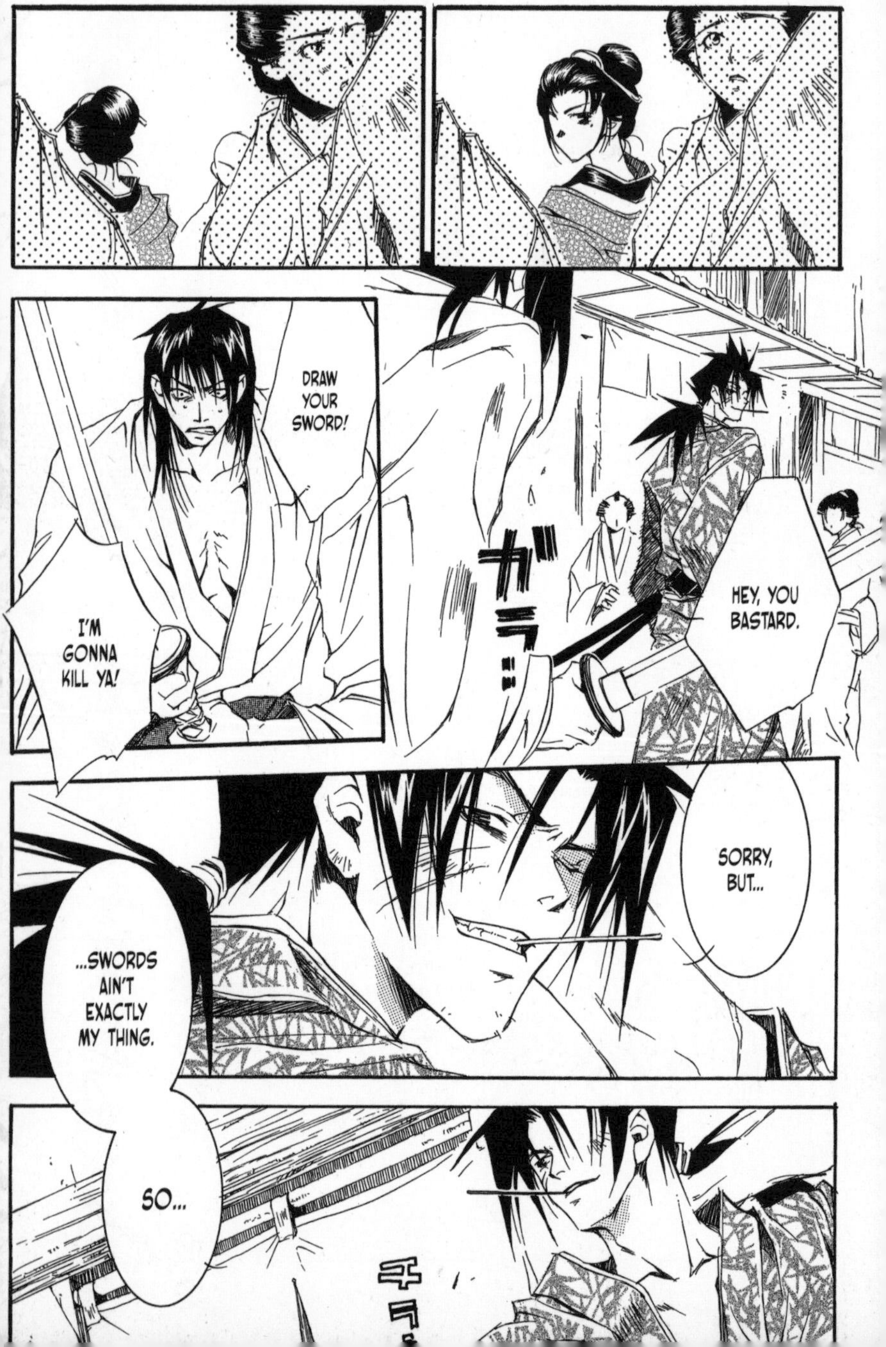
HEY, YOU BASTARD.
ガラ
DRAW YOUR SWORD!
I'M GONNA KILL YA!
SORRY, BUT...
...SWORDS AIN'T EXACTLY MY THING.
SO...

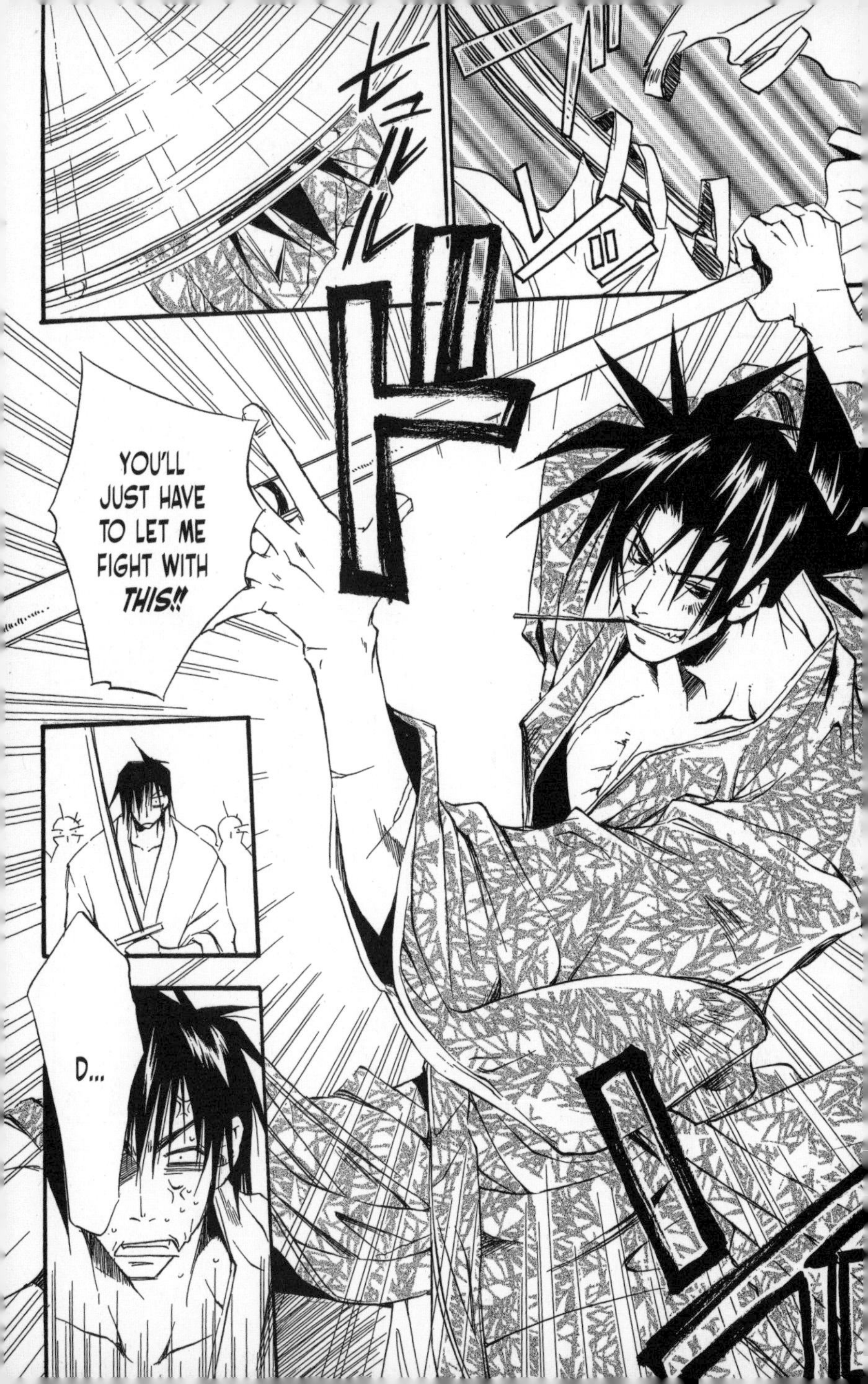
YOU'LL JUST HAVE TO LET ME FIGHT WITH THIS!!
D...

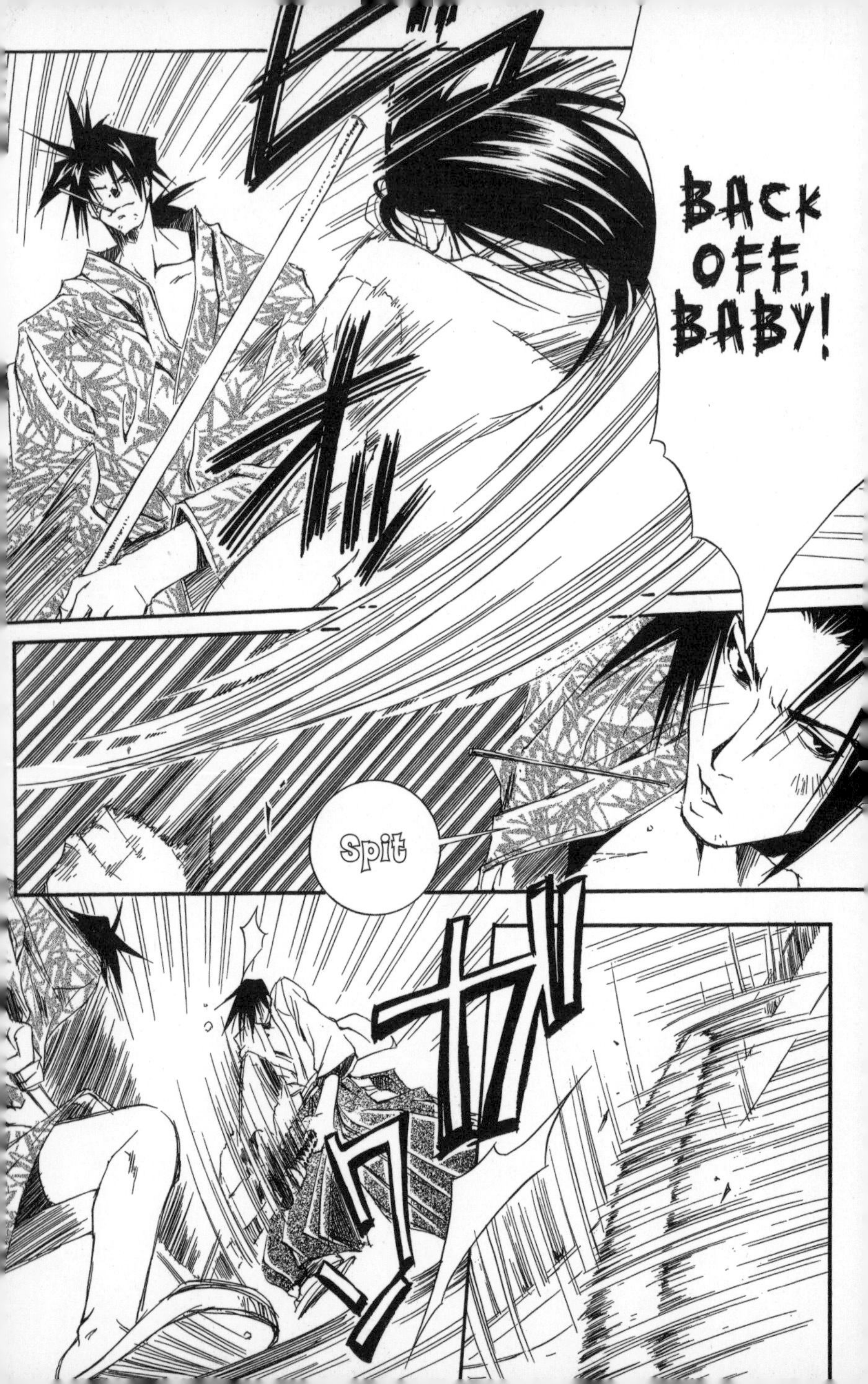
BACK OFF, BABY!
Spit

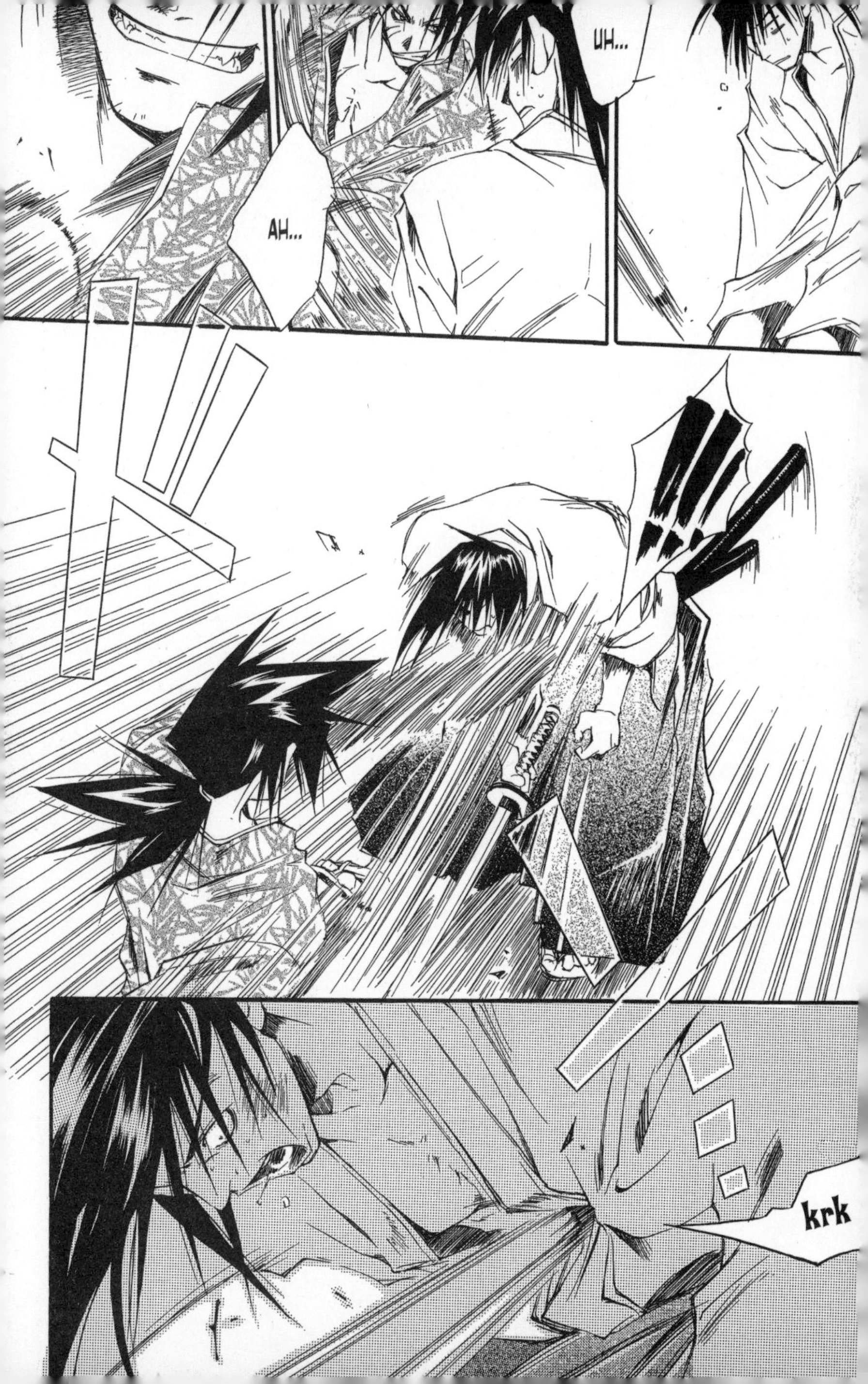
UH...
AH...
krk

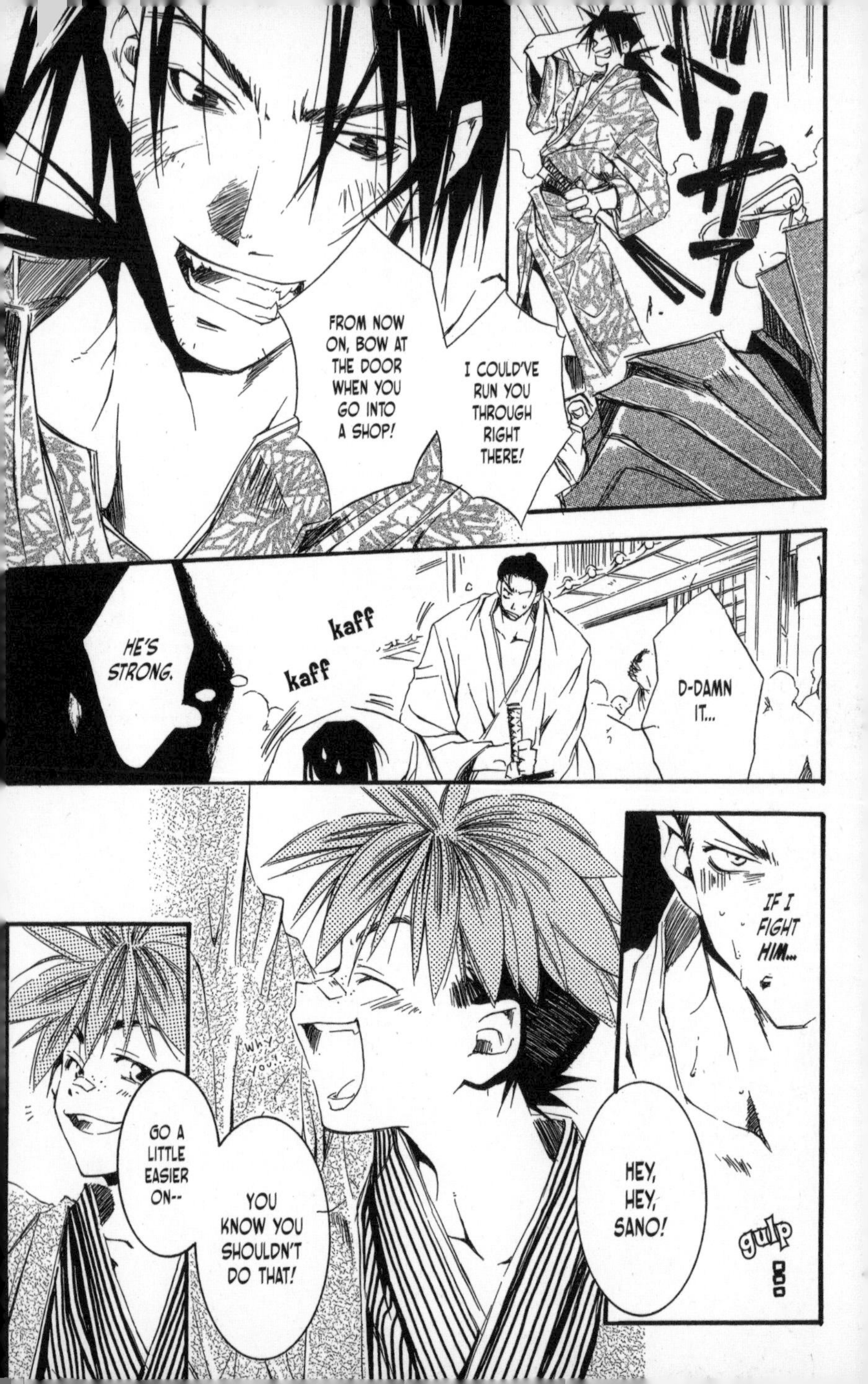

I COULD'VE RUN YOU THROUGH RIGHT THERE!
FROM NOW ON, BOW AT THE DOOR WHEN YOU GO INTO A SHOP!
D-DAMN IT...
kaff
kaff
HE'S STRONG.
IF I FIGHT HIM...
gulp
HEY, HEY, SANO!
YOU KNOW YOU SHOULDN'T DO THAT!
why you...
GO A LITTLE EASIER ON--

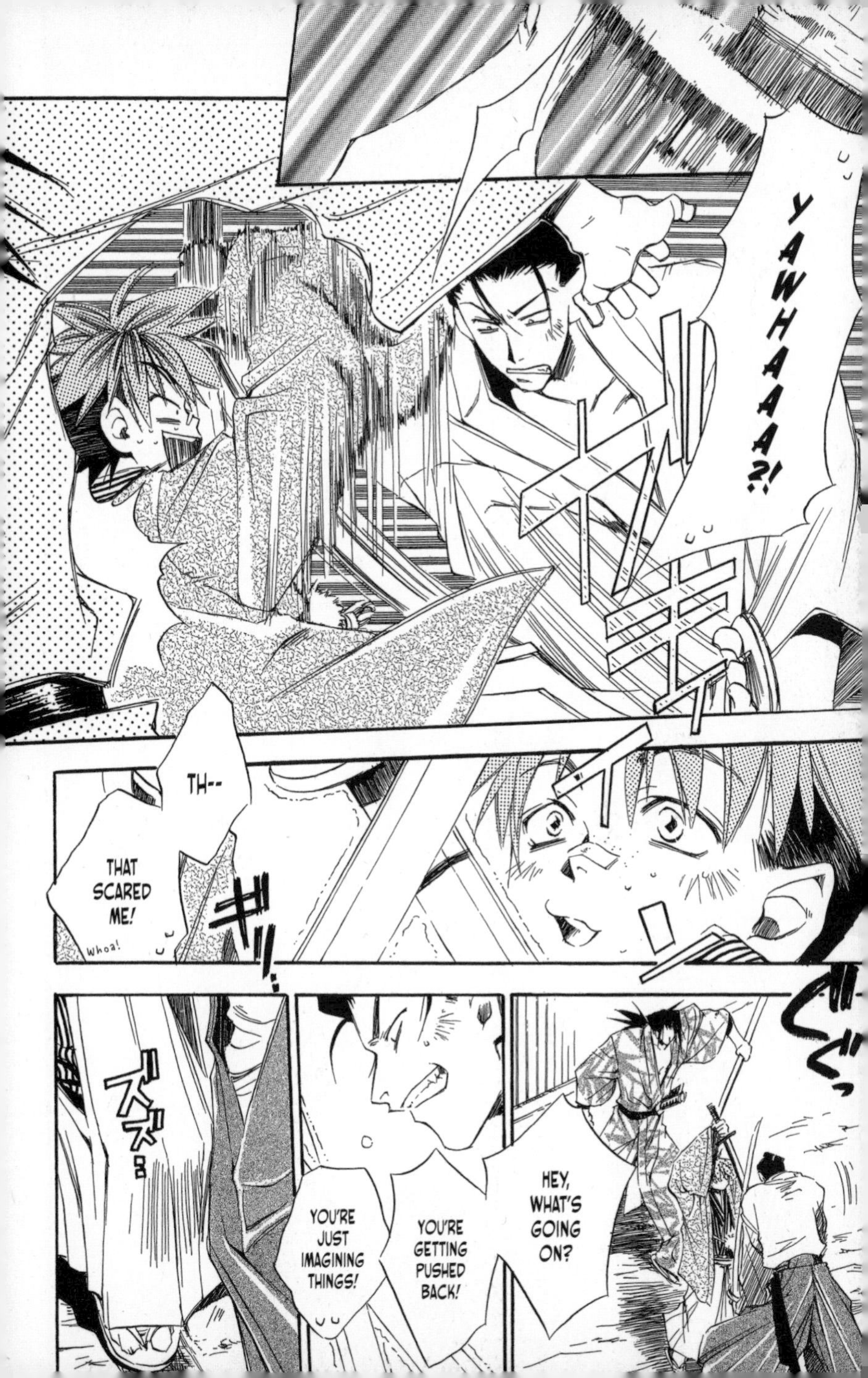
YAWHAAAAA?!
TH--
THAT SCARED ME!
Whoa!
HEY, WHAT'S GOING ON?
YOU'RE GETTING PUSHED BACK!
YOU'RE JUST IMAGINING THINGS!

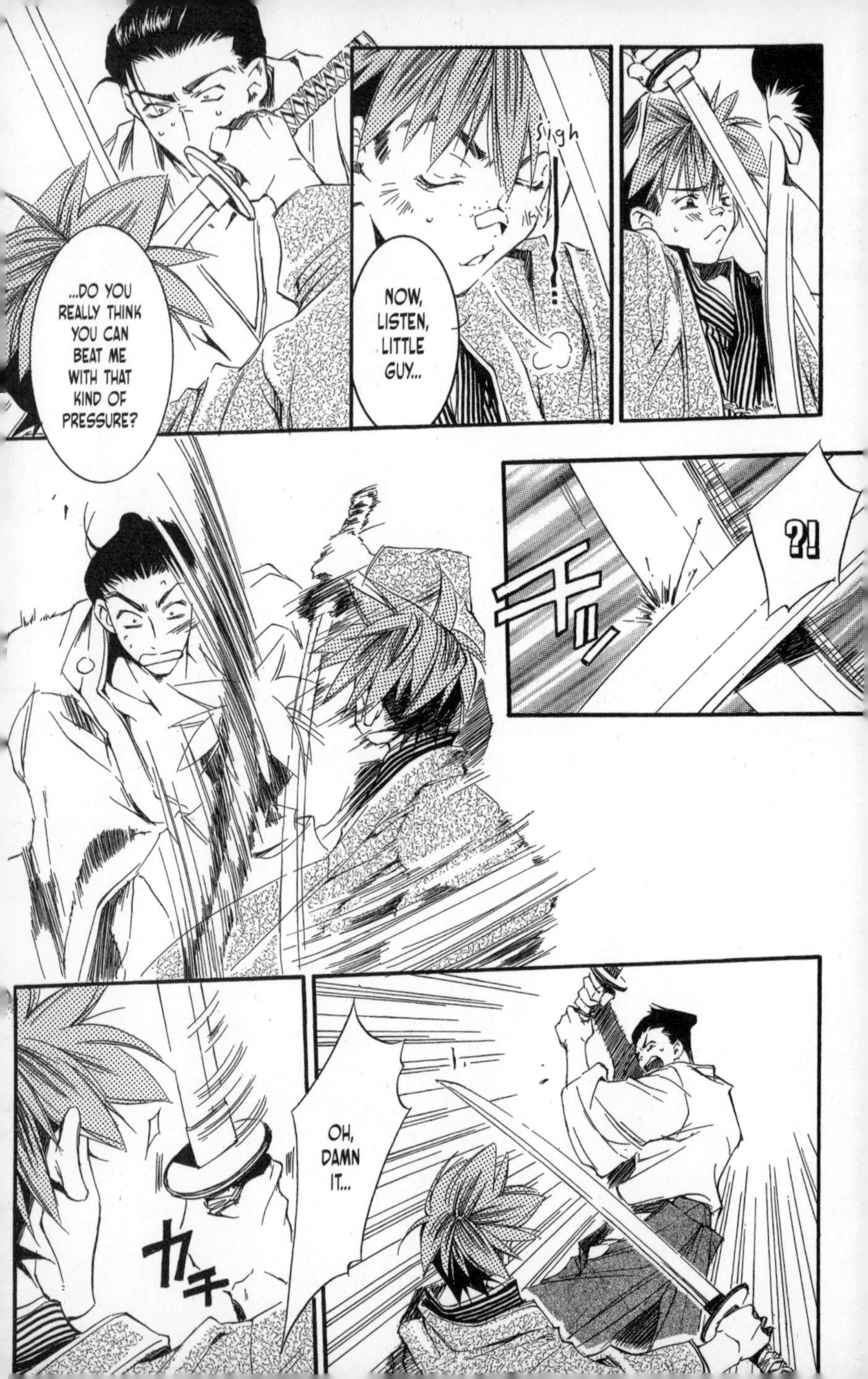
Sigh
NOW, LISTEN, LITTLE GUY...
...DO YOU REALLY THINK YOU CAN BEAT ME WITH THAT KIND OF PRESSURE?
?!
チッ
OH, DAMN IT...
カチ

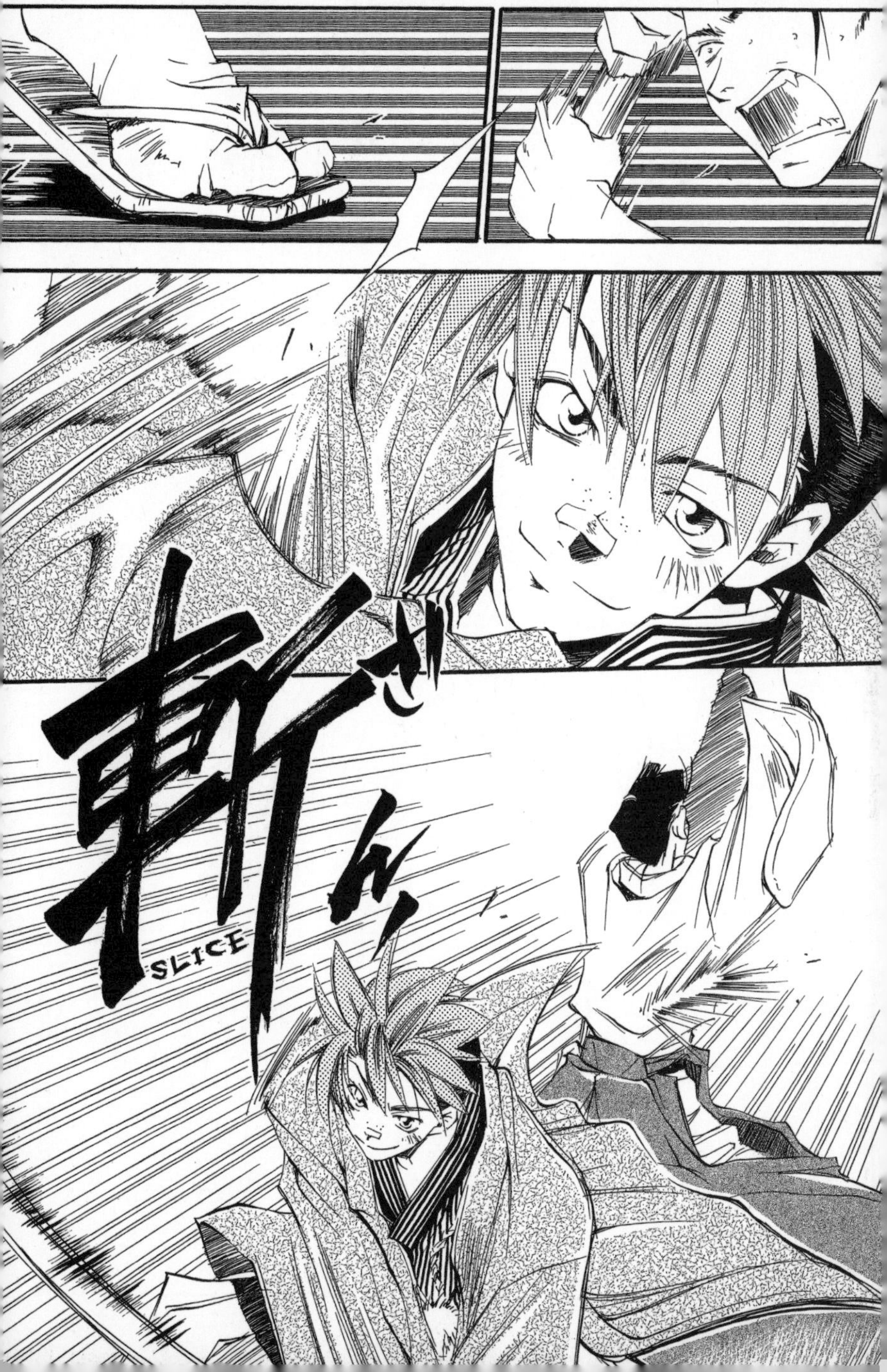
斬ん
SLICE

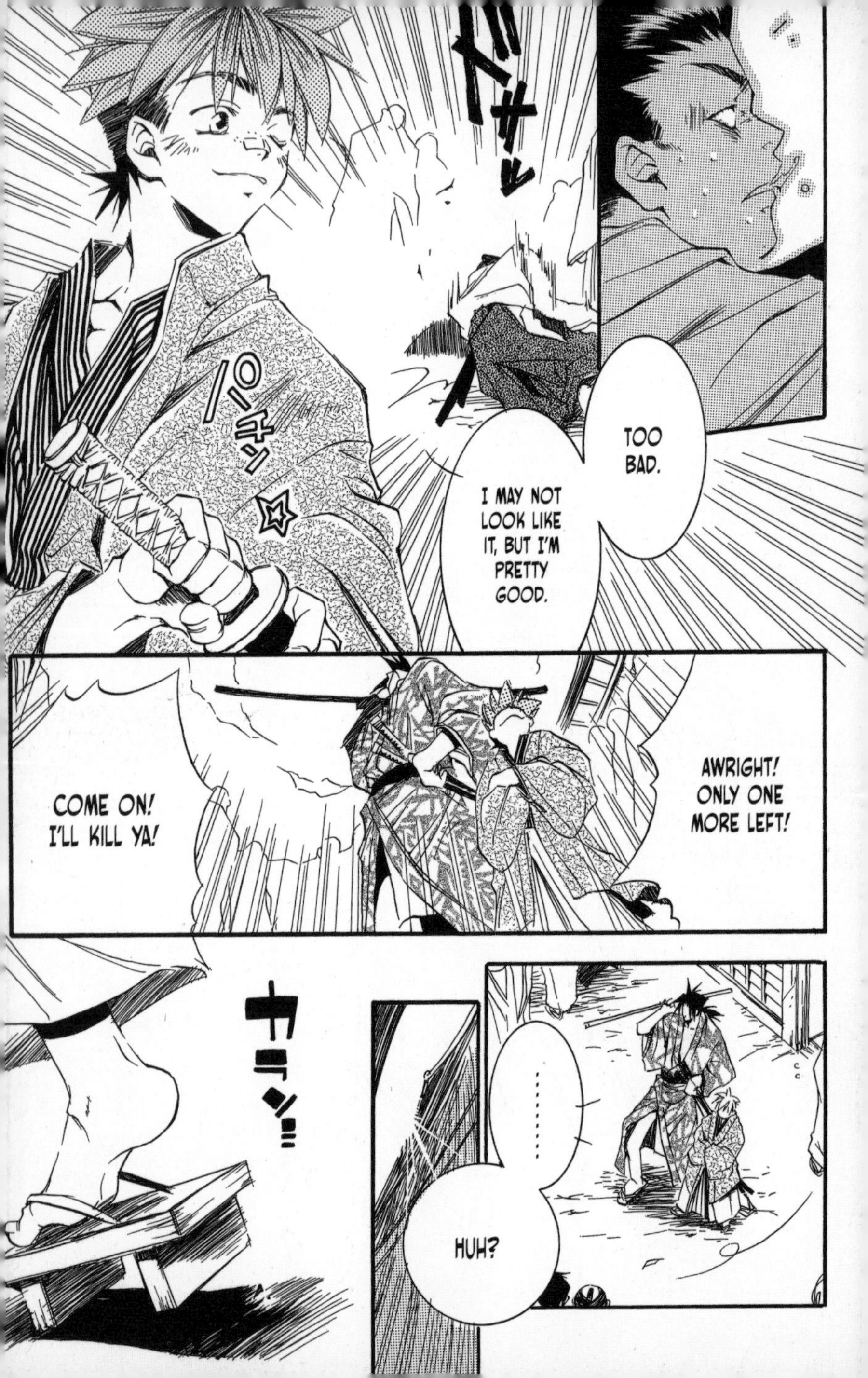
ドサッ
TOO BAD.
I MAY NOT LOOK LIKE IT, BUT I'M PRETTY GOOD.
パチン
AWRIGHT! ONLY ONE MORE LEFT!
COME ON! I'LL KILL YA!
......
HUH?
カラン!!

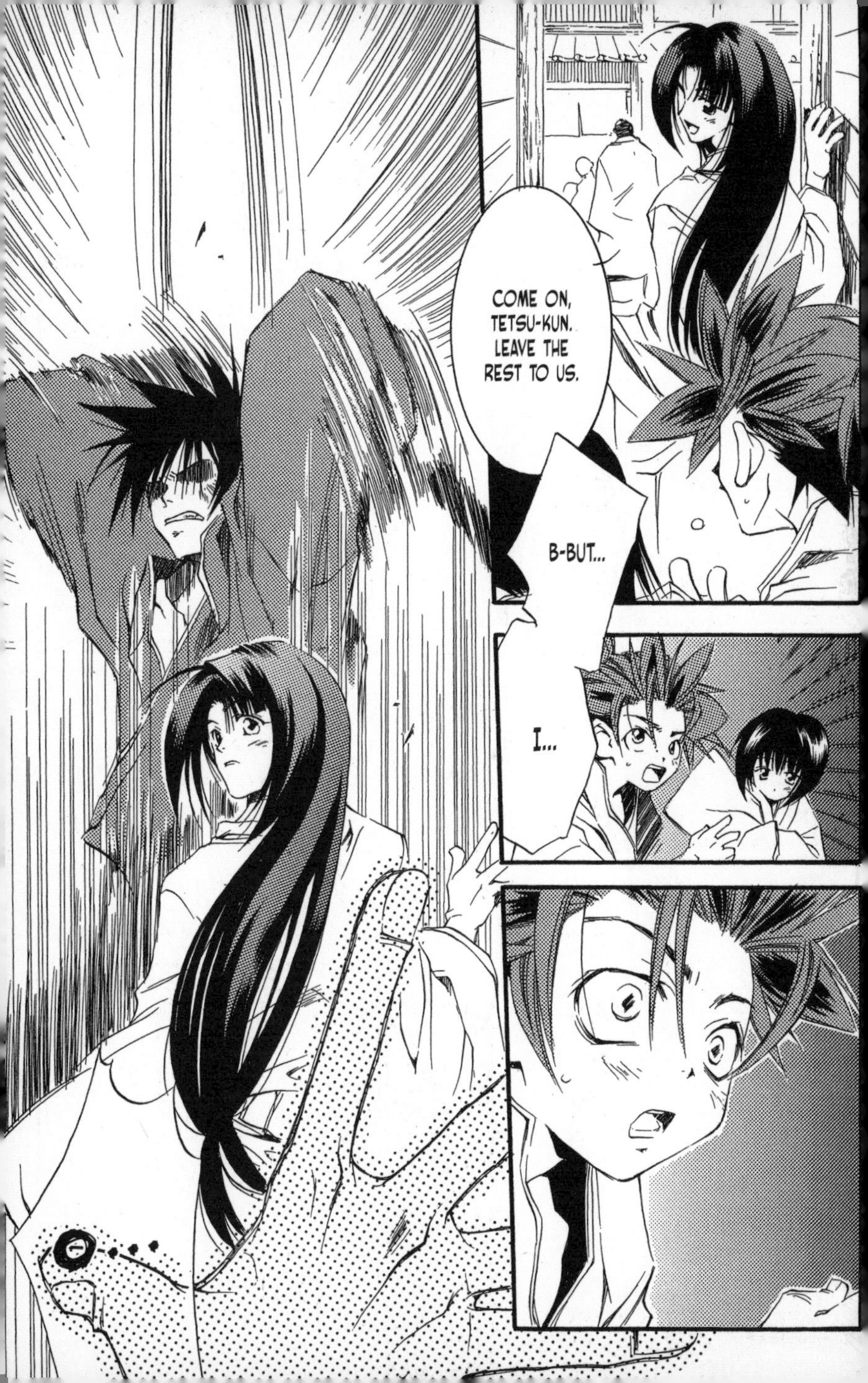
COME ON, TETSU-KUN. LEAVE THE REST TO US.
B-BUT...
I...

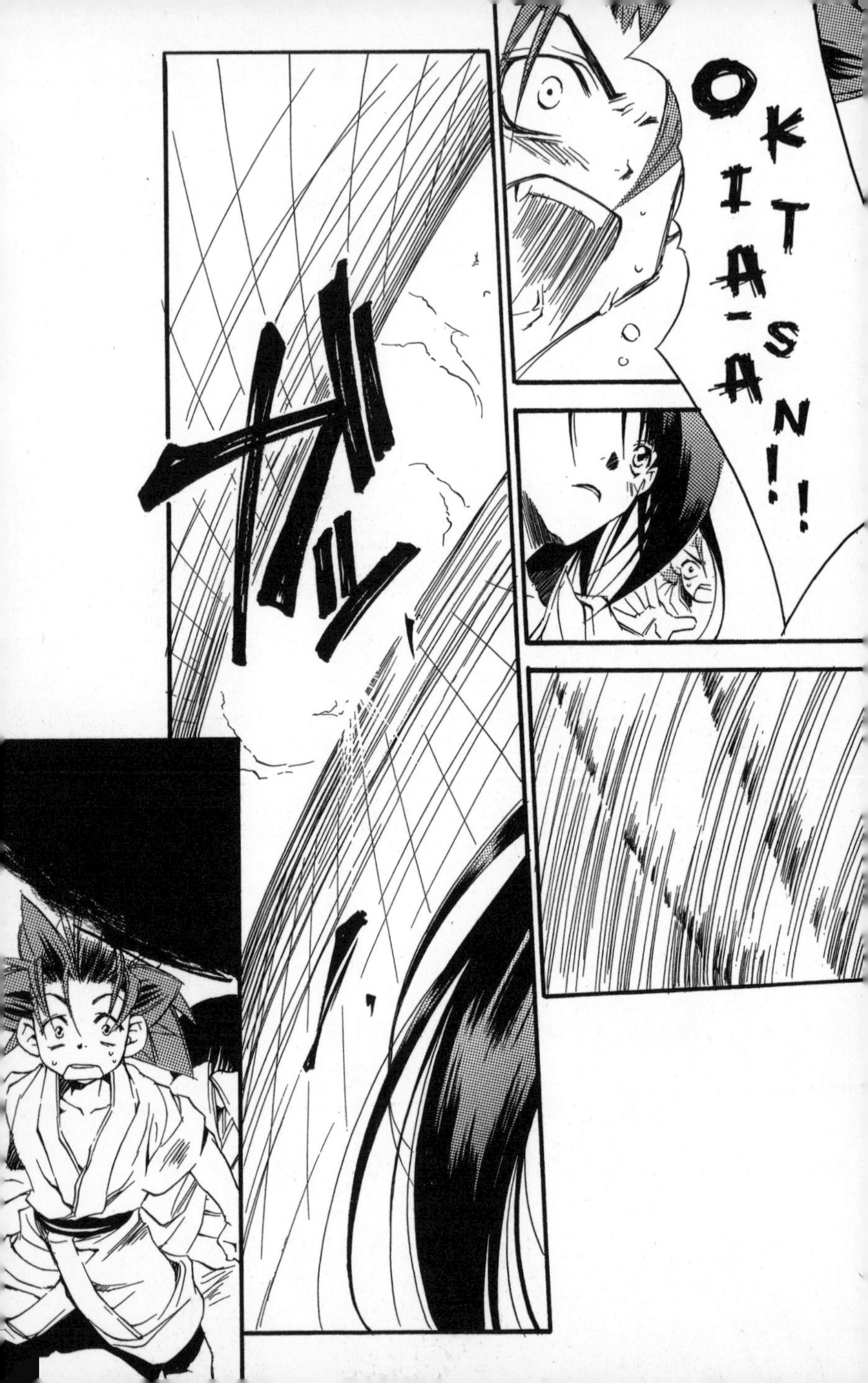
OKITA-SAN!!

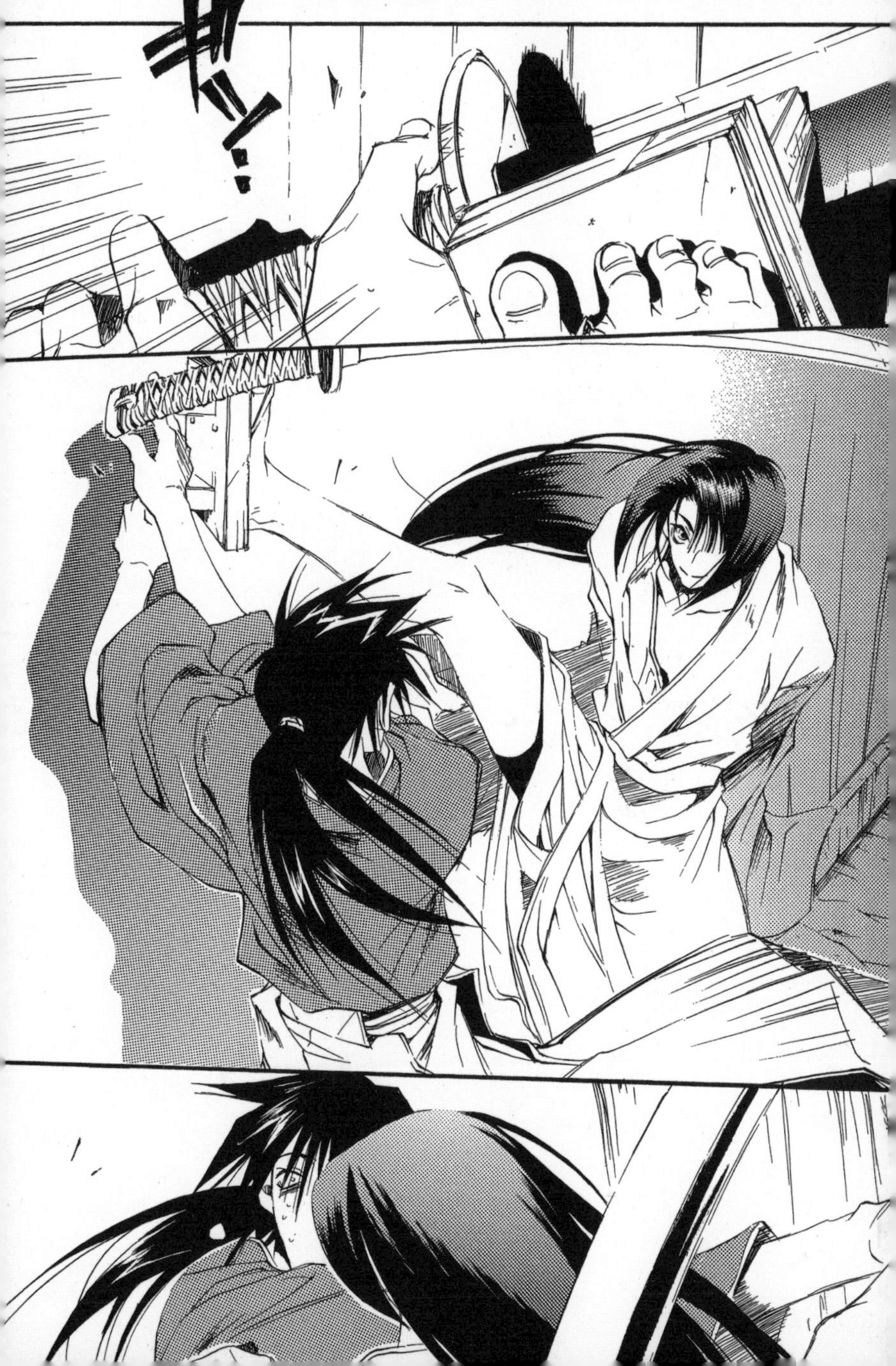
ギン!!

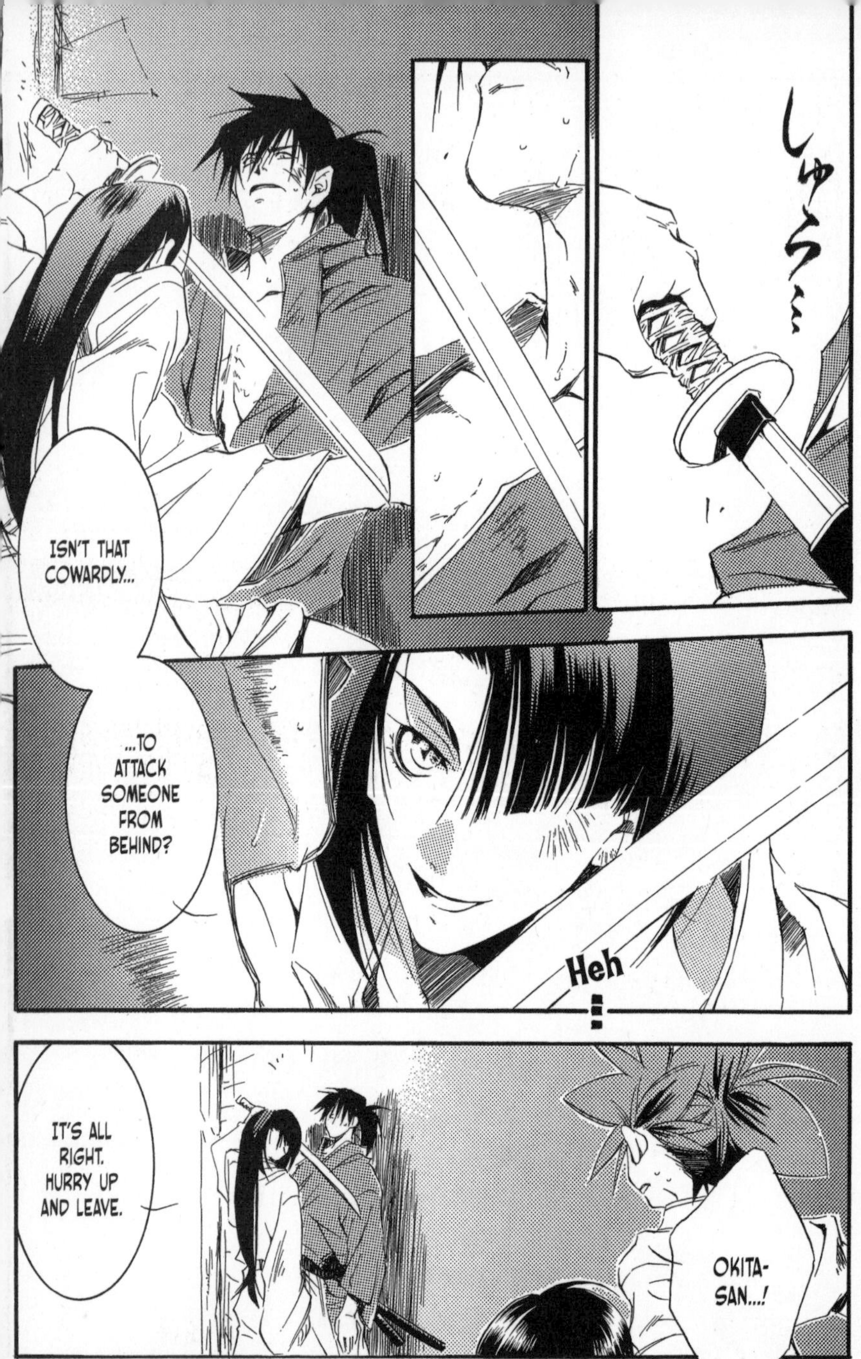
しゅら
ISN'T THAT COWARDLY...
...TO ATTACK SOMEONE FROM BEHIND?
Heh
OKITA-SAN...!
IT'S ALL RIGHT. HURRY UP AND LEAVE.

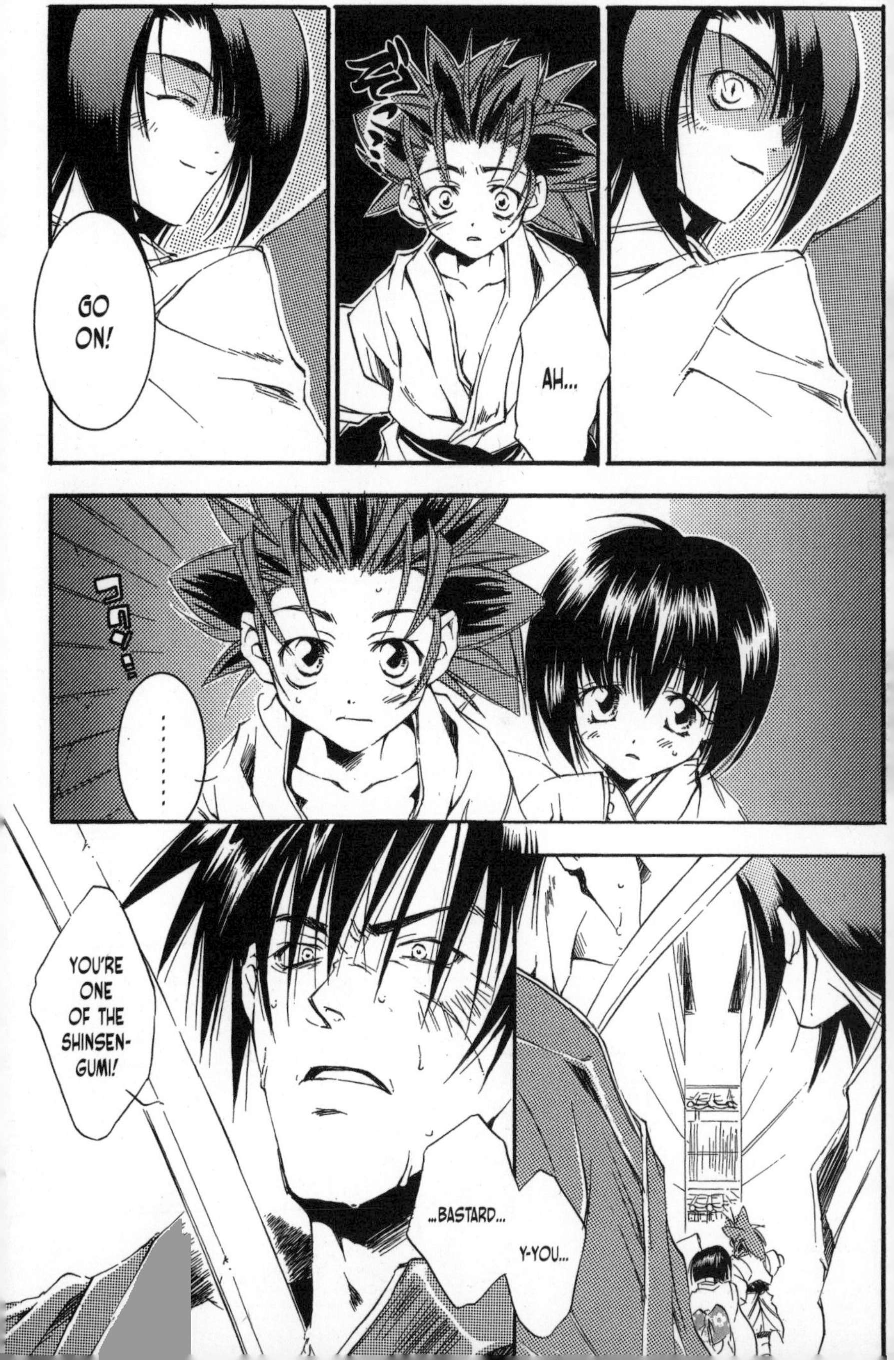
AH...
GO ON!
......
Y-YOU...
...BASTARD...
YOU'RE ONE OF THE SHINSEN-GUMI!

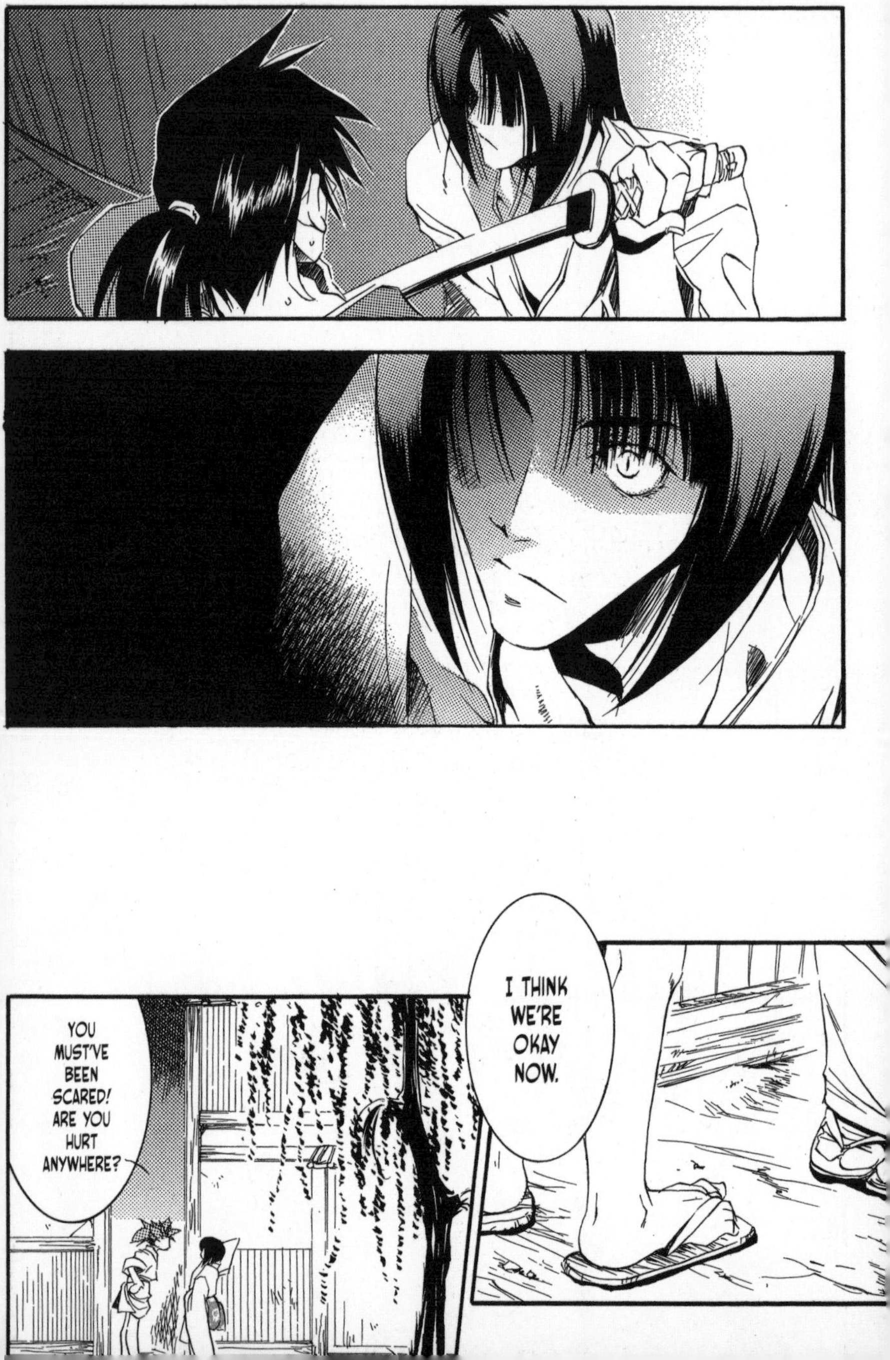
I THINK WE'RE OKAY NOW.
YOU MUST'VE BEEN SCARED! ARE YOU HURT ANYWHERE?

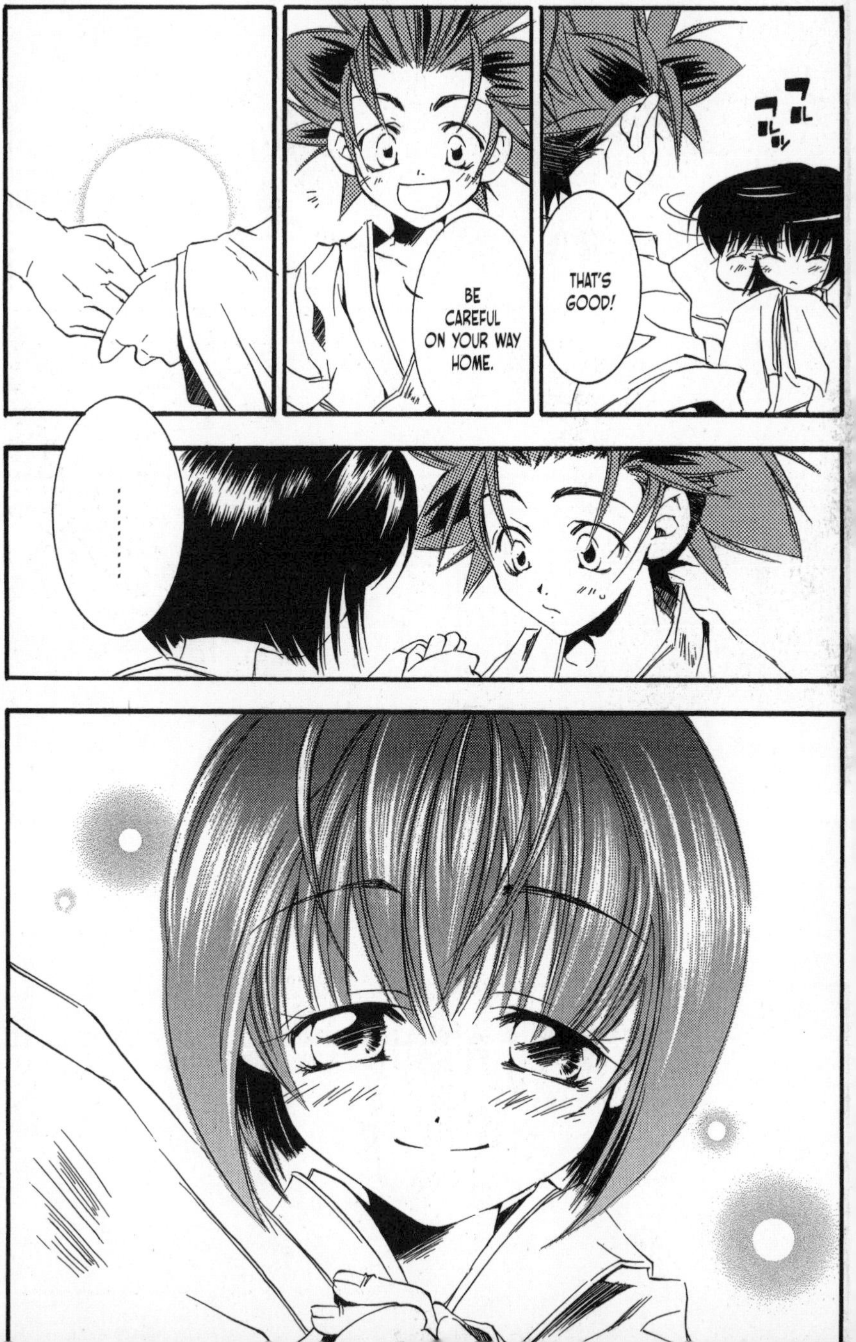
THAT'S GOOD!
BE CAREFUL ON YOUR WAY HOME.
......

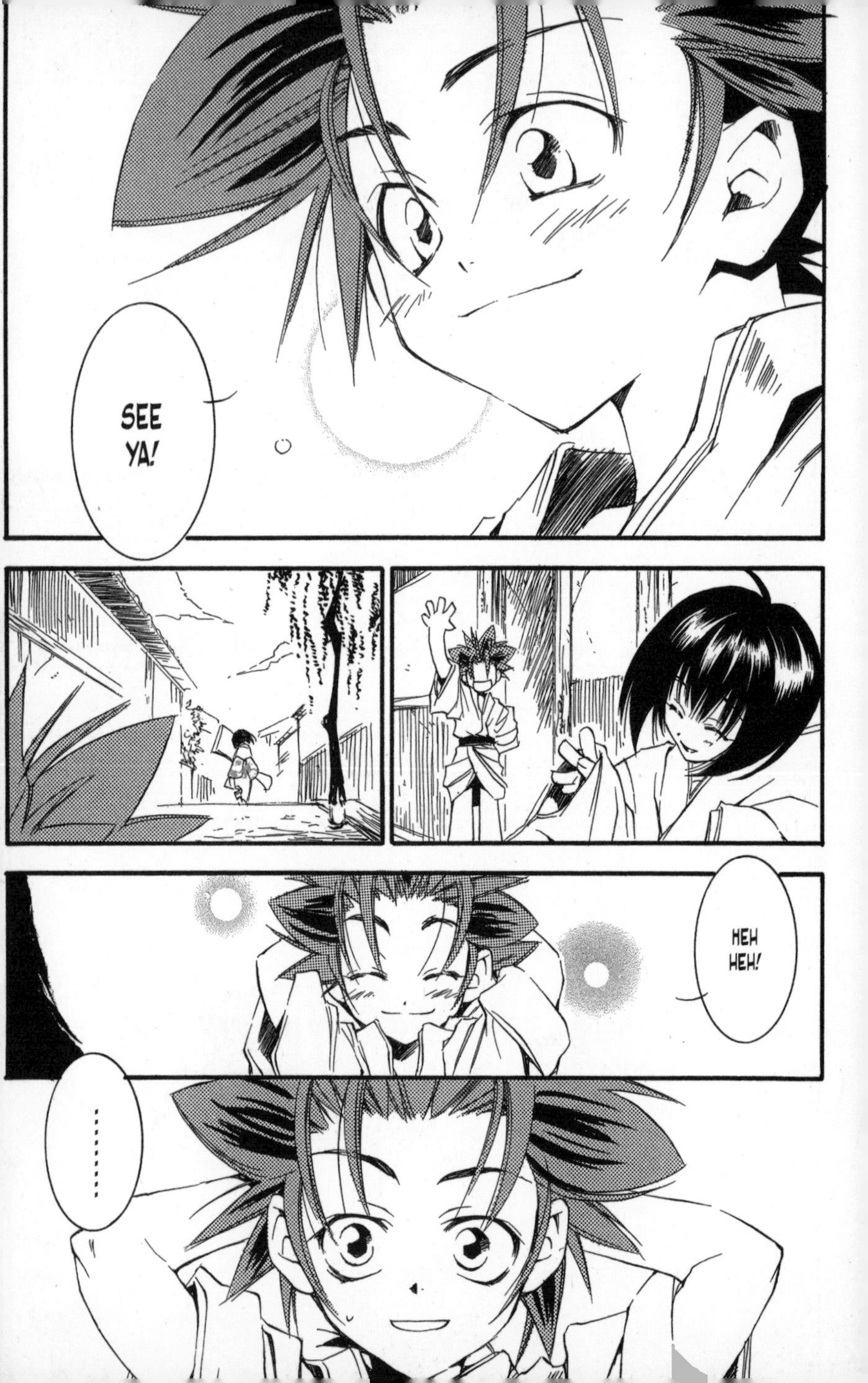
SEE YA!
HEH HEH!
......

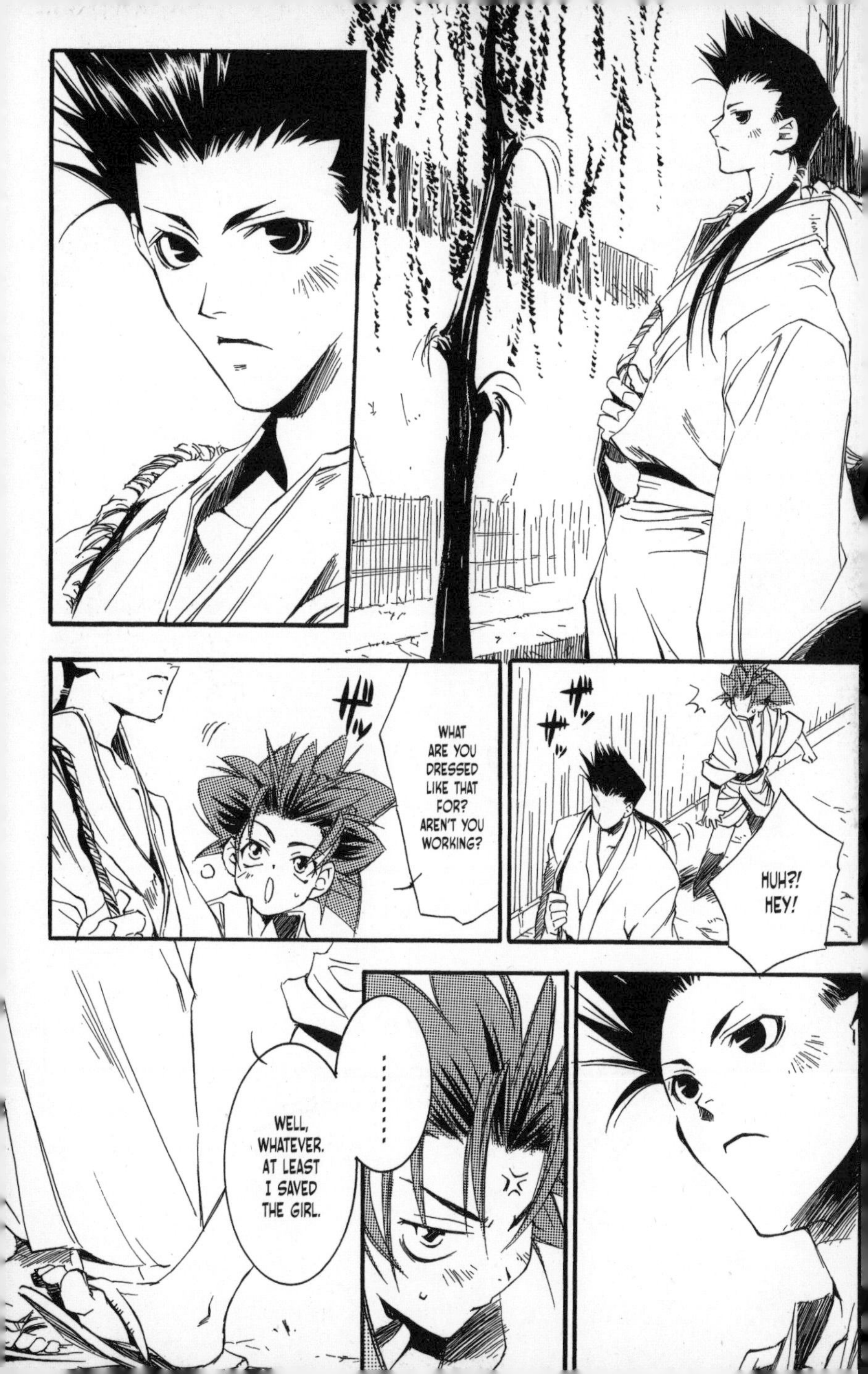
ザッ
ザッ
HUH?! HEY!
ザッ
WHAT ARE YOU DRESSED LIKE THAT FOR? AREN'T YOU WORKING?
......
WELL, WHATEVER. AT LEAST I SAVED THE GIRL.

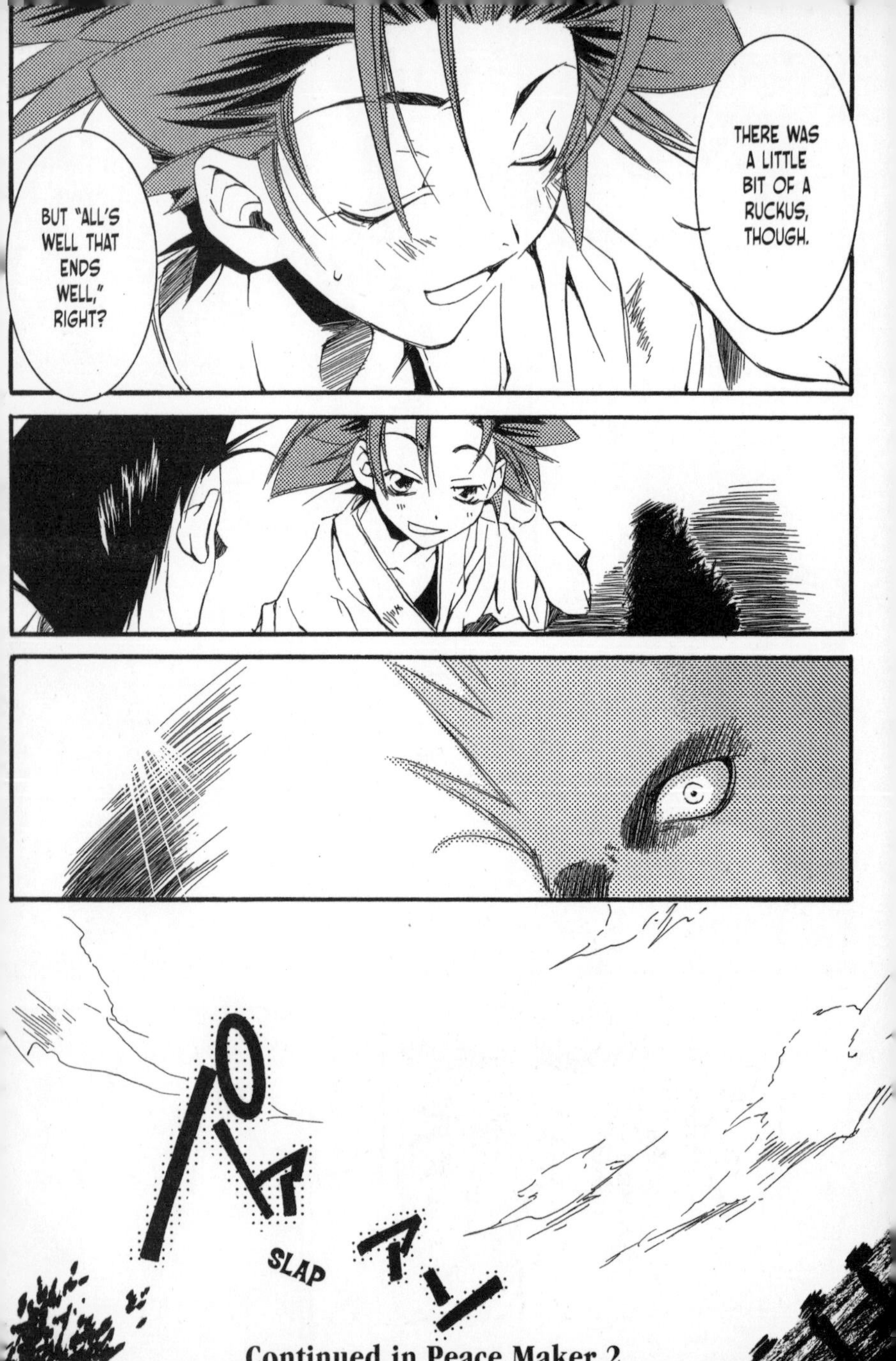
THERE WAS A LITTLE BIT OF A RUCKUS, THOUGH.
BUT "ALL'S WELL THAT ENDS WELL," RIGHT?
SLAP

Continued in Peace Maker 2

In the Next

PEACE MAKER
ピースメーカー

New comrades revealed
But beware the dark swordsman
And his pupil, too.

Coming soon!

A GUIDE TO THE HISTORICAL ERA OF *PEACE MAKER*

THE *SHINSENGUMI* WAS A SPECIAL POLICE FORCE OF THE LATE TOKUGAWA SHOGUNATE PERIOD IN JAPAN. AFTER JAPAN'S LONG HISTORY OF ISOLATION WAS BROKEN BY THE VISIT FROM U.S. COMMODORE MATTHEW PERRY IN 1853, MANY JAPANESE REACTED BY ATTEMPTING TO OVERTHROW THE SHOGUN AND RETURN TO THE ERA OF THE EMPEROR. THE INFLUENCE OF THE WEST SIGNALED THE NEARING END OF THE EDO PERIOD (SO CALLED BECAUSE THE SHOGUN RULED FROM EDO CASTLE IN THE CAPITAL CITY THAT IS NOW KNOWN AS TOKYO), AND THE CITIZENS WERE SPLIT INTO FEELING EITHER SENTIMENT FOR THE PAST OR HOPE FOR THE FUTURE.

THE SHINSENGUMI ("SHINSEN," MAY BE TRANSLATED AS "NEWLY CHOSEN," AND "GUMI" AS "GROUP") WERE MADE UP OF MASTERLESS SAMURAI, OR *RONIN*, AND WERE ORIGINALLY CALLED THE "MIBURO," OR "RONIN OF MIBU," AFTER THE TOWN WHERE THEY WERE STATIONED. ENEMIES OF THE GROUP--CHIEFLY THE IMPERIALIST-SUPPORTING CHOUSHUU CLAN--CALLED THEM THE "WOLVES OF MIBU." CHOUSHUU WAS A WESTERN PROVINCE (IN WHAT IS NOW YAMAGUCHI PREFECTURE) WHICH WAS STRONGLY *SONNOU JOUI*--MEANING THEY ADHERED TO THE DOCTRINE OF *"REVERE THE EMPEROR, EXPEL THE FOREIGNERS."* SONNOU JOUI IS STILL USED TODAY TO DESCRIBE JAPAN'S XENOPHOBIA. WHEN THE NEW MEIJI GOVERNMENT WAS ESTABLISHED, MANY OF THE TOP MEN WERE FROM CHOUSHUU.

MANY OF THE CHARACTERS IN NANAE CHRONO'S *PEACE MAKER* ARE BASED ON HISTORICAL MEMBERS OF THE SHINSENGUMI. THE SHINSENGUMI HAD TWO VICE COMMANDERS: HIJIKATA TOSHIZOU AND YAMANAMI KEISUKE (APPEARING IN FUTURE VOLUMES). HIJIKATA WAS KNOWN FOR BEING EXTREMELY STRICT AND MEAN, WHICH IS HOW HE EARNED THE NICKNAME "DEMON VICE COMMANDER." UNLIKE MOST OF THE OTHER SHINSENGUMI MEMBERS, WHO SPECIALIZED IN THE SWORD, HARADA SANOSUKE SPECIALIZED IN THE SPEAR. HARADA SANOSUKE ONCE ATTEMPTED TO COMMIT RITUAL SUICIDE BUT FAILED. IT LEFT HIM WITH A SCAR ON HIS STOMACH, WHICH HE WAS SAID TO BE FOND OF SHOWING OFF.

-CHRISTINE BOYLAN

CHERRY JUICE

FROM THE CREATOR OF INSTANT TEEN AND KEDAMONO DAMONO!

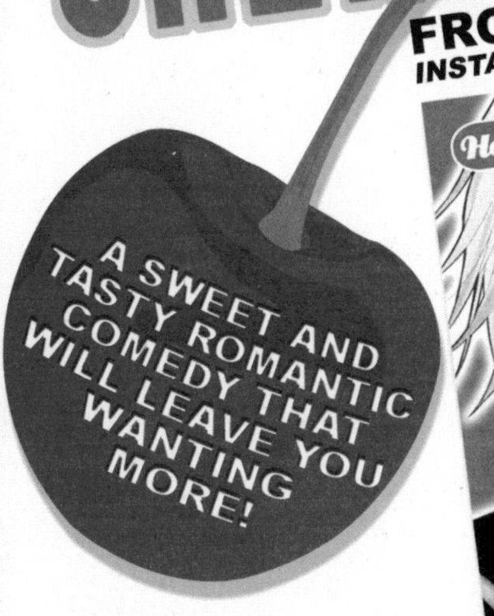
A SWEET AND TASTY ROMANTIC COMEDY THAT WILL LEAVE YOU WANTING MORE!

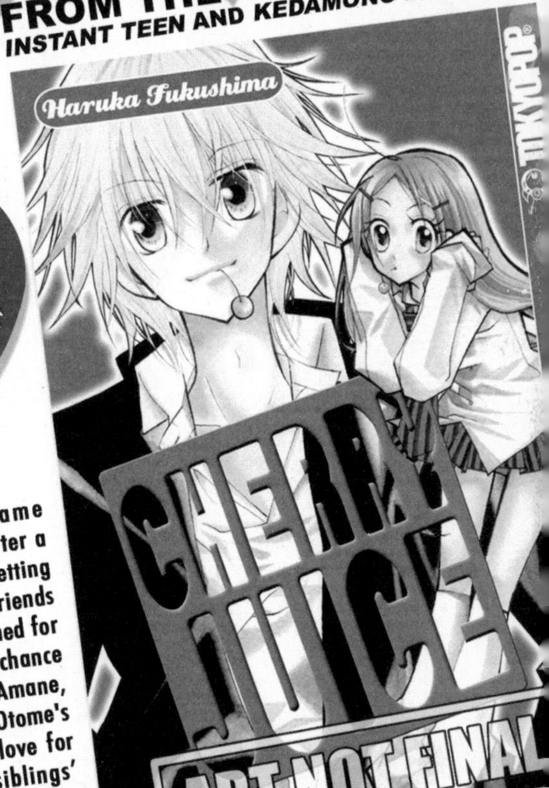
TOKYOPOP
Haruka Fukushima
CHERRY JUICE
1
ART NOT FINAL

Otome and Minami became step-siblings five years ago. After a rocky start, they are finally getting along as brother and sister. Friends believe that the two are destined for more, but Otome denies any chance of romance. But when Amane, Minami's best friend and Otome's secret crush, confesses his love for Otome, suddenly the siblings' peaceful relationship takes a turn for the worse...

DRAMA

TEEN AGE 13+

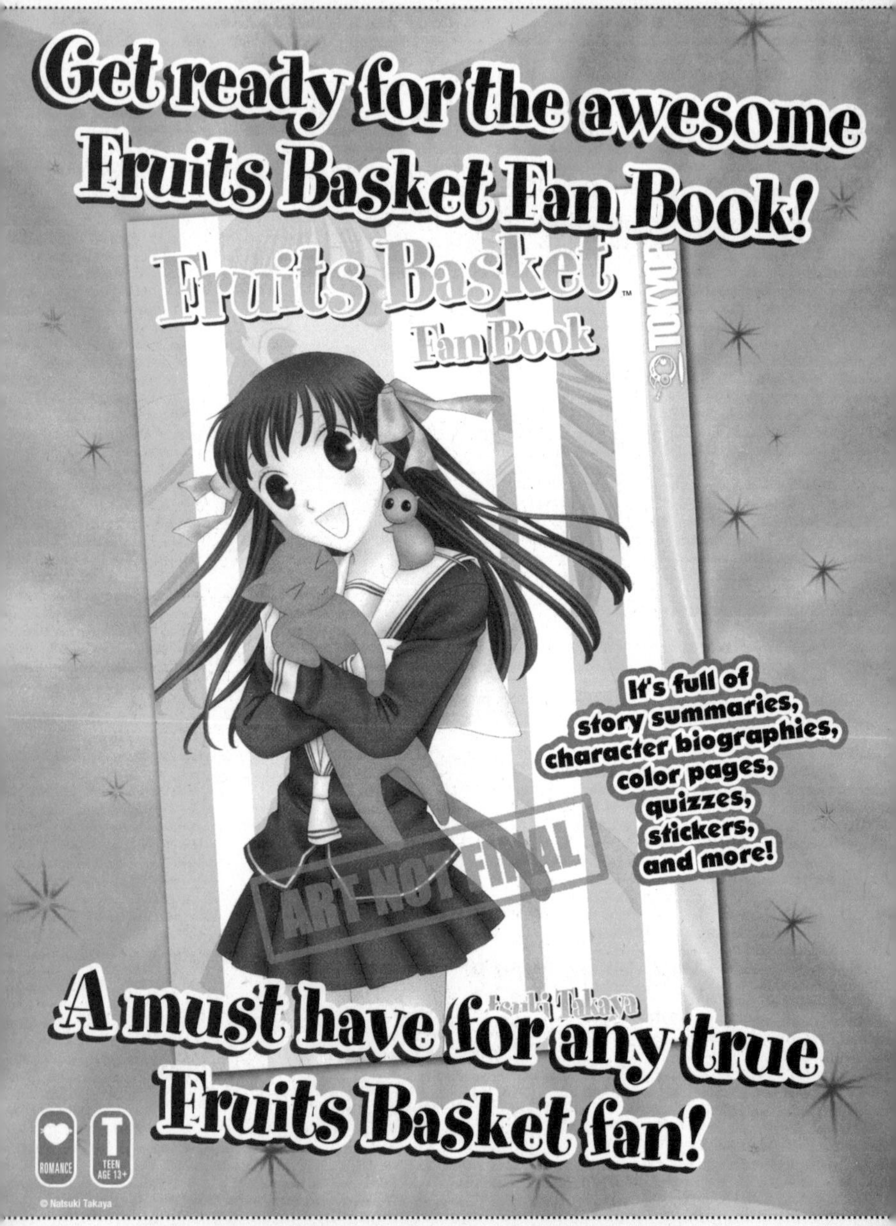
Get ready for the awesome Fruits Basket Fan Book!
Fruits Basket™
Fan Book
TOKYOPOP
It's full of story summaries, character biographies, color pages, quizzes, stickers, and more!
ART NOT FINAL
Natsuki Takaya
A must have for any true Fruits Basket fan!
ROMANCE
T
TEEN AGE 13+
© Natsuki Takaya

DARK MOON DIARY ™

After losing her parents in a tragic accident, Priscilla goes to live in a new town with her aunt's family. As if adjusting to a new family wouldn't be tough enough, her relatives turn out to be vampires who live in the ghoul-filled town of Nachtwald! Priscilla tries hard to assimilate, but with a ghost for a teacher, a witch as a friend, and food that winks at you, can she ever adapt to life in her new town? Or will she pack her garlic and head back to normal-ville?

FOR MORE INFORMATION VISIT: WWW.TOKYOPOP.COM

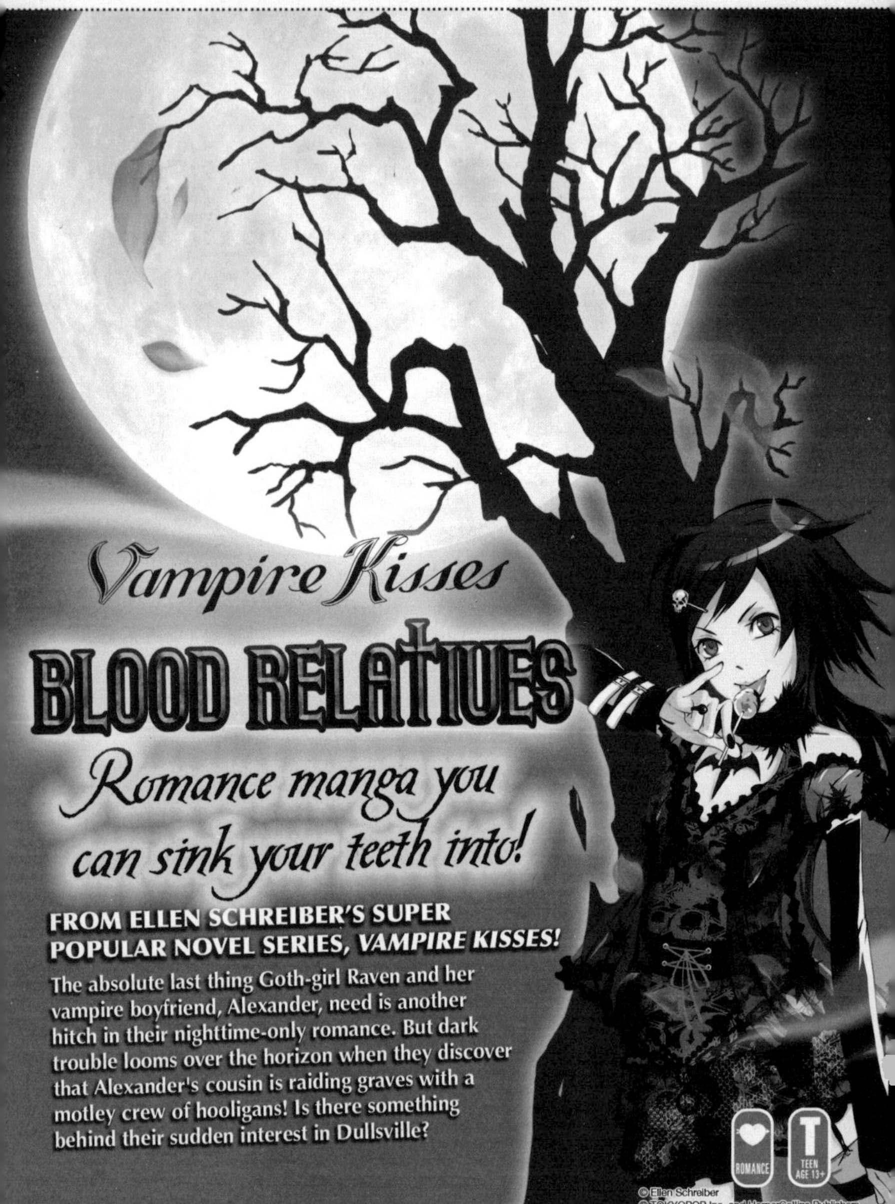
Vampire Kisses
BLOOD RELATIVES
Romance manga you can sink your teeth into!
FROM ELLEN SCHREIBER'S SUPER POPULAR NOVEL SERIES, *VAMPIRE KISSES!*
The absolute last thing Goth-girl Raven and her vampire boyfriend, Alexander, need is another hitch in their nighttime-only romance. But dark trouble looms over the horizon when they discover that Alexander's cousin is raiding graves with a motley crew of hooligans! Is there something behind their sudden interest in Dullsville?
ROMANCE
T
TEEN AGE 13+
© Ellen Schreiber
© TOKYOPOP Inc. and HarperCollins Publishers

STOP!

This is the back of the book.
You wouldn't want to spoil a great ending!

This book is printed "manga-style," in the authentic Japanese right-to-left format. Since none of the artwork has been flipped or altered, readers get to experience the story just as the creator intended. You've been asking for it, so TOKYOPOP® delivered: authentic, hot-off-the-press, and far more fun!

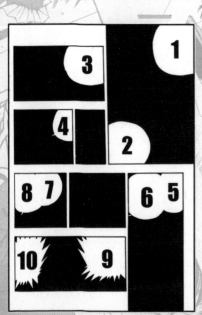

DIRECTIONS

If this is your first time reading manga-style, here's a quick guide to help you understand how it works.

It's easy... just start in the top right panel and follow the numbers. Have fun, and look for more 100% authentic manga from TOKYOPOP®!